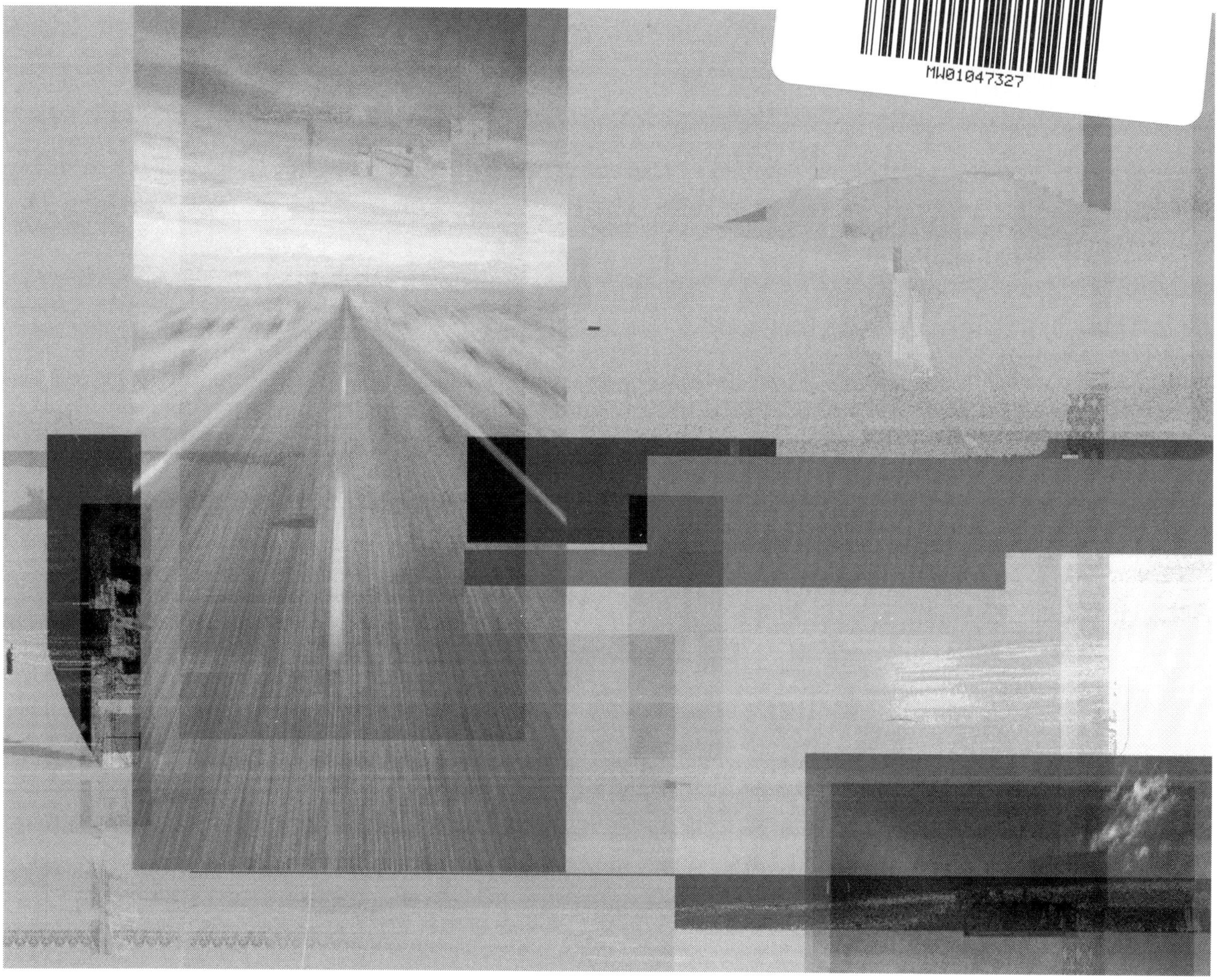

UPGRADING TO INROADS SS4

CAD Productivity Incorporated

www.cadprodinc.com

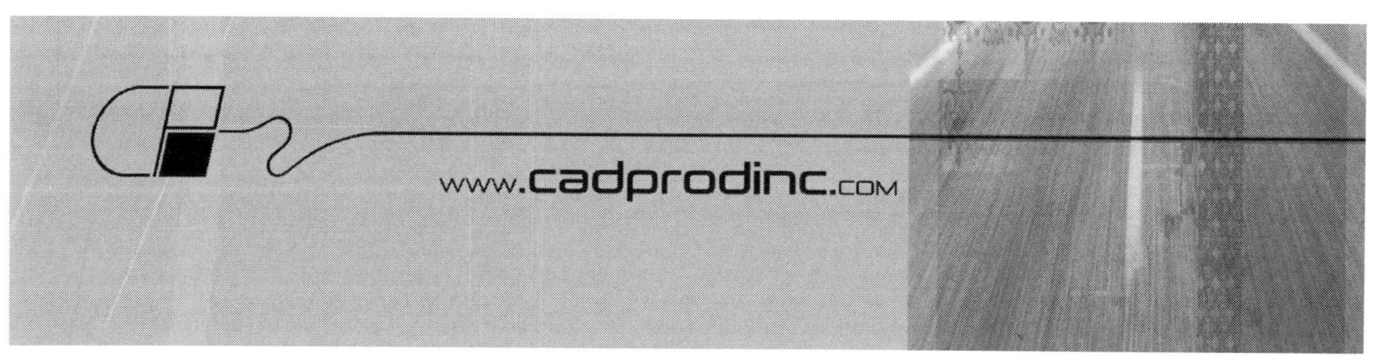

Published by CAD Productivity Incorporated, PO Box 281195, Nashville, TN 37228.

Post Office Box 281195
Nashville, Tennessee 37228

615.255.7440
615.255.7441 fax

info@cadprodinc.com
www.cadprodinc.com

09|29|16 – CP

MS Version 08.11.09.832 (SS4)
InRoads Version 08.11.09.878 (SS4)

Table of Contents

Introduction

About CAD Productivity

About this Document

Document conventions

Lab files

About InRoads SS4

1 Introduction

About CAD Productivity Incorporated

CAD Productivity Incorporated was formed in the early 1990's to provide consulting and training services for what was then Intergraph Corporation's civil engineering software (now Bentley's). Since that time, we have been dedicated to assisting our customers in becoming more productive with their software investment. With the vast array of projects that are tackled with the advanced Bentley applications, quality training is critical to the success of the software.

Quality Products and Services

We offer an array of training and consulting services for the InRoads suite civil applications as well as for MicroStation. This includes:

- Basic and Advanced MicroStation training
- Basic and Advanced InRoads training
- Version Upgrade training for MicroStation and InRoads
- CAD overview training for project managers and administrators
- Custom training plans and custom course development
- Project start-up and on-going consulting services
- MicroStation and InRoads configuration development (DGNLIBS and XIN files to match CAD standards)

CAD Productivity has extensive experience over the last 20+ years working with numerous DOTs and private engineering firms across the country to provide these quality training, consulting and customization services. CAD Productivity is proud of its reputation as ***the*** information source for MicroStation and the InRoads suite of civil engineering products.

Document Conventions

There are several conventions that are used throughout this document to indicate actions to be taken or to highlight important information. The conventions are as follows:

Symbology	Meaning
View Perimeter	a command name or a file that you are to select
Tools > Options	a command path that you are to select – usually from the pull-down menus
MS: or IR:	the command is either on the MicroStation or the InRoads Explorer menu
Key in	entering data with the keyboard
C:\train\train.xin	file or path
Note: text	information about a command or process that you should pay particular attention to
Emphasis	an important word or phrase
1 Numbered Steps	general description of an activity you are to perform with the following bulleted items
• Select	actions that you are to perform as part of the numbered lab step

Mouse Actions

<D> or Data	press the data button on the mouse
<R> or Reset	press the reset button on the mouse
<T> or Tentative	press the tentative button on the mouse

Exercise (Lab) Files

Each chapter in this book (with the exception of Chapter 1) has two sections. The first section contains concepts and/or workflows pertaining to the topic that may be used for study and reference. The second section is for working through the topics with the accompanying data set. The second section in each chapter is entitled **Exercise** …

If you do not have the accompanying data, please follow these steps.

1. Go to **www.cadprodinc.com**

2. If you have not registered as a student on our site, click **Register** on the **Home** page. If you have registered, click **Login**, provide your user name and password and then go to step 4.

3. Complete the registration form.

4. Go to the **Downloads** page from the menu.

5. Select your class files from the list to download a self-extracting zip file.

6. Unzip the files to your computer's **C:** folder.

When unzipped, a *c:\Projects* folder is created on your machine and all the files you need are in that folder and its subfolders.

About InRoads

InRoads SS3 and beyond introduces a new concept in roadway design. Dubbed 'OpenRoads Technology,' this design concept incorporates many new features that allow you to interactively change and edit your designs. It relies heavily on the MicroStation platform and stores much of the design data in DGN files.

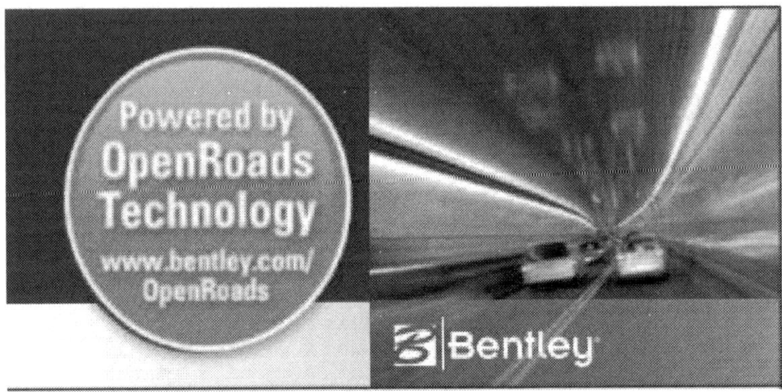

The following pages include some settings and definitions that are key to using this version of InRoads effectively.

MicroStation Preferences

Since OpenRoads is interdependent on MicroStation, there are several preferences that can be set in your workspace. Found under **MS: Workspace > Preferences > View Options – Civil**, these preferences control various temporary displays and command settings.

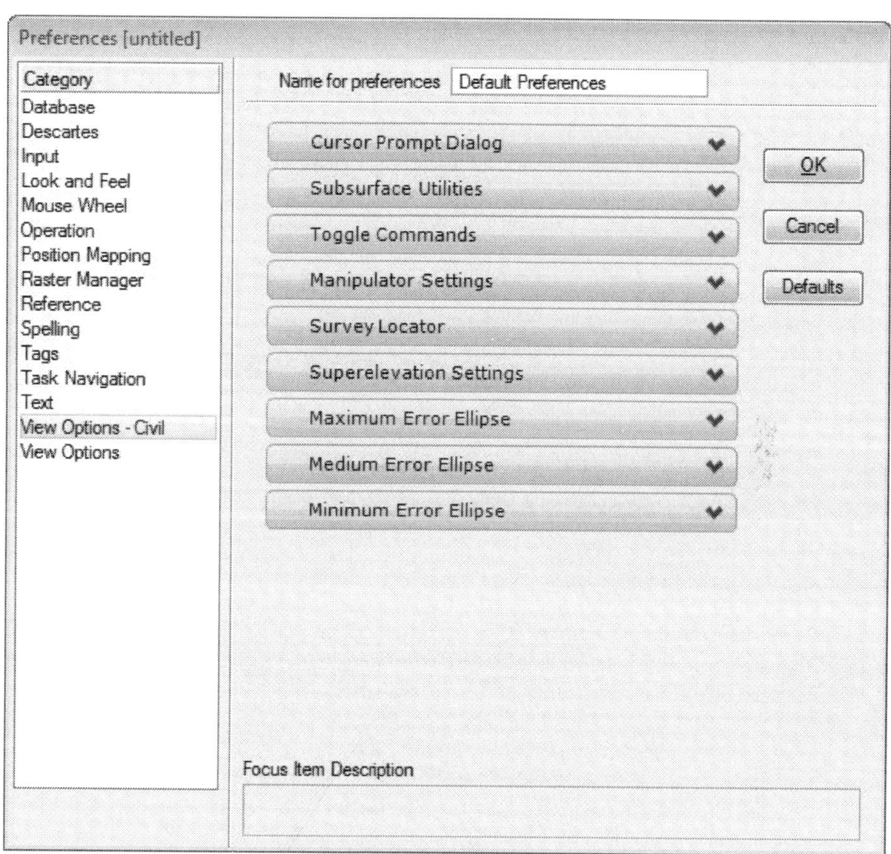

Cursor Prompt Dialog – control the display of the head-up prompts that are used during command execution as shown here.

Subsurface Utilities – controls displays in the Subsurface Utilities Engineering (SUE) software.

Toggle Commands – control the default settings for the **Features Definition Toggle Bar** commands which are used when creating features.

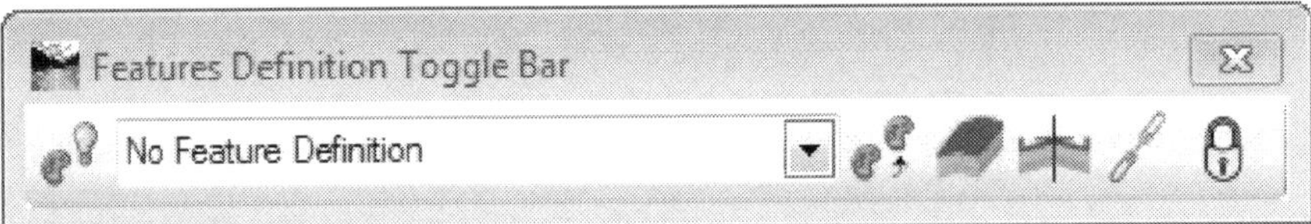

Manipulator Settings – control the display of manipulators used to review and modify Civil Geometry among other things. (Note: Manipulators are also affected by the resolution of your screen.)

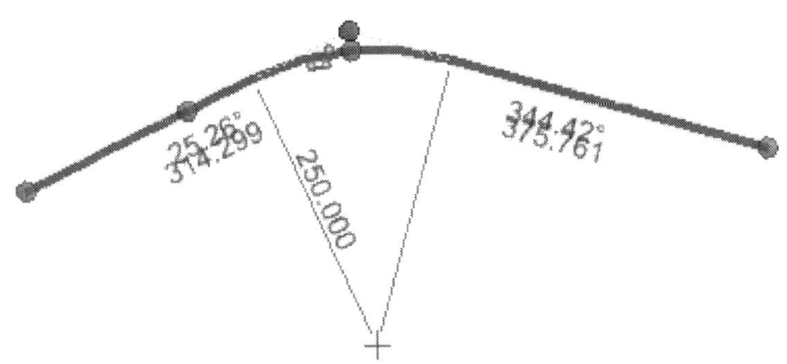

Survey Locator – controls the display of the active or highlighted survey point.

Superelevation Settings – control how Superelevation is displayed in the design file.

Error Ellipse (Maximum, Medium and Minimum) – control the display of error ellipses formed during Least Squares Adjustments.

Design Files

It is ***highly recommended*** that you start out with ***new*** design files when using this version. This means files created from seeds – not copied from previous projects. Since the data is stored graphically, it is easy to accidentally carry forward data that you do not want.

In general, use 3D MicroStation models for terrain models and 2D models for everything else. If 3D is needed, a 3D model will automatically be created and referenced to the 2D model.

Design File Settings

There are various settings that are used by Civil commands which are controlled by the design file. These settings are copied from the seed file when a design file is created.

MS: Settings > Design File Settings > Civil Formatting

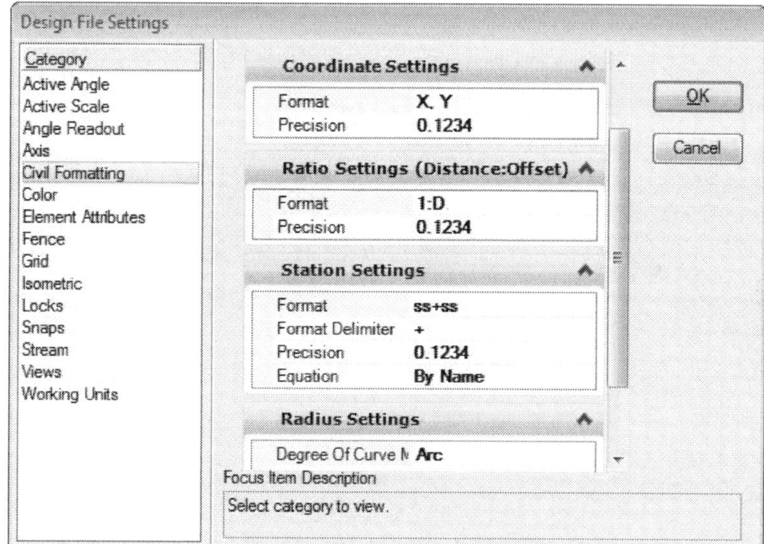

References

Since your InRoads data is now stored in the DGN, the data management workflow will need to change. Data is accessed by opening DGNs *or* referencing them. While you can create all data in the same DGN, it is recommended that you use references for clarity and so others can reference your data as well. It is also best to avoid nesting in most cases.

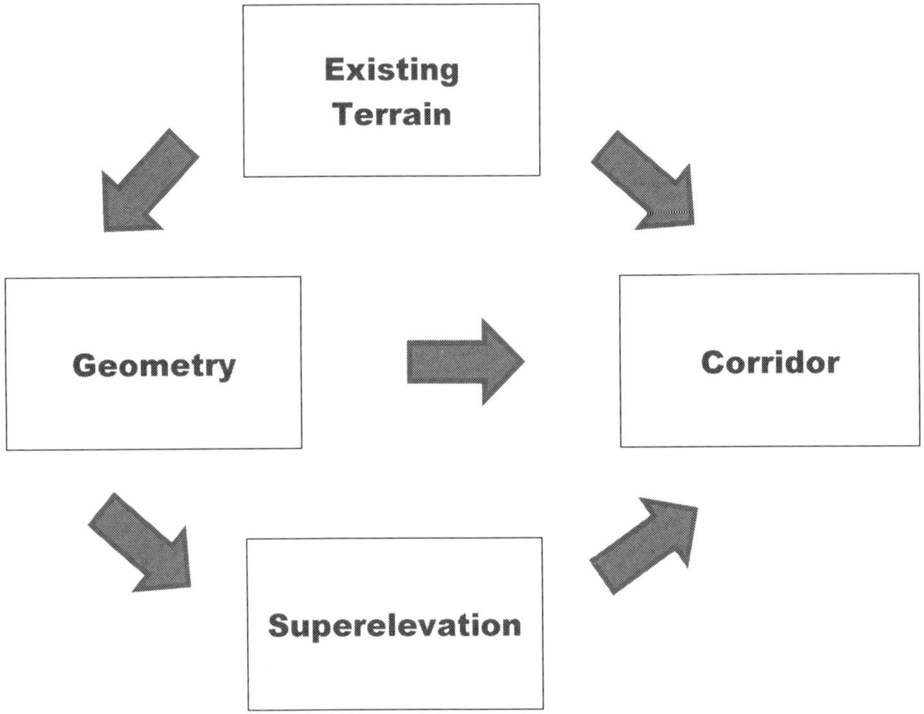

Civil Message Center

The **Civil Message Center** provides informational messages, errors and warnings. It can be docked and unpinned to take up less space but remain readily accessible.

MS: Tasks > Civil Tools > General Geometry > Civil Message Center

Project Explorer

Project Explorer is a very important interface for dealing with InRoads data, including the setup and configuration as well as project data.

MS: File > Project Explorer

If you toggle on Project Explorer and do not see tabs for **Civil Model**, **Civil Standards** and **Survey**, choose **MS: Settings > Project Explorer** and set them to **True**.

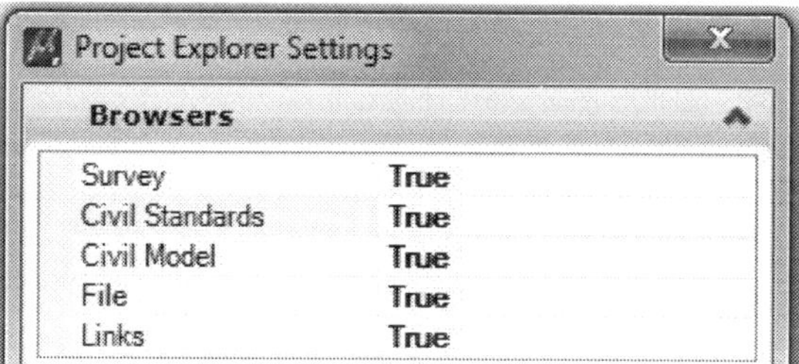

Civil Model

The **Civil Model** tab provides a look at what Civil Data is contained in the *active* MicroStation model. From here, you can modify, review, delete etc., typically through a right-click menu option. It is often handy to use this interface when editing data that is hard to identify or find in your design file.

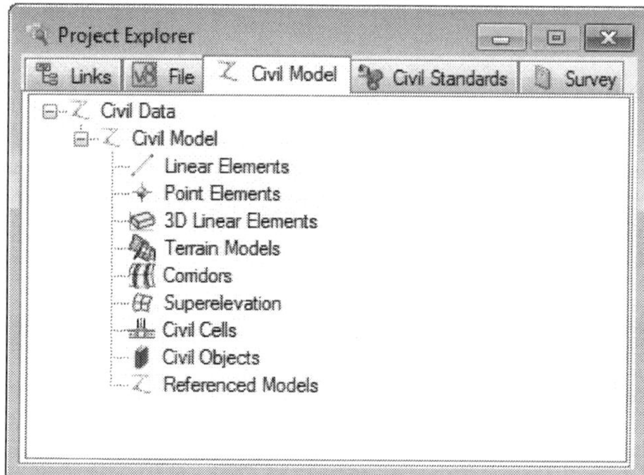

Civil Standards

The **Civil Standards** tab in Project Explorer is the interface to your organization's standards. The Libraries category contains all of the default configuration settings and cannot be modified without opening the configuration files.

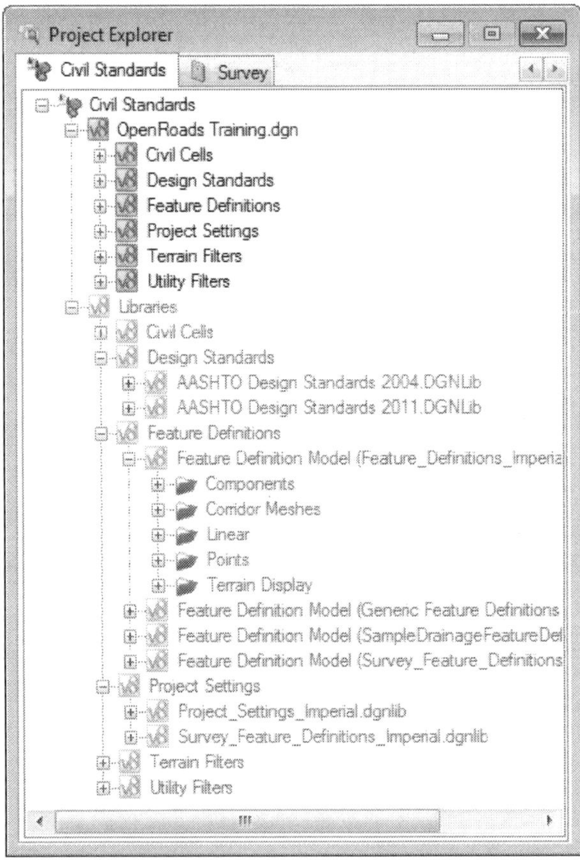

There is also a category for the current model. As you use standards, such as **Feature Definitions**, they are copied into the current model. Once copied, you can edit the local settings but should only do so when you are sure you want to change the standard for this one design.

This book was written using the Bentley delivered standards. When starting OpenRoads, select the MicroStation User ***examples*** and the project ***Bentley-Civil-Imperial***.

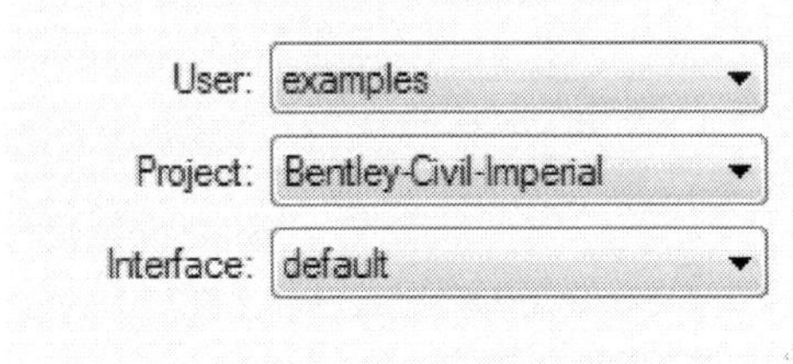

Survey

The **Survey** tab is the interface to all your survey data. From here, you create a Field Book for storing the data and can edit, display, delete or otherwise modify the data as needed. You can have as many Field Books as you need in each model.

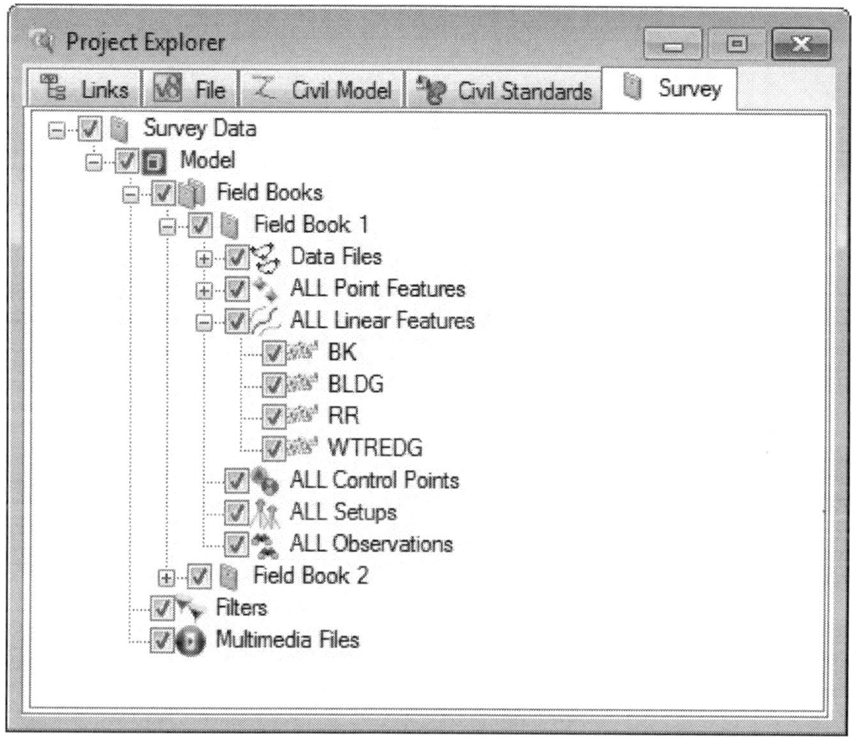

Features

A feature is a measurable entity which exists as part of your design. For example: a centerline, an edge of pavement, a terrain model, etc. They can be shown differently in different views, such as in plan, profile, 3D, etc.

A feature has a name and a feature definition.

There are various types of features:

- **Linear**: Centerlines, Shoulders, EOPs, etc.
- **Point**: Standalone point, such as tree, sign, etc.
- **Surface**: 3D such as terrain models (terrain model elements) or solids like curb, sidewalk, asphalt (components)
- **Node**: Manhole, inlet, etc.
- **Conduit**: Pipes
- **Polygon**: Catchments, Ponds

Feature Definitions

Feature Definitions are stored in DGNLIBs as part of your configuration. They define the engineering properties (for example, will it behave as a break line in a DTM) and the display characteristics of a feature. These allow the feature to represent the 'real-world' entity they are defining and to be displayed properly in different locations (plan, profile, 3D). **Feature Definitions** are similar to **Styles** from previous versions.

Feature definitions control symbology by linking to a **Native Style** (from an XIN) OR by calling **Element Templates** (from a DGNLIB). The link to the native style is by style name. It matches that name to whichever XIN is currently loaded.

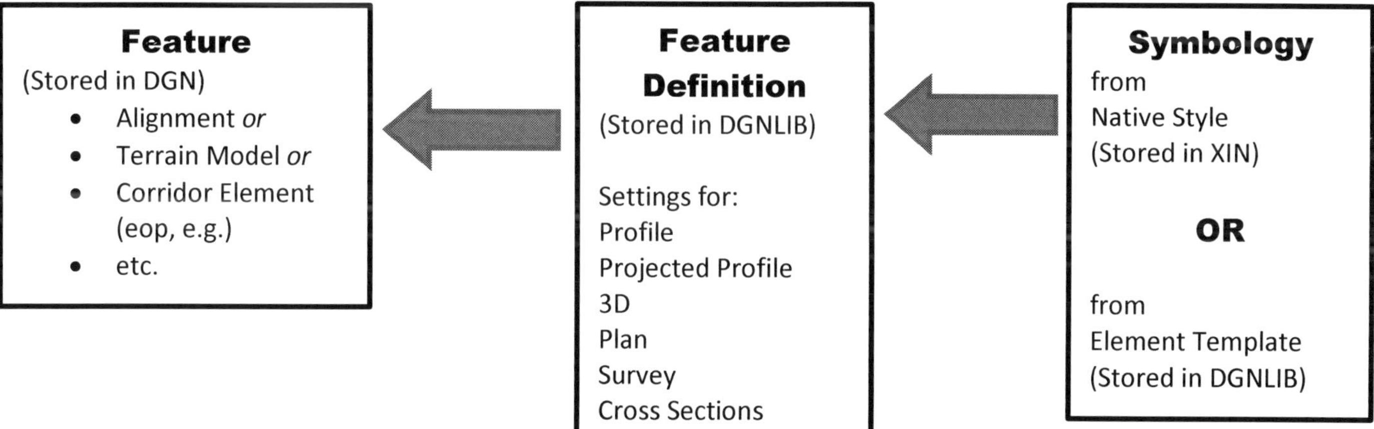

Element Information

Element Information is invaluable in allowing the edit and review of all kinds of entities within the InRoads data as well as settings from your configuration. Many times, you may right-click and select properties on an element or on data in the civil model to access **Element Information** for that particular entity.

MS: Element > Information

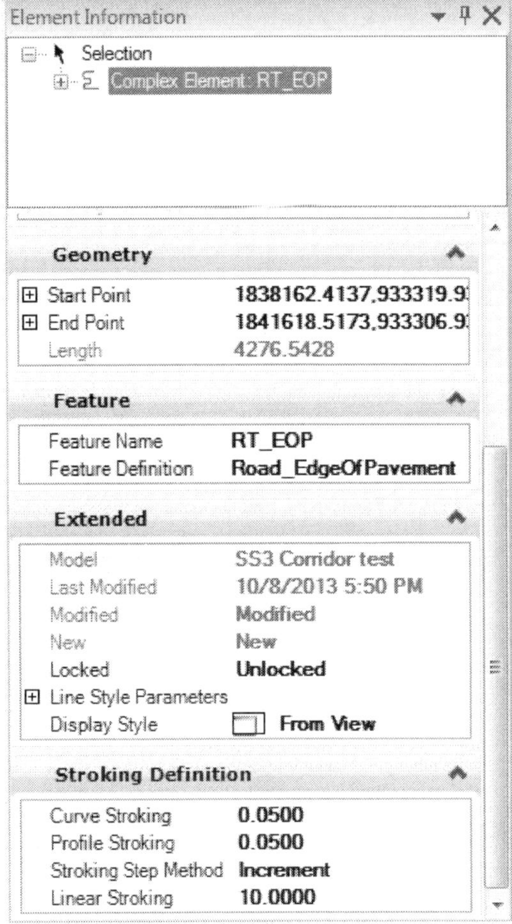

Data Files used by InRoads

In previous versions of InRoads, there was much more reliance on outside data files rather than MicroStation DGN files. Now, much of the design process will use DGN-based data. There are still items for which you need the older or legacy files and this course will cover how to convert to them as needed. Below is a table of the files used by InRoads.

File	Ext.	Format	Comes From		Contains	Method of Saving
Design File	.dgn	Binary	User created		Terrain Models Civil Geometry Corridor Setup Graphics	Saved automatically (dependent upon MicroStation settings)
Template Library	.itl	XML	Standard Make copy for project use so you can edit		Templates End Conditions Point Names	Must be saved before exiting command.
Digital Terrain Models	.dtm	Binary	Existing - Converted from Terrain Model Design – Created from Corridor	*	Topographic information for ground surface. Used for contouring, profiles, etc. **SS4 uses Terrain Models for most surface functions**	Must be saved before exiting. May use File>Save As>*.dtm
Geometry Project	.alg	Binary	Created by design and/or converted from Civil Geometry	*	Horizontal alignments Vertical alignments Cogo points **SS4 uses Civil Geometry for most geometry functions**	Must be saved before exiting. May use File>Save As>*.alg

* Legacy file type; not typically used during design in OpenRoads. Corresponding OpenRoads data is now stored in the DGN file.

Project Defaults

InRoads SS4 loads a preference file (XIN) when it starts just like previous versions. Your configuration can specify an agency XIN or you may create **Project Defaults** to have InRoads load your customized XIN automatically. If you do not load your customized one by either method, InRoads will load the default file out of the InRoads product directory and you will have to load yours through a project file (.rwk) or individually.

The **Project Defaults** also set the path that is used to open or store data files that you load or save. These paths are not absolute; they are just the starting point to which the **Open** or **Save** commands default.

Multiple **Project Defaults** may be created and stored on a machine, and you can switch between them when switching between projects.

IR: File > Project Defaults as shown below.

The Civil Tools Task Menu

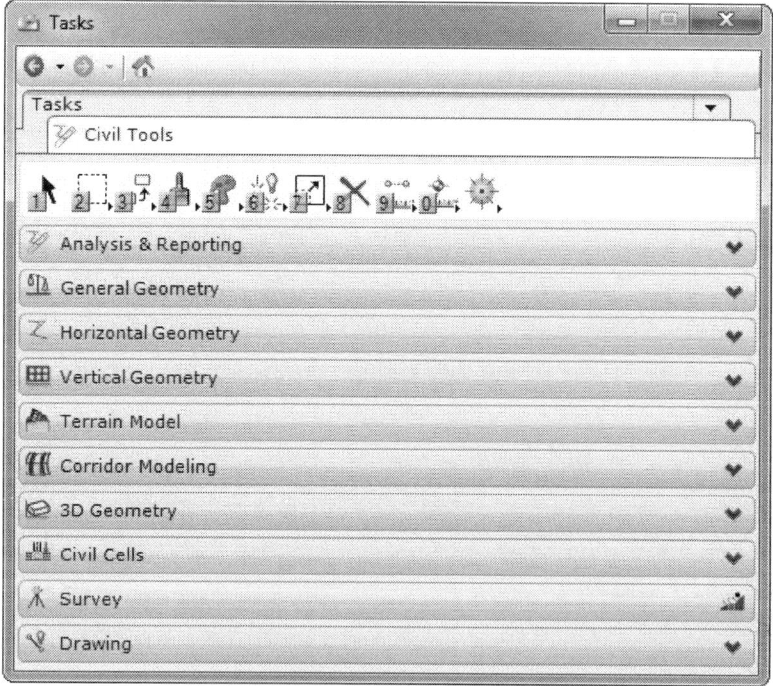

InRoads (OpenRoads) commands are found on the **MicroStation Task** menu under a workflow called **Civil Tools**. When it is expanded, there are several categories of commands.

Analysis & Reporting – commands for creating all kinds of geometry reports as well as terrain model tracking and analysis.

General Geometry – commands for setting an active Feature Definition, Importing and Exporting civil geometry, assigning actives, creating civil geometry from graphics, and unlocking or deleting rules from geometry.

Horizontal Geometry – commands for creating and editing horizontal elements. Unlike previous versions, these elements do not technically have to be 'geometry'. For example, items previously stored in the DTM, such as utilities, can now be created as geometry.

Vertical Geometry – commands for adding and editing 'Profile' or vertical information to any horizontal geometry you have created. This can include creating true vertical alignments or draping a surface to assign elevations to the horizontal for example.

Terrain Model – commands for creating and editing terrain models. In this version, a terrain model is a MicroStation element type, so it is created and edited using MicroStation-like tools.

Corridor Modeling – commands for created corridors. If you used a previous version of InRoads, this is where all of your templating and Roadway Designer commands have gone. It is also where you'll find Cross Sections and Cross Section Annotation commands as well as End Area Volumes.

3D Geometry – contains commands that are useful for site modeling, such as pond creation tools and adding templates to linear elements.

Civil Cells – allow the placement of standard civil data, similar to MicroStation cells. This can be standard geometry, such as a turnout, or a fully developed driveway entrance. They are placed based on reference geometry in the design file and can be as simple or complex as needed. Civil Cells can save a lot of time for repetitive tasks.

Survey – is a workflow that contains the basic survey commands, most of which can also be accessed through the Project Explorer. The workflow also contains the Terrain Model and Geometry commands.

Explorer Menu

InRoads legacy commands are accessed through the InRoads Explorer pull-down menus. Legacy commands are considered those commands that have been carried over from previous versions of InRoads because they do not yet have a corresponding functionality that uses OpenRoads Technology.There are times when you will need to use the data file format from previous version to complete your workflow and in that case, the Explorer is used.

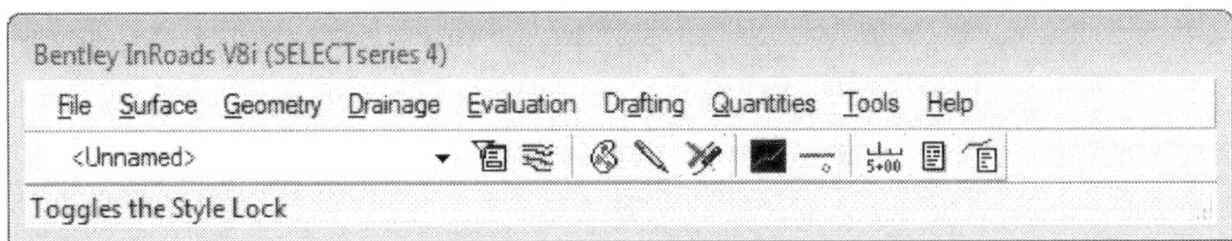

The InRoads Explorer menu may be toggled on/off from the right-click menu in MicroStation.

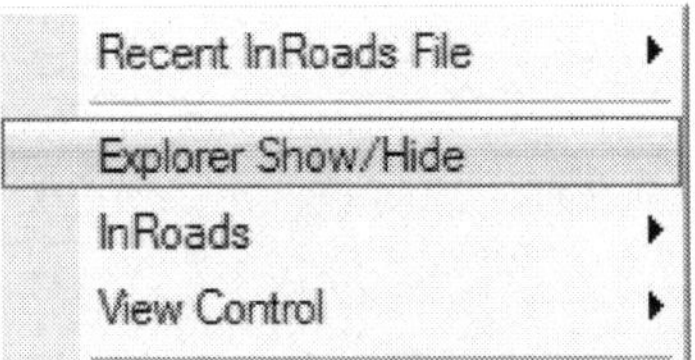

Working with Civil Data

Heads-up Displays (prompts)

The new InRoads uses fewer dialog boxes that previous versions and in most cases you can use a heads-up display instead. When using the heads-up display, command options will cycle through and allow you to toggle between choices or key in values. When keying in values, a **<Tab>** (or sometimes **<Enter>**) is used to 'lock' the value. Failing to lock the value can result in the value changing based on cursor location. The **<End>** key will unlock the value.

After each option is chosen or locked, a data point accepts the choice and moves you to the next option. If an option has an arrow beside it, you can use that keyboard arrow (up, down, left, right) to change the settings. If the option has … beside it, you can use the **<ALT>** and a down arrow to open a dialog box to make a selection.

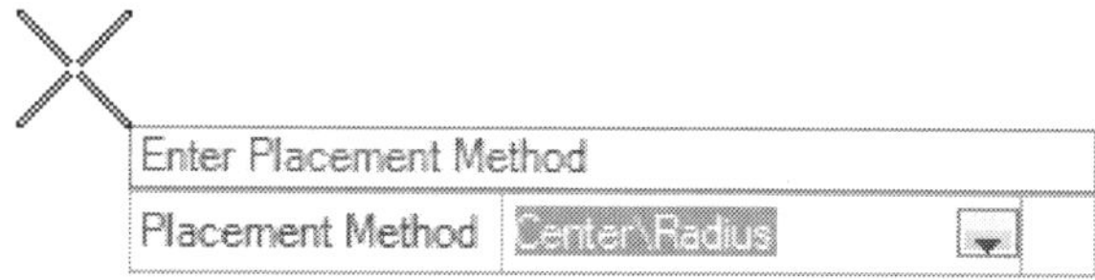

Element Selection

The **Element Selection** tool is used throughout InRoads to select and manipulate data. It is also useful to 'knock' you out of a command.

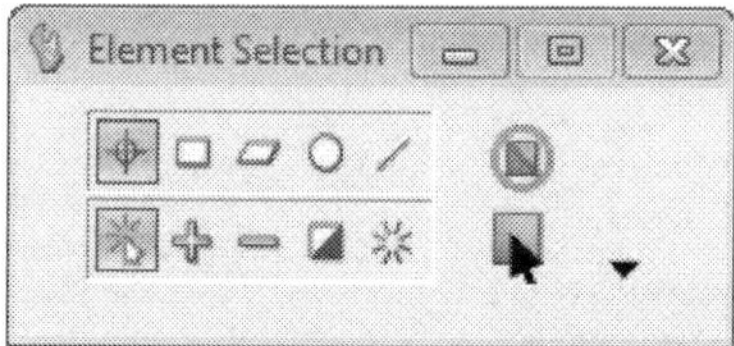

Context Sensitive Menus

There are many times that a command or an option can be selected from a pop-up menu rather than the task menu. These pop-up menus are accessed by hovering over or selecting a graphic. They are **context sensitive** meaning they will change as needed depending upon what type of civil element is selected.

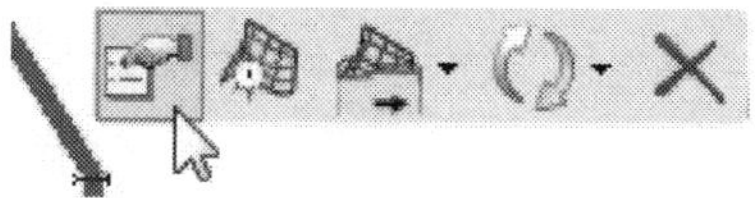

Upgrading an Existing Project

Existing InRoads SS2 projects may be upgraded to the new OpenRoads Technology in InRoads SS4. These conversions are discussed later in the book, but as a synopsis:

DTM

Digital Terrain Models (DTMs) must be converted into Terrain Models and are now stored in the DGN file.

MS: Tasks > Civil Tools > Terrain Model > Create from File

ALG

Geometry Projects (ALGs) must be converted into Civil Geometry and are now stored in the DGN file.

MS: Tasks > Civil Tools > General Geometry > Import Geometry

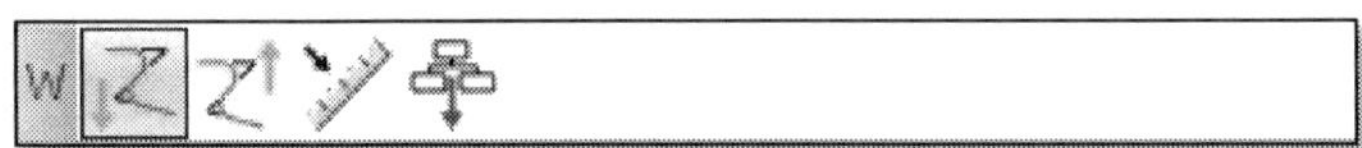

OR

MS: Tasks > Civil Tools > General Geometry > Import InRoads from Memory

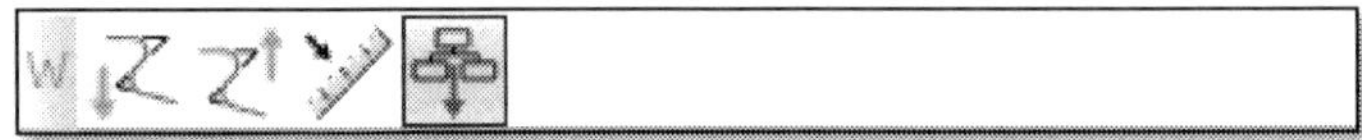

ITL

Template Libraries (ITLs) are loaded without conversion, but there are new options which should be investigated. To load a template library:

MS: Tasks > Civil Tools > Corridor Modeling > Create Template

IRD

Roadway Design files (IRDs) must be converted into corridors and are now stored in the DGN file.

MS: Tasks > Civil Tools > Corridor Modeling > Import IRD

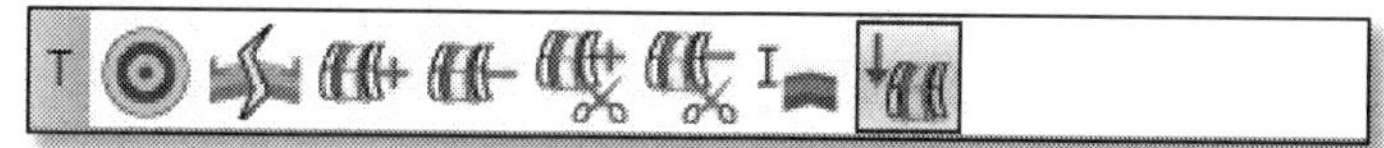

DGN

While DGN files themselves do not need to be converted to the new format, it is ***highly recommended*** that you start out with ***new*** DGN files when creating Civil Data (geometry, terrains, etc.)

2D vs 3D

In general, use 3D models to contain terrain. Use 2D models for everything else. When a 3D model is needed, it is created from the 2D model and referenced automatically.

Terrain Models

FEATURE TYPES

CREATING TERRAIN MODELS

2 Terrain Models

A **Terrain Model** is a new element type in MicroStation. Just like the previous digital terrain model (DTM), a terrain model is a series of points triangulated to create a surface. It can be made up of different point types as shown below.

Terrain Model Feature Types

Spot or Spot Elevation

Points with X,Y,Z coordinates that have no relationship to any other points. Spots can be represented with MicroStation cells, symbols or text. A Random survey shot is an example of a spot feature. Lines and line strings can also be used where the software creates a spot elevation for each vertex along the longitudinal element, although these are typically break line features.

Break Line

Break lines are used to designate linear features such as edges of pavement, curb and gutter, ditch bottoms, etc. Any longitudinal element may be defined as a break line. Triangles will not cross a break line in the terrain model.

Soft Break Line

If a soft break line crosses a break line, it is ignored in that area.

Contour

An element with points at the same elevation that is used as part of creating a terrain model. Don't confuse it with computed contours which display from the terrain.

Hole

An area defined by a closed shape that represents a region where the current terrain is ignored and the underlying terrain is utilized.

Boundary

The external limits of the terrain model. In this version, the boundary does not have to be closed. A boundary will not allow triangles to the outside.

Drape Boundary

A boundary where the elevations are calculated by draping on the underlying surface.

Void

An area defined by a closed shape where there is no data or it's an obscure area. No triangles are created inside the void areas. The void points are included in the triangulation of the surface but the lines between points are draped onto the surface and do not change the slope or elevation of the surface.

Drape Void

An area defined by a closed shape where there is no data or it's an obscure area. No triangles are created inside the void areas. The void points are *not* included in the triangulation of the surface and the void is inserted post-triangulation. The void shape is draped on the surface.

Break Void

An area defined by a closed shape where there is no data or it's an obscure area. No triangles are created inside the void areas. The vertex elevations of the shape are used in triangulation at their current elevation (unlike Void and Drape Void) and lines between points are inserted as break lines. Therefore, break voids change the slope and elevations of the surface.

Island

An area defined by a closed shape that represents a region completely inside a void. A typical example is an island in the middle of rivers or lake.

Terrain Models

Terrain models are 3D so if they are created in 2D, a 3D MicroStation model is created automatically to 'hold' the terrain and is attached to the current model as a reference. To edit the terrain model, you must be in the actual MicroStation model where the terrain resides.

When a terrain model is created, it can be assigned a **Feature Definition** for display purposes. The feature definition is one of the terrain model's properties and can be changed at any time. The feature definition controls what the initial display consists of – triangles, contours, boundary, etc.

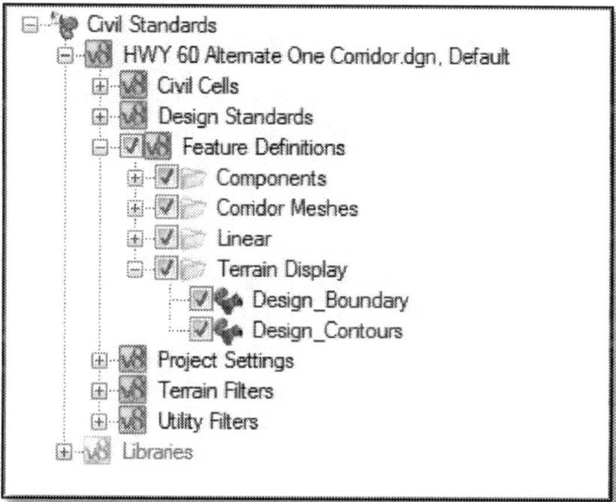

To change the display while in the model containing the terrain, hover over the terrain elements (the boundary or other displayed terrain feature) and select **Properties**

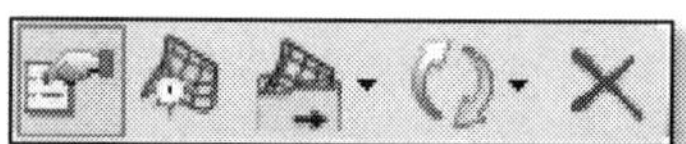

Turn on any of the other displays by double-clicking the **Off** to change it to **On**. When the change is made in this manner, the terrain will revert to whatever was originally toggled on in the feature definition any time an edit is made to the terrain.

If you want to more permanently change the display, change the **Feature Definition** to one that defaults to the display you want.

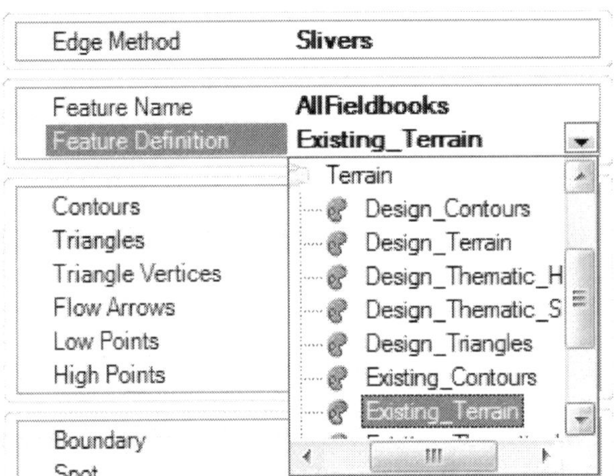

To change the display while referencing the model containing the terrain, select the terrain elements (the boundary or other displayed terrain feature) and choose **Properties**

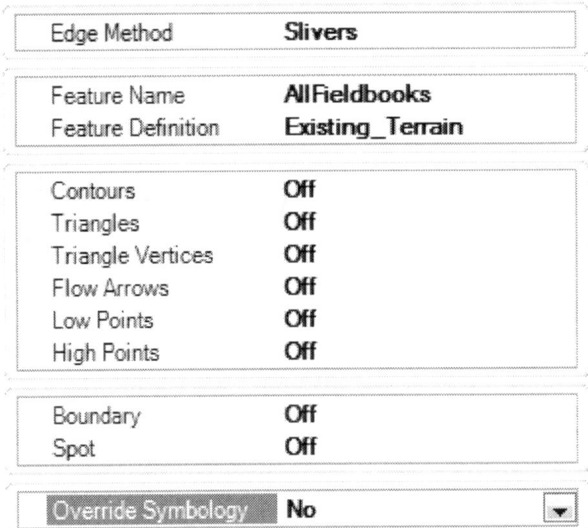

If you're in the same DGN as the model containing the terrain, you can toggle displays on and off. If you are in a different DGN, first toggle on **Override Symbology**, then any displays you wish.

The **Feature Definition** gets it's default display and symbology options from its **Element Template**. If you're in the same design file as the terrain, the element template is copied in and can be modified as another method of changing the default display.

2.1 Importing a DTM file to create Terrain Model

➢ **MS: Tasks > Civil Tools > Terrain Model > Create From File**

➢ Choose the DTM file from the hard drive

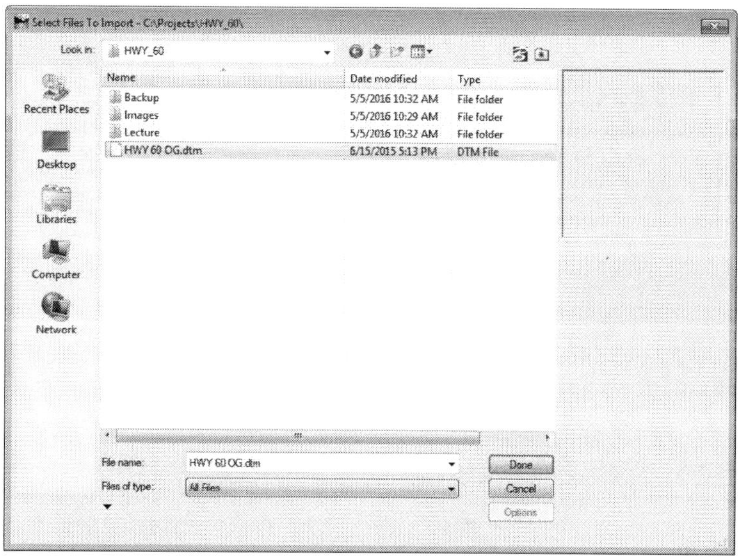

➢ Set the **Options** as necessary

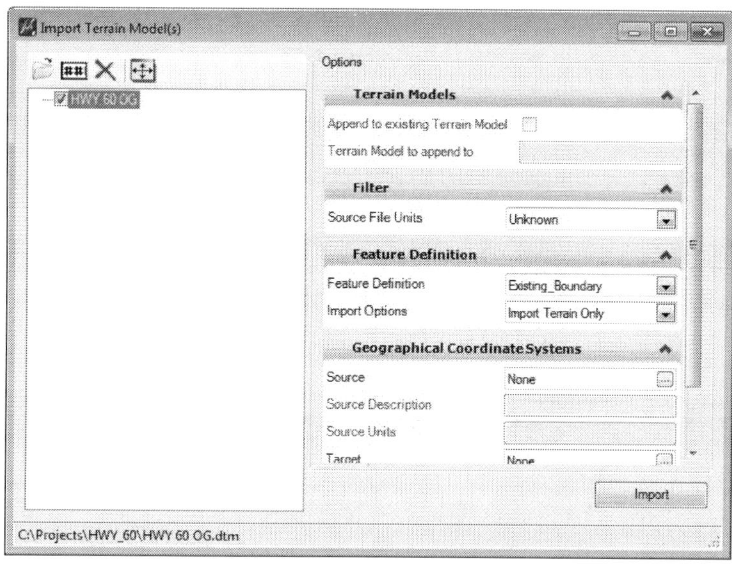

- In the **Feature Definition** category **Import Options**,
  - **Import Terrain Only** creates a terrain model element from the DTM. The individual features are part of the DTM but are not editable as such.
  - **Import Features Only** creates graphical features that are editable but no terrain model is created.
  - **Import Both** creates graphical features that are editable and adds them to a terrain model so if the features are edited, the terrain updates.
- Select **Import**
- The terrain model and/or features are imported

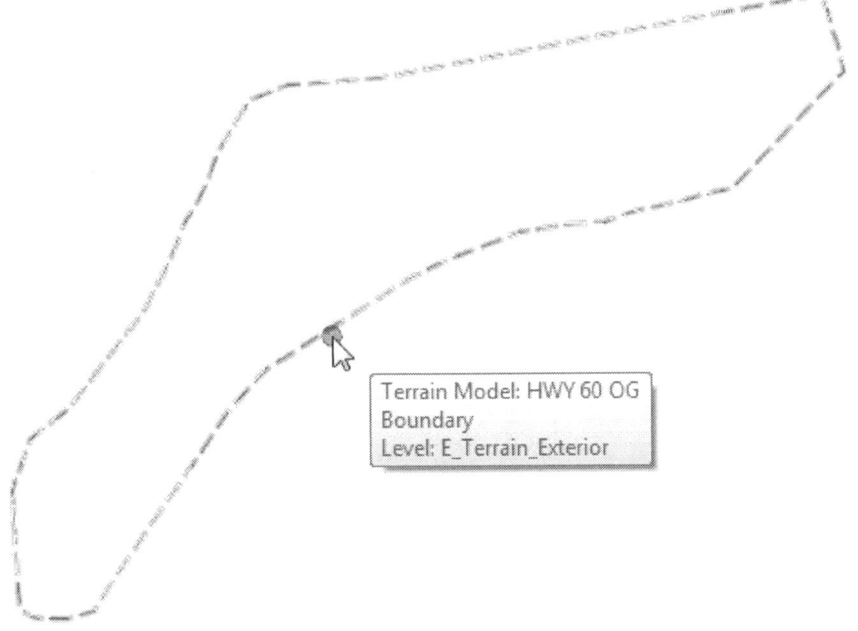

2.2 Tracking a terrain model

The MicroStation model containing the terrain model may either be the active MicroStation model, or it may be referenced to the active model

- **MS: Tasks > Civil Tools > Analysis & Reporting > Analyze Point**

- Select the terrain element

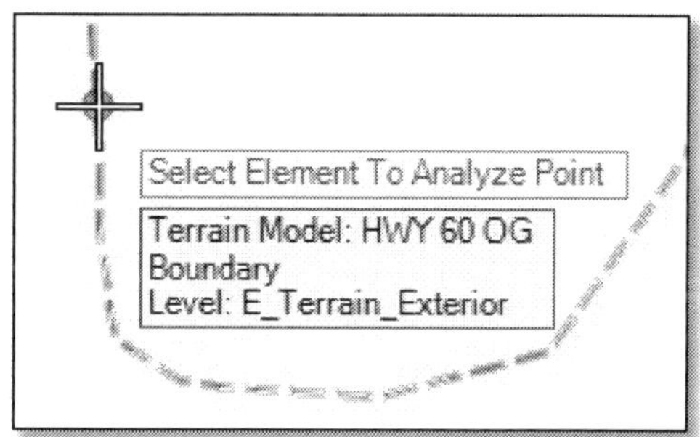

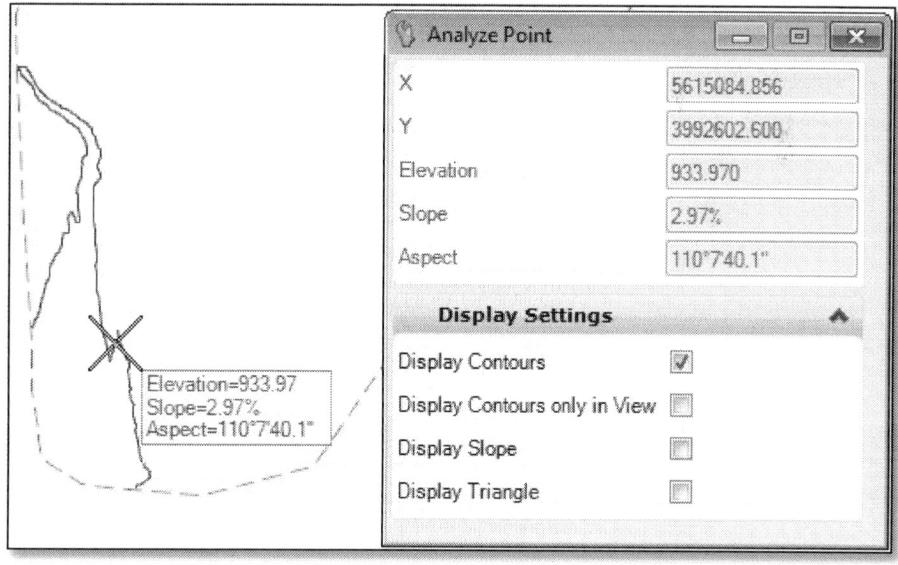

2.3 Viewing Contours

If you are in the MicroStation model containing the terrain, you can permanently change the display type of the terrain element by changing the Feature Definition.

➢ Select the terrain element and choose **Properties** from the menu

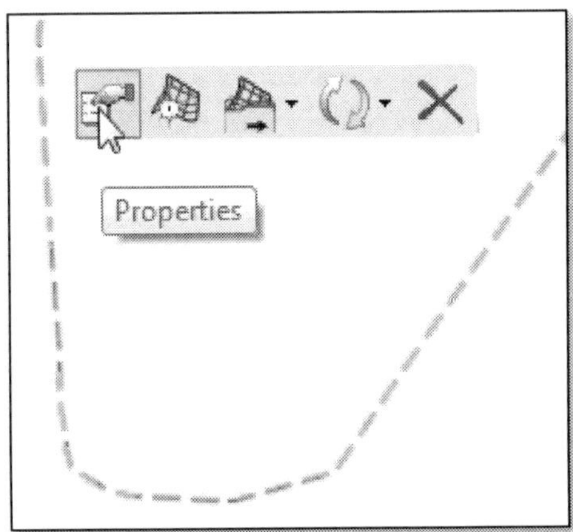

➢ Change the **Feature Definition** to the desired display

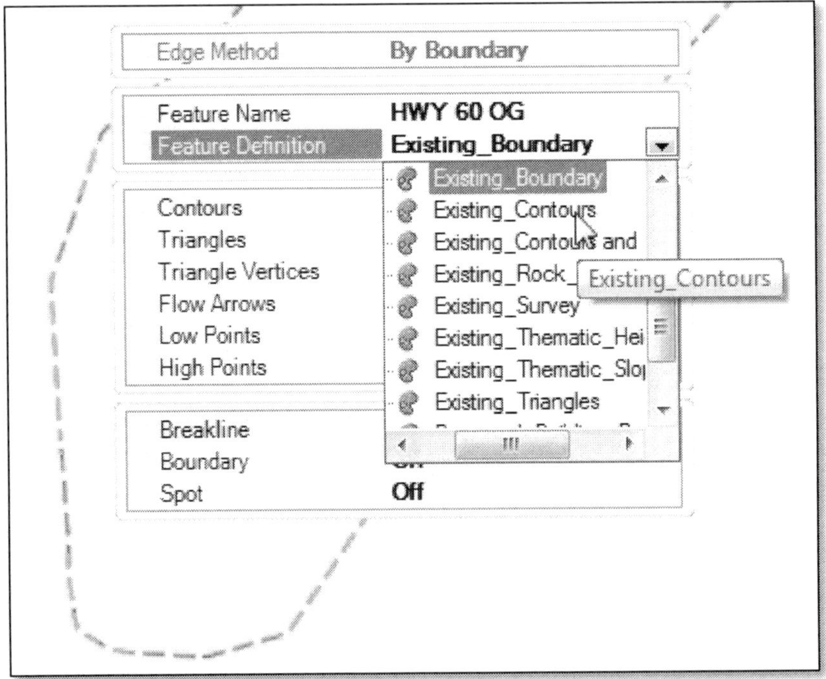

The terrain model will show the desired display until it is changed, even if the terrain is edited.

- To temporarily change the display, toggle the desired display **On** or **Off** using the toggles on the **Properties** menu.

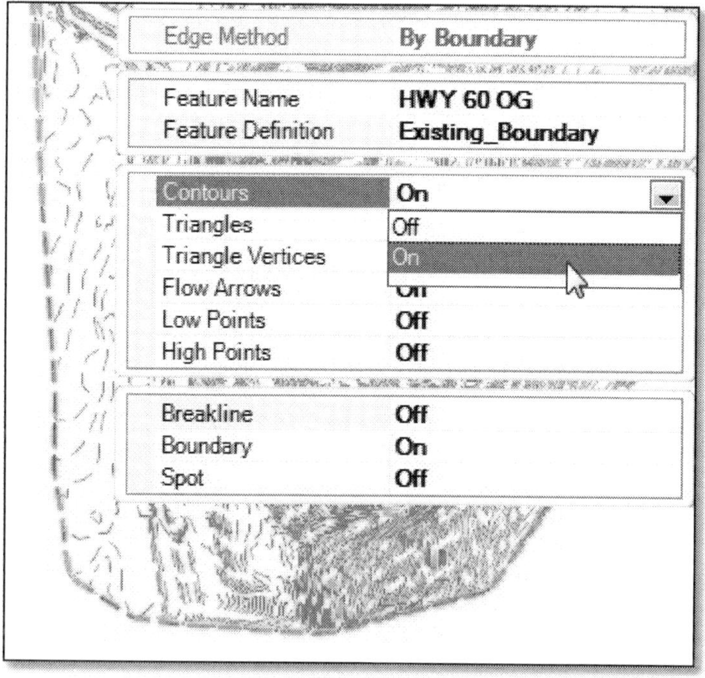

- If the terrain is referenced, toggle **Override Symbology** to Yes, then you can temporarily toggle on and off the displays. You cannot change the **Feature Definition** of a referenced terrain.

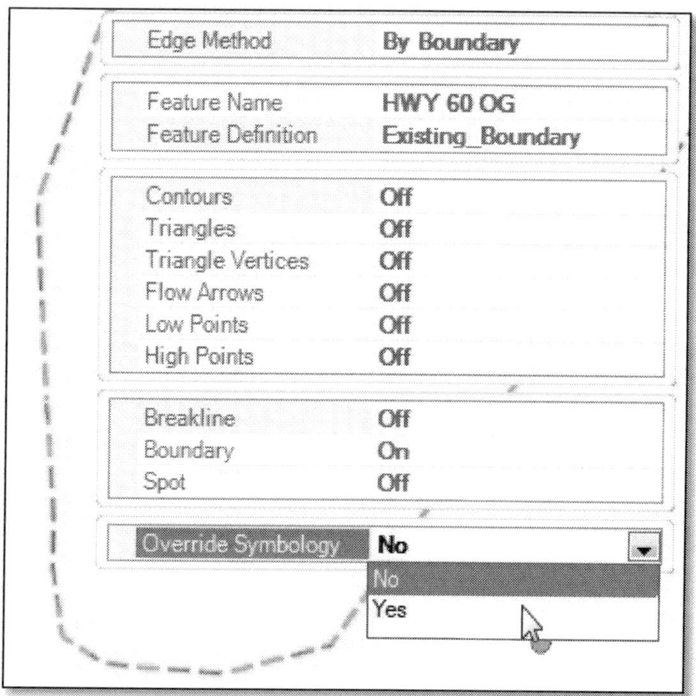

- ➢ The displays are controlled by **Element Templates**, initially found in a DGNLIB and copied into the active design file when used.
- ➢ **MS: Element > Element Templates**

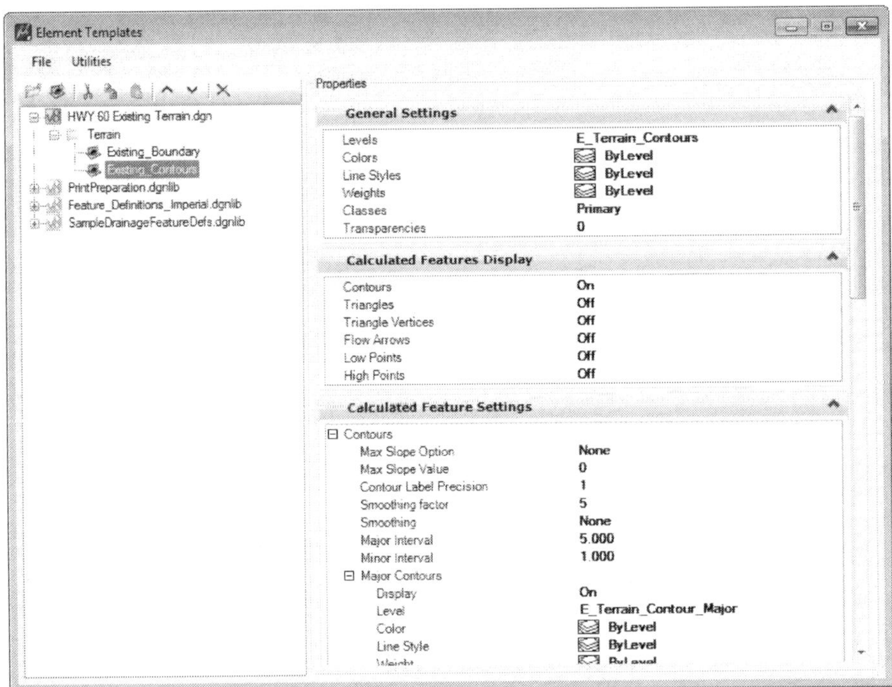

Note: Changes to the element template are for this design file only and will not affect the standards.

2.4 Adding linear features to a terrain model

Linear features can be added to an existing terrain model to create break lines, voids, etc.

The MicroStation model containing the terrain model must be active. The linear features you want to add may be in the active or a referenced model. The features can be either MicroStation graphics drawn at the correct elevations or civil geometry with profiles for the elevations. If you are tracing survey data to create the MicroStation graphics, the survey data must be in a 3D model rather than the default 2D, so the elevations can be picked up from the survey points.

➤ Select the graphical element

➤ On the context sensitive menu, select **Terrain Model > Add to Terrain Model**

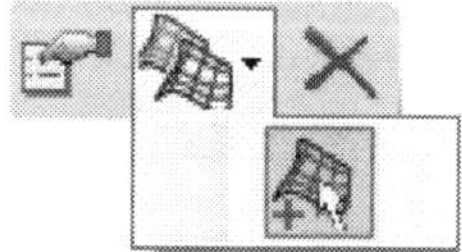

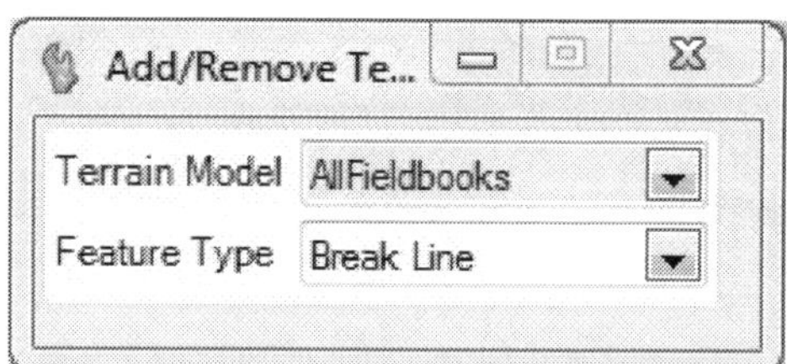

➤ Use the dialog or follow the heads-up prompts to select the **Terrain Model** and the **Feature Type**

➤ Data **<D>** to **Accept** the selections and the feature is added

You may also choose the same command from the Task menu and follow the prompts.

2.5 Combining Terrain Models

If you have two models that you wish to combine, you can create a **Complex Terrain Model**. In this example, a terrain model created from Lidar data is combined with the terrain model created from survey but this is also the procedure used to combine an existing and proposed terrain.

➢ **Text MS: Tasks > Civil Tools > Terrain Model > Create Complex Terrain Model**

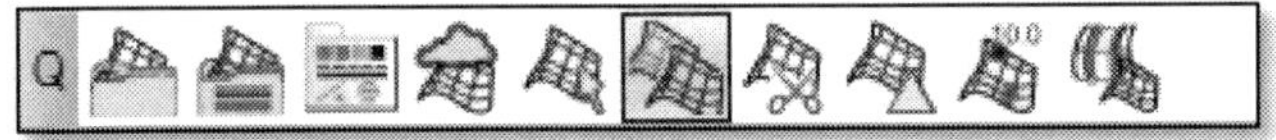

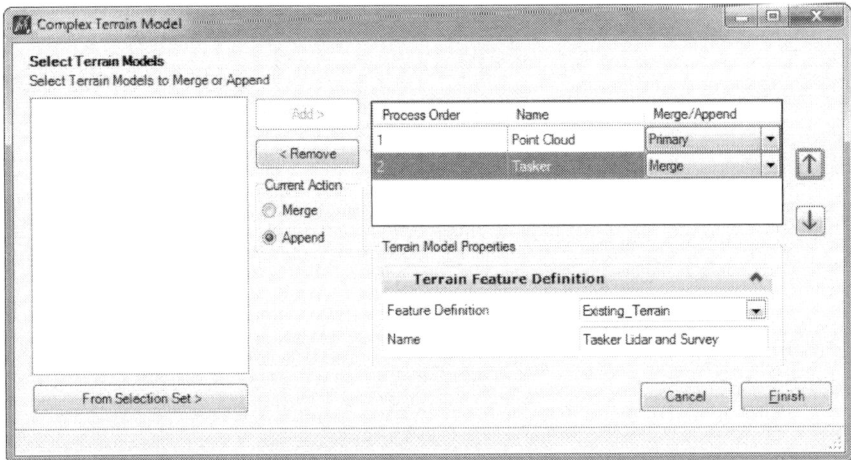

➢ Select the Point Cloud terrain model and choose **Add**

➢ Set the Point Could terrain model as the **Primary**

➢ Select the Survey terrain model and choose **Add**

➢ Set the Survey terrain model as a **Merge** or **Append**

If you want it to replace the area inside the Primary data, then Merge. If you want to add it to the Primary data, then Append.

➢ Set the Terrain **Feature Definition** and **Name** as desired

➢ Choose **Finish**

Once the combined surface is created, any changes to the original surfaces are automatically reflected in the combination.

Exercise 2: Terrain model from an existing DTM

If you have a DTM from an older version of InRoads that you need to use OpenRoads, it can be imported to create a Terrain Model. The terrain model will remain linked to the original file so that if the original is updated, the terrain model may also be updated.

Given:

- *HWY 60 OG.dtm* – Original ground digital terrain model from aerial survey

Required:

- Create a new design file
- Import the DTM to create a new terrain model
- Become comfortable with the terrain model displays

Getting Started

1 Start InRoads using the icon on your desktop or using the **Start** menu

2 In the **File Open** dialog, set the:

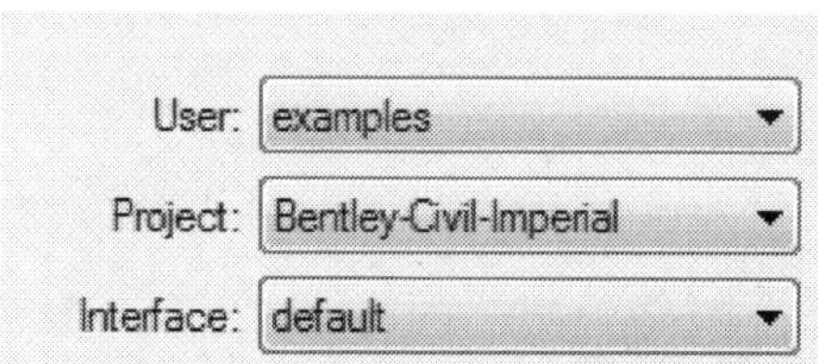

- **User**: ***examples***
- **Project**: ***Bentley-Civil-Imperial***
- **Interface**: ***default***

3 Set the Look in folder to *C:\Projects\HWY_60*

4 Select the **New File** icon

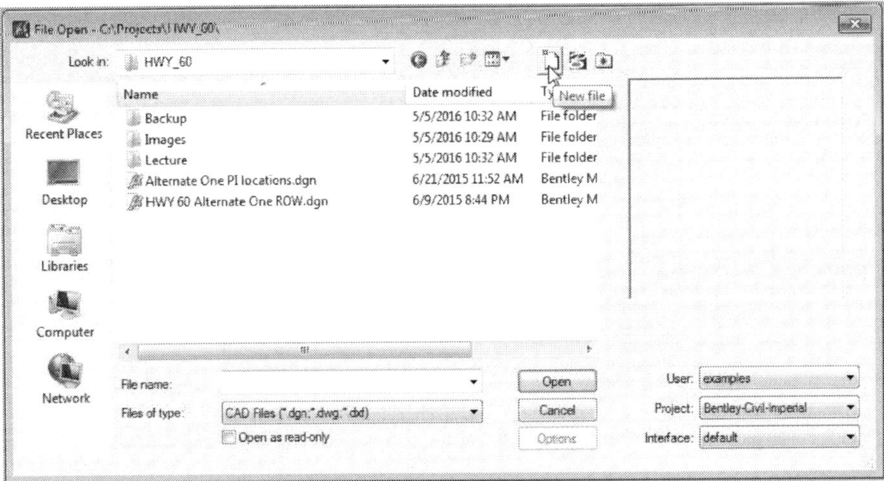

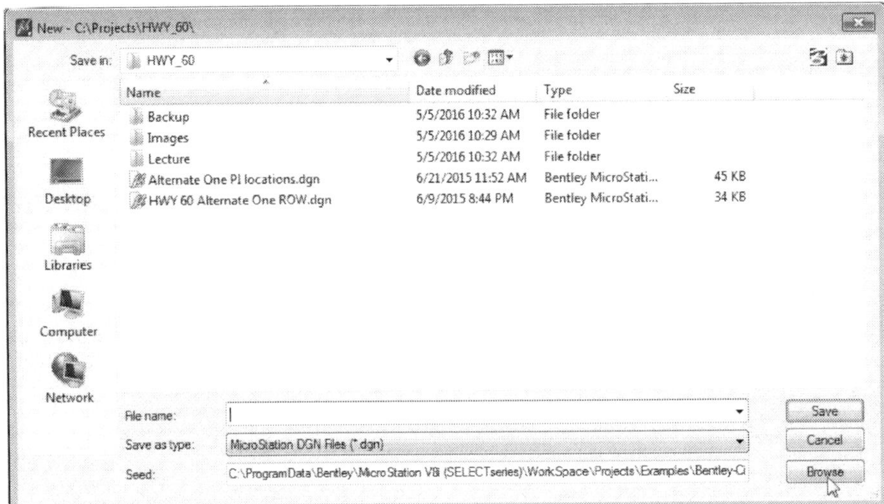

- Choose **Browse** next the Seed file

- The correct folder should open by default, but if not navigate to:

C:\ProgramData\Bentley\MicroStation V8i (SELECTseries)\WorkSpace\Projects\Examples\Bentley-Civil-Imperial\seed\

- Select the seed file *Seed3D-InRoads-Imperial.dgn* and select **Open**

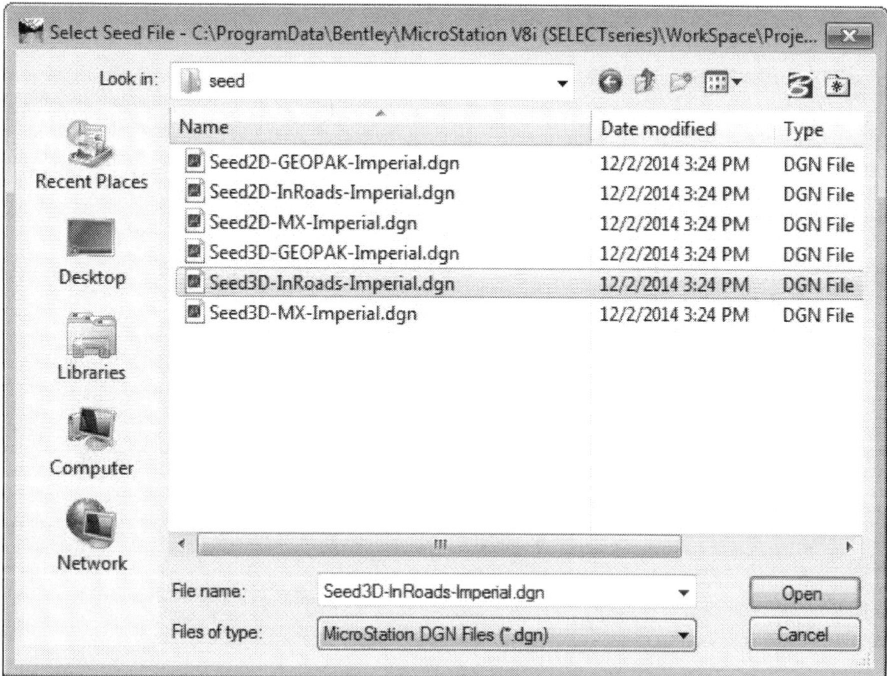

- Key in the File Name: *HWY 60 Existing Terrain.dgn*
- Select **Save**

5 **Open** the new file

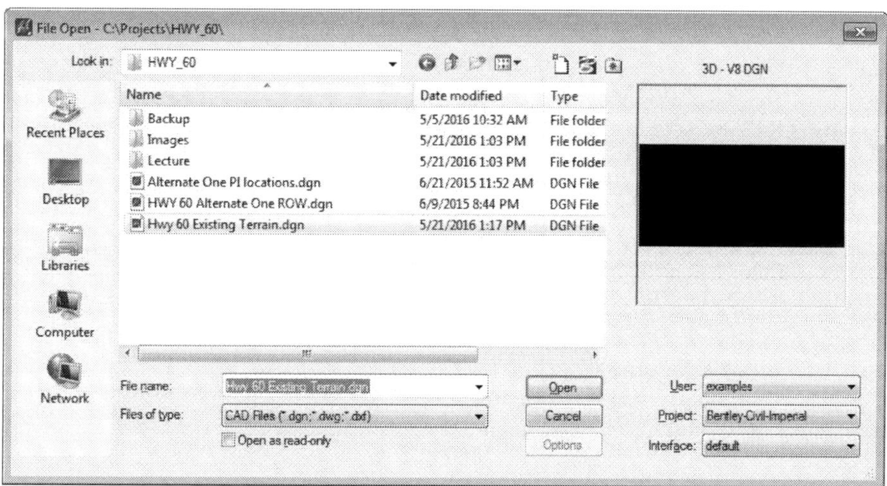

Importing a DTM

6 Import the DTM to create a terrain model

- **MS: Tasks > Civil Tools > Terrain Model > Create From File**

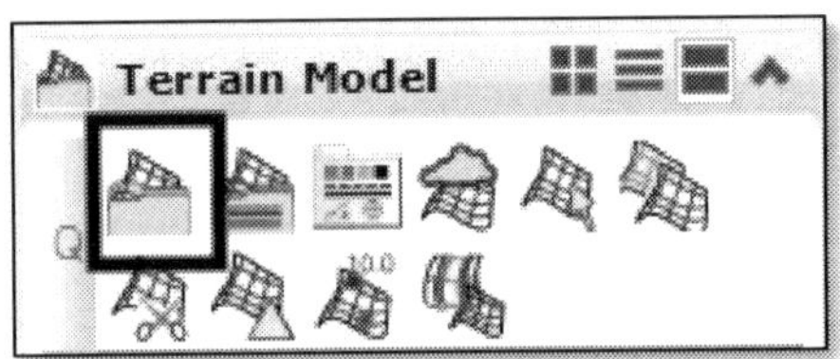

- Verify the Look in folder is set to *C:\Projects\HWY_60*
- Select the file *HWY 60 OG.dtm* and then **Done**
- On the **Import Terrain Model(s)** dialog,

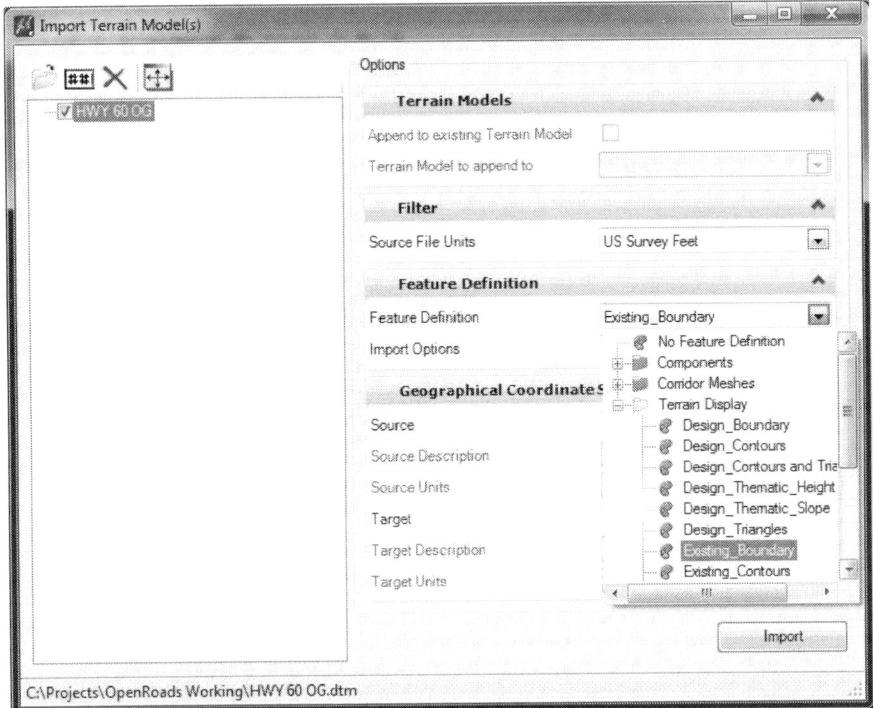

- **Filter**: Source File Units: ***US Survey Feet***
- **Feature Definition**: ***Terrain Display > Existing_Boundary***

  This will show only the boundary of the terrain by default

- **Import Options**: ***Import Terrain Only***

  This will import the terrain but the individual features will not be available for editing.

- Select **Import**
- **Close** the dialog

7 **Fit** the MicroStation view

An outline of the terrain model is displayed in the file.

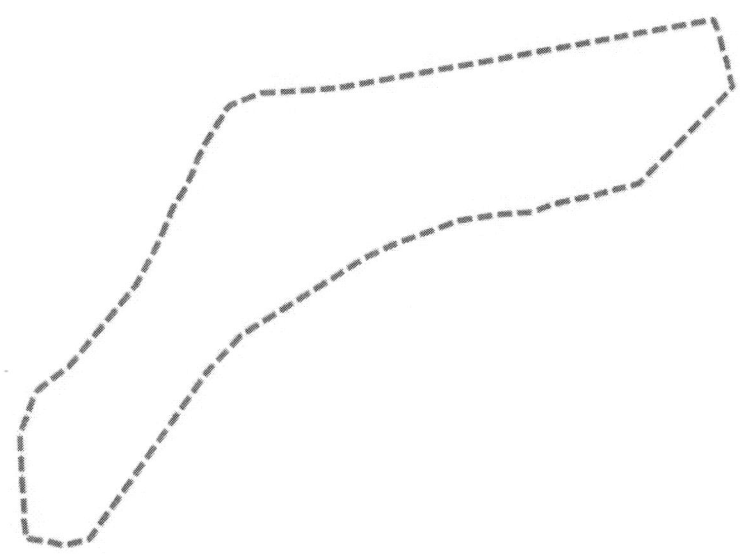

If the outline in your file does not appear like the one shown, or if in the future the DTM file is updated and you want to update the terrain model:

- Select the boundary
- On the context-sensitive menu that pops up, choose **Update from Source** and select the file you imported.

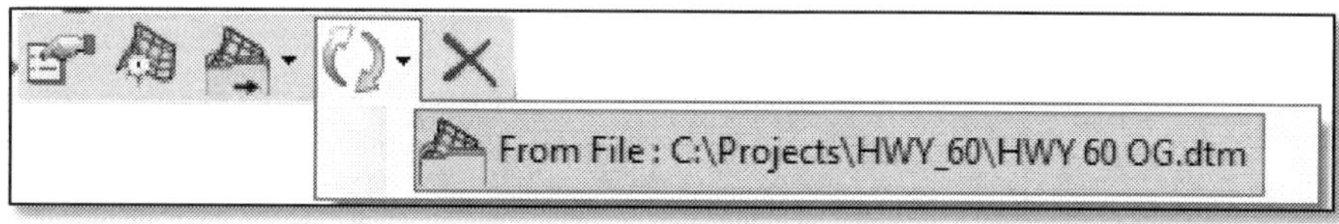

The boundary should update and appear as shown.

Terrain Model Displays

8 Work with Terrain Displays

- Select the boundary and choose **Properties**

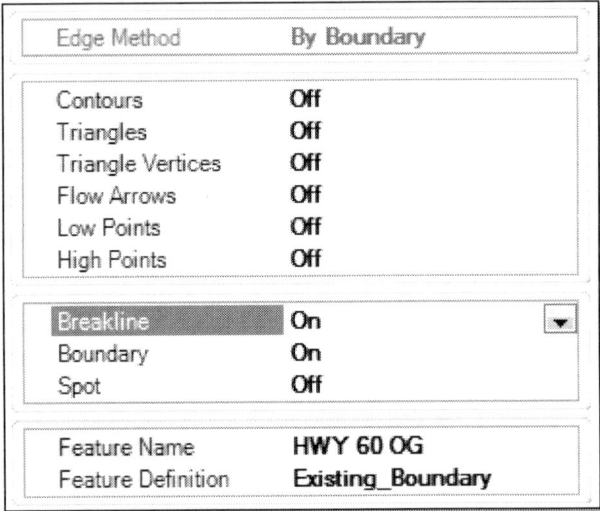

- Toggle on the ***Breakline*** display by either using the drop-down, or double-clicking **Off** to toggle it to **On**

Even though the original break lines are not displayed by default, they are in the terrain and affect the triangulation.

- Toggle **Off** ***Breakline*** and **On** ***Triangle*** display by either using the drop-down, or double-clicking **Off** to toggle it to **On**

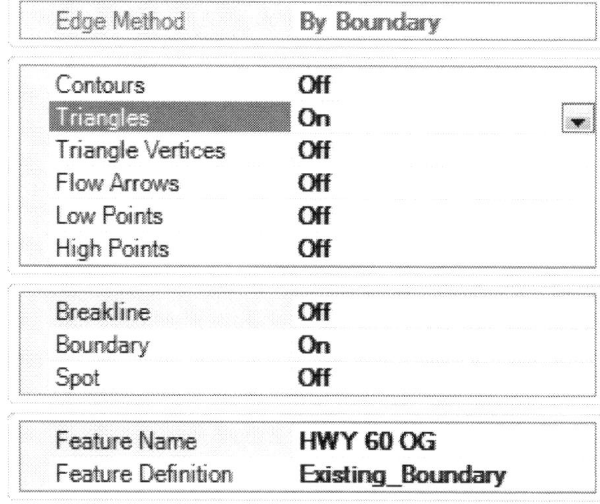

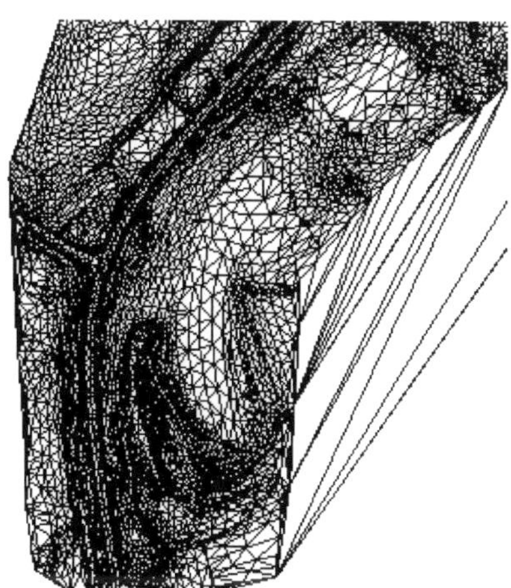

- Toggle **Off** the ***Triangle*** display and toggle **On** ***Contours***

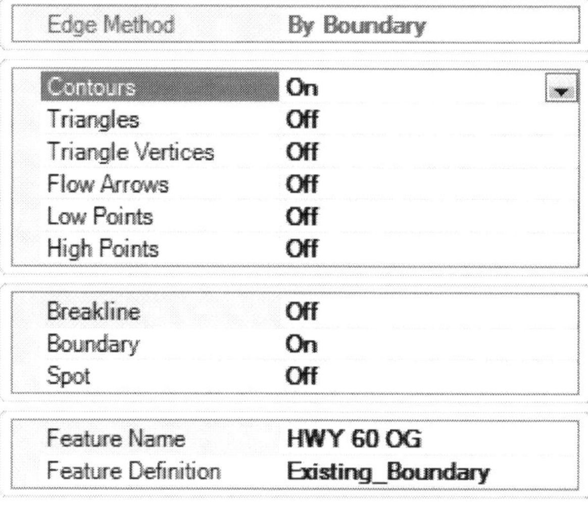

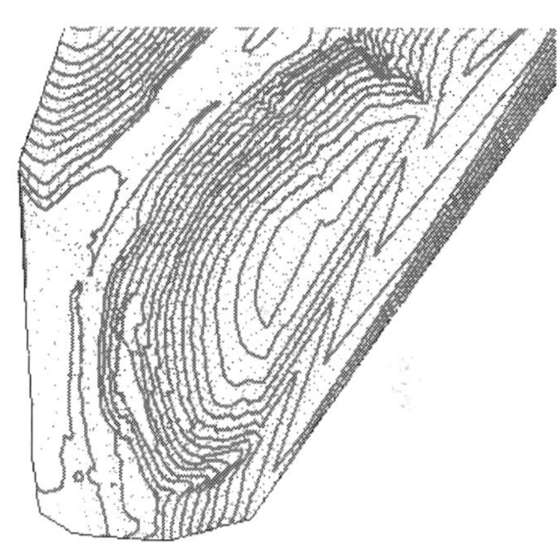

- Select **MS: Element > Element Templates**
- Expand the category for the current design file and select the element template *Existing_Boundary*

  Note the Element Template for the terrain has been copied into this file. As element templates are used, they are copied from the standards and can be modified for this particular file if necessary. The element template controls the displays including settings and symbology.

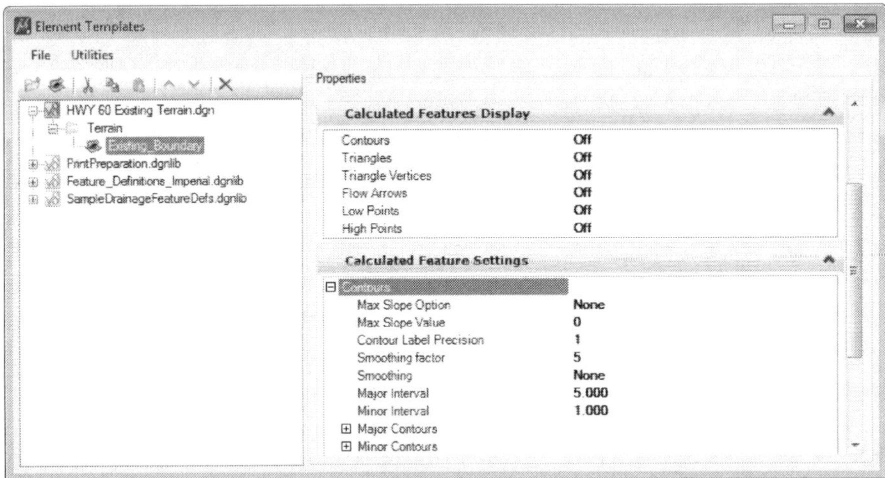

- Expand the ***Calculated Feature Settings*** category if not already expanded
- Change the ***Major Interval*** to **100** and ***Minor Interval*** to **10**
- Since the default setting for **Contours** is **Off**, you must turn them back **On** under **Properties** after making a change

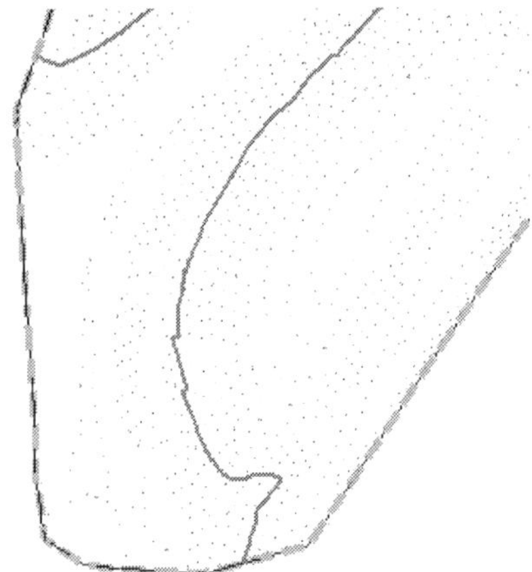

- Change the ***Major Interval*** to **10** and the ***Minor Interval*** to **2**
- Close the **Element Template** dialog

9 Try out some different **Feature Definition** options

> *When you change the* ***Feature Definition****, the settings 'stick' as opposed to just toggling a display on or off in which case the terrain always reverts back to the* ***Element Template*** *called by the assigned* ***Feature Definition****.*

- Select the boundary and then choose **Properties**

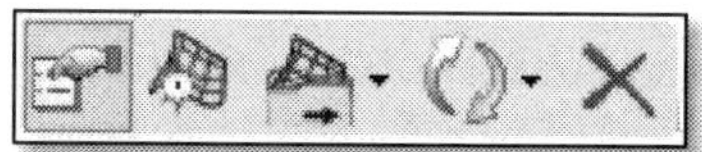

- Change the assigned ***Feature Definition*** to ***Existing_Contours***.

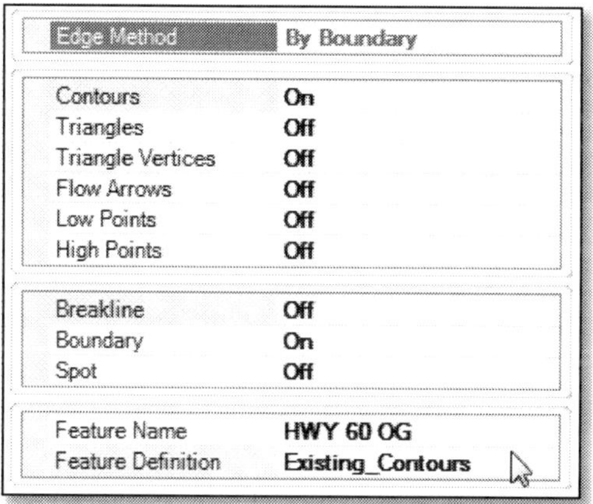

- Look at **Element Templates** and note a new one has been copied into the file.

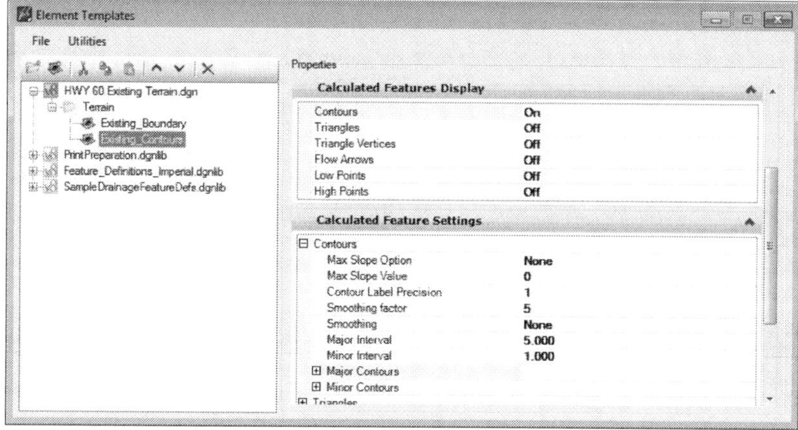

- Make a change to the ***Interval***

> *Notice the contours update but do not disappear as before. This is because the assigned Feature Definition calls an Element Template that has the contours turned on by default.*

- Close the **Element Template** box when done experimenting

Terrain Model Boundaries

10 Modify the Boundary

- Select the boundary and choose **Properties**

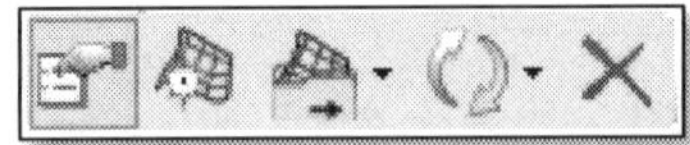

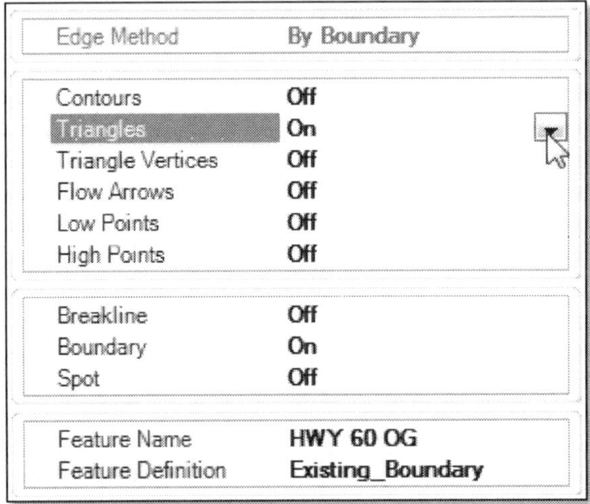

- Change the ***Feature Definition*** back to **Existing Boundary**
- Notice the ***Edge Method*** is set to **By Boundary**

  The Edge Method (Exterior) is assumed to be the edge or boundary of the triangulation from the DTM, even though the DTM does not actually have an exterior boundary.

- Toggle **On** the ***Triangle*** display and toggle **off** the ***Contours***

  Note there are extraneous triangles around the edge of the surface. In order to remove these triangles, the Boundary must be deleted.

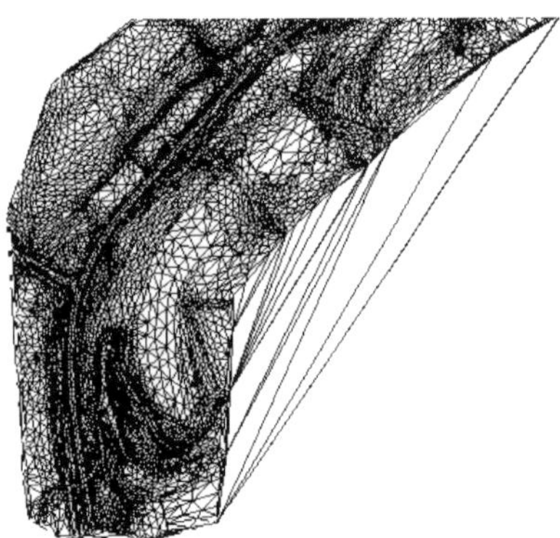

- **MS: Tasks > Civil Tools > Terrain Model > Remove Terrain Model Boundary**

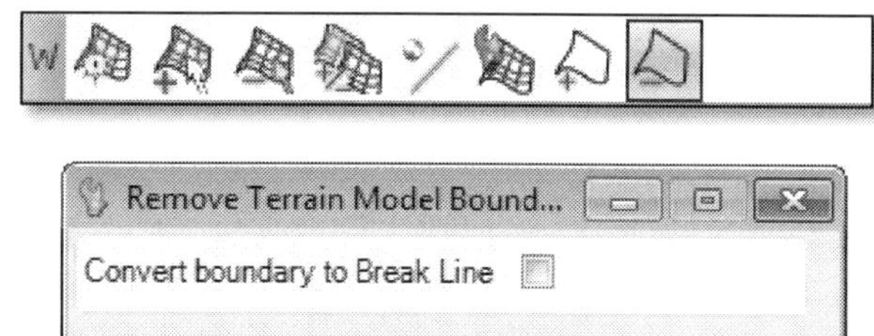

- Select the Terrain Model
- **Accept**

  Note the triangles disappear. This is again because the default setting for the Feature Definition is for triangles to be Off.

- Change the **Feature Definition** so that triangles default **On**

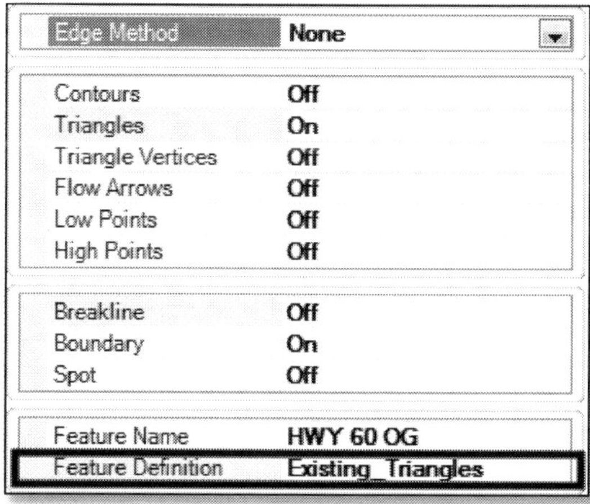

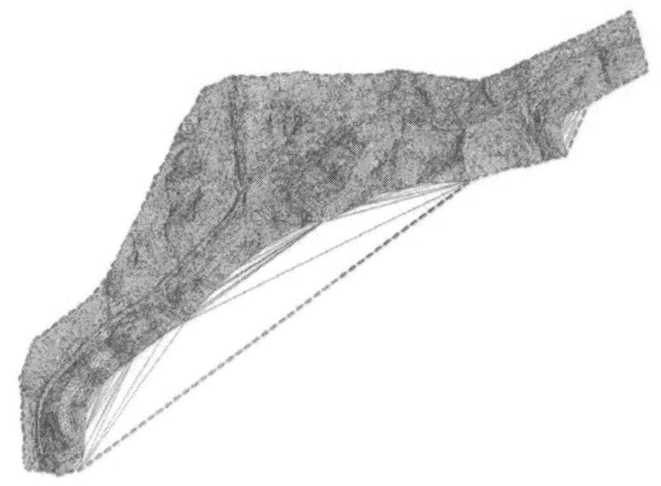

- In the Terrain's Properties, change the ***Edge Method*** to **None** and then back to **Slivers** and notice the change

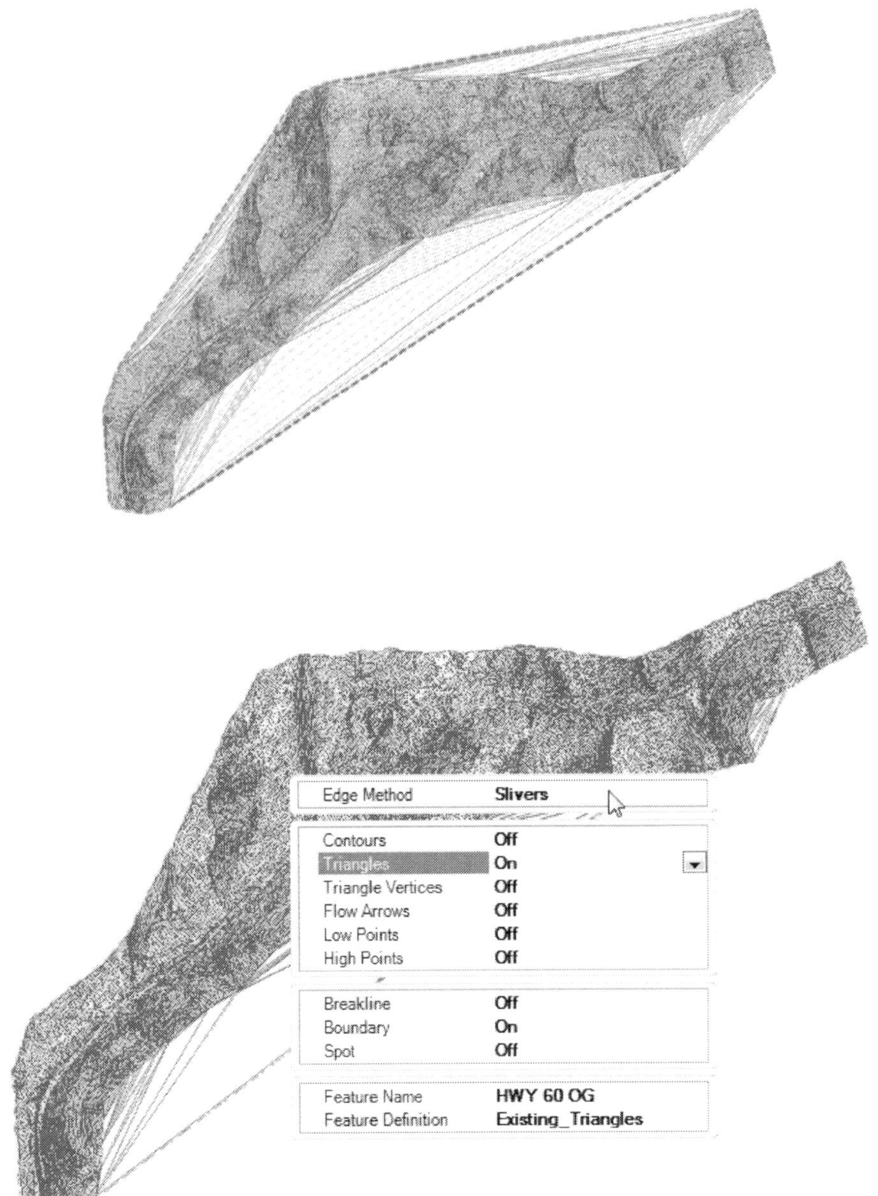

Note the Slivers option helped in some areas, but not in others.

- Change the ***Edge Method*** to ***Max Triangle Length*** and enter **25**

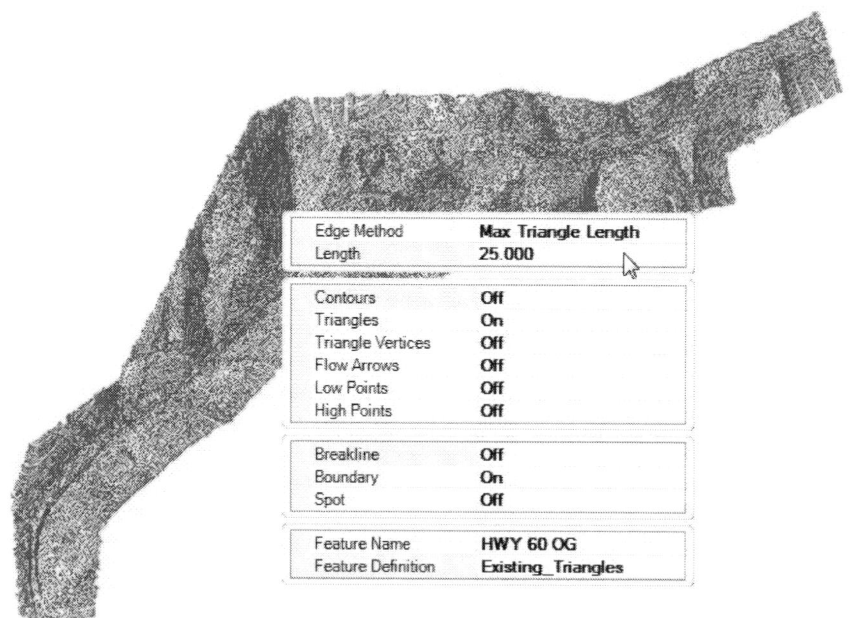

The Max Triangle Length now affects only the perimeter triangles, but you may still have areas where a small value in this setting eliminates triangles you want to keep.

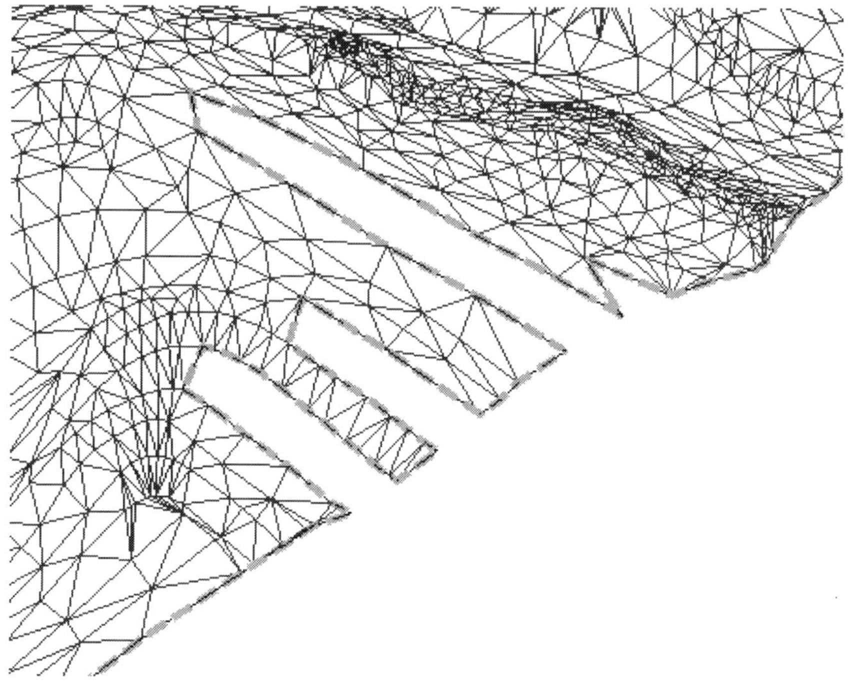

- Continue experimenting with ***Max Triangle Length*** until you find one that is satisfactory (100 is a pretty good value for this terrain).

- Change the assigned ***Feature Definition*** back to **Existing_Boundary**

Edge Method	**Max Triangle Length**
Length	**100.000**

Contours	**Off**
Triangles	**Off**
Triangle Vertices	**Off**
Flow Arrows	**Off**
Low Points	**Off**
High Points	**Off**

Breakline	**Off**
Boundary	**On**
Spot	**Off**

Feature Name	**HWY 60 OG**
Feature Definition	**Existing_Boundary**

11 Try out some different **Feature Definition** options

- Toggle on Contours
- Try some of the other displays

12 Make the elevation difference more apparent

- In **View Attributes**, set the **Display Style** to **Thematic Height**

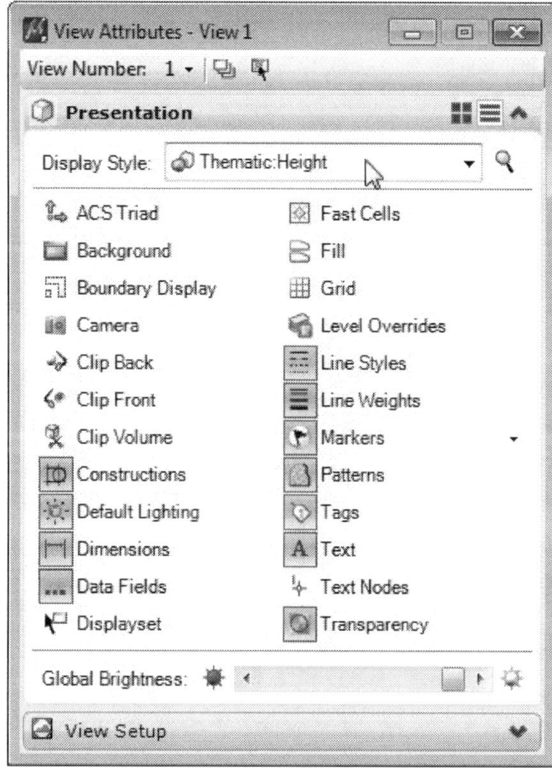

- Change the assigned ***Feature Definition*** to ***Existing_Thematic_Height***

  Be sure to de-select the terrain to see the results.

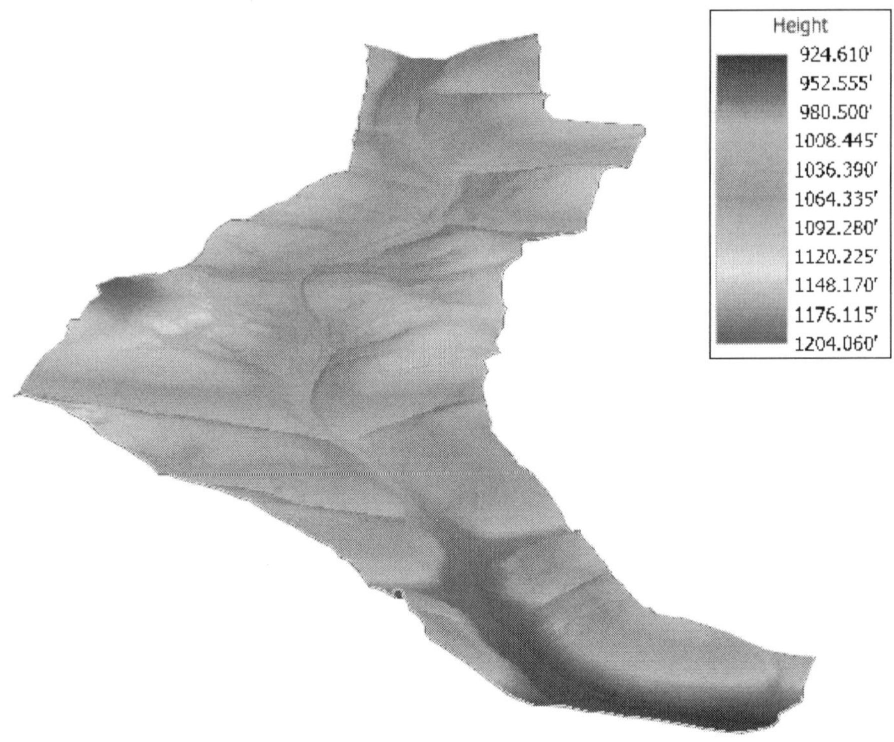

- Set the **Display Style** back to Wireframe

13 Try some of the other **Feature Definitions** of your choice

14 When done, change the assigned ***Feature Definition*** back to ***Existing_Boundary***

Remember, the terrain always reverts back to the assigned Feature Definition upon any edit.

15 **Fit** the view

Ending

16 Choose **Save Settings**

17 **Exit** MicroStation

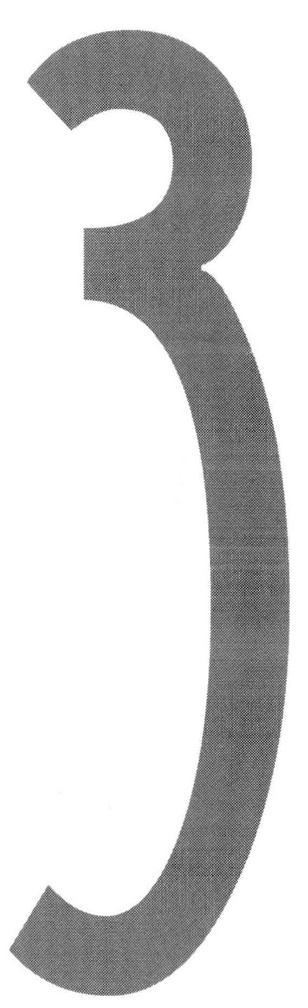

Horizontal Geometry

IMPORTING CIVIL GEOMETRY (CG)

GEOMETRY REPORTS

CREATING CIVIL GEOMETRY ALIGNMENTS

EDITING CIVIL GEOMETRY

3 Geometry

There are two ways to store geometry (alignments, etc.) in InRoads. Civil Geometry tools, found on the MicroStation menu, store geometry in the DGN file. This is the type of geometry that will be used for designing and modeling corridors.

Previous versions of InRoads, and some current commands, use a geometry project, or ALG binary file to store geometry and only use the DGN file as a viewer for the data. These commands are called legacy commands since they are hold-overs from the past, but are still used for creating profiles to plot and for use with **Plan and Profile Generator**.

Civil Geometry (CG)

The modeling portion of InRoads uses what is known as **Civil Geometry**. **Civil Geometry** (CG) is very similar to geometry stored in the ALG with a few key differences. With CG, the data is stored in the MicroStation DGN file rather than the external ALG. The model containing the geometry can be referenced to other models and used, but geometry can only be created or modified in the active model. The tools to create civil geometry are not on the InRoads Explorer menu, but a part of the MicroStation menu, and they function more like MicroStation commands. Since the geometry is made up of MicroStation elements, it can be accessed through **Element Information** and edited through element selection.

Another advantage of civil geometry is its ability to remember design intent. For example, if you create an alignment and then parallel it, the parallel alignment will adjust with the original. Or, if you create an alignment that ties into another at a particular angle, that angle is maintained when the geometry is adjusted. These 'rules' can be toggled off or removed if you wish to disassociate the geometry.

> ***Warning**: If you have been using geometry with the ALG, you know that the MicroStation graphics can be easily reproduced by simply viewing the data. This is NOT the case with civil geometry. The MicroStation graphic IS the geometric data; delete it and the geometry is gone. (Undo will recover it, however.)*

3.1 Creating CG from an ALG

From an ALG currently loaded

- **MS: Tasks > Civil Tools > General Geometry > Import InRoads from Memory**

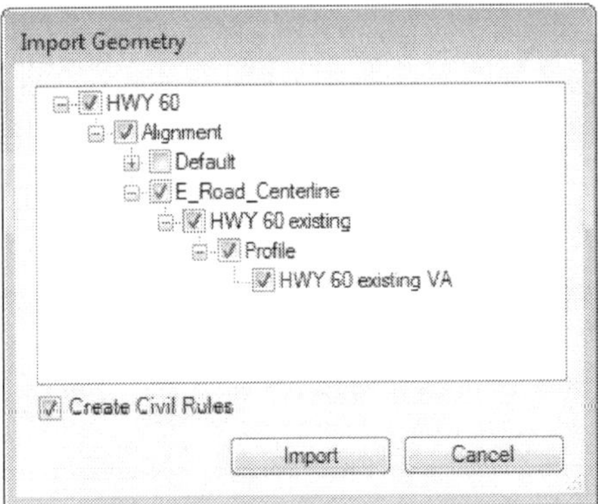

- Drill through the list and toggle on the Alignment(s) you want to import
- Toggle on **Create Civil Rules** if you want to be able to edit the alignment using the **Element Selection** options
- Select **Import**

  *The alignment is imported and is now civil geometry. However, it still exists in the ALG. Any edits using civil geometry will NOT be updated in the ALG unless you have **Auto Persist** toggled on in the Feature Definition assigned to the civil geometry. By default the Feature Definition assigned is the same name as the Style originally assigned to the alignment in the ALG if that same name is available in the Feature Definition list.*

- **Cancel**

From an ALG not currently loaded

- **MS: Tasks > Civil Tools > General Geometry > Import Geometry**

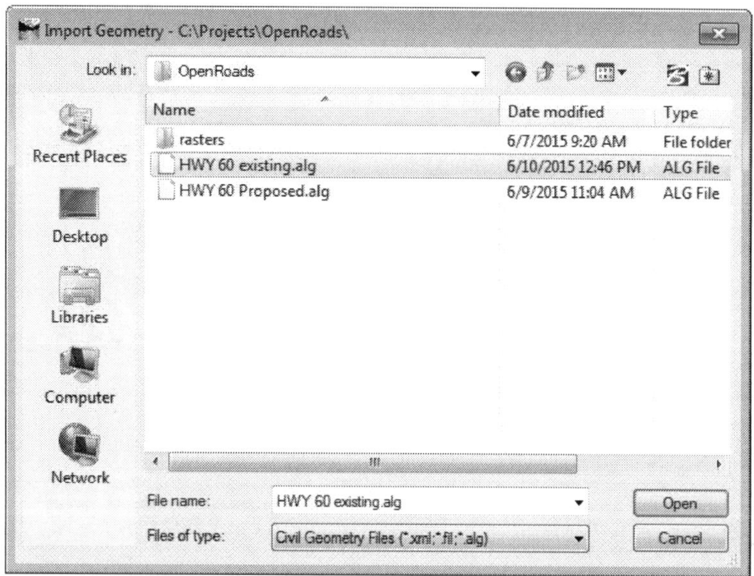

- Navigate through the file structure and select the *ALG* you want to import

- Drill through the list and toggle on the Alignment(s) you want to import

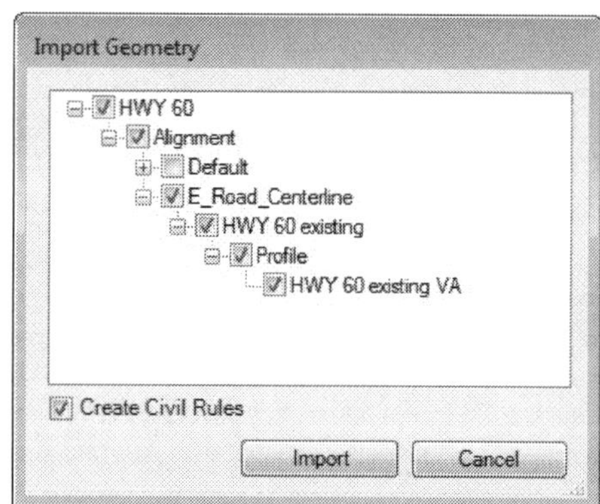

- Toggle on **Create Civil Rules** if you want to be able to edit the alignment using the **Element Selection** options

➢ Select **Import**

The alignment is imported and is now civil geometry. However, it still exists in the ALG. Any edits using civil geometry will NOT be updated in the ALG unless you have ***Auto Persist*** *toggled on in the Feature Definition assigned to the civil geometry.*

In this configuration, by default the Feature Definition assigned is the same name as the Style originally assigned to the alignment in the ALG.

➢ **Cancel**

➢ Once the alignment is imported, you can set or change the feature definition by selecting the alignment and choosing either **Properties** from the context sensitive menu or **Element Information**.

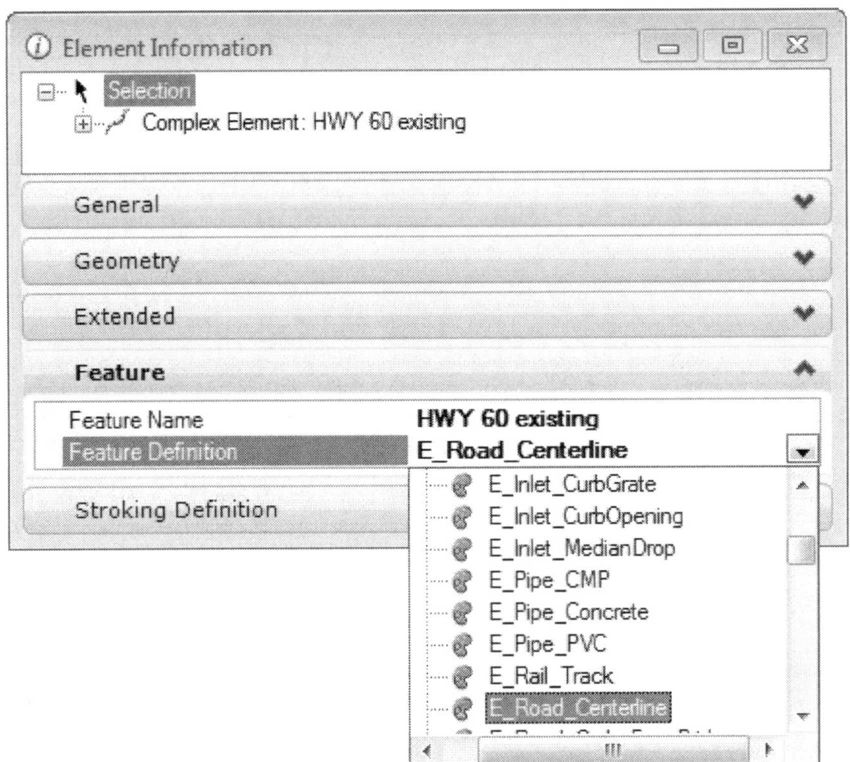

3.2 Creating a CG Alignment from PIs

- Open the design file which will contain the alignment
- Set the **Feature Definition**

  You can set the feature definition for each command within Civil Geometry, or you can set a default feature definition for this design session. Here, we'll set a default.

- **MS: Tasks > Civil Tools > Horizontal Geometry > Feature Definition Toggle Bar**

- In the drop-down list, choose the **Feature Definition** you wish to use for the geometry

- To make the Feature Definition the default for this session, toggle on **Use Active Feature Definition**

➢ **MS: Tasks > Civil Tools > Horizontal Geometry > Complex by PI**

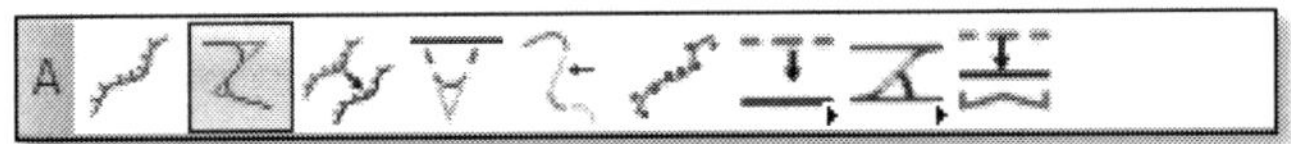

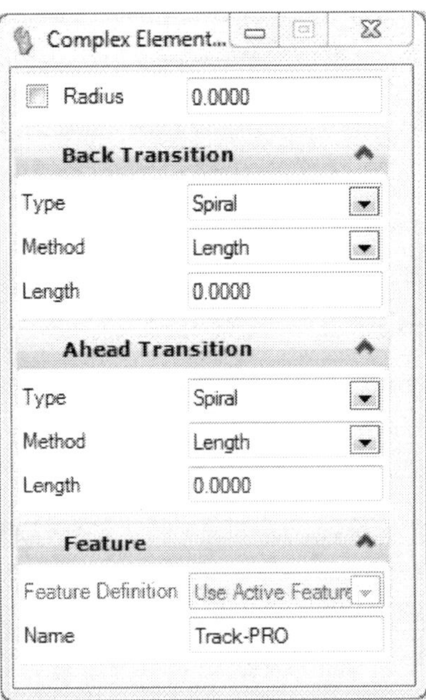

You can enter the Radius and Spiral information in the dialog, or use the heads-up display.

➢ If using Heads-up, key in the desired **Radius** and **<TAB>** or **<ENTER>** to lock

➢ Use the left or right Arrow Key to move to the Back or Ahead Spiral field, key in the desired value and **<TAB>** or **<ENTER>** to lock

➢ Use the left or right Arrow Key again to move to the opposite Spiral field, key in the desired value and **<TAB>** or **<ENTER>** to lock

➢ Define the Point of Beginning

This can be accomplished by snapping to a location in the DGN file, or by using one of the standard MicroStation key-ins such as XY= or NE= to specify a location. Subsequent points can be entered the same way, or you may also use a DI= key-in to specify a distance,direction. As an alternative to the MicroStation key-ins, you may use AccuDraw or Civil AccuDraw to define the PI locations.

➢ Continue defining the PIs as needed, changing the Radius and Spirals where necessary

➢ **<R>** when done

➢ To edit the alignment, use the MicroStation **Element Selection** tool and select the alignment

➢ Manipulators appear allowing for the graphical editing of the alignment. The values that appear for Radii, Spiral lengths, Distances and Directions may also be selected and edited.

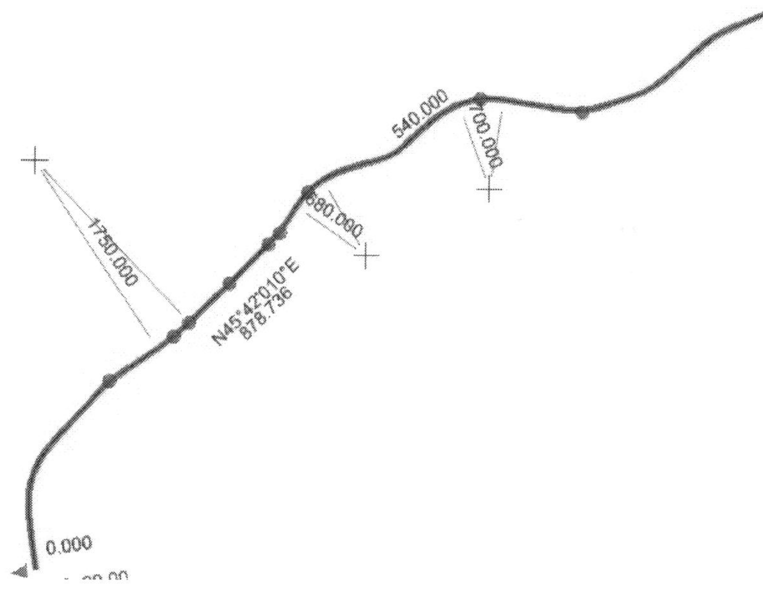

The alignment is stored in the DGN file. MicroStation Undo and Redo commands will affect the actual geometry, not just graphics.

3.3 Beginning Station in CG

- **MS: Tasks > Civil Tools > Horizontal Geometry > Start Station**

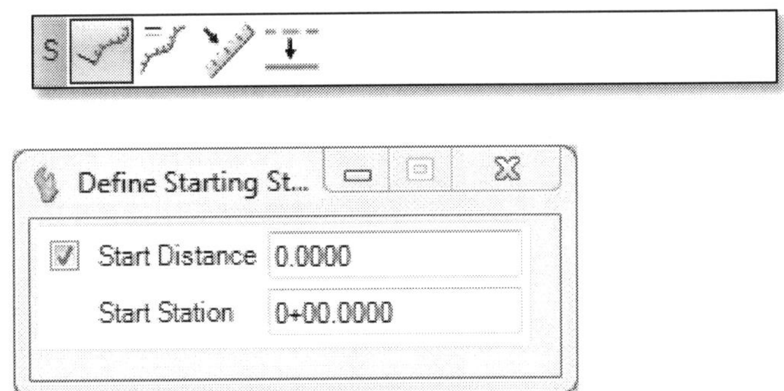

You can enter Start Distance and Start Station in the dialog, or use the heads-up display.

- If using Heads-up, key in the desired Start Distance and **<TAB>** or **<ENTER>** to lock (you can use your cursor to define the location instead of keying it in)

The Start Distance is the distance from the end of the alignment where the station you are assigning should occur. If you know the starting station, the distance is 0.

- **<D>** to Accept

- Use the left or right Arrow Key to move to the **Station** field, key in the desired value and **<TAB>** or **<ENTER>** to lock

After the stationing is assigned, the start station value is part of the manipulators and can be edited when the alignment is selected using the MicroStation Element Selection tool.

3.4 Tracking

The **Analyze Point** command allows you to track features in your file. The readouts change depending upon what type of feature you are analyzing. For example, if you analyze a terrain model element, the readout will include elevation, slope, etc. If you analyze civil geometry, the readout will be location, offset, etc. If the civil geometry has stationing assigned, it includes stationing. If it has a vertical assigned, the readout includes the elevation and vertical grade.

- **MS: Tasks > Civil Tools > Analysis & Reporting > Analyze Point**

Also found here:

- **MS: Tasks > Civil Tools > Terrain Model > Analyze Point**

- Select the element you want to analyze or track

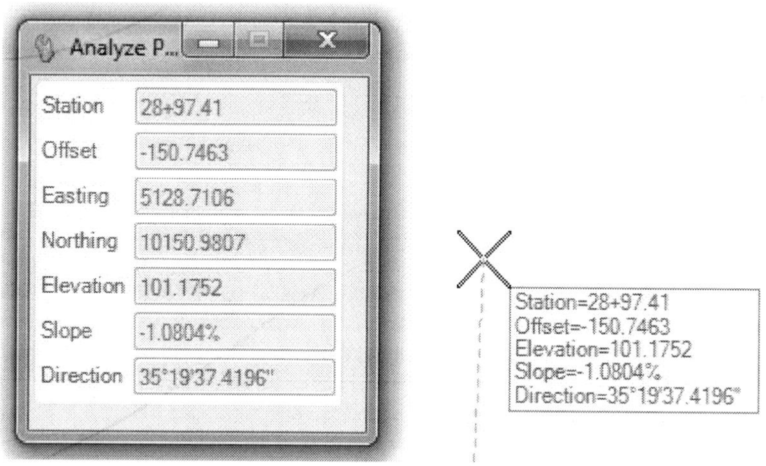

In this picture, the alignment has stationing assigned and already has a vertical alignment (profile) active.

3.5 Reviewing CG

- **MS: Tasks > Civil Tools > Horizontal Geometry > Horizontal Geometry Report**

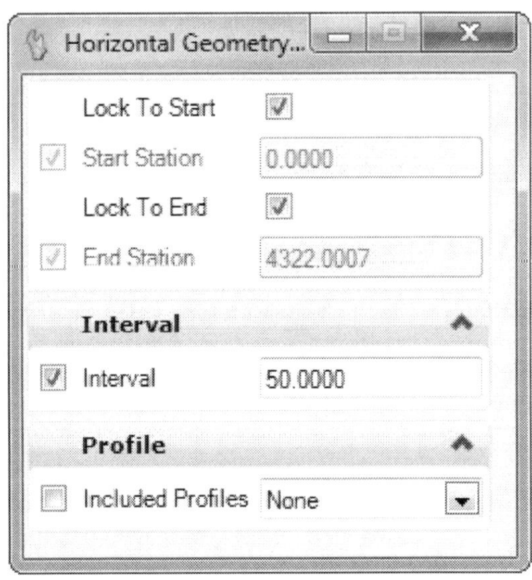

You can use either the dialog or the heads-up prompts.

- When prompted to **Locate First Element**, **<D>** on the alignment
- When prompted to **Locate Next Element**, **<D>** on another alignment if you wish to report on more than one
- **<R>** when all alignments have been selected
- Use your mouse to locate the first station for the report or **<Alt>** to **Lock to Start**
- **<D>** to **Accept**
- Repeat to locate the last station for the report
- Key in an **Interval**
- **<D>** to **Accept**
- If a profile exists and you want to report on it, use your down arrow for the proper selection

➢ **<D>** to Accept

Alignment Name: Track-PRO2
Alignment Description:
Alignment Style: Track-PRO-ALG

		Station	Northing	Easting
Element: Linear				
POB	( )	0+00.00	597865.792	589133.970
TS	( )	14+36.86	598412.976	590462.562
Tangential Direction:		N 67°36'56" E		
Tangential Length:		1436.8606		
Element: Clothoid				
TS	( )	14+36.86	598412.976	590462.562
SPI	( )	14+57.53	598420.847	590481.672
SC	( )	14+67.86	598424.723	590491.251
Entrance Radius:		0.0000		
Exit Radius:		2500.0000		

The report can be printed and/or saved to the hard drive.

Exercise 3: Create a Horizontal Alignment

Given:

- *HWY 60 OG.dgn* – Original ground terrain model created in previous lab
- *Alternate One PI Locations*.dgn

Required:

- Create a new design file
- Attach the terrain model as a reference
- Create horizontal geometry for a proposed bypass

Getting Started

1 Create a new design file

- Start InRoads using the icon on your desktop or using the Start menu

2 On the MicroStation manager, set the:

- **User**: ***examples***
- **Project**: ***Bentley-Civil-Imperial***
- **Interface**: ***default***

3 Select the **New File** icon

- Browse to select the seed file *Seed2D-InRoads-Imperial.dgn* and select **Open**

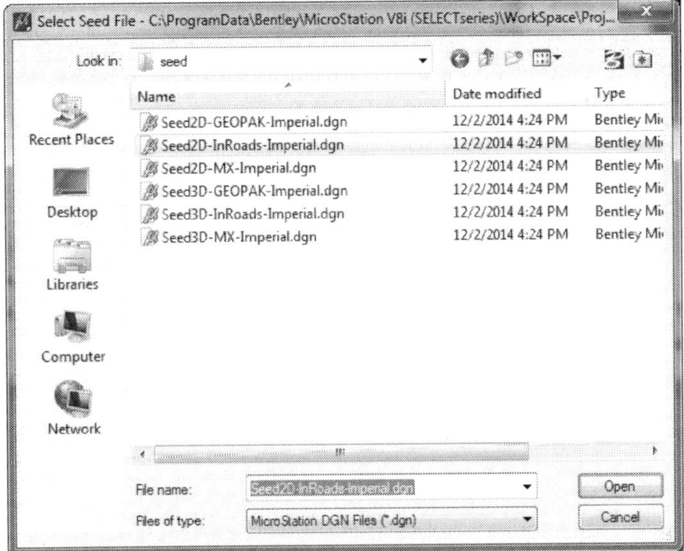

- Key in the File Name: *HWY 60 Existing Geometry.dgn*
- Select **Save**

4 **Open** the new file

Importing an ALG

5 Import Geometry

- **MS: Tasks > Civil Tools > General Geometry > Import Geometry**

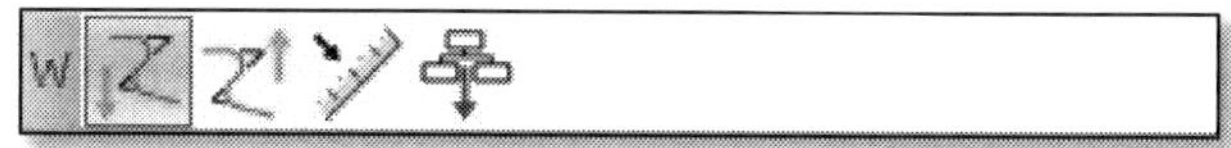

- Select *HWY 60 existing.alg* from the *C:\Projects\HWY_60* folder

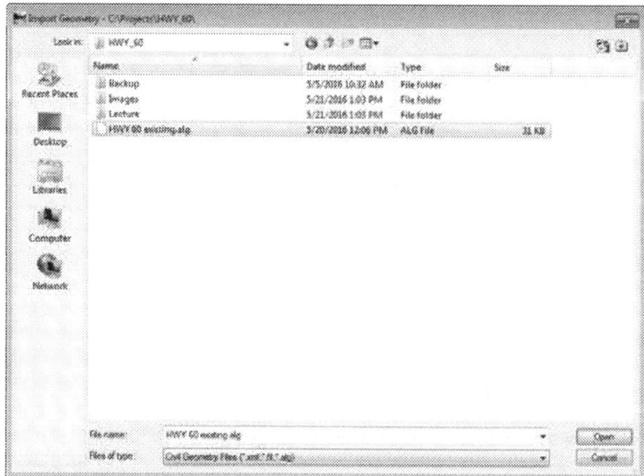

- Choose **Open**
- Drill through the list and toggle on *HWY 60 existing VA* (all previous branches will toggle on as well)
- Toggle on **Create Civil Rules** so that you can see the edit options, even though you will not be editing the alignment.

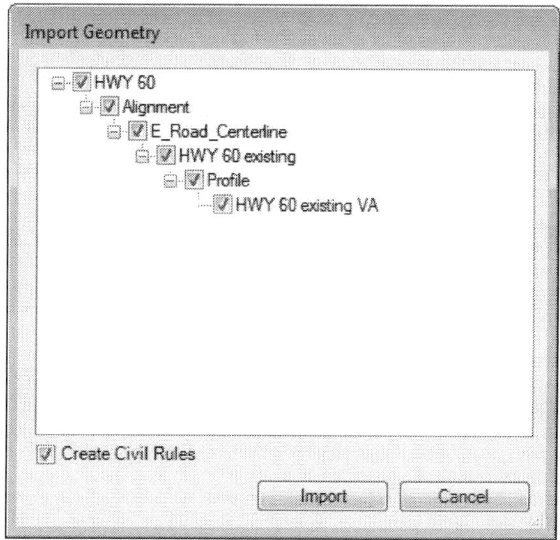

- Select **Import**

- **Fit** the View

  The alignment is imported and is now civil geometry. However, it still exists in the ALG. *Any edits using civil geometry will NOT be updated in the* ALG *unless you have* **Auto Export** *toggled on in the* ***Feature Definition*** *you're using.*

  By default the Feature Definition assigned is the same name as the Style originally assigned to the alignment in the ALG.

- Select the alignment and note the Manipulators.

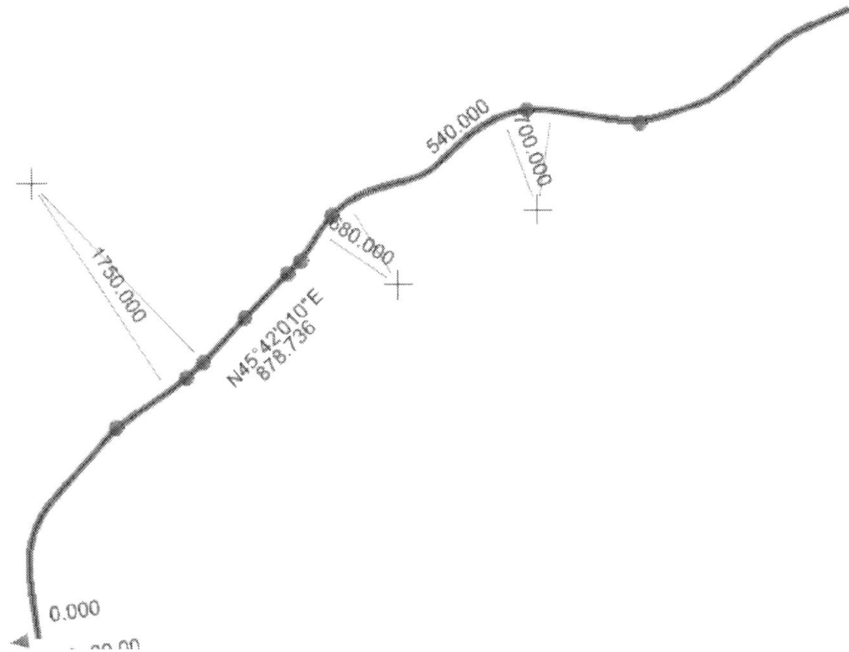

The manipulators may look different depending upon how far in you're zoomed. They allow you to modify the alignment and update surrounding elements based on the civil rules. Since this alignment was imported, it cannot remember true design intent as we will see in alignments created with Civil Geometry.

- The default manipulator color may be hard to see. If you want to change it, select **MS: Workspace > Preferences > View Options – Civil**. Under ***Manipulator Settings*** change ***Normal Color*** as desired.

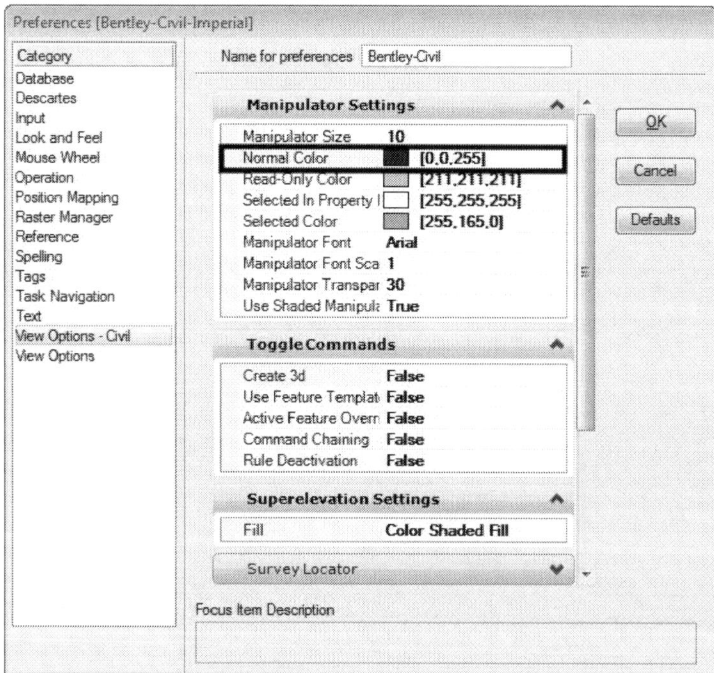

- Select the alignment and choose **Horizontal Geometry Report** from the context sensitive menu

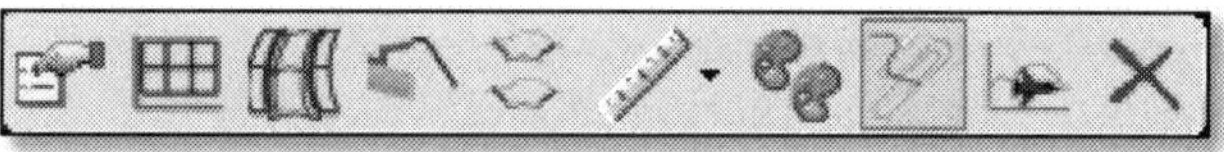

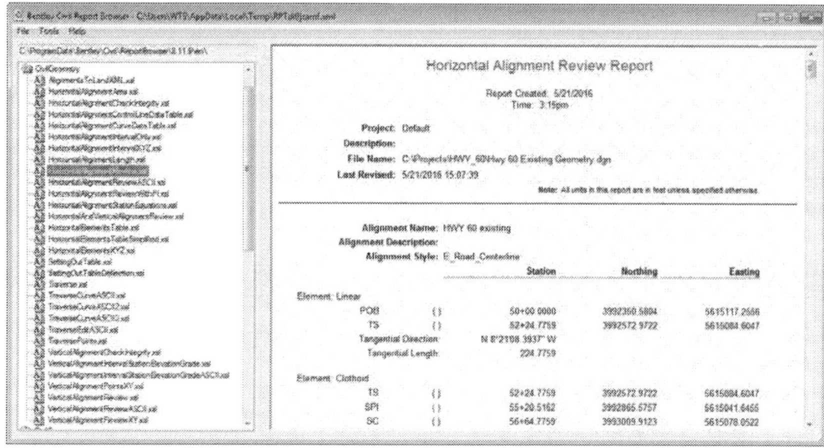

Notice the alignment picked up the starting station from the ALG.

- **Close** the report after reviewing

Working with Civil Geometry (CG)

6 Create a new design file for working with Geometry

- **MS: File > New**
- If necessary, **Browse** to select the seed file *Seed2D-InRoads-Imperial.dgn* and select **Open**

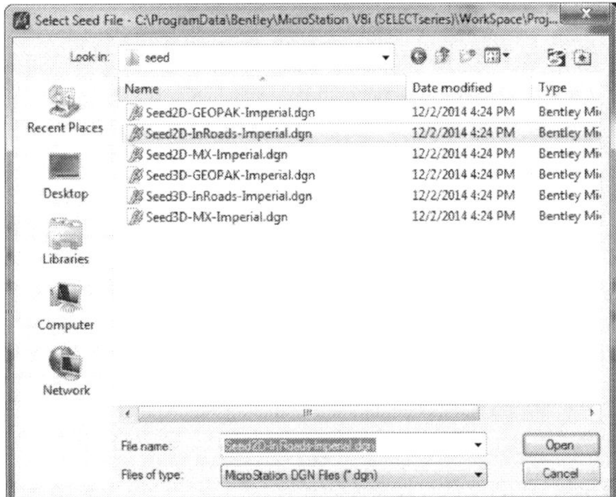

- Key in the **File Name**: *Working Geometry.dgn*
- Select **Save**

  The new file opens

7 Reference the existing geometry

- **MS > Project Explorer > Links**
- In the drop-down, select **Active Directory**, then expand **Design** until you see *Default [HWY 60 Existing Geometry.dgn]*

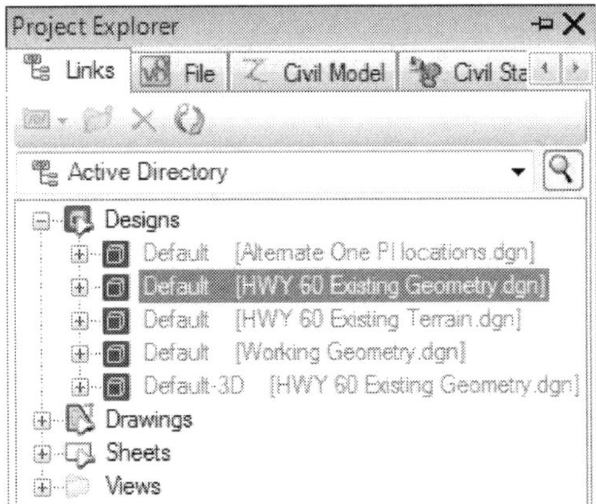

- Drag this model over to your view and drop it

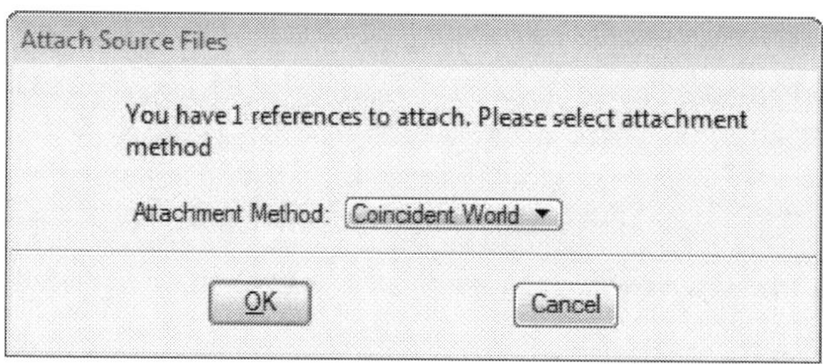

- When the **Attach Source Files** dialog appears, set the **Attachment Method** to ***Coincident World*** and choose **OK**.

  You may also use standard referencing commands.

- **Fit** the View
- Select the horizontal alignment

  Since the alignment is in a reference file it is not editable.

8 Reference the existing terrain

- Repeat the previous step to reference *HWY 60 Existing Terrain*

9 Set the active feature definition for creating alignments

- **MS: Tasks > Civil Tools > General Geometry > Features Definition Toggle Bar**

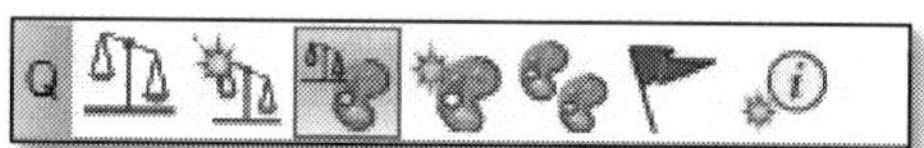

- On the **Features Definition Toggle Bar** (it may be docked above in MicroStation)

- Use the drop-down to select ***Linear > Geometry > Geom_Centerline***
- Toggle on **Use Active Feature Definition**

  By setting the Active Feature Definition and toggling it on, this feature definition will be the default in subsequent commands.

- Make certain the **Chain Commands** is toggled on as well.

  This allows the end of one line to automatically be the beginning of the next.

Creating CG Elements

10 Create the Tangent segments of an alignment

- **MS: Tasks > Civil Tools > Horizontal Geometry > Line Between Points**

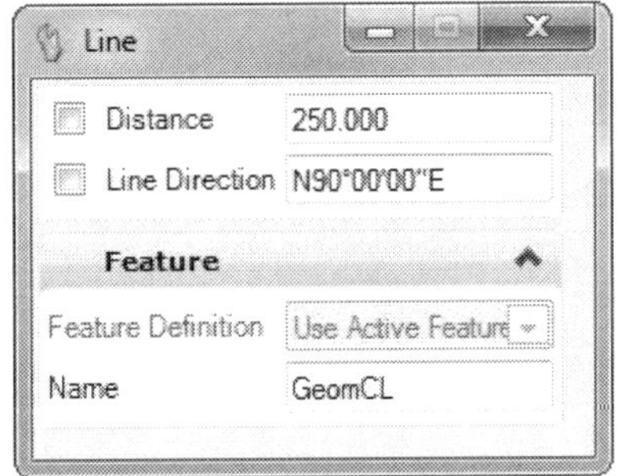

- Sketch in the lines similar to what is shown here.

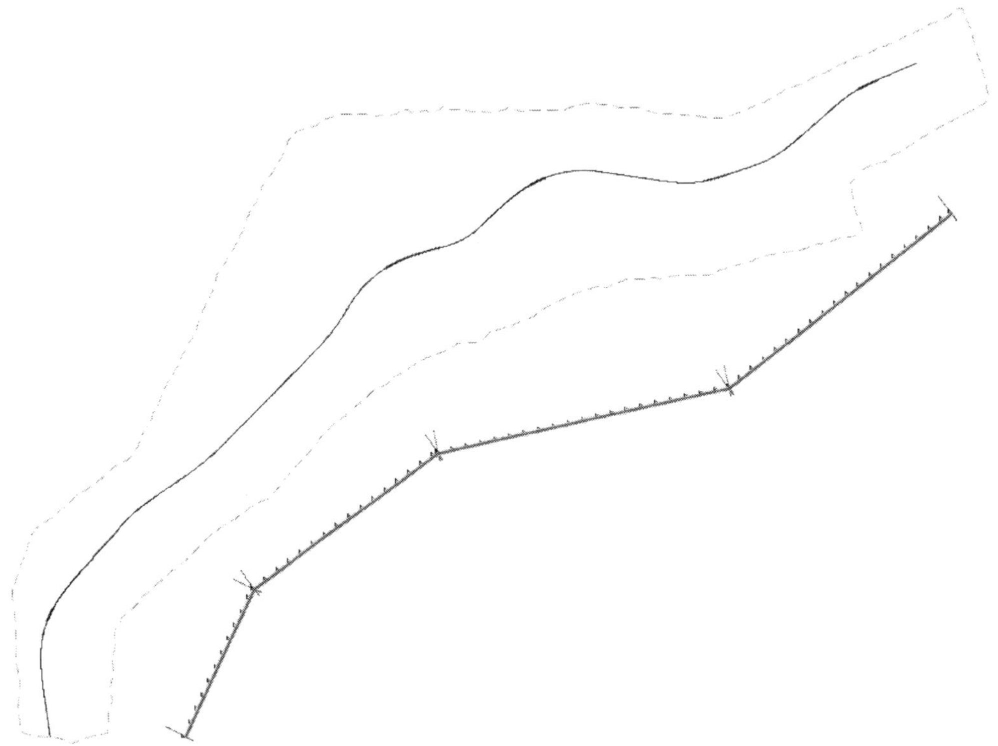

Note the Geom_Centerline feature definition is set up to automatically station the alignment. This is accomplished by the **Auto Annotate** *toggle in the Feature Definition.*

It is also set to **Auto Export***, so there is an alignment for each line created in the current* ALG.

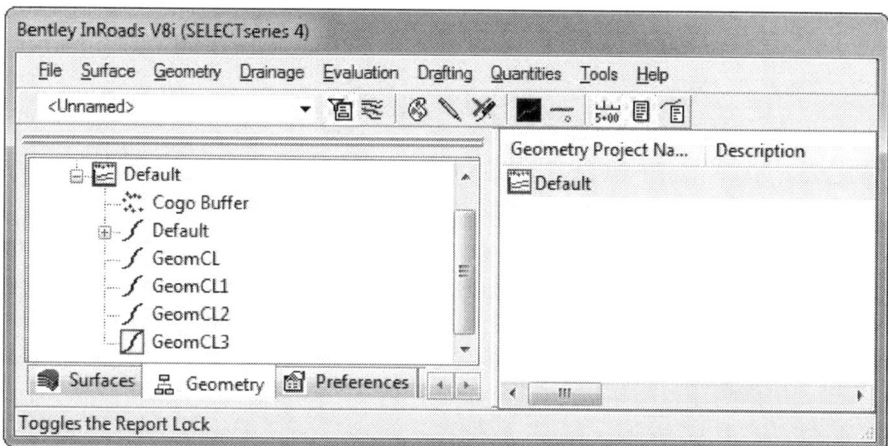

11 Edit the Feature Definition

- Select the **Civil Standards** tab in **Project Explorer.**

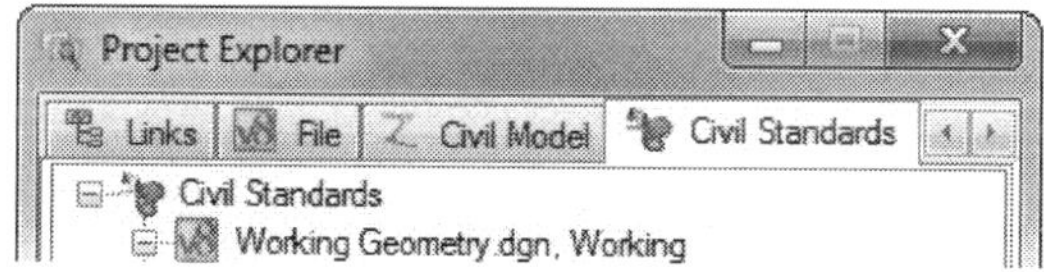

- If you don't see the **Civil Standards** tab turn it on by selecting **Settings > Project Explorer** and changing ***Civil Standards*** from **False** to **True**. Repeat for ***Civil Model*** if necessary.

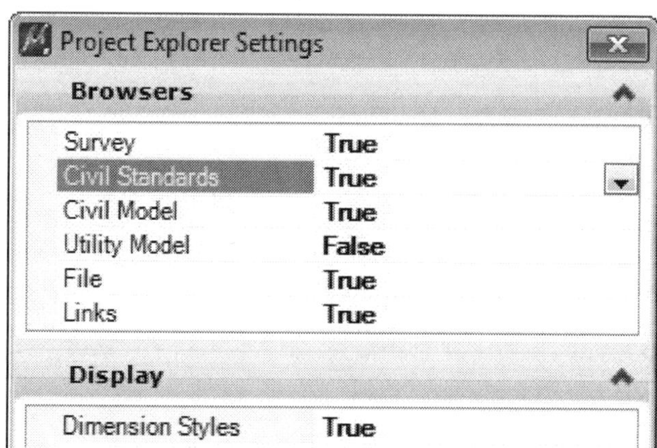

*Note: You may have to re-open the Project Explorer after making these changes (**MS: File > Project Explorer**).*

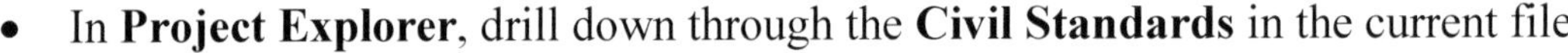

- In **Project Explorer**, drill down through the **Civil Standards** in the current file

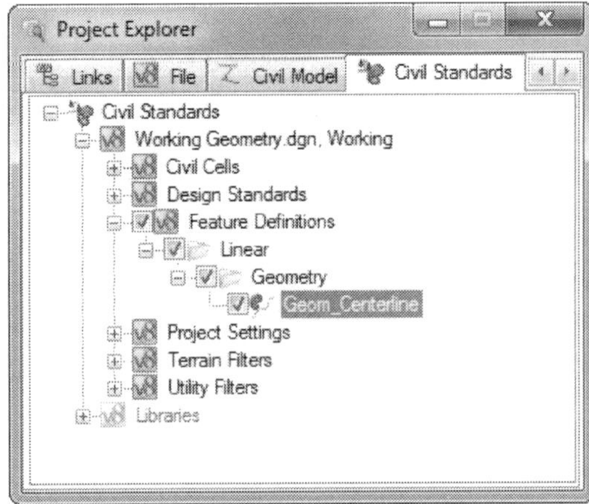

Note the Feature Definition has been copied into this DGN.

Right-click on **Geom_Centerline** and choose **Properties**.

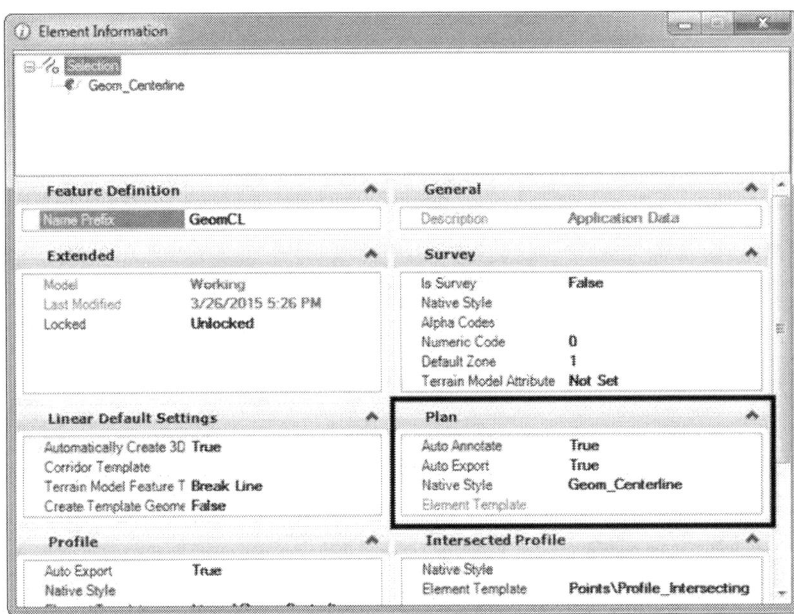

- In the **Plan** area, Change **Auto Export** to ***False*** then **Close Element Information**

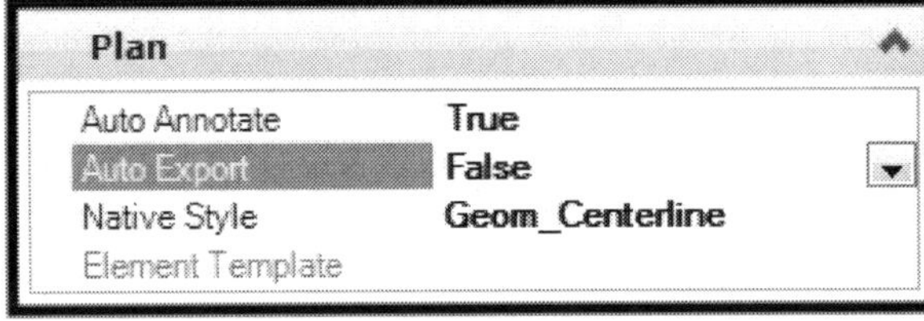

12 Add curves to the alignment

- **MS: Tasks > Civil Tools > Horizontal Geometry > Simple Arc**

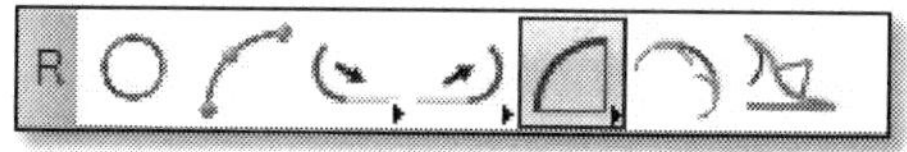

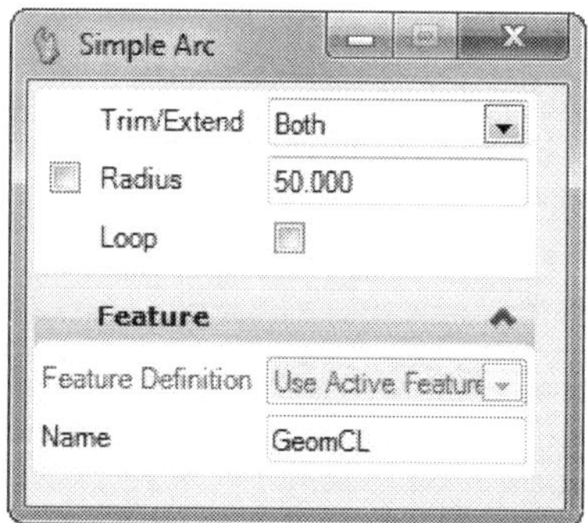

- Toggle off **Radius** and **Loop**

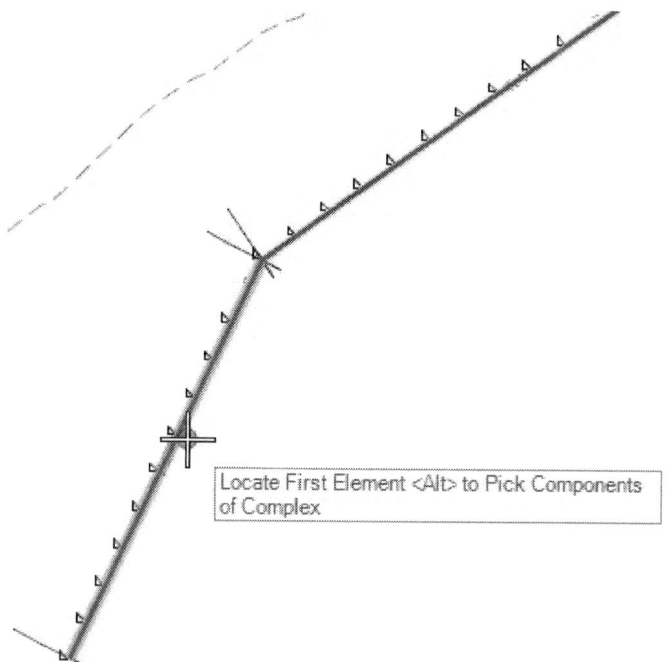

- **<R>** until prompted to **Locate First Element**
- **<D>** on the first tangent
- When prompted to **Locate Second Element**, **<D>** on the second tangent

- Enter a **Radius** of **960** and **<TAB>**

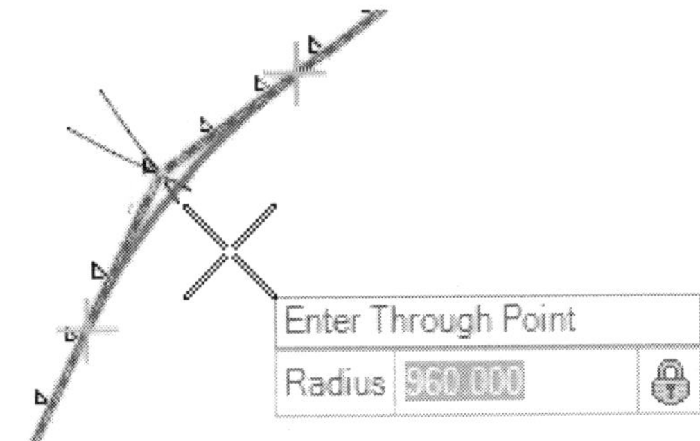

- Move your cursor to the inside quadrant
- **<D>** to Accept.

- When prompted for the **Trim/Extend Option**, be certain it's set to **Both** and **<D>** to Accept.

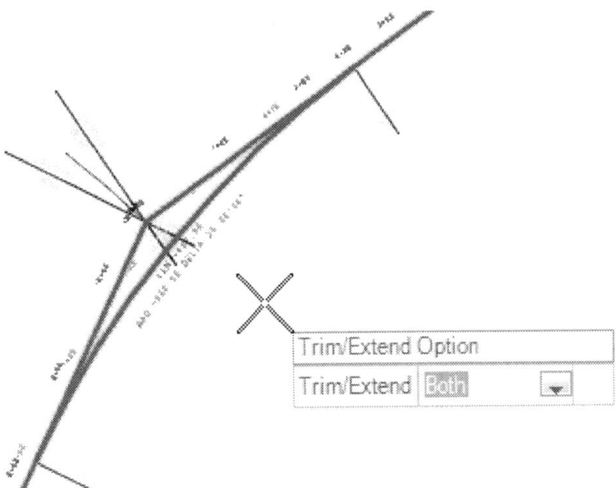

- Continue placing curves for each of the PIs using a radius of **960**

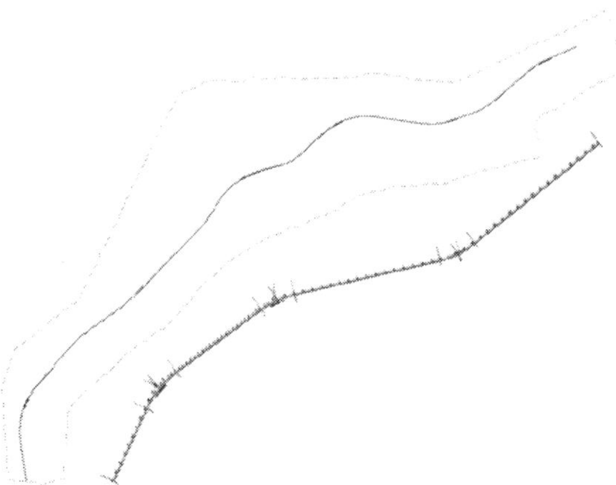

13 Modify a Curve

- Select one of the curves

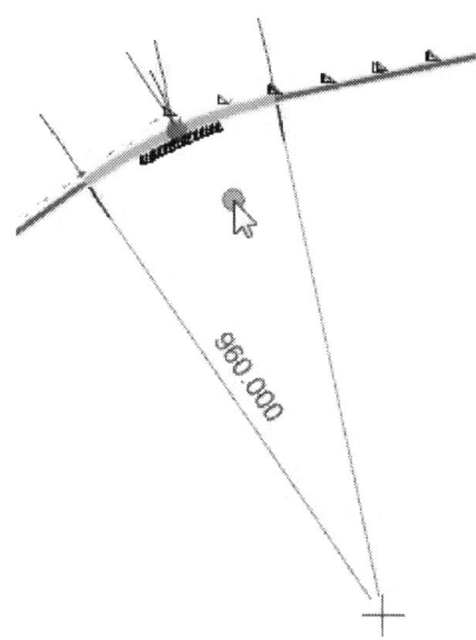

Manipulators appear allowing you to modify the curve.

- Select the text '960.000'
- A key-in field opens

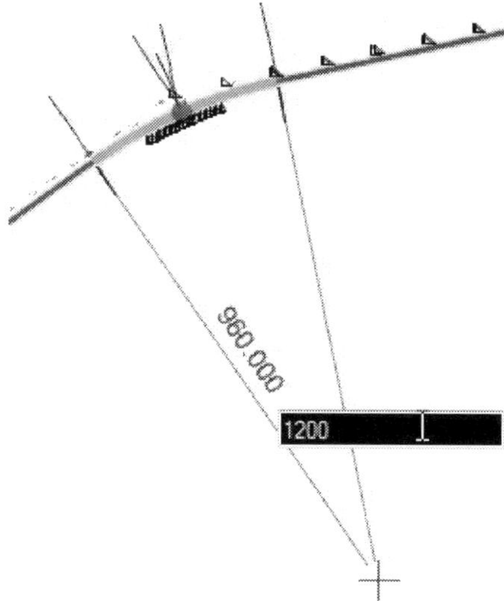

- Type in a new Radius and **<ENTER>**

  The curve is updated and the tangents are adjusted accordingly. However, the alignment is still made up of individual pieces. Next, you'll complex the alignment.

14 Create an alignment from multiple small alignments

- **MS: Tasks > Civil Tools > Horizontal Geometry > Complex by Elements**

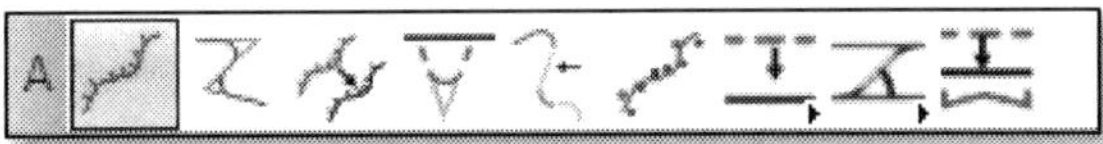

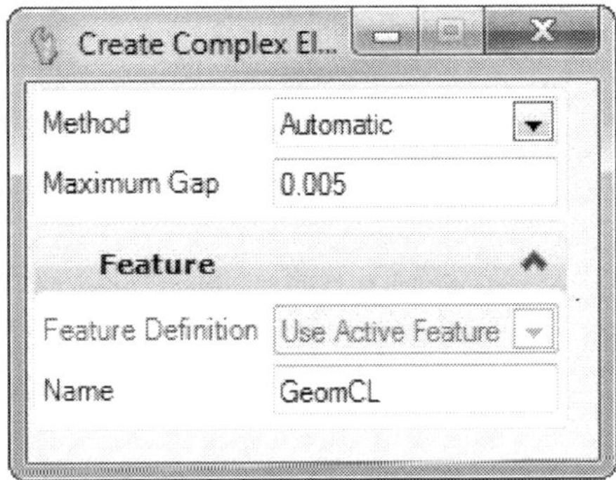

- Hover over the first element

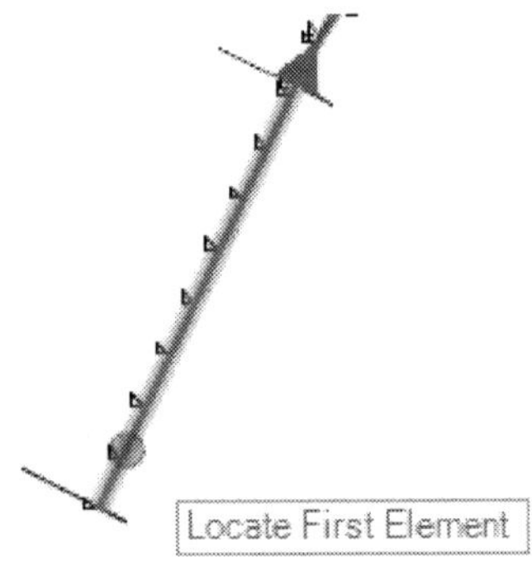

Notice the directional arrow at the end of the element. This tells the direction of the new alignment.

- Make certain the arrow is pointing toward the next element and **<D>** to choose the first one
- **<D>** again to accept the complex and all the pieces highlight correctly

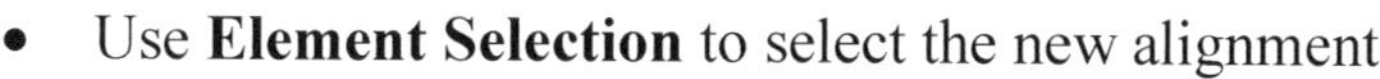

- Use **Element Selection** to select the new alignment

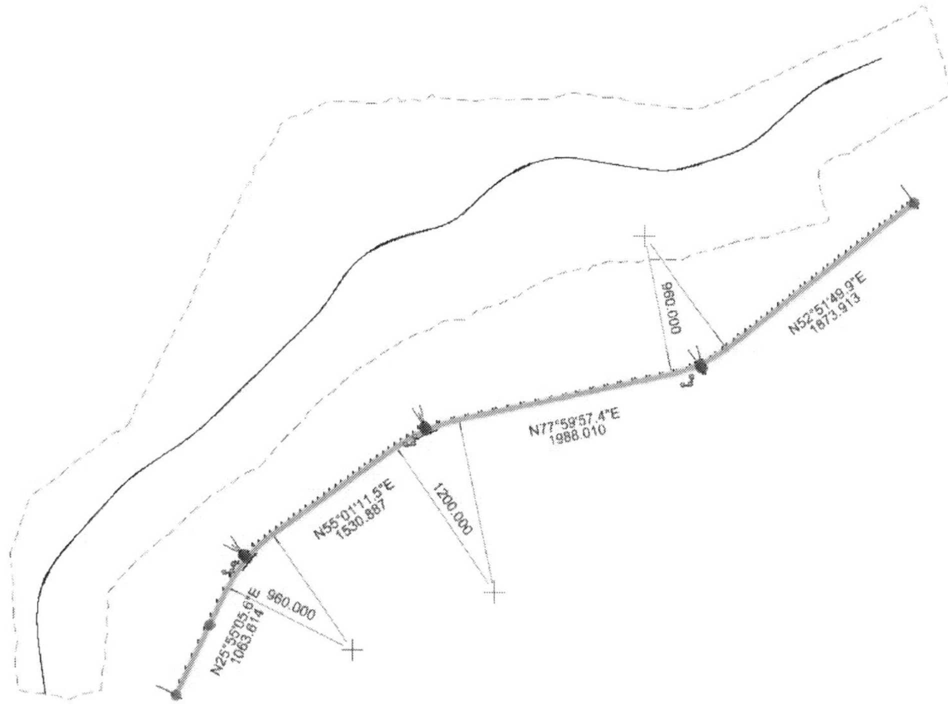

Note the entire alignment highlights and the manipulators are available for editing.

- Make some changes to the alignment to see how it can be modified.
- Again, select the alignment
- Hover over the selected alignment

A context sensitive menu appears with multiple options.

- Choose **Properties**

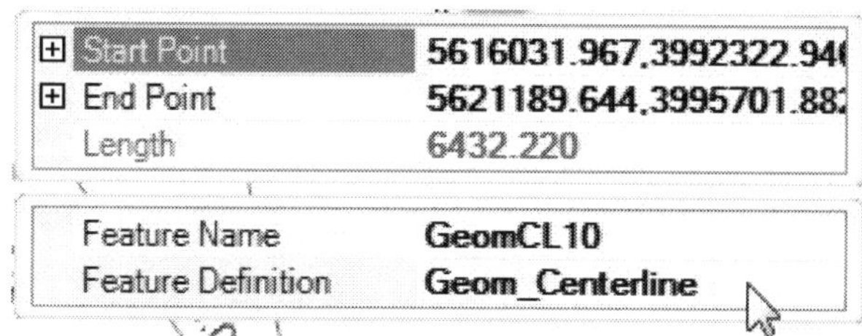

⊞ Start Point	5616031.967,3992322.94
⊞ End Point	5621189.644,3995701.88
Length	6432.220
Feature Name	GeomCL10
Feature Definition	Geom_Centerline

From this pop-up menu, you can make changes such as the name of the alignment or the Feature Definition.

- On **Project Explorer**, select the **Civil Model** tab.

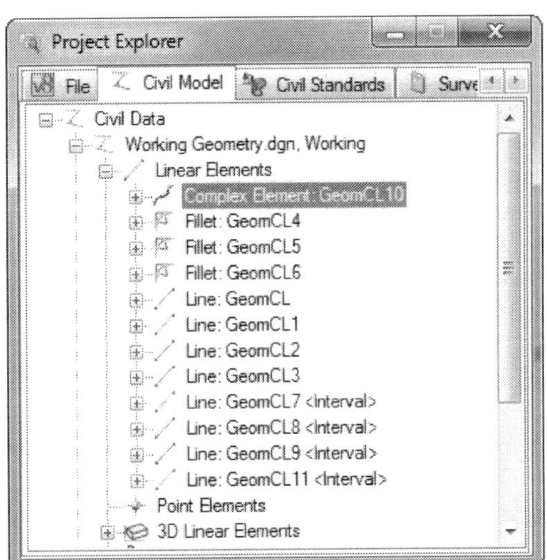

- Expand the *Working Geometry.dgn* category as shown

  Note the Complex Element is made up of all the different pieces you originally created.

Creating CG with PIs and curves

15 Create an alignment defining curves as you go

- **MS: Tasks > Civil Tools > Horizontal Geometry > Complex by PI**

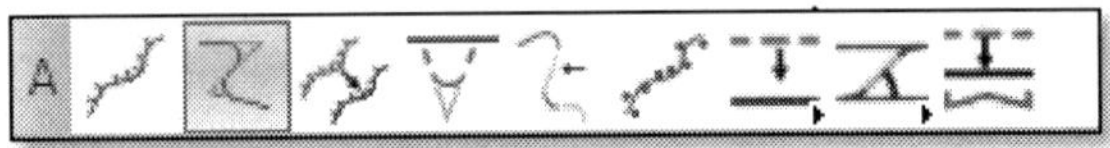

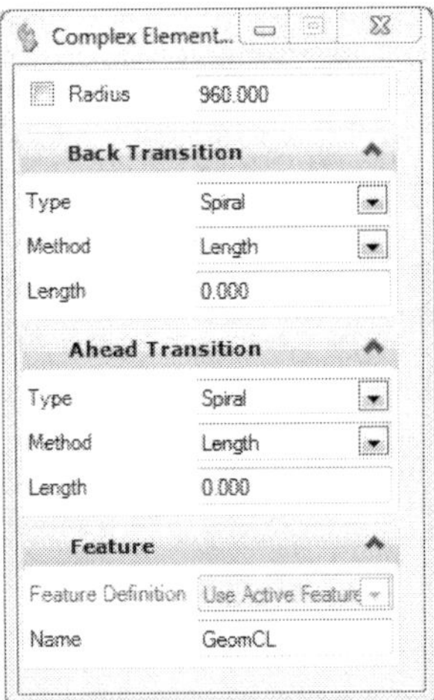

- Set both ***Transition Type*** to **None**

- Following the prompts, create an alignment similar to the one shown.

- Use **960** for the Radius of the first two curves and **1200** for the third
- Select the alignment and change the middle curve to a **Radius** of **500**
- Clear the selection set
- Then, you can **Undo** if you need to start over (it may crash if you don't clear the selection)

Design Checks

16 Using **Design Checks**, compare the alignment you created to the 55MPH, 8% Superelevation design criteria

- **MS: Tasks > Civil Tools > Horizontal Geometry > Design Standards Toolbar**

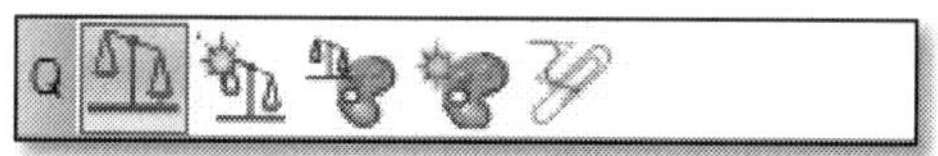

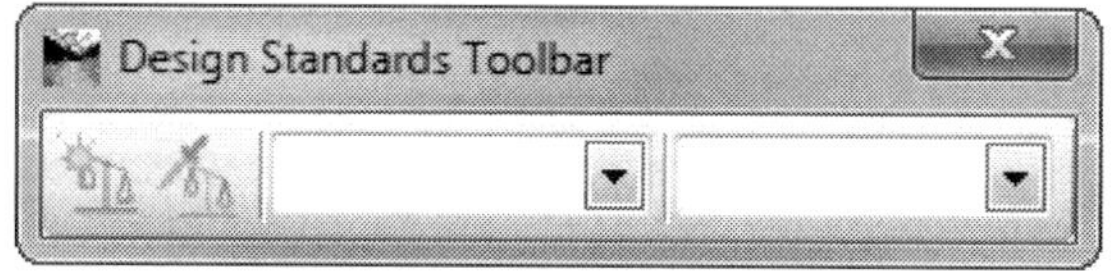

- Using the Drop-down, choose the *2 Lane AASHTO Design Standards 2004.DGNLib* and drill down to the ***2Lane\8%Super\55MPH design***.

- On the toolbox, toggle on the first icon **Set Design Standard**

- Follow the prompts and select the alignment you just modified.
- Zoom in to the 500' Radius curve and hover over the warning symbol.

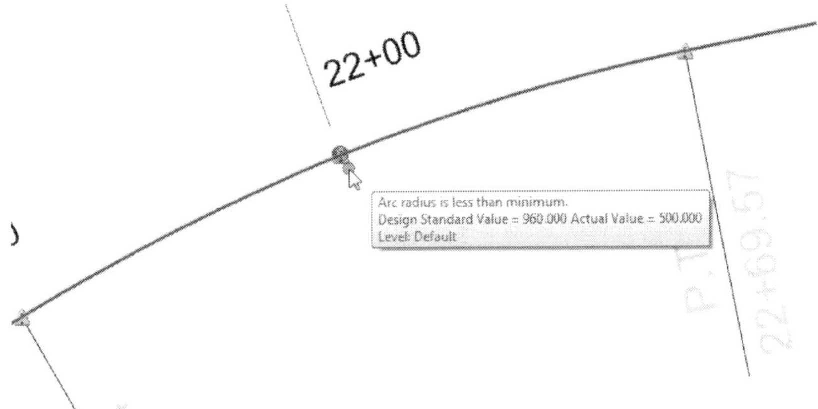

- If the **Civil Message Center** is not on, choose **MS: Tasks > Civil Tools > General Geometry > Civil Message Center**

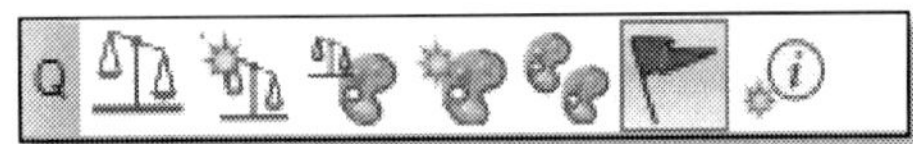

- **Click the Civil Message Center** tab (lower left) to open and make sure that the **Warnings** and **Error** tabs are toggled **on** (you may need to scroll to see all of the warnings)

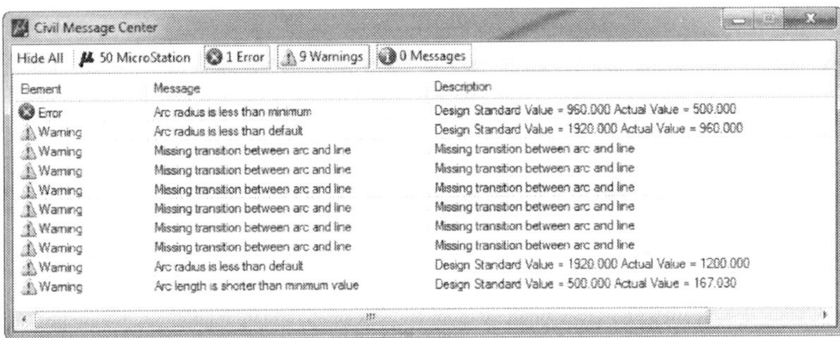

Note the Warnings that the radii are smaller than the Design Standard Value, and the Error when it's below the minimum. There are also warnings since the design calls for spirals and none have been used. Your warning may vary since your alignment will not be identical to what is shown here.

- Select the alignment again and change the 500' Radius back to **960**.

  Notice the Error symbol and message disappear.

17 Automatically add curves during placement

If you want to have curves placed automatically, you can use the Design Standards and the default radius for the selected criteria will be placed as your alignment is created.

- On the **Design Standards Toolbar**, turn on **Toggle Active Design Standards**.

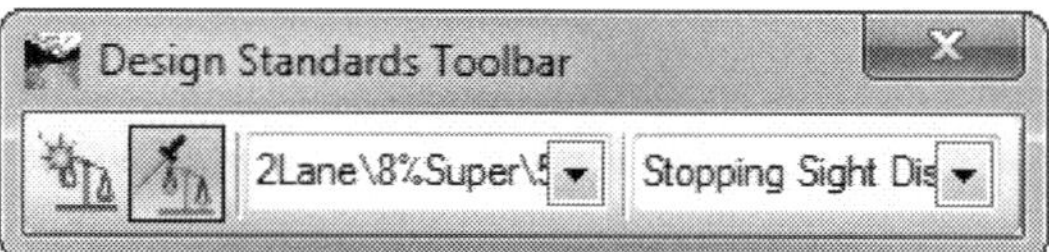

- **MS: Tasks > Civil Tools > Horizontal Geometry > Complex by PI**

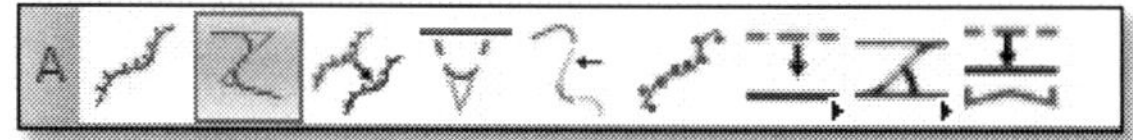

- Sketch another alignment similar to the one shown here

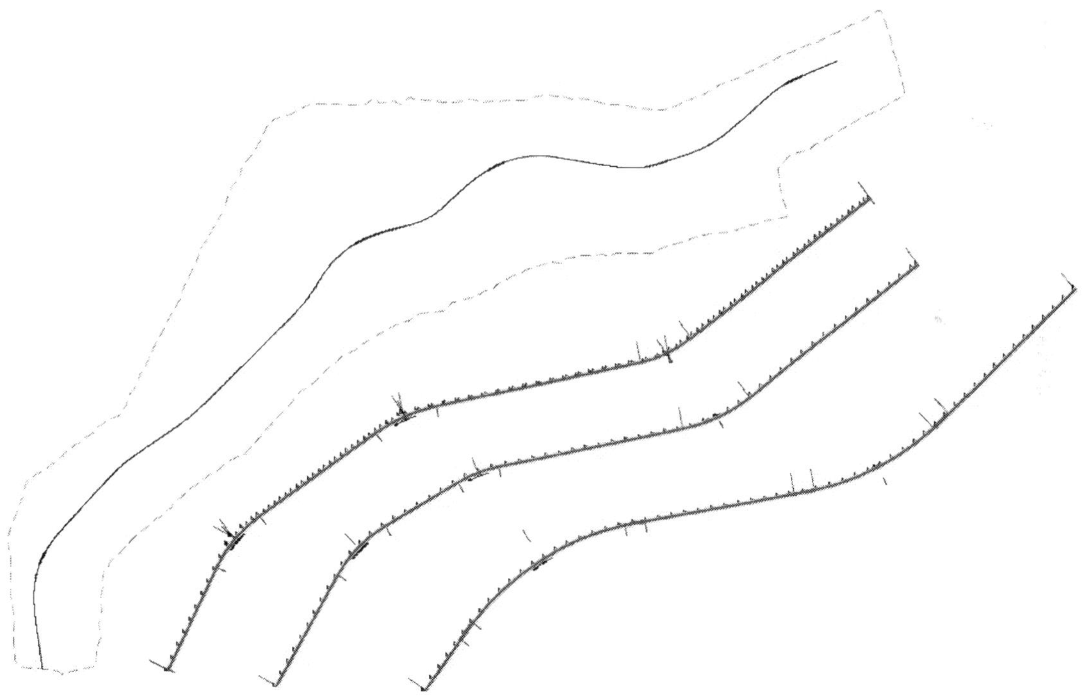

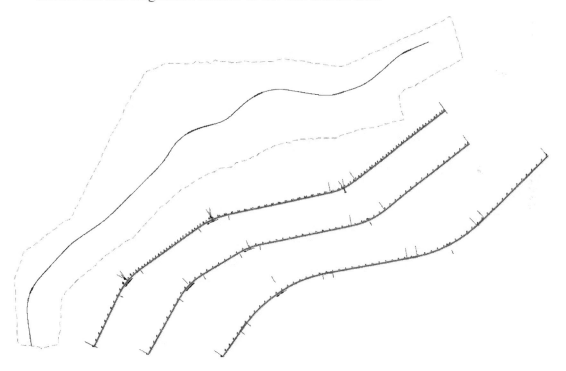

Note that the curves are automatically placed along with spirals, and the curves are not using the minimum radius of 960'. Instead they are using a default radius of 1920'.

- On the **Civil Standards** tab in **Project Explorer**, drill down into the **Design Standards**.

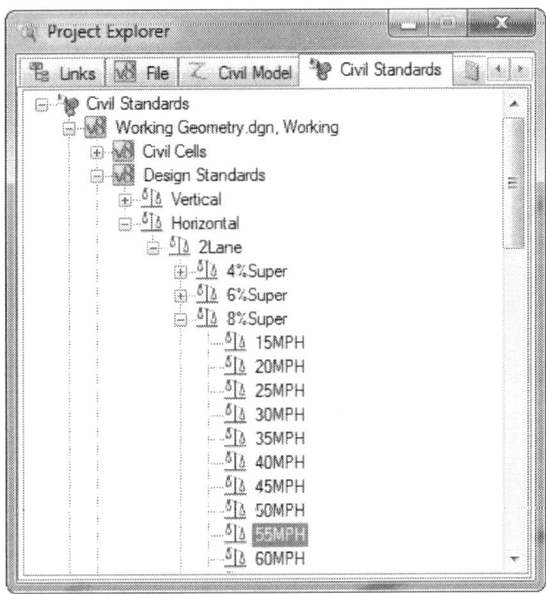

- Right-click on **55MPH** and choose Properties

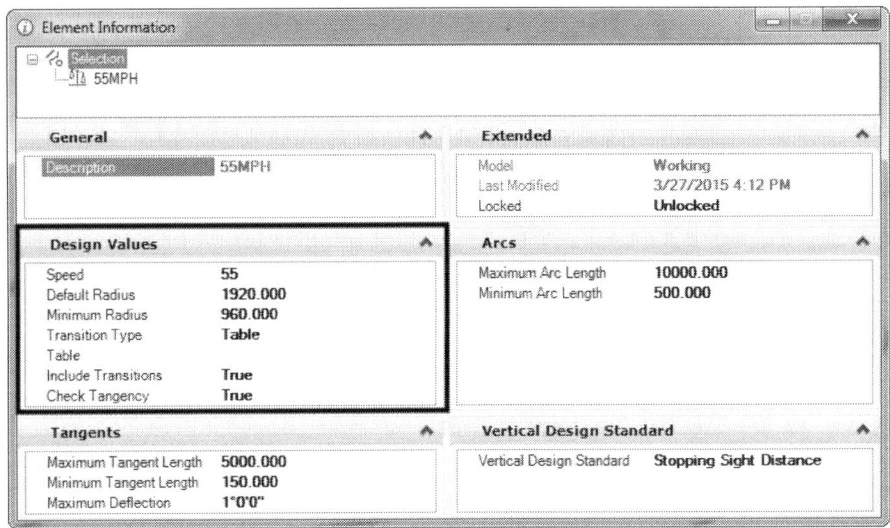

*Notice the **Default Radius** is **1920** and the **Include Transitions** is toggled to **True**. Since the Design Standard for 55 MPH has now been copied into the DGN file, you can edit these options if desired. You can also edit the curves after they're placed.*

Alternate One

18 Create a new design file for Alternate One geometry

- Select **File > New**
- Browse to select the seed file ***Seed2D-InRoads-Imperial.dgn*** and select **Open**

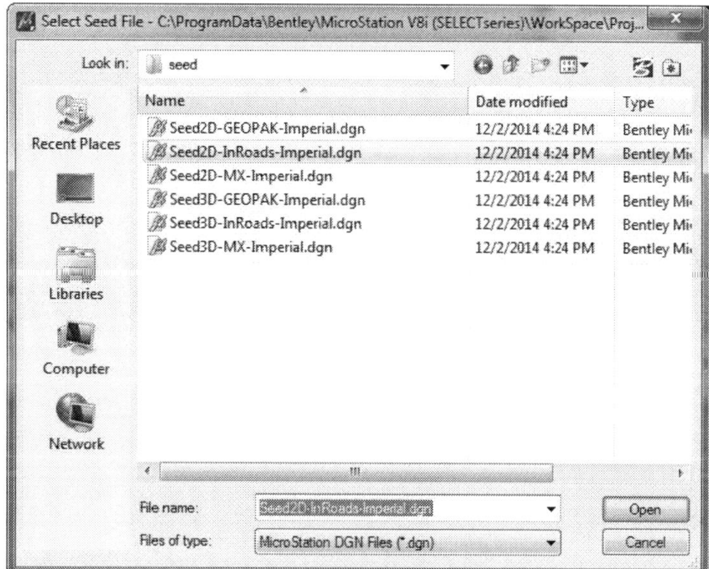

- Key in the File Name: **HWY 60 Alternate One Geometry.dgn**
- Select **Save**, which will **Open** the new file

19 Establish the Beginning and Ending from existing

- **MS: Tasks > Civil Tools > General Geometry > Import Geometry**

- Select *HWY 60 existing.alg* and **Open**

- Toggle on the horizontal alignment as shown. Be sure to toggle **off *Profile*** and ***HWY 60 existing VA*** to only import the horizontal alignment and not the vertical.

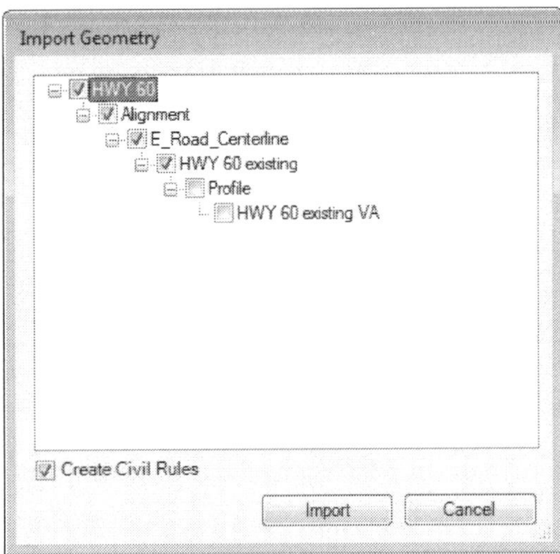

- Select **Import**
- **Fit** the view

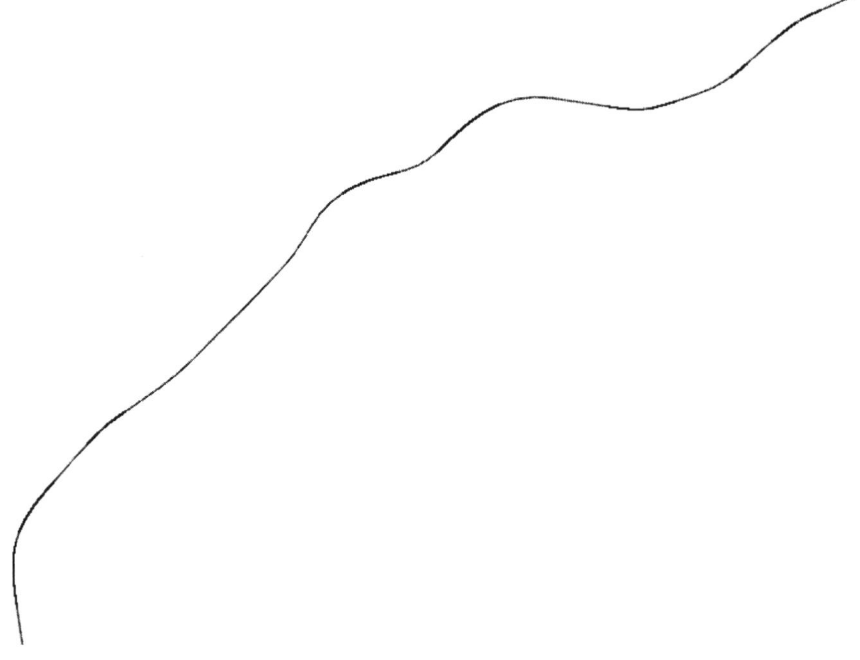

- Drop the complex chain. **MS Tasks: Main > Drop Element**

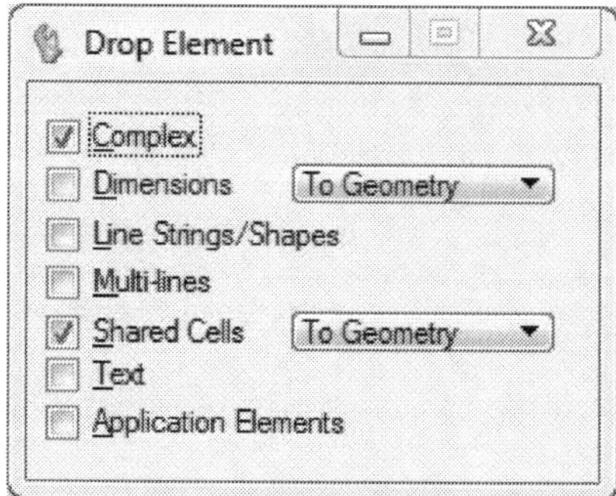

- Select and **Accept** the graphical alignment.
- Use MicroStation to **Delete** all parts of the alignment except the first and last elements.

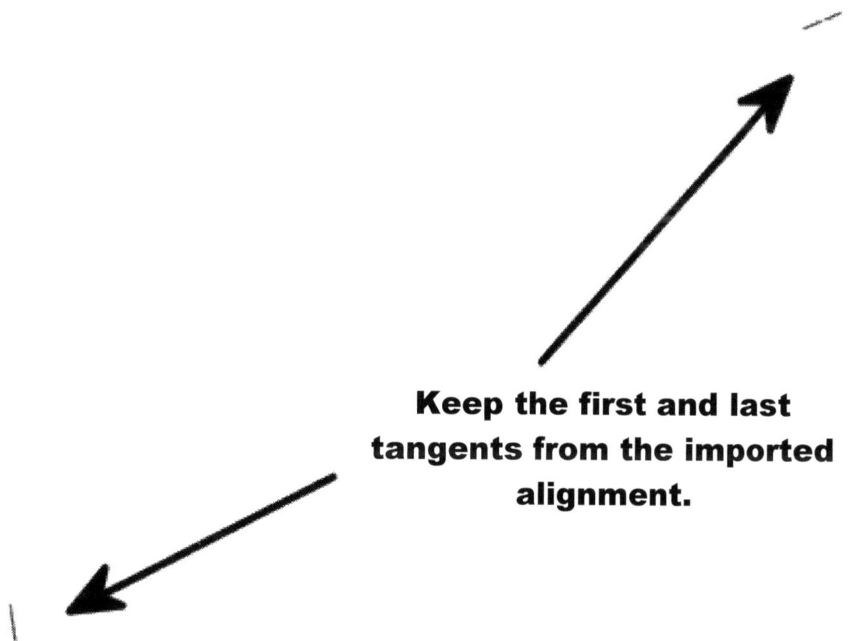

Keep the first and last tangents from the imported alignment.

These will be the tie-in tangents for the new horizontal alignment.

20 Reference Alternate One PI locations.

- Choose **Project Explorer > Links**
- In the drop-down, select **Active Directory**
- Expand the ***Designs*** category

- Drag and drop the **Default** model from *Alternate One PI locations.dgn* onto View 1

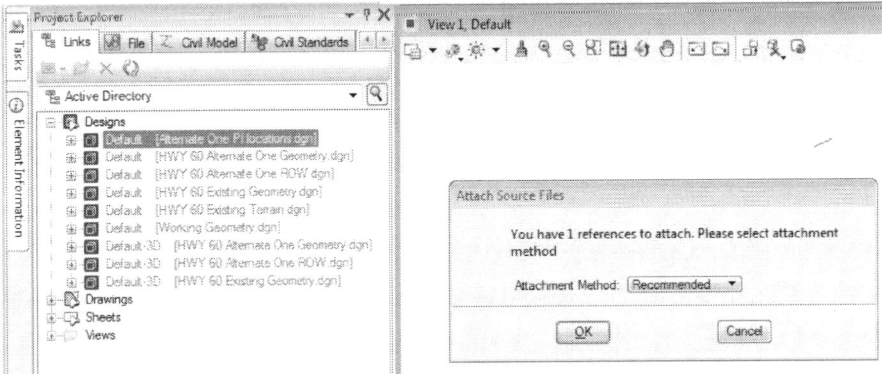

- Change the attachment method to **Coincident World** and select **OK**

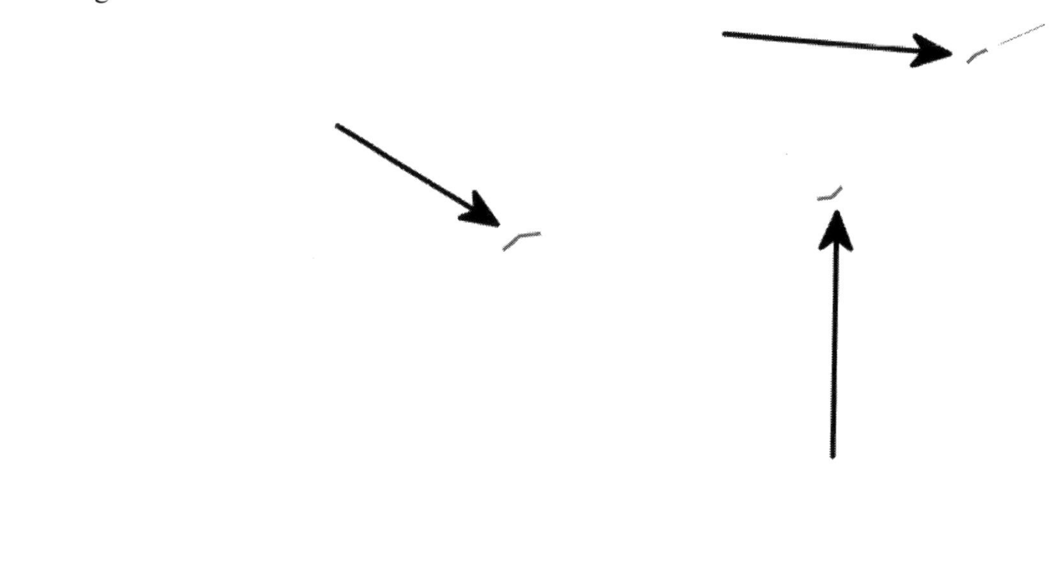

The locations for 4 PIs will appear.

21 Add tangents between the new PI locations

- Set the **Active Feature Definition** to ***Linear > Geometry > Geom_Scratch***

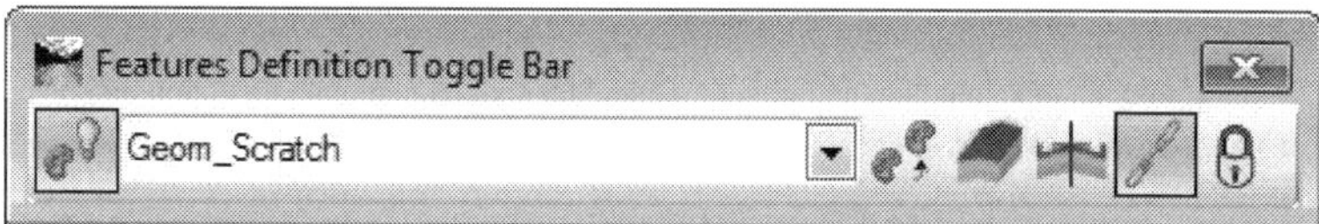

- Make certain **Use Active Feature Definition** and **Chain Commands** are both toggled on.
- **MS: Tasks > Civil Tools > Horizontal Geometry > Line Between Points**

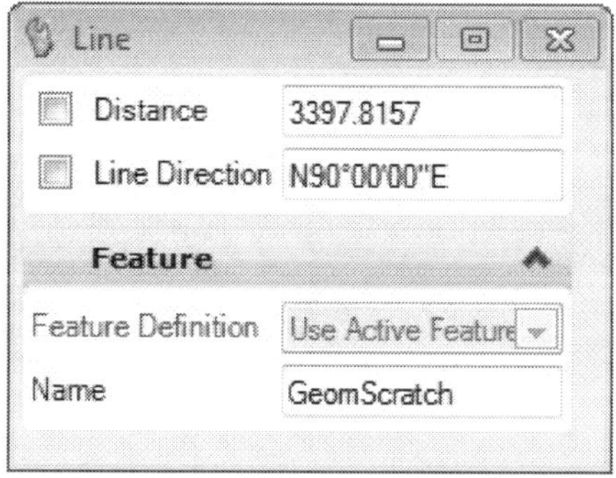

- Make certain **Distance** and **Line Directions** are off.
- Beginning with the first referenced PI location, AccuSnap to each in order to create three tangents as shown here. You only need to create the three middle tangents since the first and last ones from the original alignment will be used.

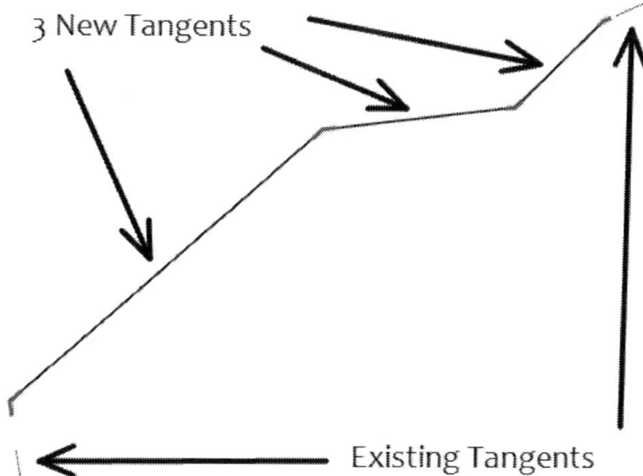

22 Add Curves to the Alignment

- **MS: Tasks > Civil Tools > Horizontal Geometry > Simple Arc**

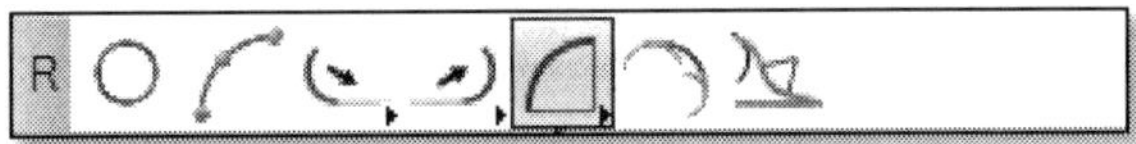

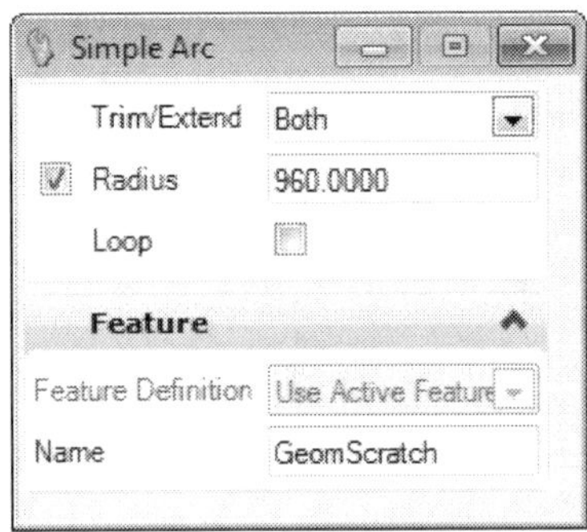

- Using what you learned about this command earlier, add **960'** Radius curves to each PI location, including the beginning and end where there are gaps between the original tangents and the new ones. (The gaps will close with the **Trim/Extend** option set to **Both**.)

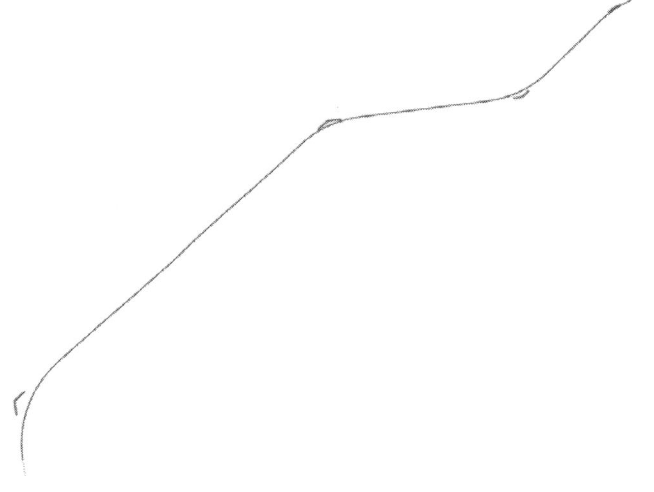

24 Complete the alignment

- Set the **Active Feature Definition** to ***Linear > Geometry > Geom_Centerline***

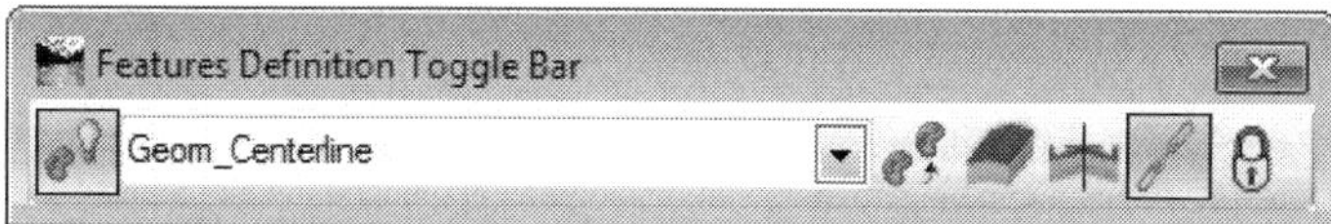

- Choose **MS: Tasks > Civil Tools > Horizontal Geometry > Complex by Elements**

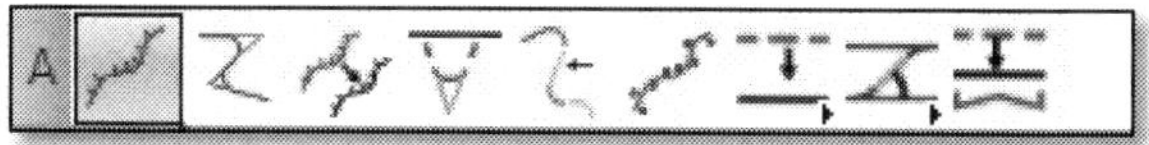

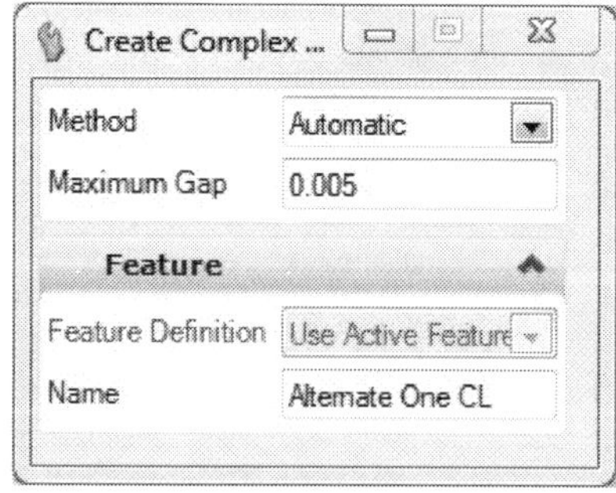

- Change the **Name** to **Alternate One CL**

- Using what you learned about this command earlier, start with the first element from the **existing** geometry and complex the elements together to form the finished alignment. Be certain the arrow is going the correct direction when you start the chain!

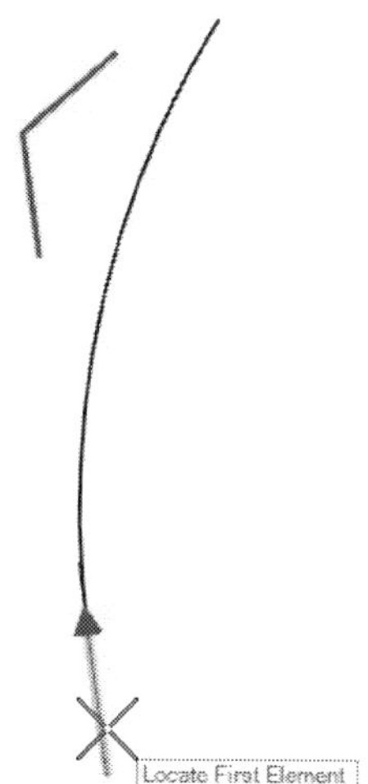

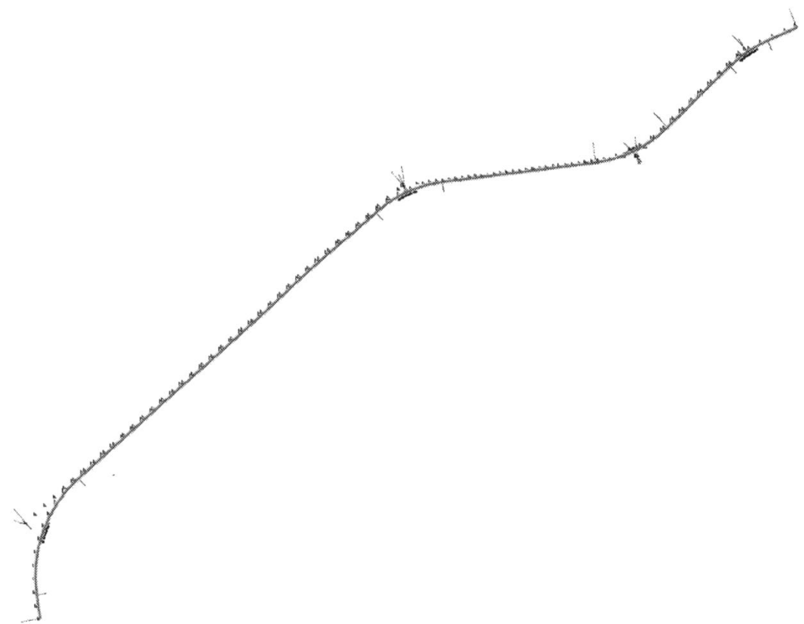

25 Repeat the process of attaching references (use **Interactive** and set the **Nested Attachments** to ***No Nesting***):

- Reference the **Default** model from *HWY 60 Existing Geometry.dgn*
- Reference the **Default** model from *HWY 60 Existing Terrain.dgn*

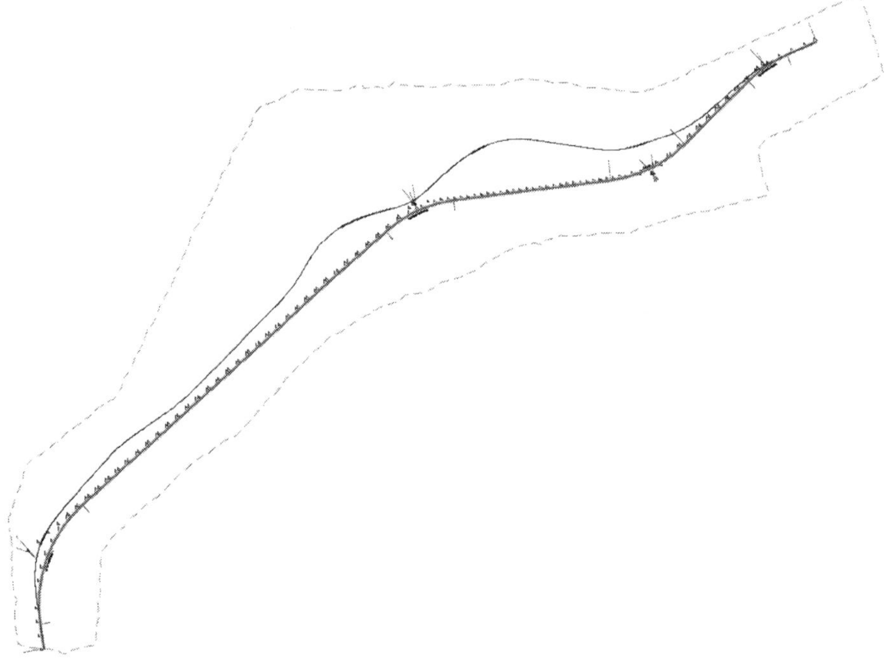

26 Revise the alignment

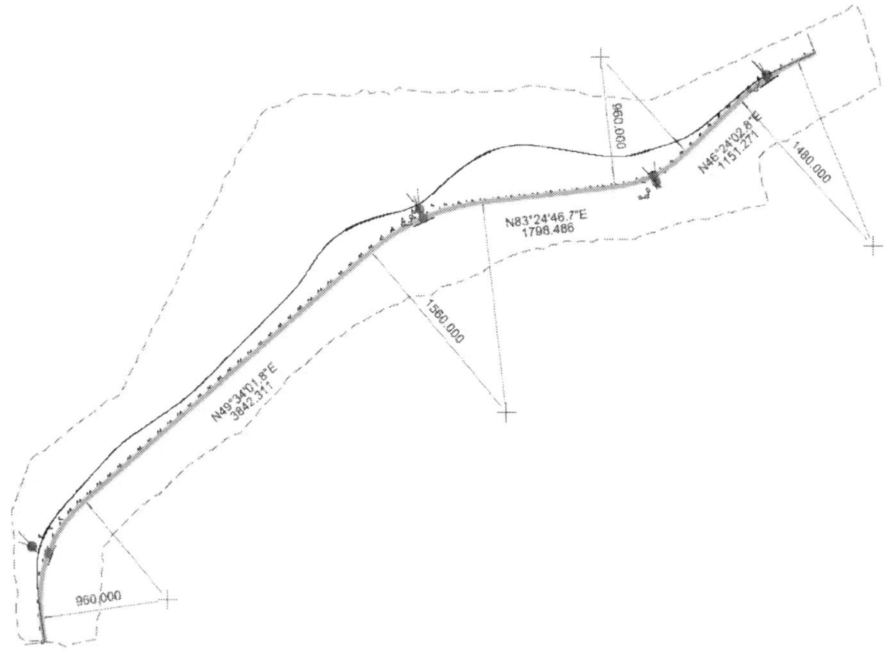

27 Change the second curve radius to **1560** and the fourth curve radius to **1480**.

Beginning Station

28 Set the Beginning Station

- **MS: Tasks > Civil Tools > Horizontal Geometry > Start Station**

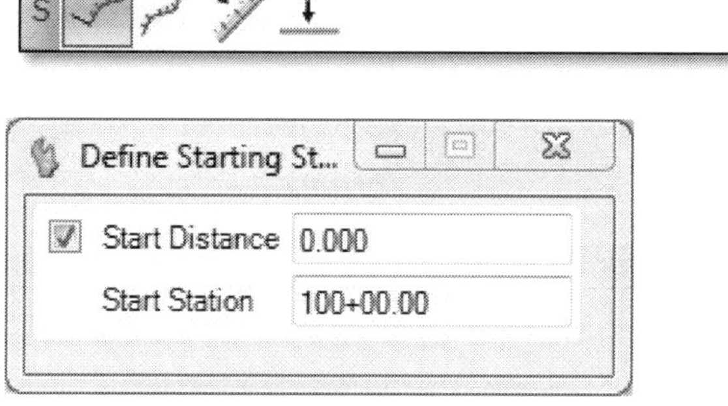

- Set the **Start Station** to **100+00**.

  You can either use the dialog or the heads-up prompts to enter the data.

- When prompted, choose the Alignment.
- **<D>** to Accept the Start Station Position with a **Start Distance** of **0**

This is the distance from the POB to the position where you are defining the station. Here, you're setting the station of the POB, so the distance is 0.

- Enter the **Starting Station** if you did not use the dialog.
- **<D>** to **Accept** the **Start Station**.

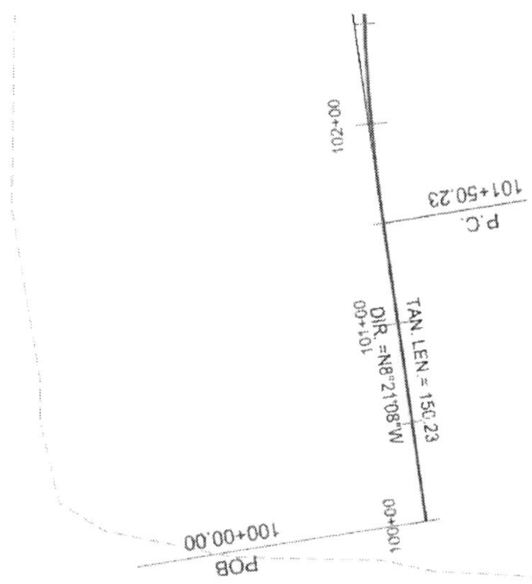

CG Report

29 Generate a report of the alignment and save it to your *C:\Projects\HWY_60* project folder

- Select the alignment and choose **Horizontal Geometry Report**

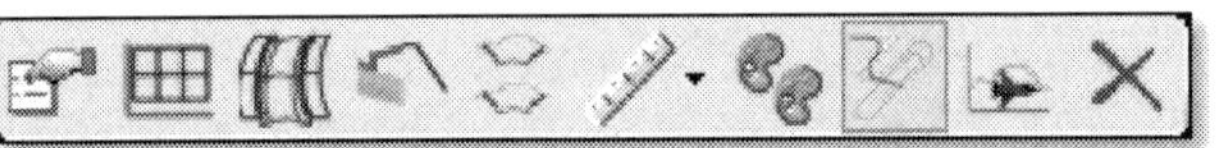

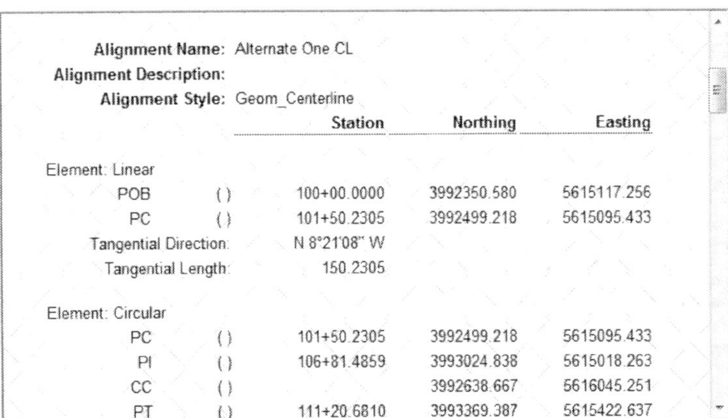

Alignment Name: Alternate One CL
Alignment Description:
Alignment Style: Geom_Centerline

		Station	Northing	Easting
Element: Linear				
POB	( )	100+00.0000	3992350.580	5615117.256
PC	( )	101+50.2305	3992499.218	5615095.433
Tangential Direction:		N 8°21'08" W		
Tangential Length:		150.2305		
Element: Circular				
PC	( )	101+50.2305	3992499.218	5615095.433
PI	( )	106+81.4859	3993024.838	5615018.263
CC	( )		3992638.667	5616045.251
PT	( )	111+20.6810	3993369.387	5615422.637

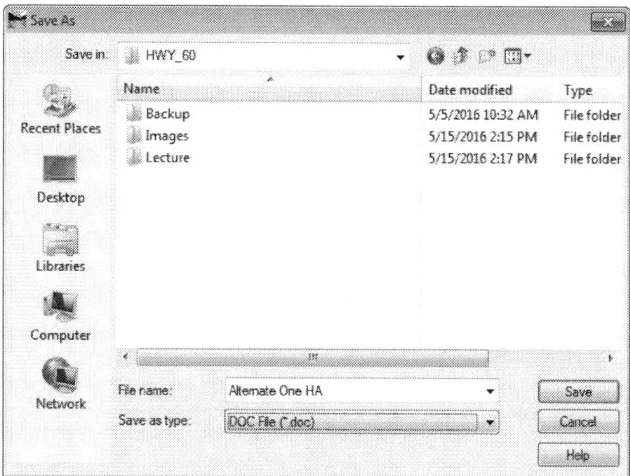

- Close the **Report Browser**
- **Fit** your view

Ending

30 Detach the *Alternate One PI locations.dgn* file

- When prompted about the dependencies, choose **Yes**

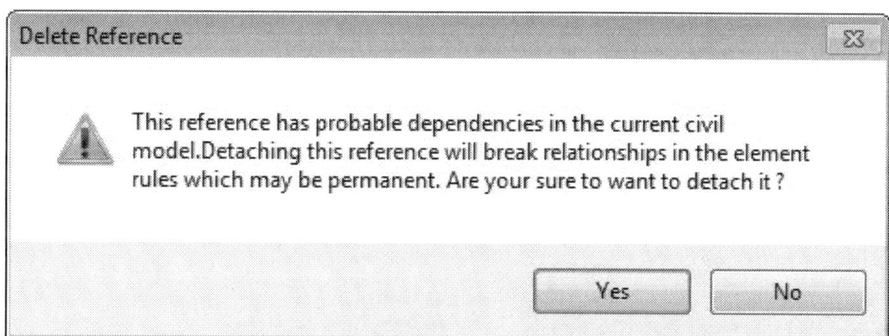

Since you snapped to the PI locations, the graphics now control the location of the alignment. We do not need to maintain this rule, so detaching the file is fine.

31 **Save Settings**

32 **Exit** MicroStation – do not save the geometry project.

Exercise 3: Challenge

1. Create a new design file
2. Attach the terrain model as a reference
3. Create horizontal geometry for an Alternate Two alignment of your choice. You may turn on contours and rasters for reference if desired.

Profiles & Vertical Alignments

CREATING PROFILES

CREATING CG VERTICAL ALIGNMENTS

4 Profiles and Vertical Alignments

In this version of InRoads, profiles come in two forms. Temporary profiles are used for evaluation and design, while permanent profiles are used for plan production. The same information may be seen on both, but only the permanent profiles can be fully annotated and/or plotted.

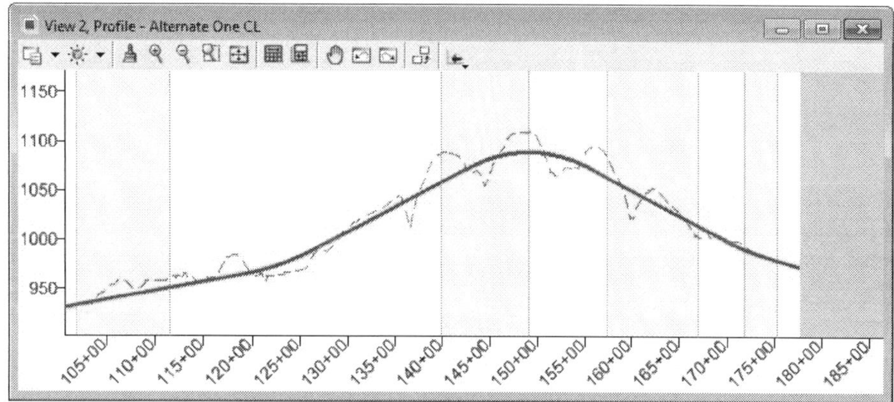

The temporary profile, shown here with a vertical alignment, is created from an alignment's pop-up menu. The shaded areas indicate where there is a curve in the corresponding horizontal alignment.

Vertical Alignments are created with the **Civil Geometry** tools. They take on the symbology of the horizontal by default, but you can assign an **Element Template** to override that symbology if you prefer. In this version, Vertical Alignments are typically known as Design Profiles or just Profiles, while the Temporary Profile is known as the Profile View.

4.1 Creating a CG Vertical Alignment from PIs

Create the Profile

➢ Make the existing terrain active

- Use **Element Selection** to select the terrain element
- On the pop-up menu, select **Set As Active Terrain Model**

➢ Create a Profile View

- Use **Element Selection** to select the horizontal geometry
- On the pop-up menu, select **Open Profile Model**

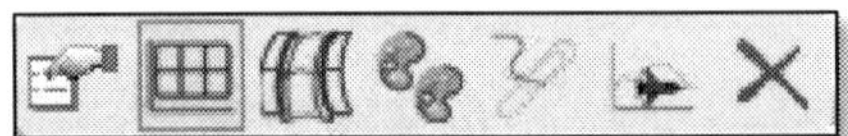

- Select a MicroStation View for the profile (you can open another view before selecting if necessary)

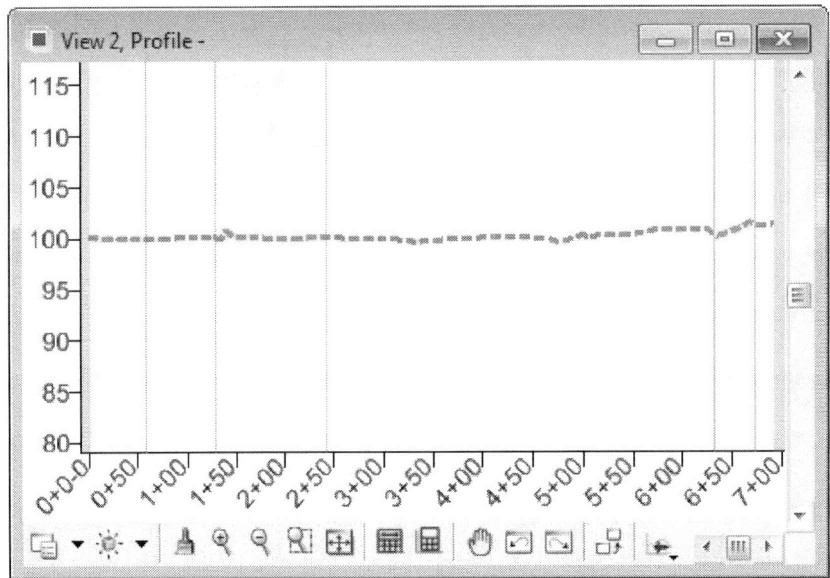

Create the alignment

➢ **MS: Tasks > Civil Tools > Vertical Geometry > Profile Complex by VPI**

There are many vertical curve tools for creating more complex vertical geometry, but for this workflow, we'll create one using VPI command.

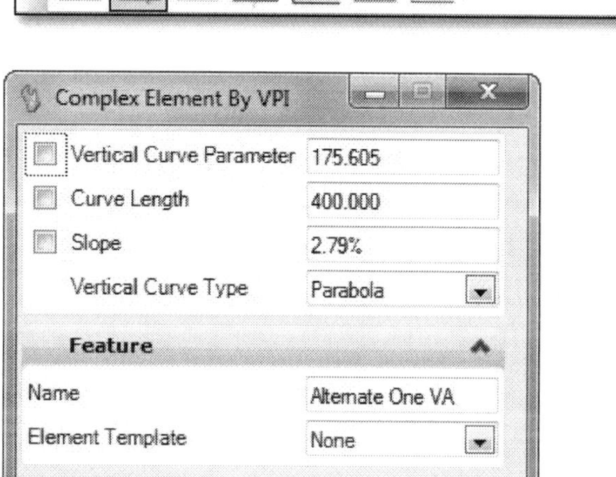

➢ In the **Feature** category, set the **Name** and select an **Element Template** for the display (if you do not choose an element template, the symbology is taken from the horizontal alignment's symbology)

➢ You can use either the dialog or the heads-up prompts to set the **Parameter** (parameter definition is determined by your Design File Settings), the **Curve Length** and the Slope. **<Ctrl>** switches between the **Vertical Curve Types**

➤ Identify the PI locations (if you want to use SE= key-ins, toggle on Civil AccuDraw)

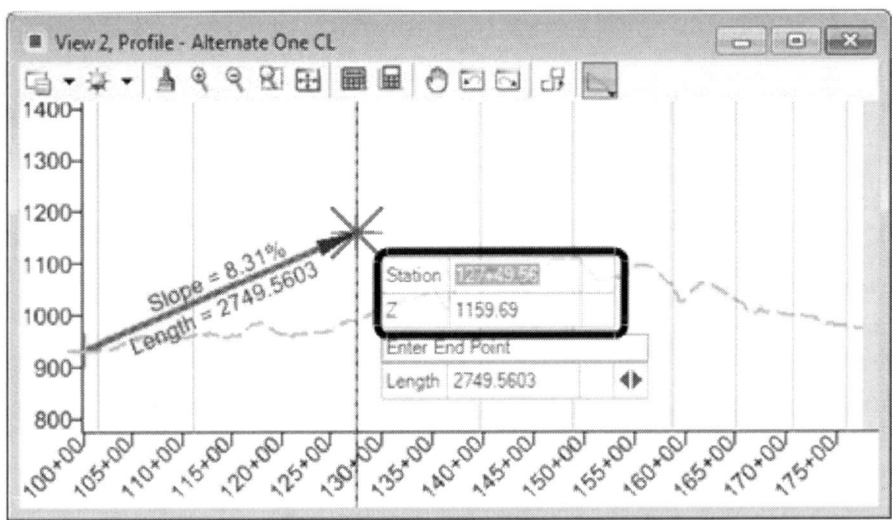

If you AccuSnap to the existing ground to place a PI, it will create a 'rule' and remembers to always match the ground elevation, even if the horizontal changes.

➤ **<R>** when done

Exercise 4: Profiles and Vertical Alignments

Given:

- *HWY 60 Alternate One Geometry.dgn* – Alternate One horizontal geometry (created in previous exercise – use the Backup file if Alternate One was not completed)
- *HWY 60 OG.dgn* – Original ground terrain model (referenced to the above file)

Required:

- Create vertical geometry for a proposed bypass

Getting Started

1 Start InRoads using the icon on your desktop or using the **Start** menu

2 On the MicroStation manager, set the:

- **User**: ***examples***
- **Project**: ***Bentley-Civil-Imperial***
- **Interface**: ***default***

3 **Open** the file *HWY 60 Alternate One Geometry.dgn*

Profile View

4 Create a Profile View

- Select the boundary line of the terrain model
- On the menu that pops up, choose **Set As Active Terrain Model**

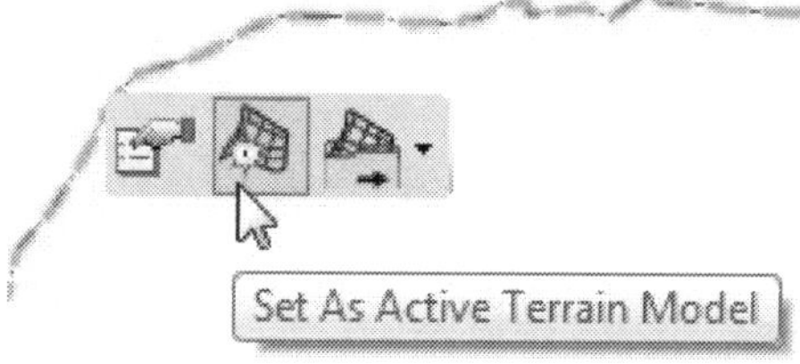

- Select the *Alternate One* alignment and on the context sensitive menu, choose **Open Profile Model**

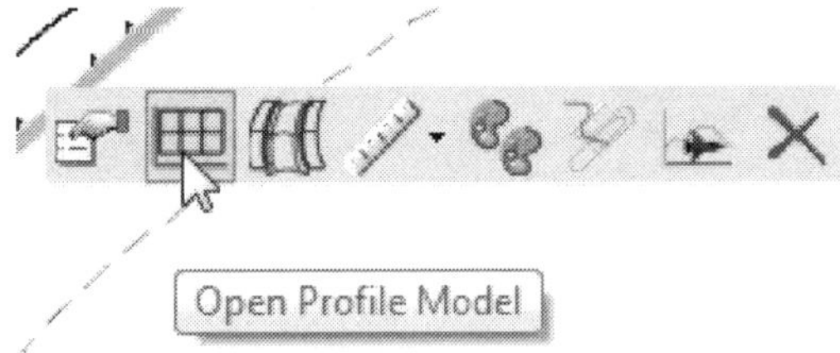

- Open View 2 and **<D>** in the view for the location of the profile.

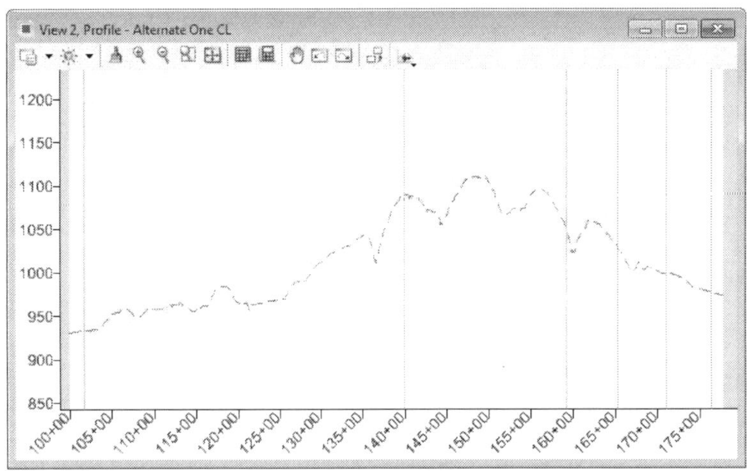

Since this is not a profile that can be plotted, the location you're giving it is really just the view to use for showing the profile. The Active Terrain Model shows on the profile grid. Areas where horizontal curves occur show as shaded in the profile – teal for circular, purple for spirals.)

- Use your scroll wheel to zoom in and out.
- Hold <**SHIFT**> and Scroll.

  The vertical exaggeration changes.

- Hold **<Ctrl>** and Scroll.

  The horizontal exaggeration changes.

- Hold <**ALT**> and Scroll.

  The profile pans.

- Click and drag with your wheel

  The profile pans, just like a regular MicroStation view.

- From View 2, select ***View Attributes***

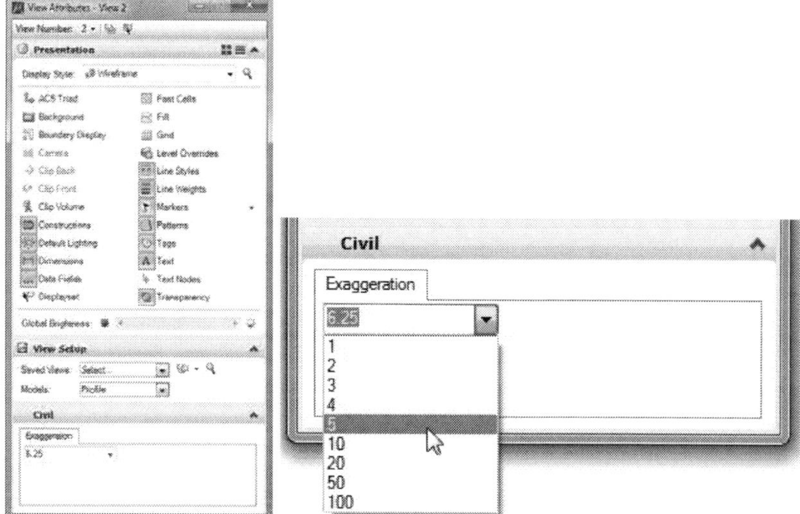

- At the bottom of the dialog, change the vertical **Exaggeration** to ***5***

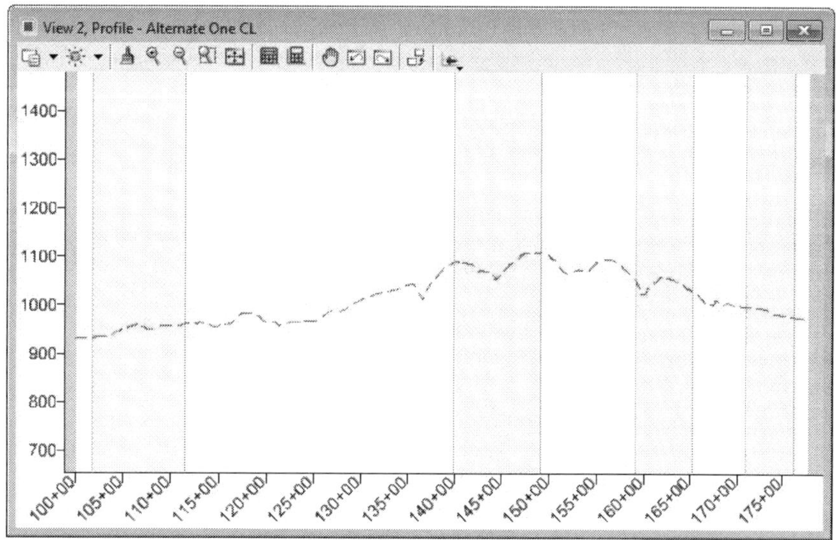

- Close **View Attributes**

In the view control menu bar, notice there are some additional commands.

- Change the zoom of the plan view to include just a portion of the horizontal alignment.

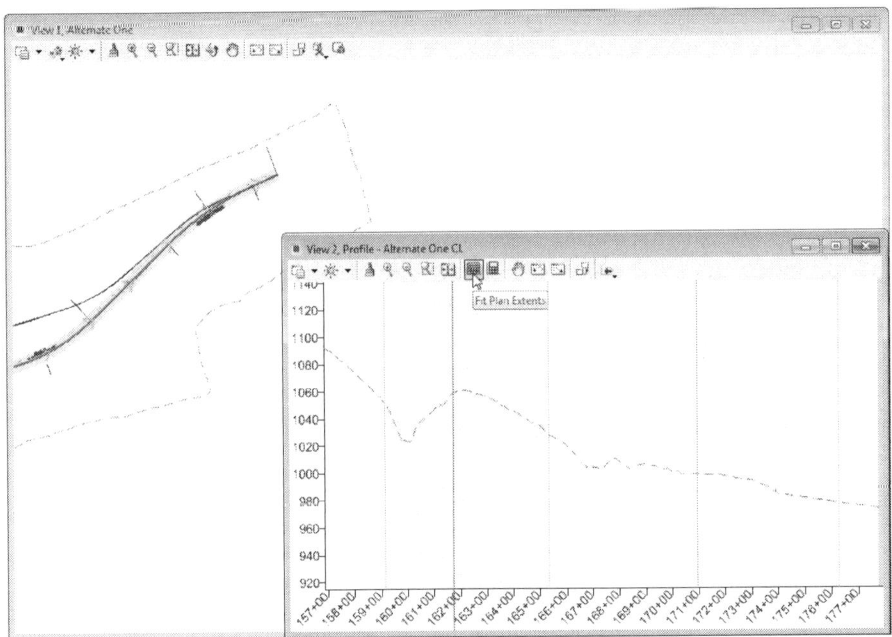

- Select **Fit Plan Extents** and **<D>** in the plan view.

  The profile fits just the station range that is shown in plan.

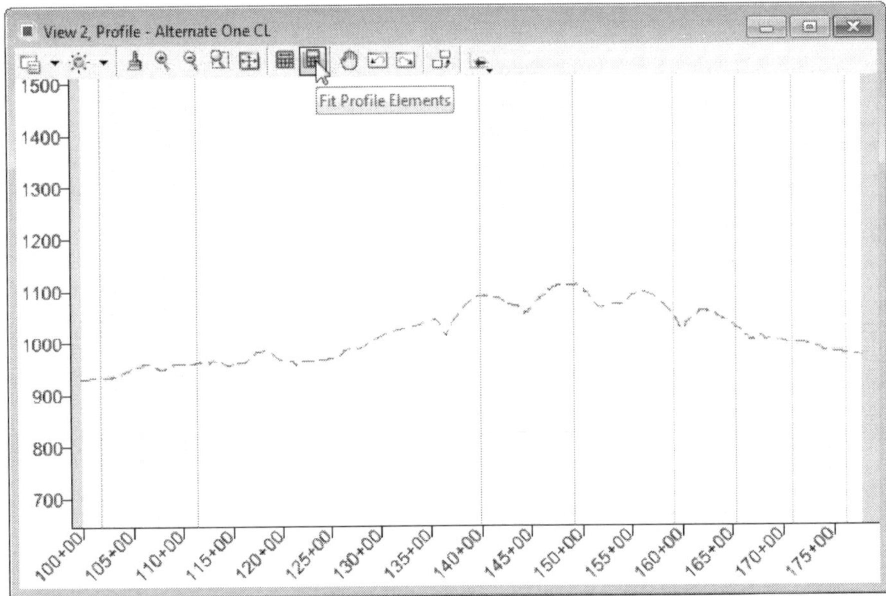

- Select **Fit Profile Elements**

  The entire profile is shown in the profile view.

Vertical Geometry (Profile)

5 Create Vertical Geometry

If you would like to enter Station and Elevation or Distance and Grade values to create the Vertical PIs, then you will need to toggle on Civil AccuDraw.

- On the **Main** task, choose **Activate Civil AccuDraw toolbar**

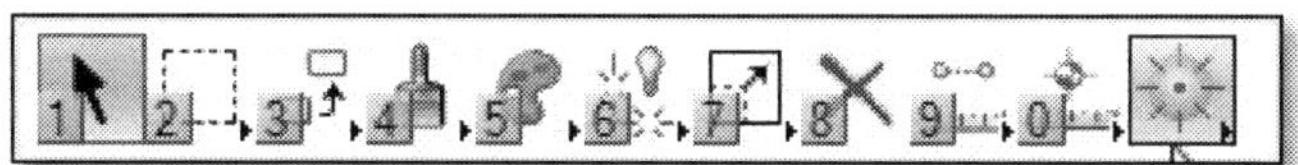

If you don't see the Civil AccuDraw toolbar, it may be docked.

- Toggle on **Civil AccuDraw** and the Z option as shown.
- If you see different options for Civil AccuDraw, click on the Profile view to activate.

  Civil AccuDraw has different options depending upon the model you're working in – i.e. Plan or Profile.

- Make certain **AccuSnap** is toggled on and the default snap is **Keypoint**.

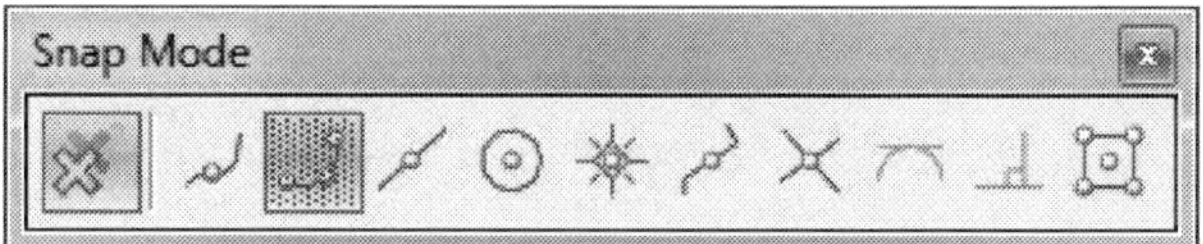

- Click and hold the last icon in the menu bar at the top of the Profile view.

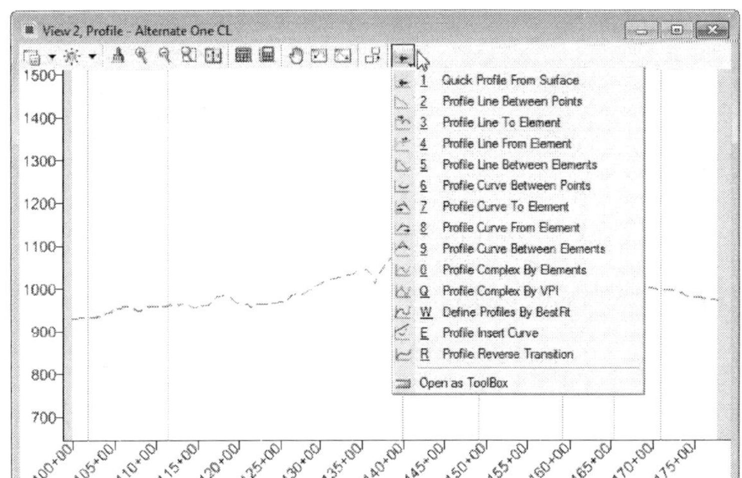

These are some of the more commonly used Vertical Geometry commands. You can access them here, or on the Task Menu.

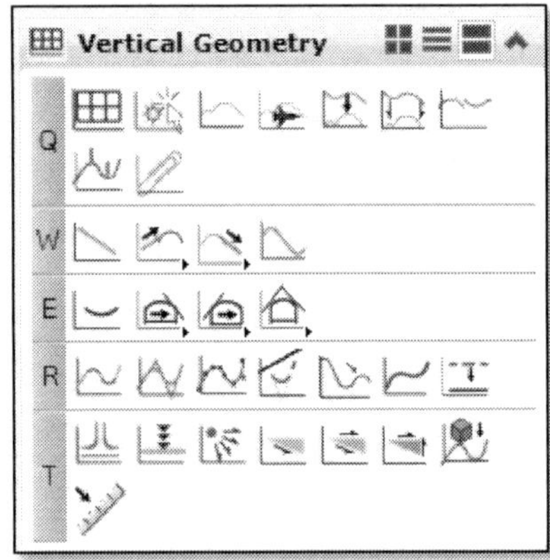

- Choose **Profile Complex by VPI** from either menu.

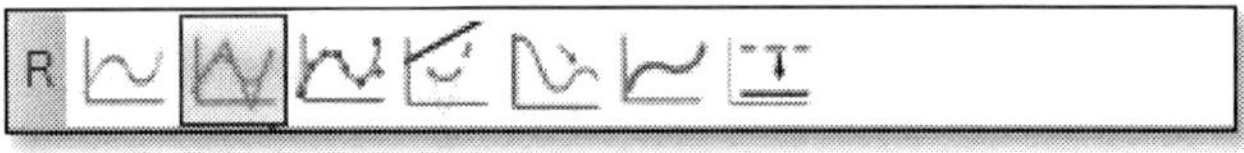

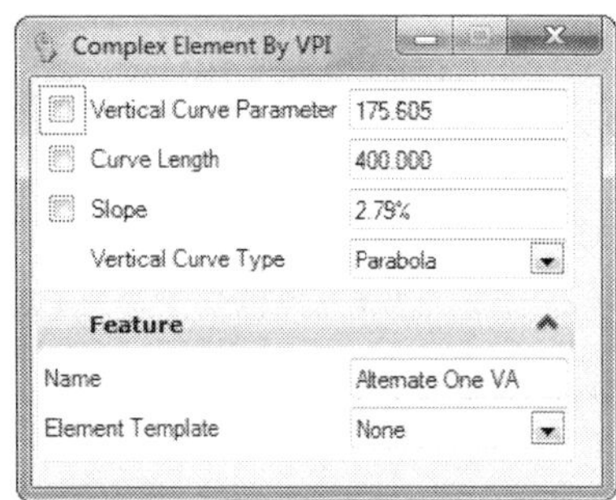

- Make certain all toggles are off and change the **Name** to **Alternate One VA**.

- As you move your cursor, you should see the heads-up display. If not, try clicking on the Profile view and/or Resetting with your mouse. Still nothing? Try toggling Civil AccuDraw off and back on.

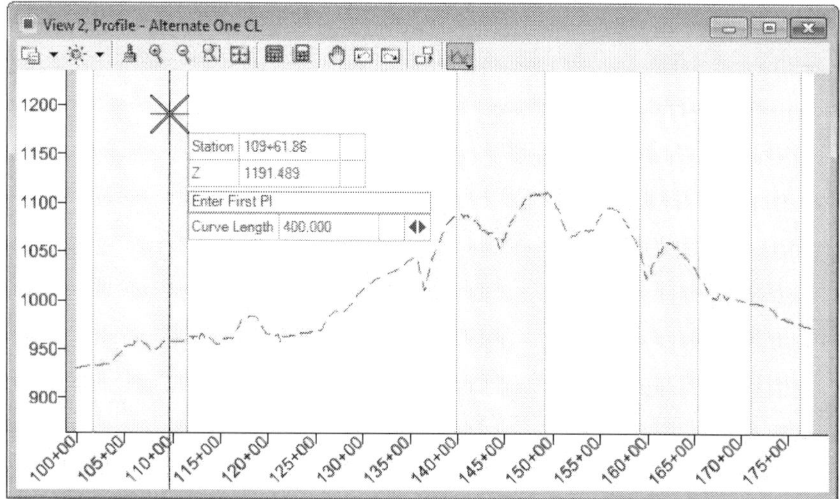

Watch your prompt – if the Profile window is not active, you are asked to pick it.

6 For the first VPI

- Use **AccuSnap** to lock onto the ground line at the beginning of the profile – you can zoom in close if you'd like

  Note: Using a tentative IS NOT THE SAME AS ACCUSNAP!

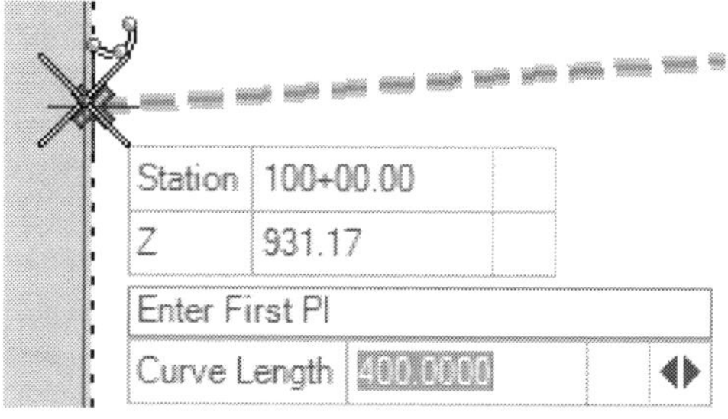

The station should default to 100+00 and the Z to 931.168 (the Z value is rounded to two decimal places in the picture).

- Accept the AccuSnap

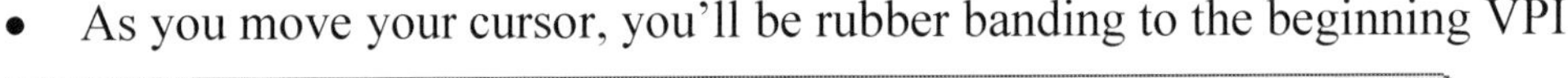

- As you move your cursor, you'll be rubber banding to the beginning VPI

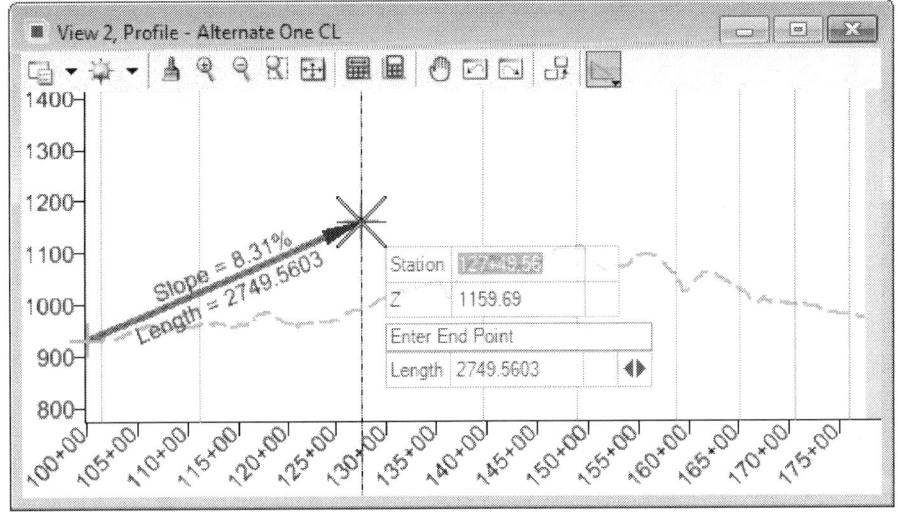

7 For the next VPIs, use the heads-up prompt to enter (Tab to get to the Station field if necessary):

- **Station**: **123+00 <Tab>**
- **Z**: **972 <Tab>**
- **<D>** to Accept.

- **Curve Length**: **750 <Tab>** *(This is the curve for the previous PI that is accepted when this PI is placed)*
- **Station**: **149+13 <Tab>**
- **Z**: **1106 <Tab>**
- **<D>** to Accept.

- **Curve Length**: **1300** *continue tabbing after each entry*
- **Station**: **171+77**
- **Z**: **990**
- **<D>** to Accept.

8 For the last VPI,

- Key in the **Curve Length** of 400
- AccuSnap to the end of the surface line

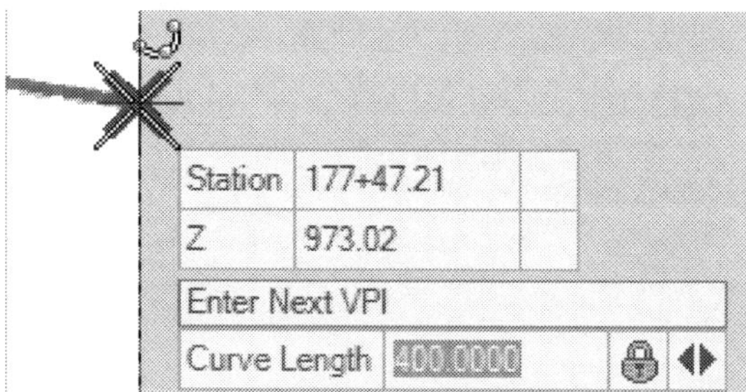

- **<R>** out of the command.

Your vertical geometry should look like the one shown here.

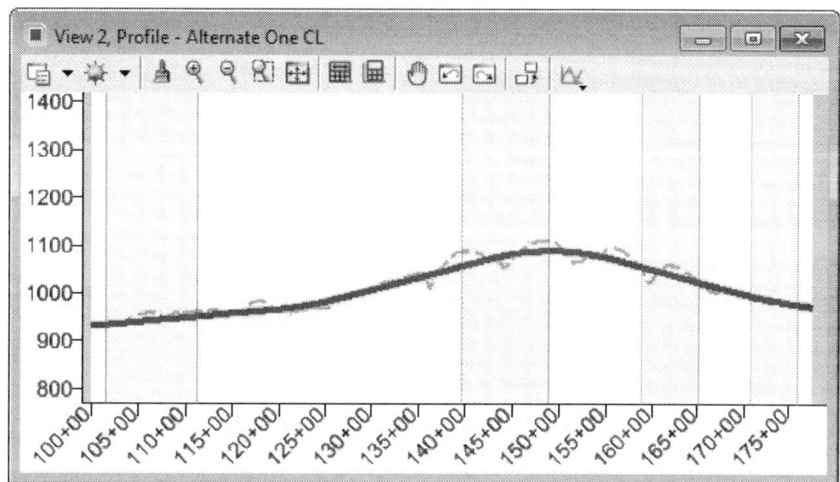

9 Select the Vertical Alignment and on the pop-up menu, select **Set as Active Profile**

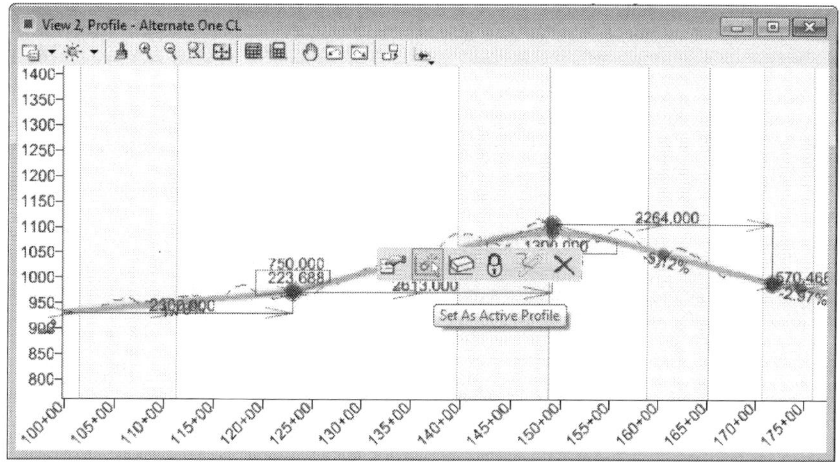

10 Generate a report for the Vertical Alignment

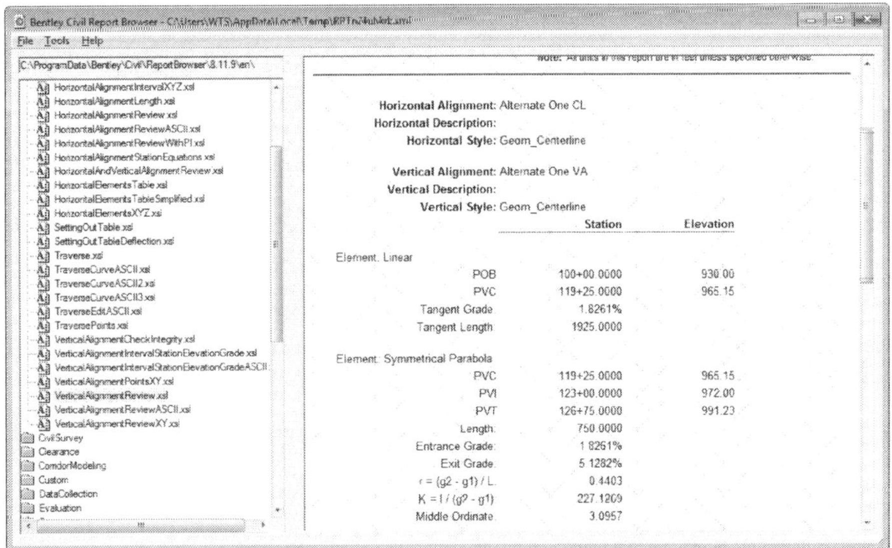

11 **Close** the Report Browser

Ending

12 **Save Settings**

13 **Exit** MicroStation.

If prompted to save changes to the geometry project, select ***No***

Exercise 4: Challenge

1 Create a Profile and Vertical Geometry for the Alternate Two alignment you created in the last lab's challenge.

Templates

CREATING TEMPLATE LIBRARIES

NEW TEMPLATE OPTIONS

PROJECT TO CLOSEST COMPONENT

SUPERELEVATION FLAG

5 Templates

Templates are in effect, just typical sections that are used for modeling a proposed corridor. They are made up of building blocks called components. Each component contains a series of points which become longitudinal break line features when the template is processed during the corridor modeling phase of the project. Templates are stored in an .itl file.

The process of creating templates is essentially unchanged from the previous version and the old ITLs may be directly loaded. There are a few enhancements however, which are covered here. The Superelevation flag is most important as it must be set for Superelevation to work properly.

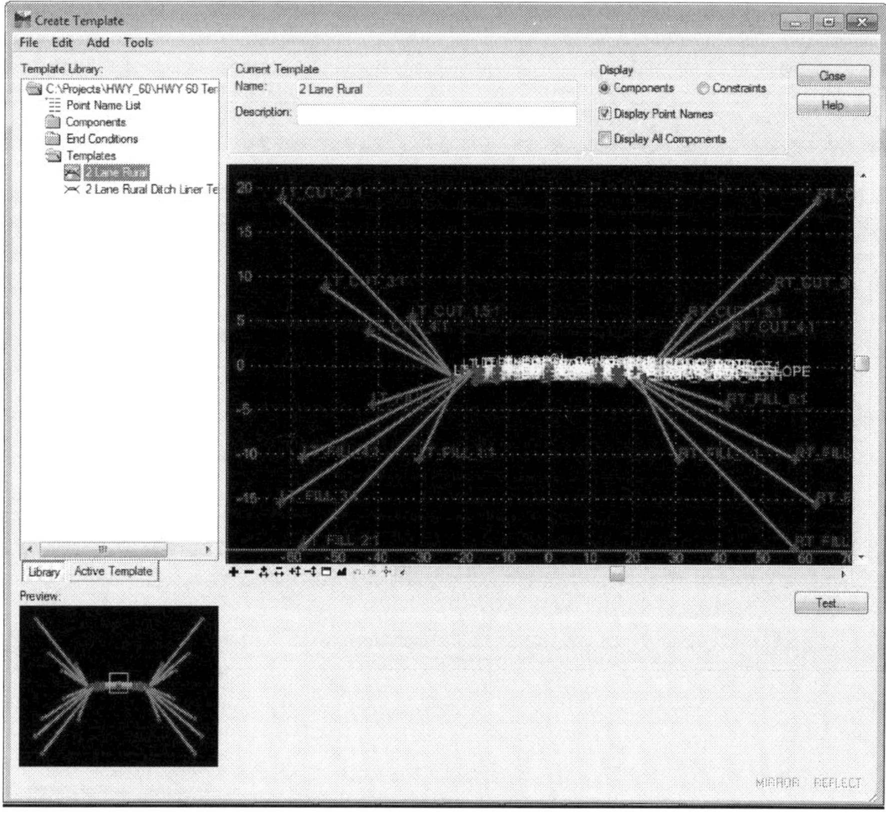

5.1 Creating a Template Library

Most organizations have a set of standard typicals you can use as a starting point for each project. The standards should be copied into a project template library and archived with your project.

- **MS: Tasks > Civil Tools > Corridor Modeling > Create Template**

- On the resulting dialog, select **File > New > Template Library**
- Navigate to your project data folder and key in the library name
- Select **Save**

The new library is created and opened. Next, you'll copy over some standard names, components and templates.

- On the **Create Template** dialog, choose **Tools > Template Library Organizer**
- On the left side of the resulting dialog, you'll see the current library. On the right, you can load another library or previously defined corridor that contains templates you wish to copy.
- Select the **Browse …** button on the right
- Navigate to the template library folder in your standards and select your desired ITL file
- Choose **Open**

The standards are now on the right side and can be drug over to the left to populate your project template library. You can copy point names, individual templates and/or entire folders.

- Drag over the **Point Name** list, being careful to drop it on the current Point Name list (which is empty)

  You may want to do this twice as there is no visual assurance the copy occurred until you drag over the list onto a list that is already populated. Once you receive the message that you're about to overwrite an existing list, you'll know the names have been copied.

- Drag over any templates or folders of templates you think you might need on the project

  You can repeat this process later in the project if you discover a template is needed that you did not originally copy. You can also copy template from other projects if needed. Should you find that you're often copying a template from project to project, you should inquire about having it added to the standards.

- When done copying, select **OK** and select **Yes** to **Save**.

New Options

Closest Component

The **Project to Design** constraint now has an option to select if you want it to tie into the **Closest End Condition** (the only option in SS2) or the **Closest Component**. This allows more flexibility, especially when the side slope contains non-end condition components such as walls or liners.

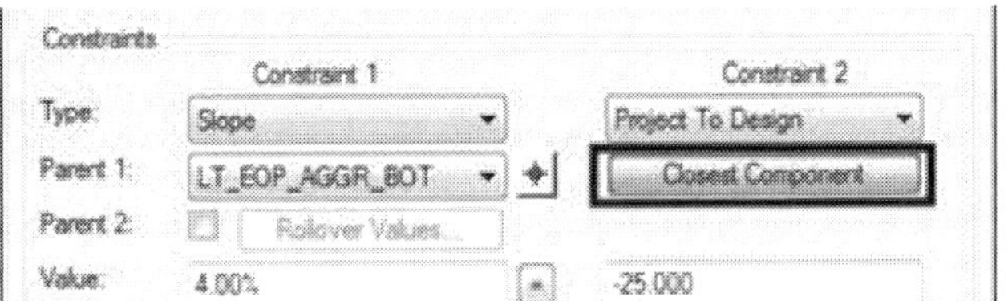

Superelevation Flag

A Superelevation 'flag' is used to determine the portion of the template that is inside the super range. Setting the flag will prevent the wrong point from being used. When setting up Superelevation, you will give it a width for the Superelevation lane. If there are multiple points near this designated width, there is a likelihood the wrong point could be used and therefore a flag should be established. It is good practice to go ahead and set the flag whether you think it will be needed or not.

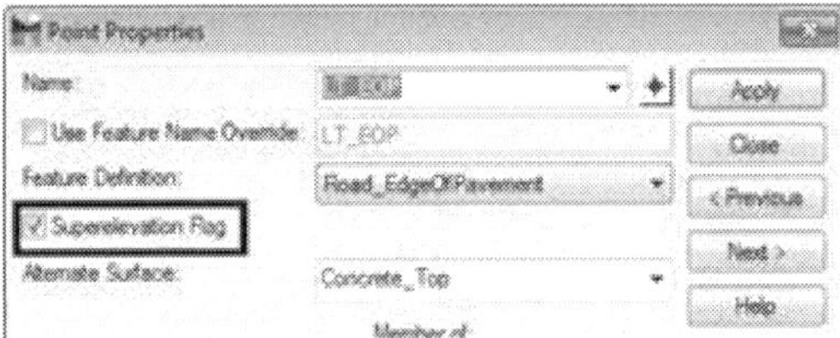

End Condition Targets

There are a few changes to the targets for end conditions. ***Active Surface*** has been replaced with ***Terrain Model***, ***Alignments*** with ***Linears*** and ***Styles*** with ***Feature Definitions***. There is no longer a separation between Features and Alignments

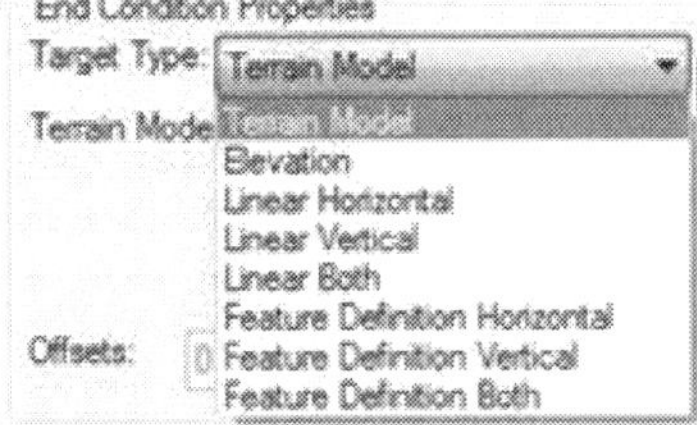

Exercise 5: New Template Options

Given:

- *HWY 60 Alternate One Geometry.dgn*
- *HWY 60 Templates.itl*

Note: In this lab, you'll be working on the Templates in an ITL, so the design file is inconsequential.

Required:

- Review new options in the templates
- Use the new Project to Design option
- Add a Superelevation Flag to your templates

Getting Started

1 Start InRoads using the icon on your desktop or using the Start menu

2 On the MicroStation manager, set the:

- **User**: ***examples***
- **Project**: ***Bentley-Civil-Imperial***
- **Interface**: ***default***

3 Open the File: *HWY 60 Alternate One Geometry.dgn*

4 Load the template library

- **MS: Tasks > Civil Tools > Corridor Modeling > Create Template**

Note: The Bentley template library is loaded by default. This is controlled by a configuration variable, so you could switch it if you prefer. However, you probably do not want to load your actual standards ITL since templates could easily be modified and overwritten.

- In the **Create Template** dialog, choose **File > Open** and select the *HWY 60 Templates.itl* file
- **Open**

Exclude from Mesh

5 Review a template

- Make the **CP / 2 Lane Rural** template active.

- Edit any one of the components and notice the **Exclude from Top/Bottom Mesh** option. This has replaced the **Exclude from triangulation** option in the previous version.

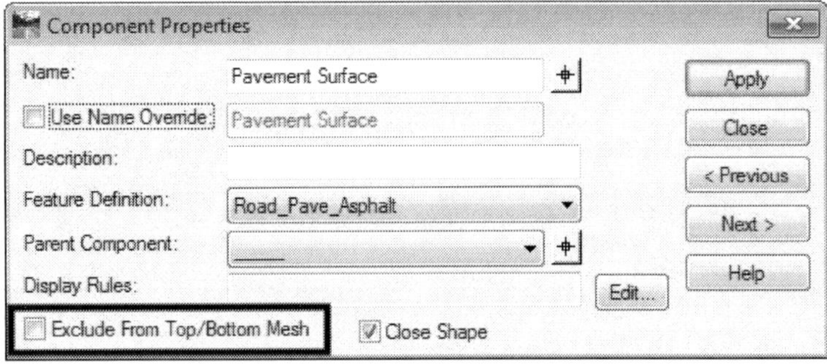

- **Close** the **Component Properties**
- Select the **Active Template** tab at the bottom of the folder hierarchy area.

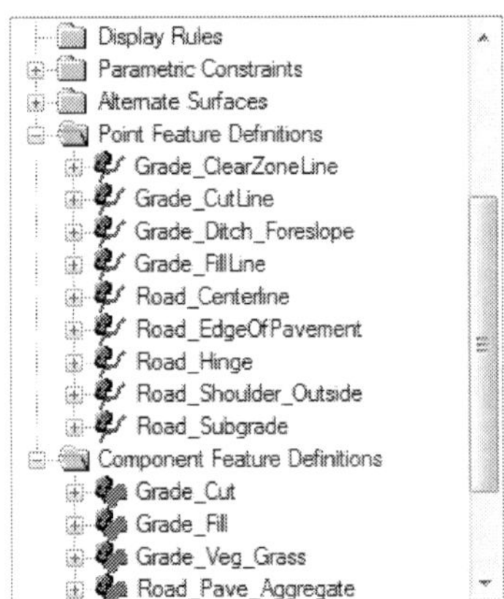

Note the new options for the Point Feature Definitions and Component Feature Definitions. You can expand either to see the Feature Definitions used in the template, and which points use each definition.

Project to closest component

6 Copy a template

- Select the **Library** tab at the bottom of the **Active Template** area.
- In the *CP* folder, highlight **2 Lane Rural**
- Right-click and select **Copy**
- Right-click again and select **Paste**
- Change the name of the new template to **2 Lane Rural - Ditch with Liner**
- Make the new template active
- Toggle on **Tools > Dynamic Settings**
- Delete the End Conditions

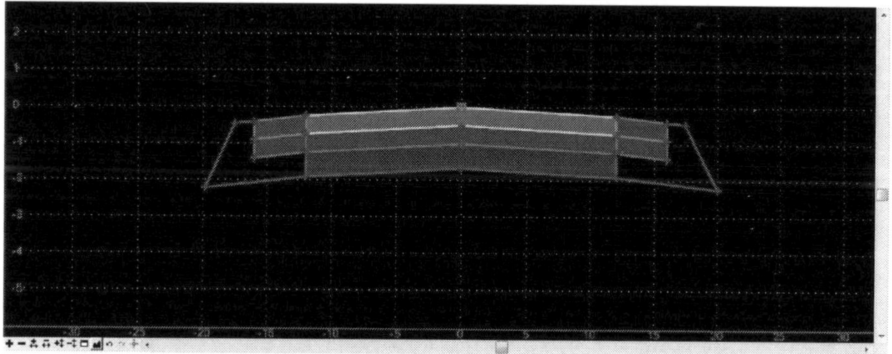

7 Add the ditch with a Liner

- Make certain **Apply Affixes** is toggled on

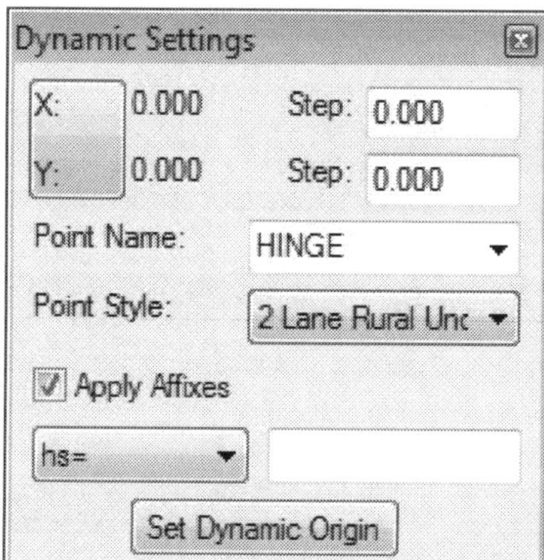

- Drag the *FB Ditch with liner* from the *End Conditions > Cut* folder onto the Hinge
- While dragging, right click and toggle on **Mirror**

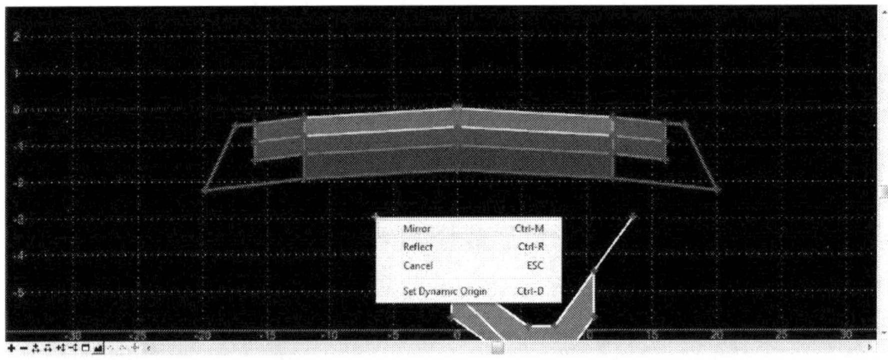
Mirror Ctrl-M
Reflect Ctrl-R
Cancel ESC
Set Dynamic Origin Ctrl-D

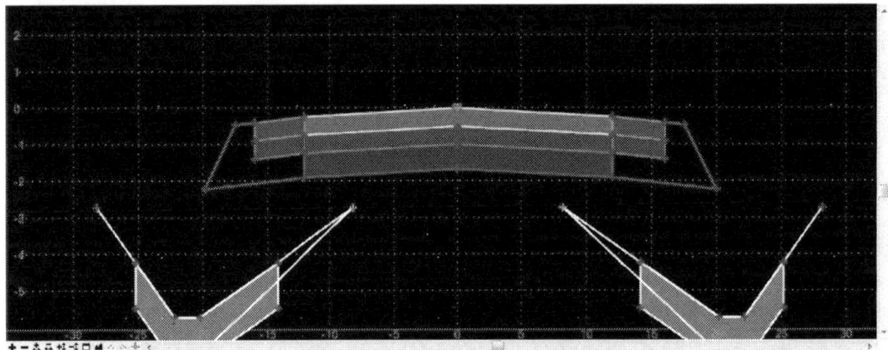

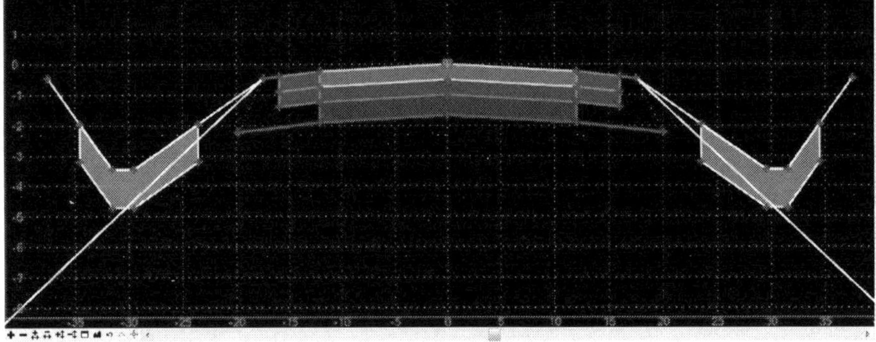

8 Test the template and note the component extends through the liner

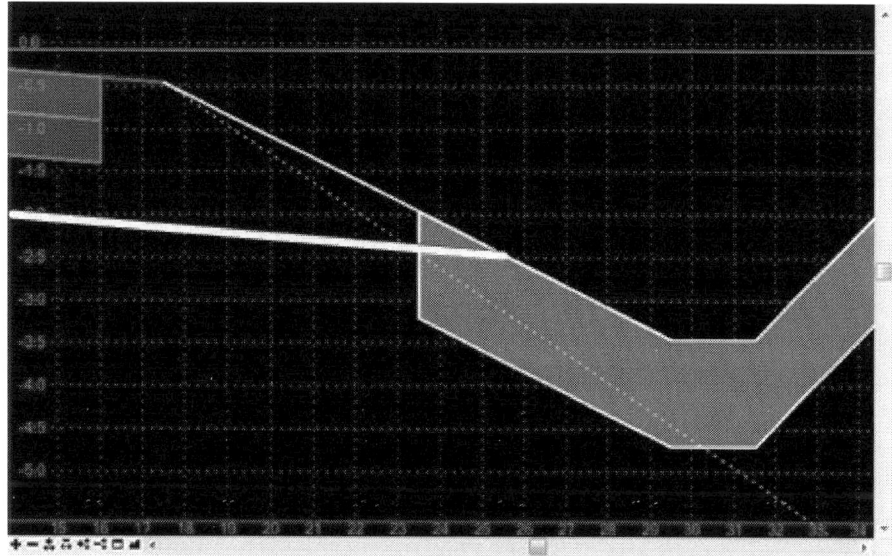

9 Edit the RT_SHDR_AGGR_BOT point

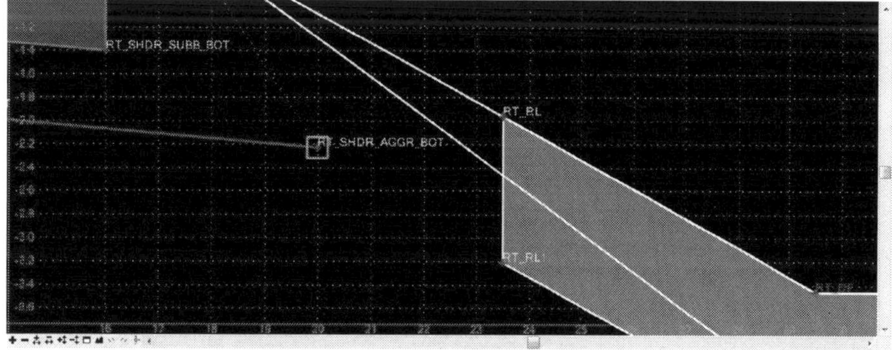

- Change the **Project to Design** constraint to tie into the **Closest Component** instead of the **Closest End Condition**.

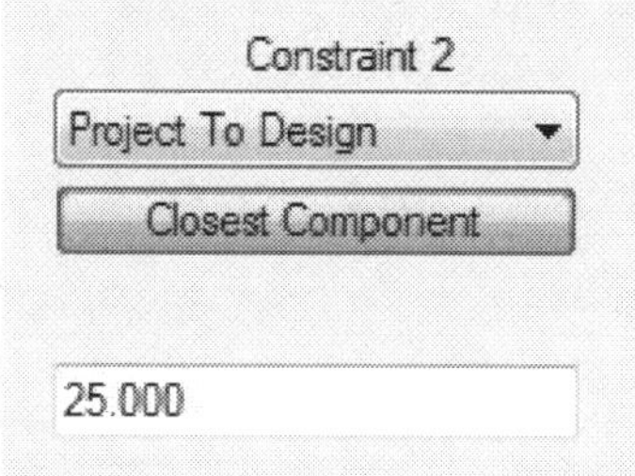

10 Test the template and note the subgrade now stops at the liner.

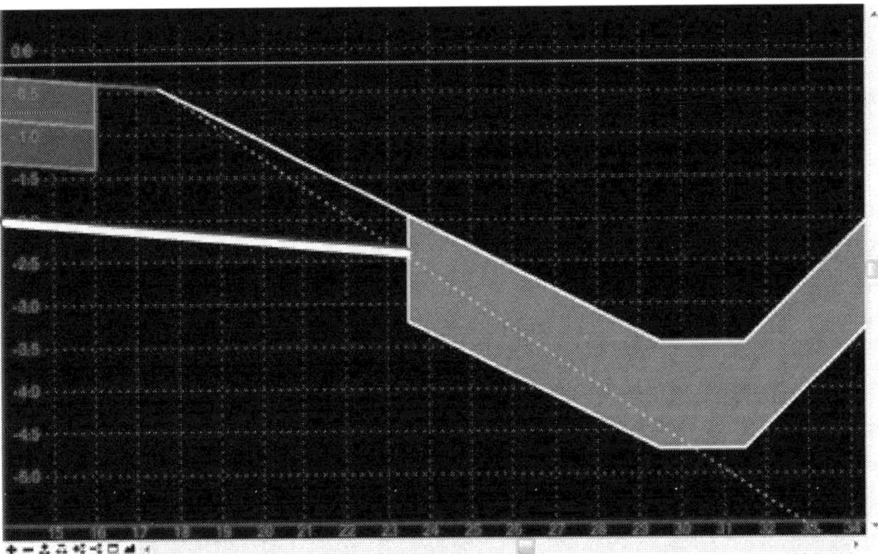

11 Change the other side and Test if desired

12 Save the ITL

Superelevation

13 Add a superelevation flag

- Make the **CP / 2 Lane Rural** template active.

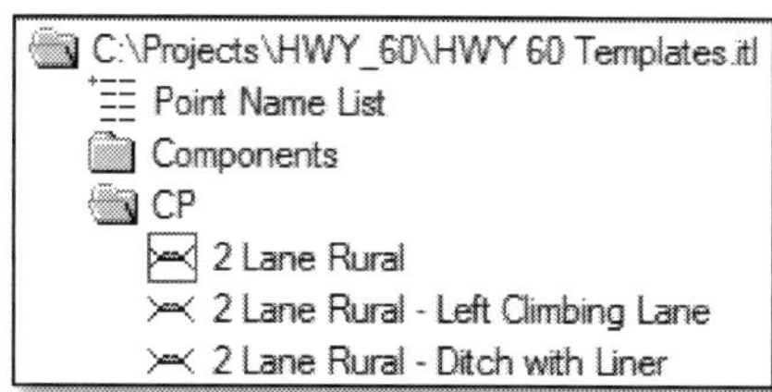

- Edit the **LT_EOP**
- Toggle on the **Superelevation flag**

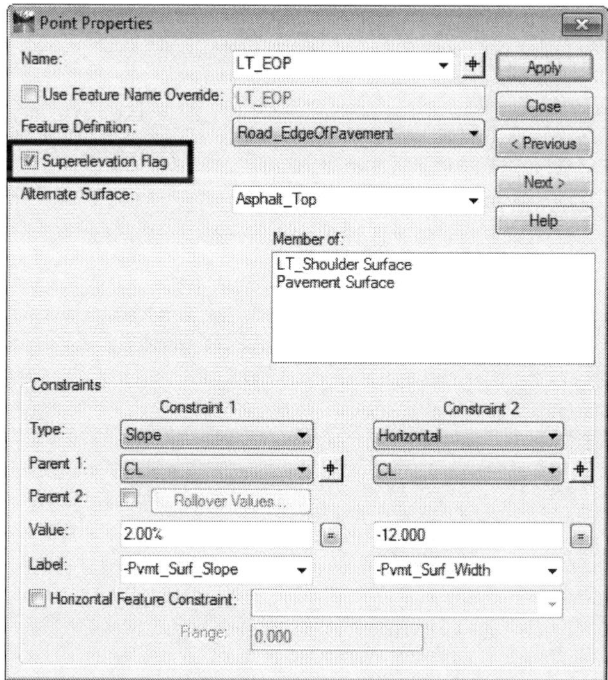

- Choose **Apply**
- Repeat for the **CL** and the **RT_EOP**

The Superelevation flag is used to determine the portion of the template that is superelevated. When the points are close together, this can prevent the wrong one being used when the Superelevation is assigned to the corridor.

14 Save the *ITL*

Rollovers

Rollovers may be handled two different ways in InRoads. They can be treated as a separate superelevated lane with different criteria, or the template can be set up to automatically roll the shoulder under certain criteria. Here, we'll set the template up for rollovers.

15 Establish rollovers in the template

- Set the **2 Lane Rural** template active
- Edit the **LT_SHDR**
- In the **Constraints** section, toggle on **Rollover Values**

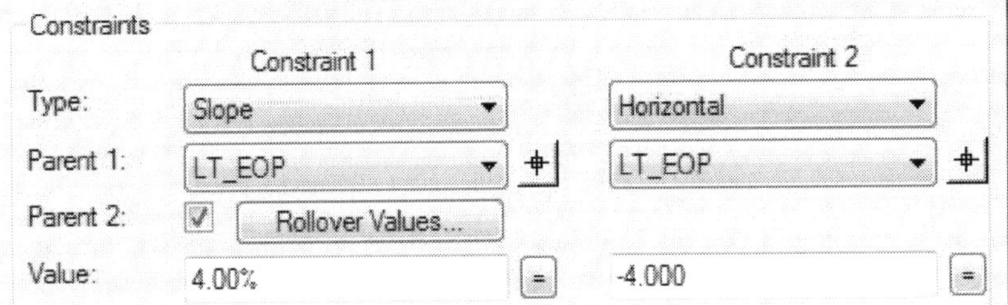

- Select the **Rollover Values** Button
- Set the **High Side** to **7.0%**
- Set the **Low Side** to **0.0%**
- Set the **Reference Point** to ***CL***

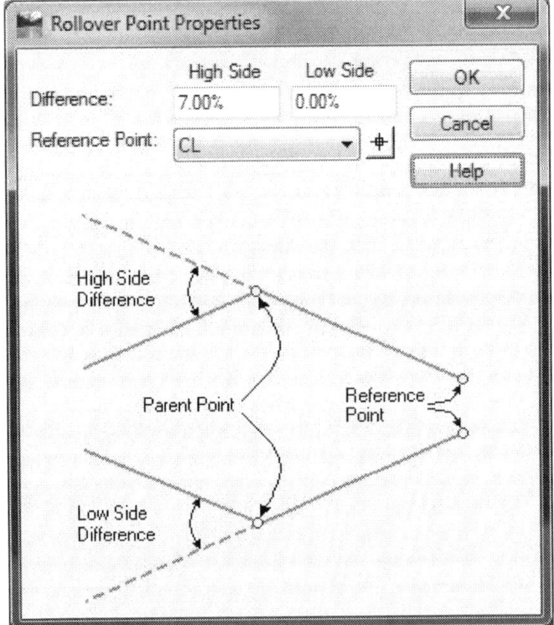

- Select **OK**, then **Apply** the changes
- Repeat for the **RT_SHDR**

  Now, whenever the Pavement is rotated, the shoulder will follow suit when the rollover difference is reached. This will also cause the shoulder to roll when the rollover cross slope is reached for other reasons than Superelevation, such as when you are matching an intersection roadway's cross slope.

Ending

16 Save the *ITL* and **Close**

17 **Exit** MicroStation

Corridor Modeling

DESIGN STAGES

CREATING A CORRIDOR

DYNAMIC SECTIONS

6 Corridor Modeling

Corridor Modeling is an interactive approach to creating a model of your design. With it, you assign templates to follow the horizontal and vertical geometry, resulting in a 3D model using the same basic workflow as creating a corridor in an IRD from previous versions.

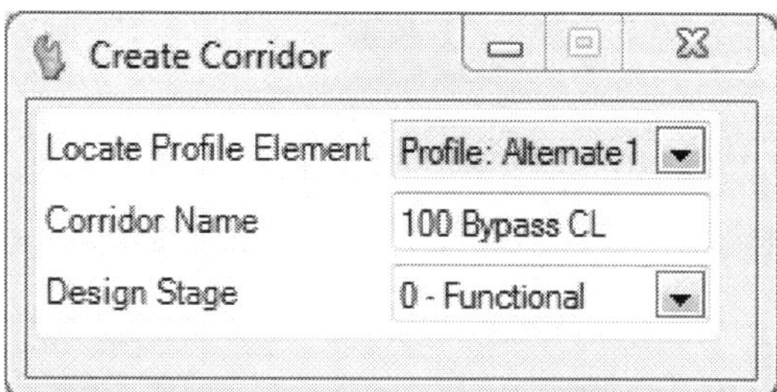

Design Stages

The **Design Stage** can be set based upon the amount of detail you need or what the result of the model needs to be. Initially, one of the lower numbered **Design Stages** may be used, as they process faster which can help in preliminary design especially with long complicated corridors. As more detail is desired, one of the higher numbered **Design Stages** can be used.

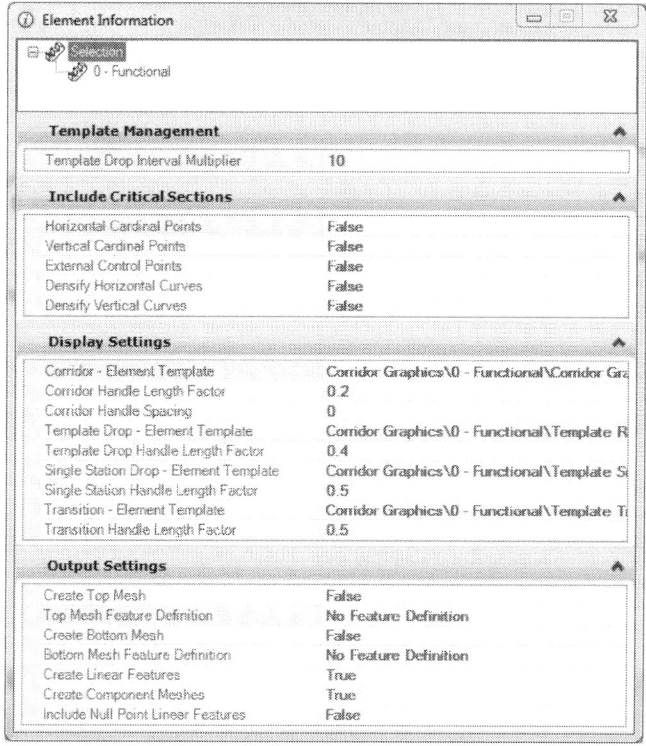

When you establish a corridor, you specify the template interval for the frequency of template drops. In the Design Stage, an Interval Multiplier is used to increase the interval, so lower stages will process faster with less detail. Contributing to less detail is the lack of using Critical Sections at the early Stages.

Display Settings control the Handle symbologies, locations and lengths. When there is less detail displayed, you may opt for fewer, smaller handles for example.

Output Settings control what is created from the modeling process. Options include a Top Mesh (typically finished grade), a Bottom Mesh (typically subgrade) Features and Components.

> *Note: Terrain Models are not automatically created as output, but may be created later.*

The Design Stages are part of your configuration.

Dynamic Sections

During the modeling process, you can create Dynamic Sections to see cross sections for the models. These dynamic sections are displayed in a different model and MicroStation View. They automatically update with any changes to the design. They are not used for plotting, but for evaluation of the design only.

6.1 Converting an IRD to a Corridor

Previously, the IRD file contained corridors for modeling. In the current InRoads, these corridors are stored graphically in the DGN file. In order to convert an IRD to this format, in the Active Design File or in a reference, you must have:

- The horizontal and vertical geometry converted to Civil Geometry
- All Point Control dependencies (alignments, corridors, etc.) in the new formats
- A 3D Model in the current file

➢ Set the active MicroStation level to your Superelevation level

➢ **MS: Tasks > Civil Tools > Corridor Modeling > Import IRD**

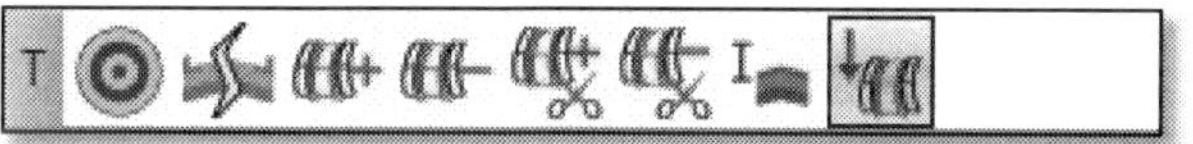

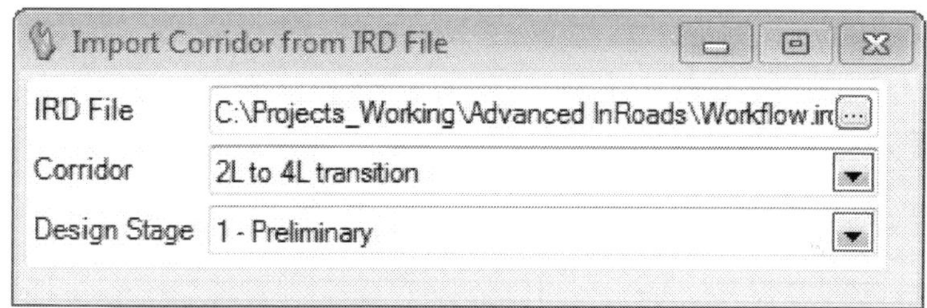

- Browse and choose the IRD file
- Choose the Corridor from the drop-down
- Choose a Design Stage from the drop-down
- Accept each of these with a **<D>** following the heads-up prompts

The IRD is imported. Any dependencies that are not found will be reported.

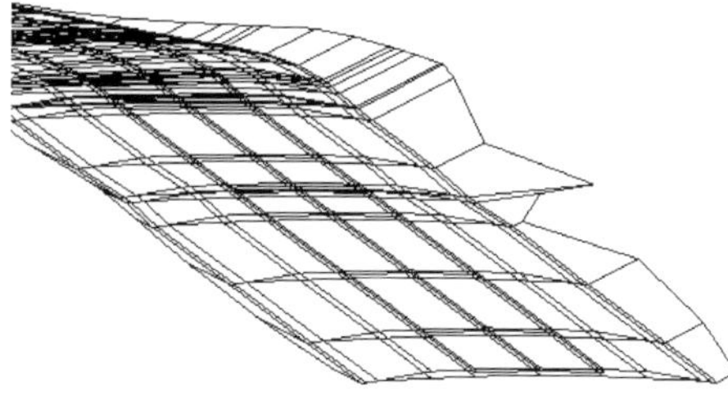

6.2 Creating a corridor

- You must have a civil geometry horizontal alignment with a vertical profile (alignment) (either in the active MicroStation model or referenced)
- Use **Element Selection** to select the horizontal alignment
- On the context sensitive menu, select **Create Corridor**

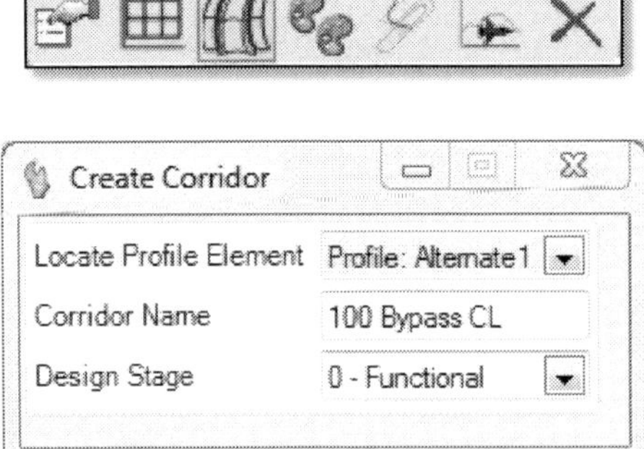

- Use the dialog box or cycle through the heads-up prompts to select the **Profile Element**, establish a **Corridor Name** and set the initial **Design Stage**
- After accepting each with a **<D>** the **Create Template Drop** box appears

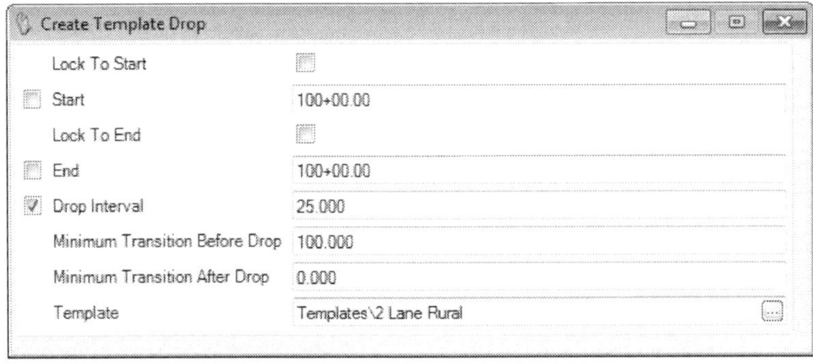

Again, you may continue by using the dialog or the heads-up prompts

- If using heads-up, **<Alt>** locks the **Start** and/or **End** to the limits of the alignment; **<End>** unlocks
- The **Drop Interval** is for the later Design Stages

- Minimum Transitions will automatically establish a transition if there is an adjacent template drop
- Proceed through the prompts, accepting with a **<D>**
- Upon the final acceptance, the corridor is created and displayed

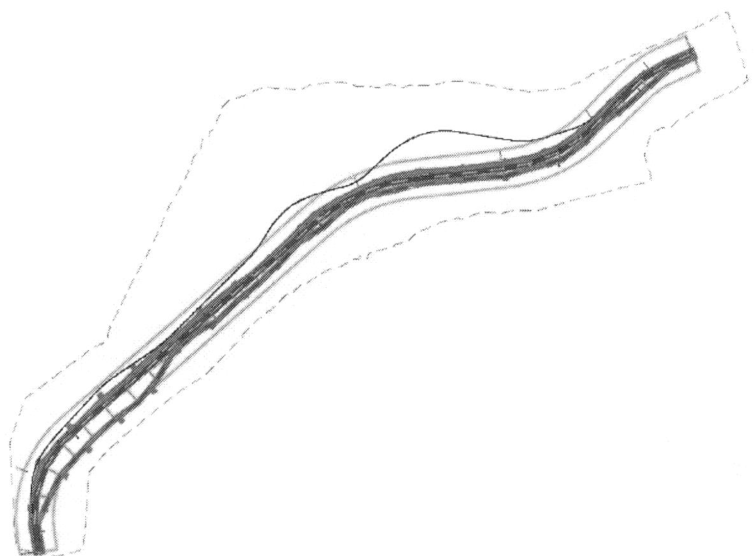

- To make edits to the corridor, you can select the corridor (use one of the handles if you have problems selecting) and choose an option from the context-sensitive menu that pops up

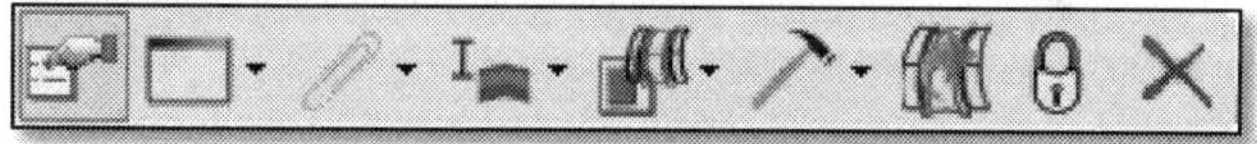

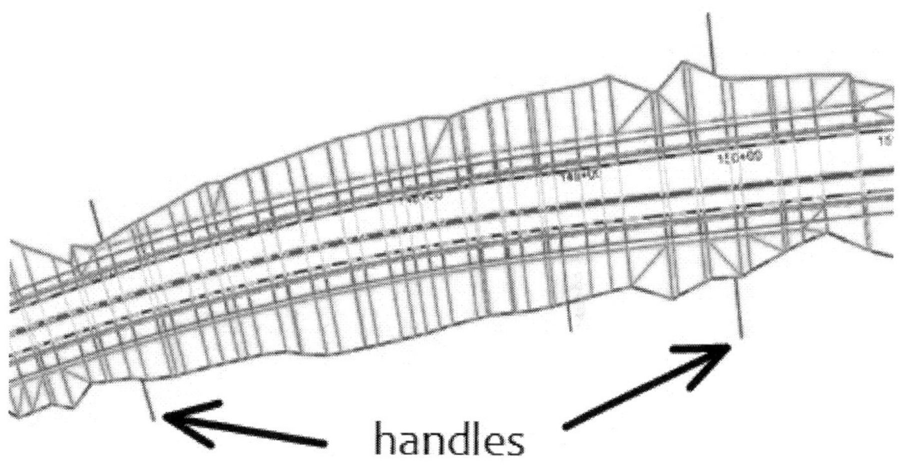

6.3 Changing the Corridor's Design Stage

➢ Select one of the handles and choose **Properties** from the context-sensitive menu that pops up

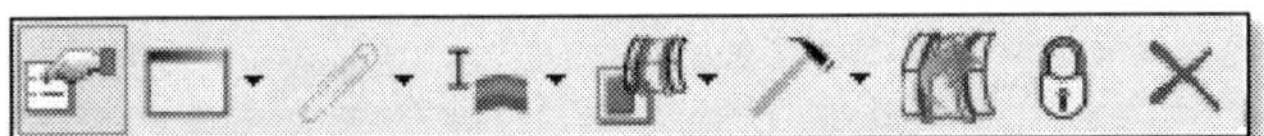

➢ Use the **Design Stage** drop-down menu to choose one of the other **Design Stages**

➢ The corridor processes and graphics immediately update with the display of the new Stage. If you want a mesh for display or for creating a Terrain Model, choose one of the **Mesh** options.

Design Stage	**0**	**1**	**2**	**3**	**4**	**5**	**6**	**7**	**8**
Template Drop Multiplier	10	5	2	1	1	1	1	1	1
Critical Sections									
Horiz Cardinals	F	T	T	T	T	T	T	T	T
Vert Cardinals	F	T	T	T	T	T	T	T	T
External Controls	F	T	T	T	T	T	T	T	T
Densify Horiz	F	T	T	T	T	T	T	T	T
Densify Vert	F	F	F	T	T	T	T	T	T
Output Settings									
Top Mesh	F	F	F	F	T	T	F	F	F
Bottom Mesh	F	F	F	F	T	F	T	F	F
Linear Features	T	T	T	T	T	F	F	T	F
Components	T	T	T	T	T	F	F	F	T
Null Points	F	F	F	F	F	F	F	F	F

6.4 Preparing features for sections

Features such as ROW or utilities can be shown on both dynamic sections and on cross sections you cut to plot. There are several methods of preparing the features for sections.

If you have 2D graphics already

➢ **MS: Tasks > Civil Tools > General Geometry > Set Feature Definition**

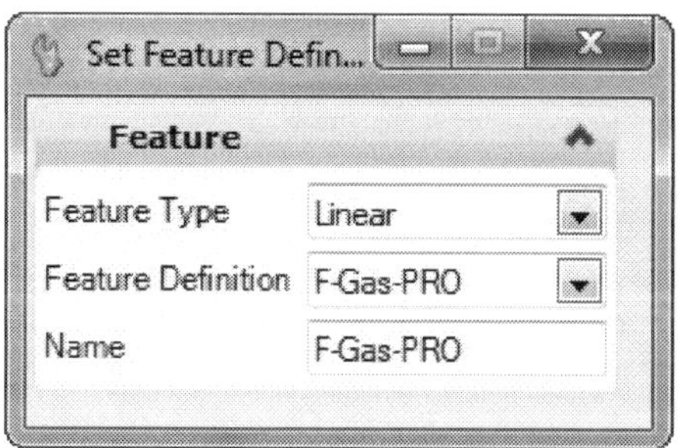

➢ Choose the feature and the **Feature Definition** is assigned

Next, you'll need to add the elevation information to the feature

If you are creating the graphics

- Use any of the **Civil Geometry** tools to create the desired feature, assigning the appropriate feature definition

➢ To assign the elevation (profile)

- Use any of the **Vertical Geometry** tools

➢ If you want to pull the elevations from a terrain model (drape), there are two commands you should be familiar with

- **MS: Tasks > Civil Tools > Vertical Geometry > Profile from Surface**
- **MS: Tasks > Civil Tools > Vertical Geometry > Quick Profile from Surface**

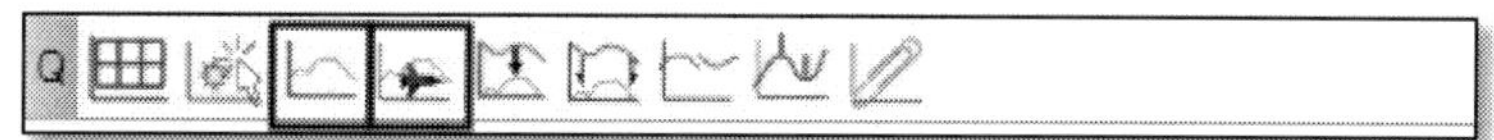

***Profile from Surface** allows options for offsets, while **Quick Profile from Surface** does not.*

➢ Once the profile is created, you must make the profile active before the feature will show up on sections. To do that, you can either go through **Element Information**,

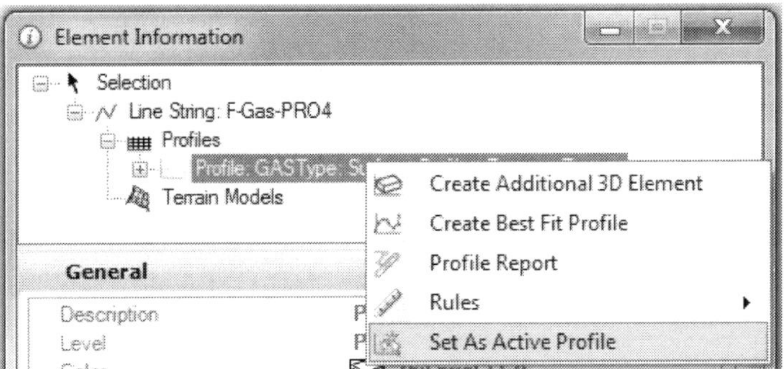

Or open a profile view for the feature and right-click on the profile.

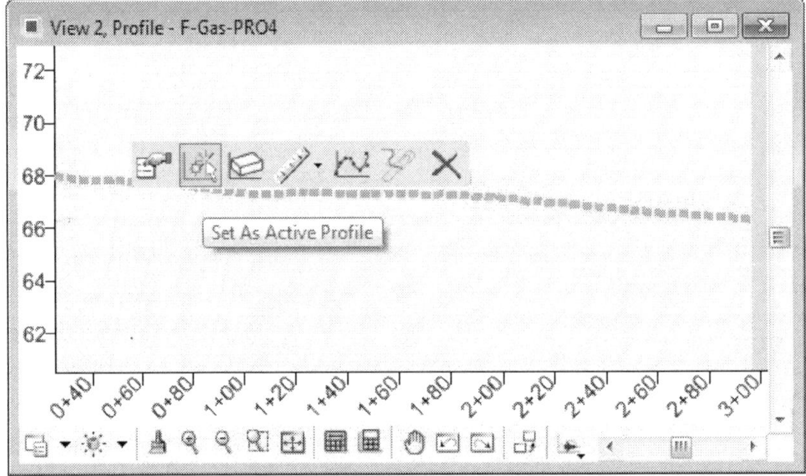

6.5 Creating dynamic sections

To create **Dynamic Sections**, you must already have an alignment and/or a corridor established.

- ➢ Select the corridor
- ➢ On the context-sensitive menu that pops-up, choose **Corridor Views**

- ➢ From the drop-down, choose **Open Cross Section Model**

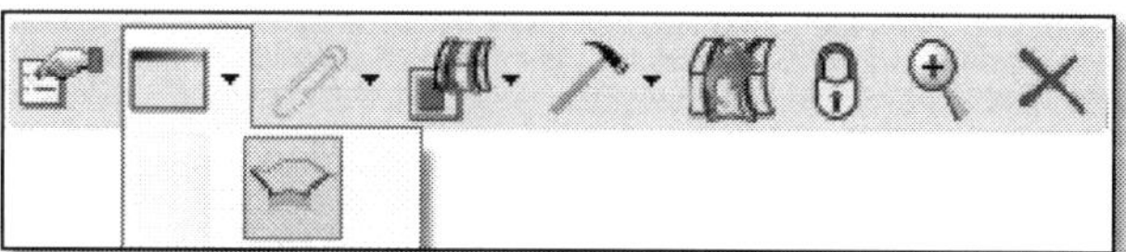

- ➢ Open another MicroStation view if you don't have one open already
- ➢ Select the View with a **<D>**

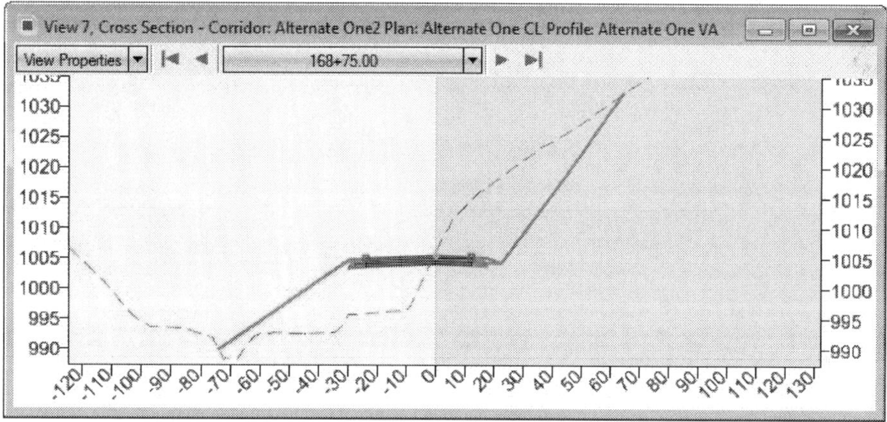

The section view is created. You can step through the sections, change the View Properties, etc.

Note: To create from an alignment, select the command from the Task menu, then follow the prompts to establish offsets, etc.

Exercise 6: Corridor Modeling

Given:

- *HWY 60 Alternate One Geometry.dgn* – Alternate One horizontal geometry
- *HWY 60 OG.dgn* – Original ground terrain model (referenced to the above file)

Required:

- Create a new design file HWY 60 Alternate One Corridor.dgn
- Attach the Geometry as a reference
- Attach the Terrain Model as a reference
- Create a Corridor for Alternate One
- Review the Corridor in 3D
- Review the Dynamic Cross Sections

Getting Started

1 Start InRoads using the icon on your desktop or using the **Start** menu

2 On the MicroStation manager, set the:

- **User**: ***examples***
- **Project**: ***Bentley-Civil-Imperial***
- **Interface**: ***default***

3 Create a new file

- Select the **New** File icon

- Browse to select the seed file *Seed2D-InRoads-Imperial.dgn* and select **Open**

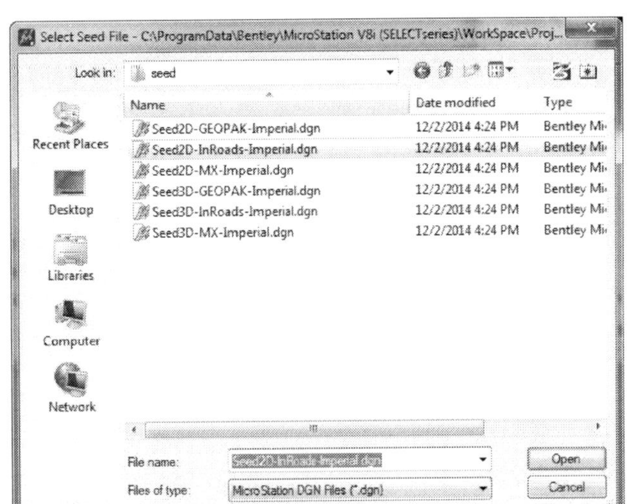

- Key in the **File Name**: *HWY 60 Alternate One Corridor.dgn*
- Select **Save**

4 **Open** the new file

5 Attach references

- On the **Project Explorer Links** tab, drag and drop the *HWY 60 Alternate One Geometry* file. Set the **Attachment Method** to ***Interactive*** and select **OK**

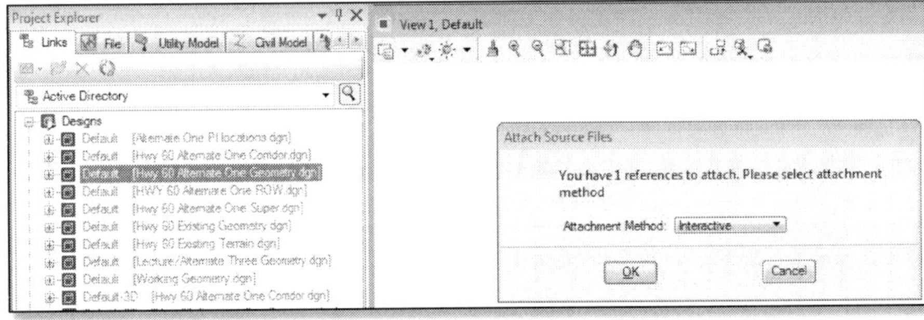

- Make sure the **Orientation** is set to ***Coincident World*** and **Nested Attachments** is set to ***No Nesting***. Set other options as shown and select **OK**

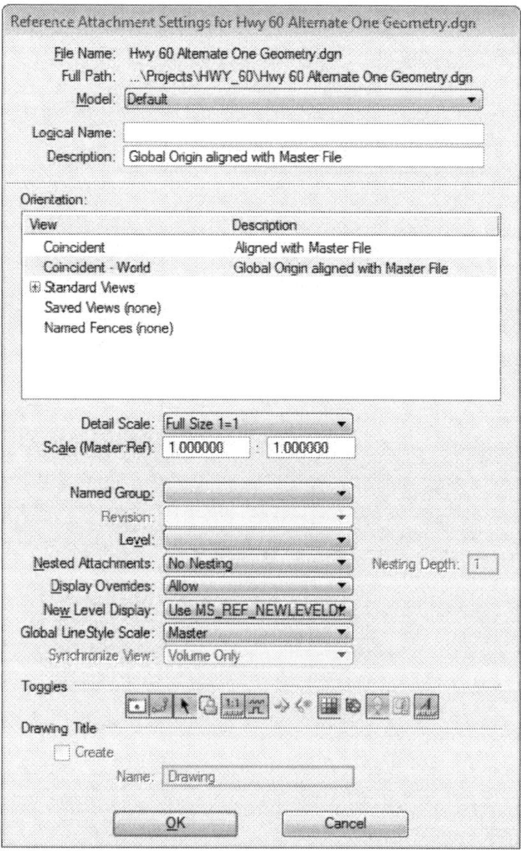

- Repeat the process to reference *HWY 60 Existing Terrain*

6 Make the Terrain Model Active

- Use **Element Selection** to select the Terrain Model
- On the context sensitive menu that appears, choose **Set as Active Terrain Model**

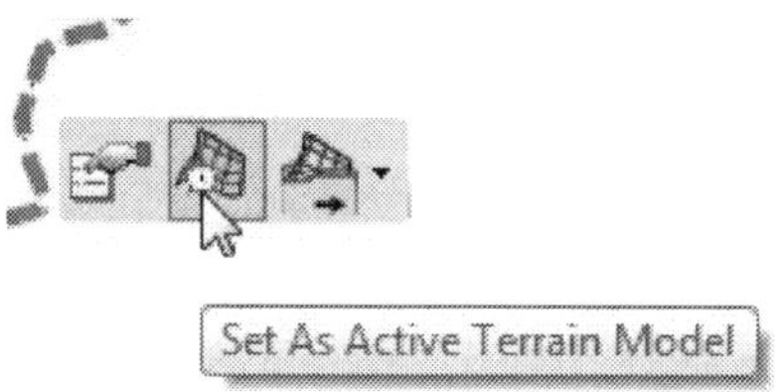

7 Load the template library

- **MS: Tasks > Civil Tools > Corridor Modeling > Create Template**
- In the **Create Template** dialog, choose **File > Open** and select the *HWY 60 Templates.itl* file and then select **Open**
- **Close** the **Create Template** dialog box

Creating corridors

8 Create a corridor

- Use **Element Selection** to select the horizontal alignment
- On the context sensitive menu, select **Create Corridor**

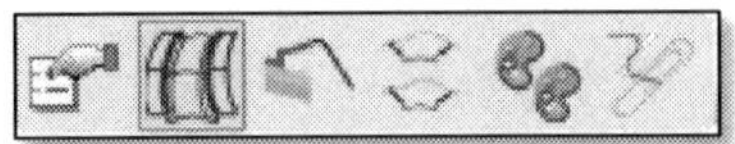

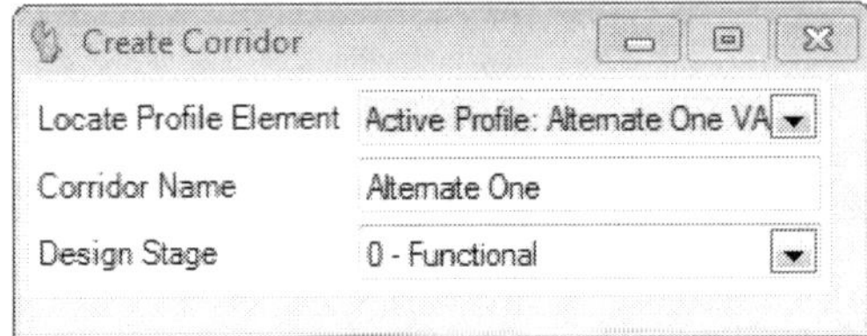

- When prompted to *Locate Profile*, use the dialog to select **Alternate One VA**

  Since it is the Active Profile, you could also **<R>** *for that option but if you are planning additional profiles such as for ditches, you may wish to specify the actual name of the profile.*

- **Corridor Name**: **Alternate One** accept with a **<D>**

  The Create Template Drop Box appears

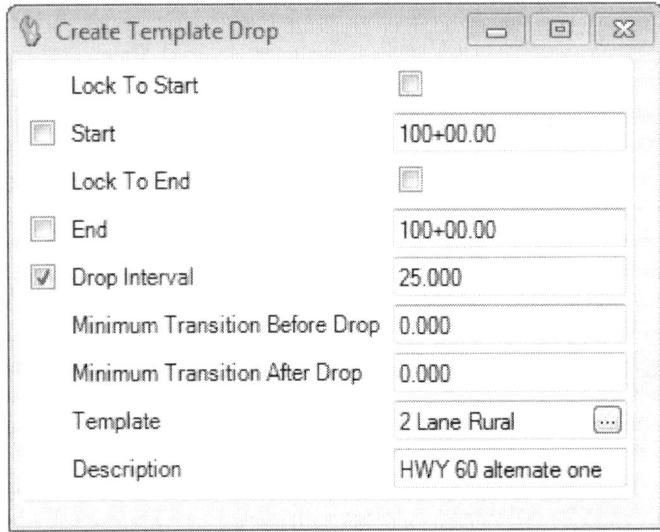

Again, you may continue by using the dialog or the heads-up prompts. These steps assume heads-up.

As you proceed through the prompts, accept each with a **<D>**

- Use **<Alt>** down arrow to select the **2 Lane Rural** template from the *CP* folder

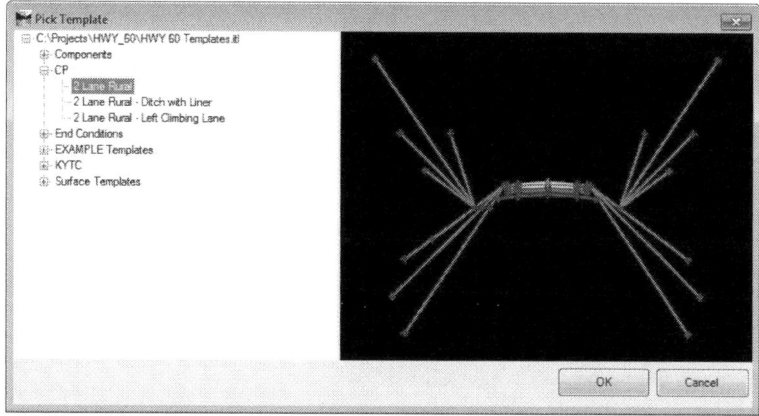

- **OK**
- Use **<Alt>** to lock the **Start** station to the beginning of the alignment
- Use **<Alt>** to lock the **End** to the end of the alignment
- Set the **Drop Interval** to **25**
- Set the **Minimum Transition** Before to **100**
- Set the **Minimum Transition** After to **100**

  Minimum Transitions will automatically establish a transition if there is an adjacent template drop. Here there is initially one template drop so these values will not affect the corridor.

- For **Description** enter **HWY 60 Alternate One**

  Upon the final acceptance, the corridor is created and displayed

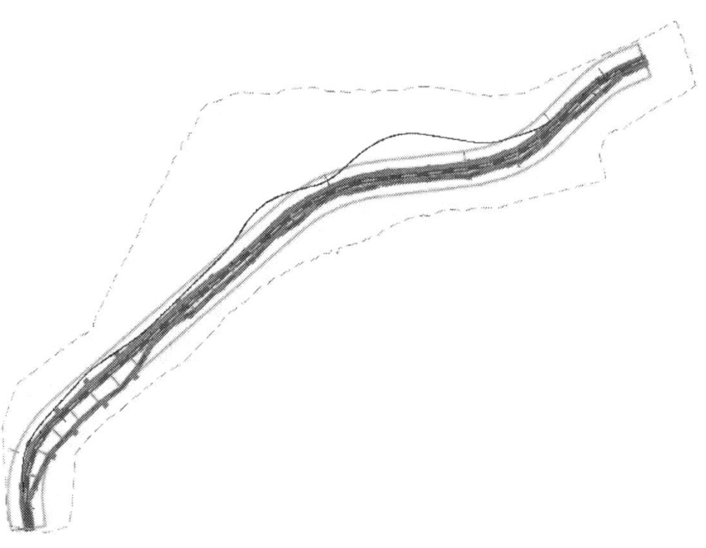

To make edits to the corridor, you can select the corridor (you may find it easiest to use one of the handles) and choose an option from the context-sensitive menu that pops up

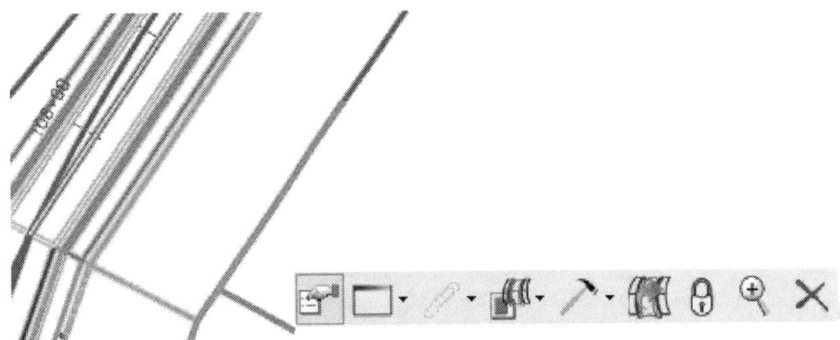

9 View the 3D Model

When you create a corridor, InRoads automatically creates a corresponding 3D model which can be viewed at any time.

- Open View 8
- Under **View Attributes > View Setup**, choose ***Default-3D*** for the Model

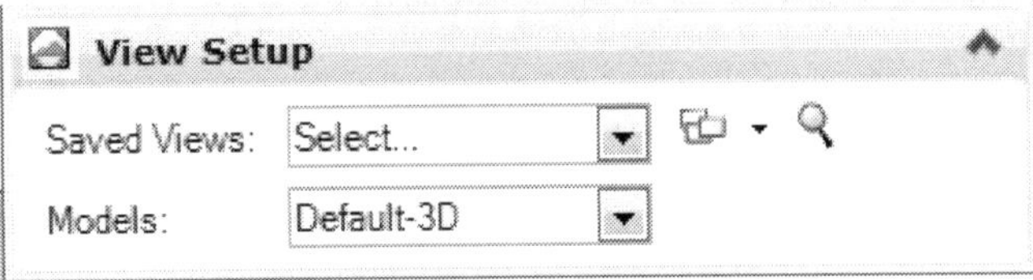

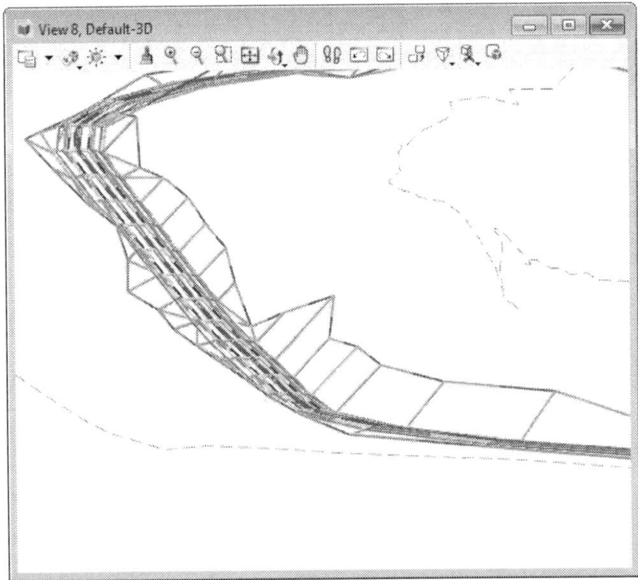

- Rotate the view to better see the 3D Model.

10 Change the **Design Stage**

Notice the model is not very smooth. The Design Stage controls the template drop interval, applying a factor to the one established when the corridor was created. In this case, the 0-Functional *stage applies a Template Drop Multiplier of 10 as seen in the* ***Civil Standards > Project Settings > Corridor Design Stages****.*

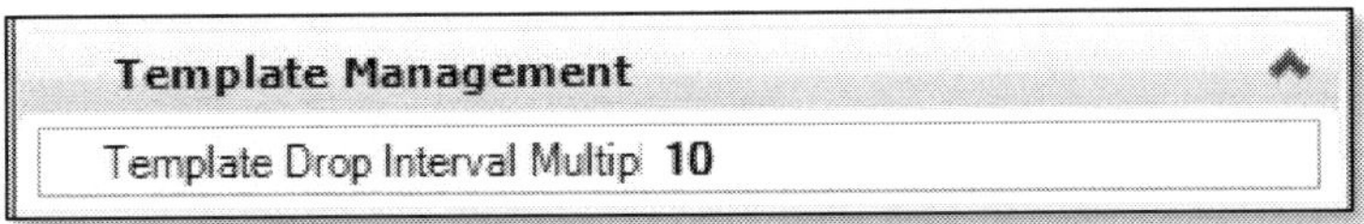

Next, you'll change the Design Stage to see the results.

- In View 1, select one of the handles of the corridor and choose **Properties** from the context-sensitive menu that pops up

- Use the **Design Stage** drop-down menu to choose ***1 - Preliminary***

Name	**Alternate One**
Horizontal Name	GeomCL
Use Active Profile	**True**
Profile Name	Alternate One VA
Design Stage	**1 - Preliminary**

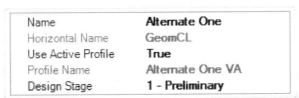

The corridor processes and graphics immediately update with the display of the new Stage. If you want a mesh for display or for creating a Terrain Model, choose one of the Mesh options.

Warning: The Design Stage also controls what is shown when cross sections are cut. For example, if you choose a Design Stage the only shows linear features, you will not see the components on the sections.

- Experiment with other **Design Stages** as you wish, then return the corridor to ***2 – Design***

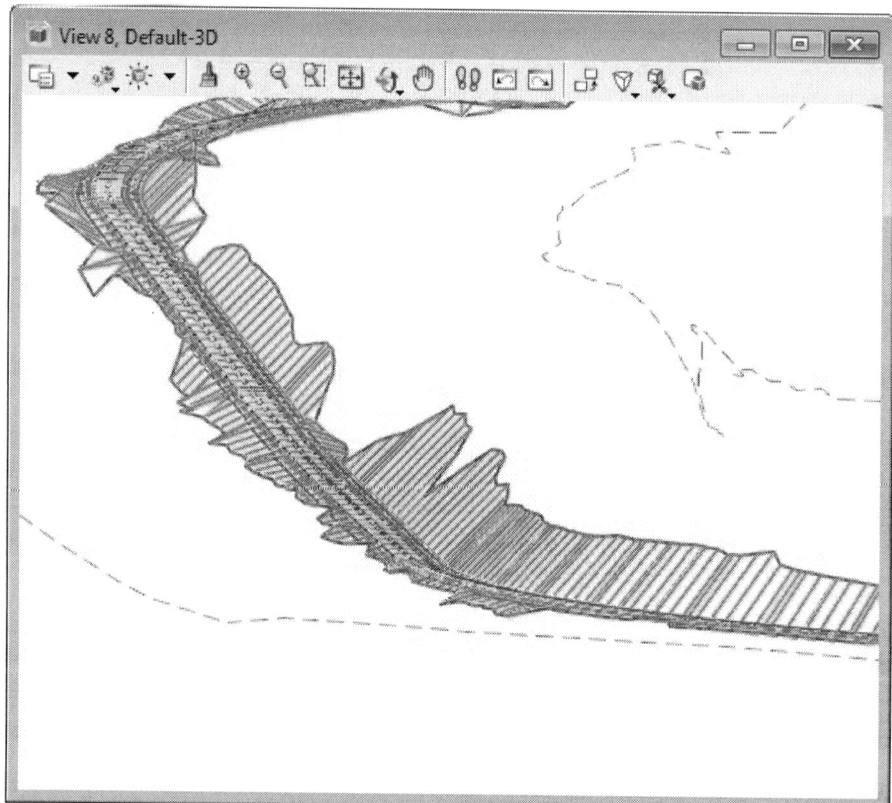

- In the 3D view, change the **View Attributes** to one of the shaded **Display Styles**

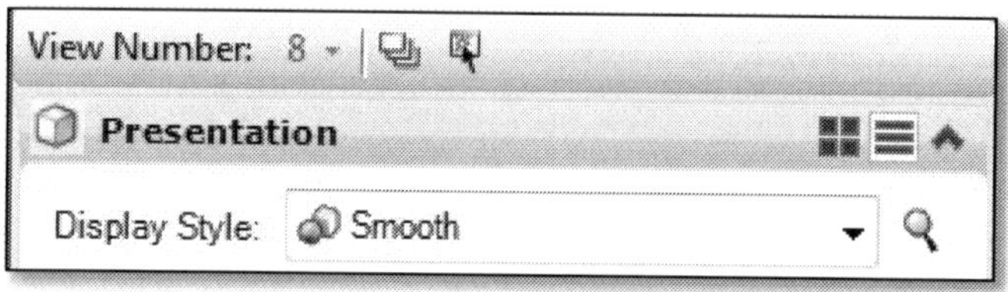

To see the shaded image better, you can brighten the view.

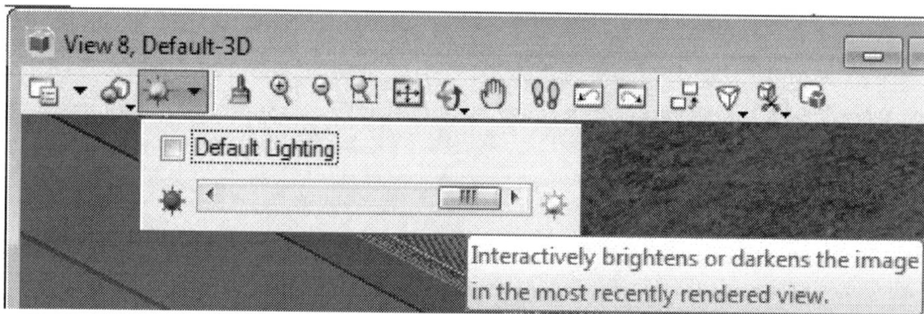

Synchronize a Template

Just like in the previous version, if you change the template in the ITL, you must synchronize to have that template updated in the corridor.

11 Edit the template's end conditions

- **MS: Tasks > Civil Tools > Corridor Modeling > Create Template**

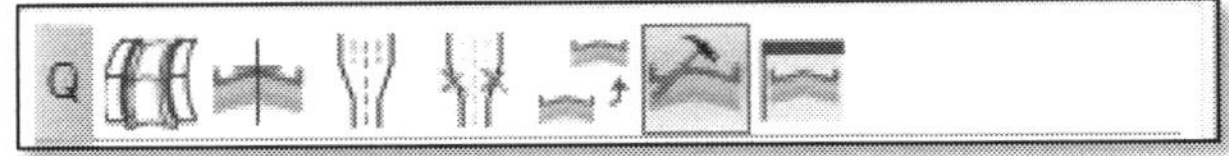

- Make the *CP/2Lane Rural* template active

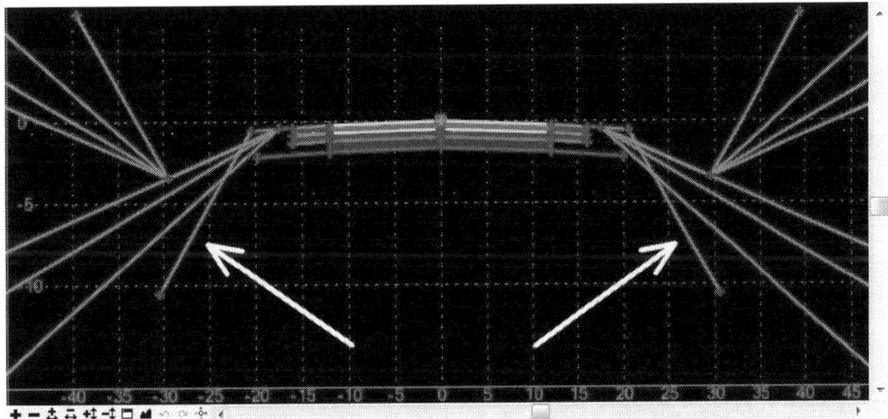

- **Delete** the steepest fill slope on each side

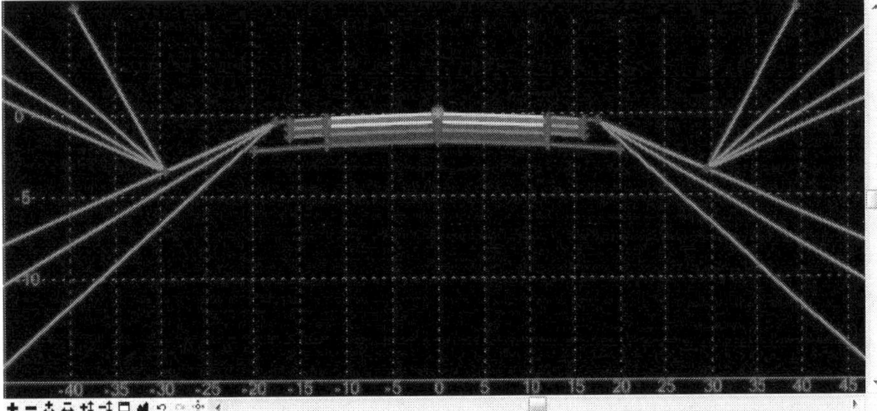

- Edit the ***LT_FILL_2:1*** point and toggle on ***End Condition is Infinite***

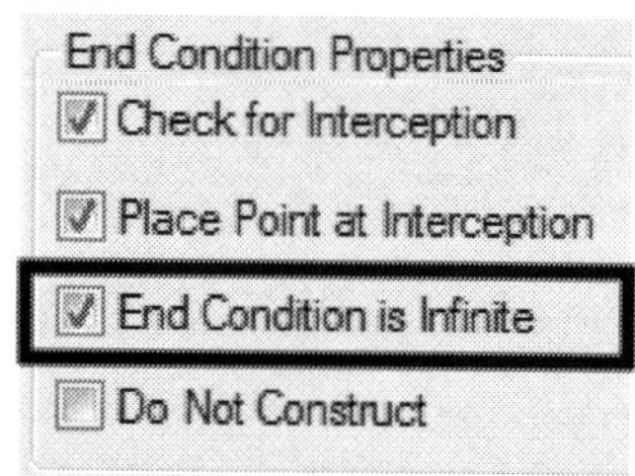

- Choose **Apply**
- Repeat for the ***RT_FILL_2:1*** point
- **Close** the **Template Editor** and **Yes** to **Save** the changes

12 Synchronize the Template

At the beginning and at the end of the corridor, there is a template drop handle in addition to the corridor one.

- Highlight the template drop and choose **Synchronize with Library** from the context sensitive menu

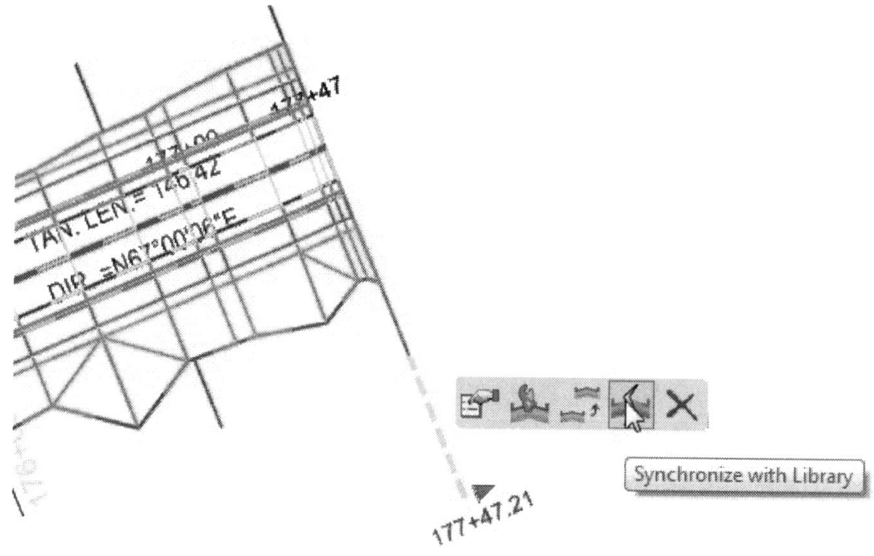

Be patient. InRoads goes into a processing mode and re-applies the template to the entire corridor

Features to show on Sections

13 Prepare the ROW to show on sections

- **Save Settings**
- Open the design file *HWY 60 Alternate One ROW.dgn*

  The ROW is already in the file as regular MicroStation graphics at an elevation of 0.00. Here, we'll give it an elevation based on the surface and add a feature definition so it will show on sections.

- Attach *HWY 60 Existing Terrain.dgn* as a reference with NO Nesting.

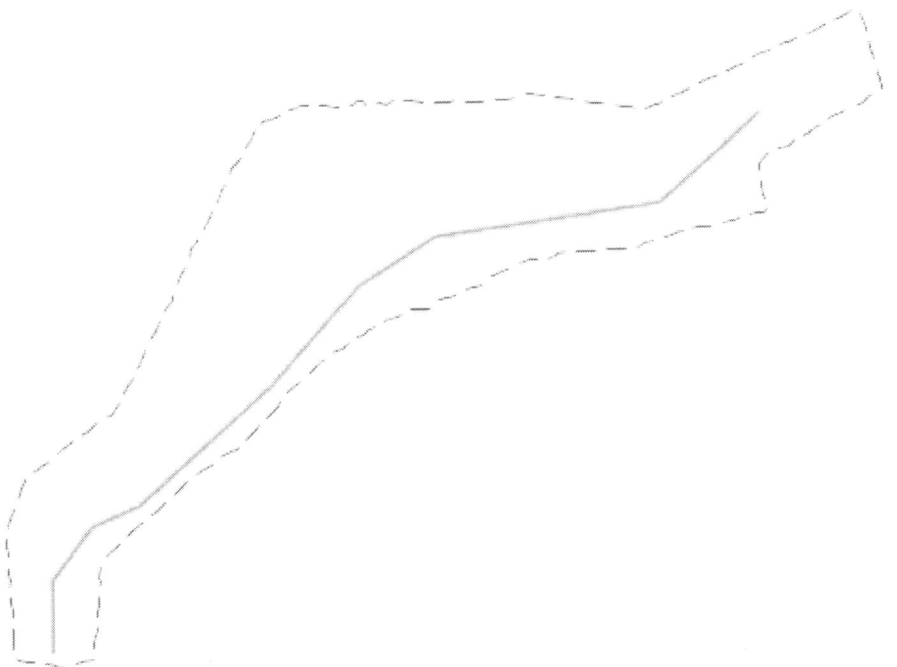

- **MS: Tasks > Civil Tools > Horizontal Geometry > Set Feature Definition**

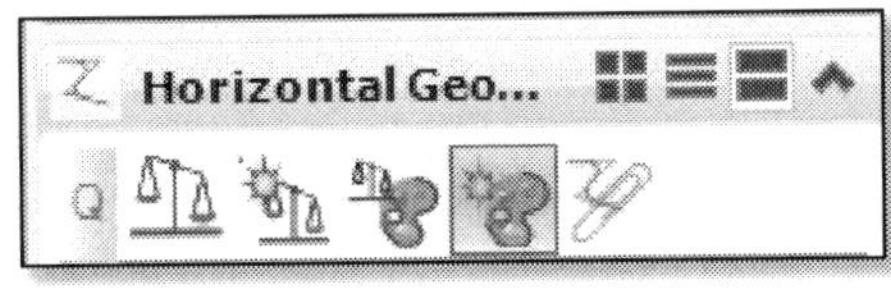

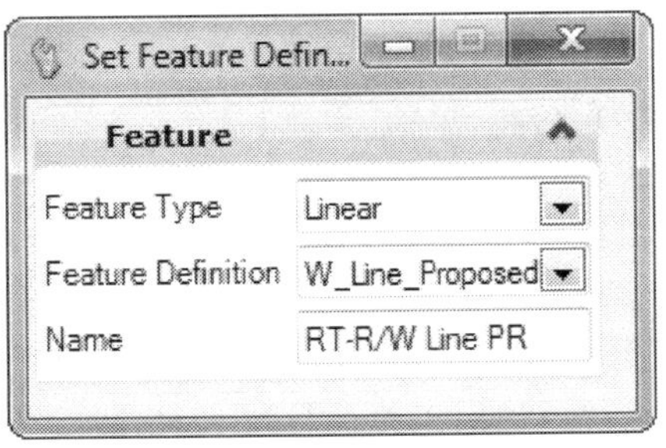

- Set the **Feature Type** to ***Linear***
- **Feature Definition** to ***Linear > Right of Way > RW_Line_Proposed***

  You may use the default name or use a more descriptive one, such as prefixing with an RT-.

- Select the graphic element. If using the generic name, you could continue selecting (or you could have created a selection set first) or if you're using more descriptive names, **<R>** after the first selection.
- Here, we just have one, so **<R>**
- Choose **Element Selection** and hover over the line

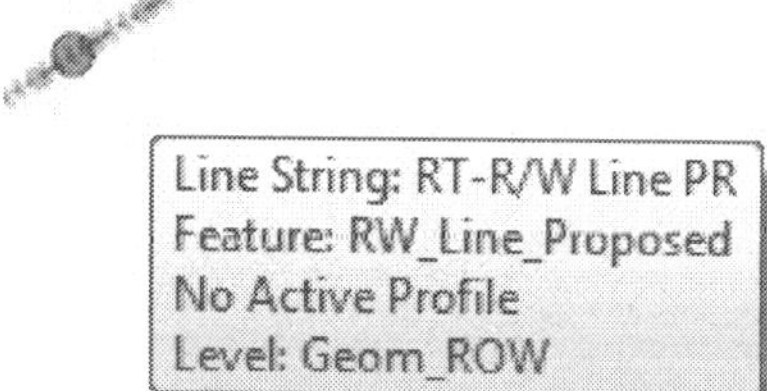

Note it is now a feature, but does not have an Active Profile

- **MS: Tasks > Civil Tools > Vertical Geometry > Quick Profile from Surface**

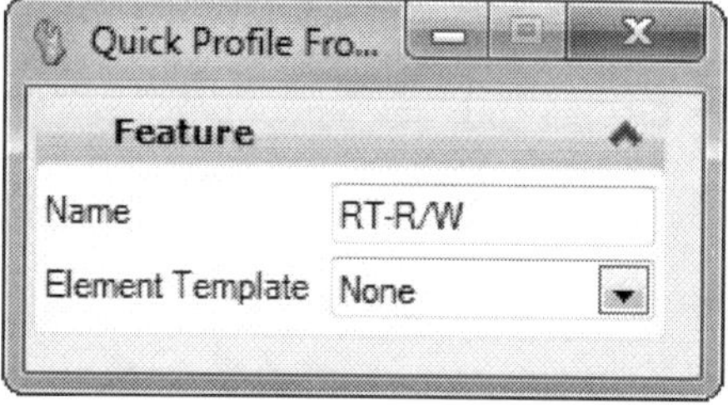

- For the **Name**, key in **RT-R/W**
- Leave the **Element Template** set to ***None***
- When prompted to *Locate Reference Element*, select the graphic for the ROW
- When prompted to *Locate Reference Surface*, select the Terrain Model
- **<R>** when done

  The ROW now has a profile (would have been called a vertical alignment in previous versions) associated that is draped on the terrain. However, it is not active.

14 Make the Profile Active

- Select **Element Information** and choose the ROW line

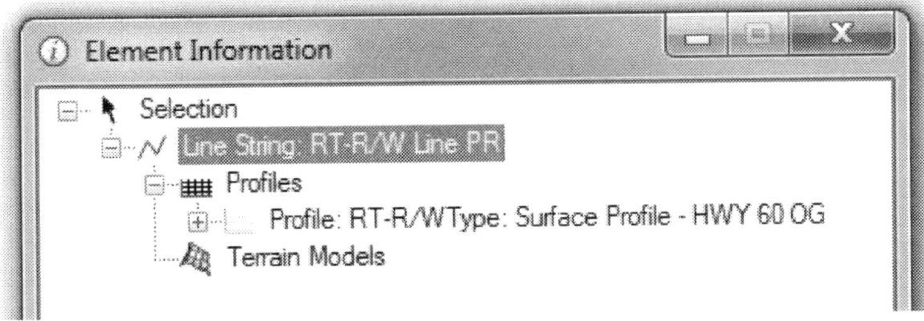

- Expand the Selection until you see the ***Profile***

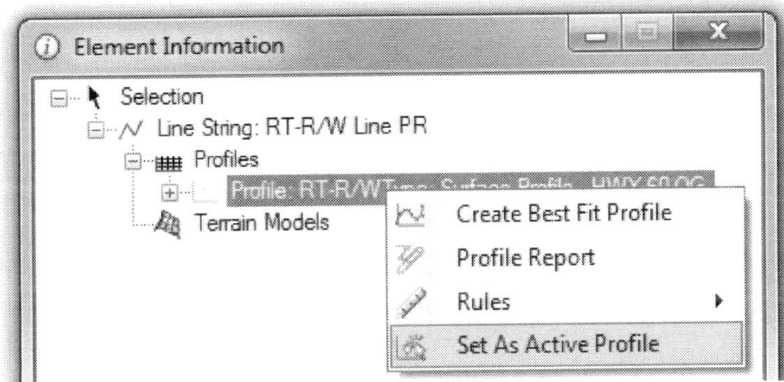

- Right-click on the ***Profile*** and choose ***Set As Active Profile***
- Close **Element Information**
- Use **Element Selection** to hover over the ROW Line

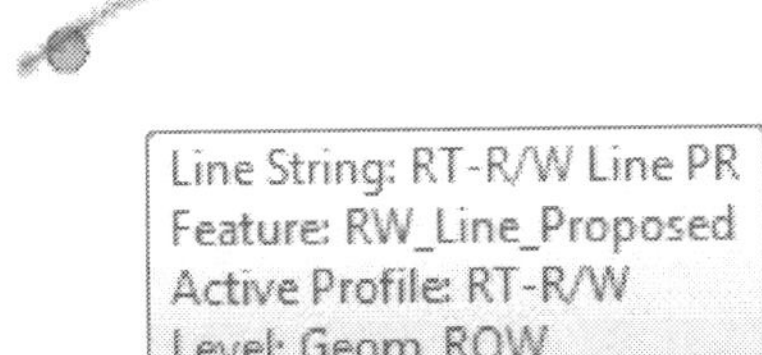

You should now see that it has an Active Profile

15 Select **File > Save Settings**

- A Default-3D Model was automatically created. You can open it and rotate to see the elevations of the ROW line.

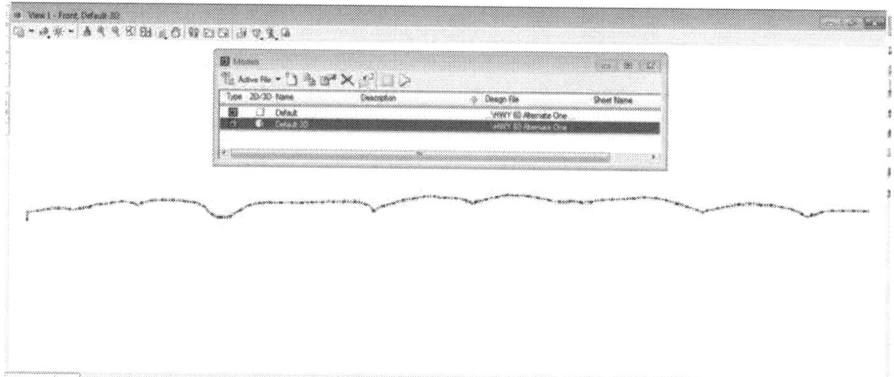

16 Open the design file *HWY 60 Alternate One Corridor.dgn*

- **Fit** the View
- Click in the Plan view to make it active
- Attach *HWY 60 Alternate One ROW.dgn*'s **Default** Model (***not*** Default-3D) with ***No Nesting***

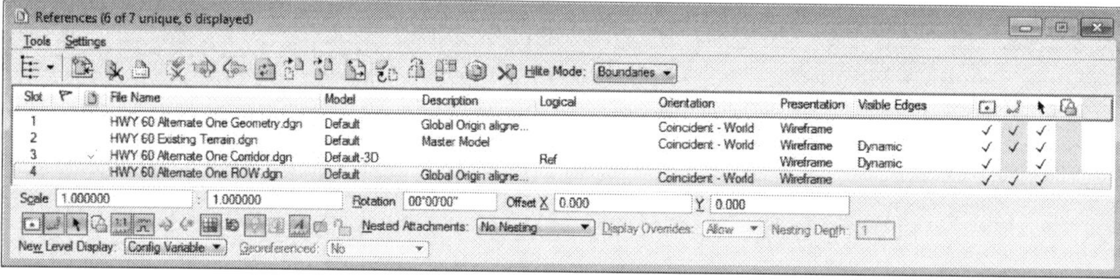

17 Create dynamic sections

- Open View 7
- Select the corridor again
- On the context-sensitive menu that pops-up, choose **Corridor Views**

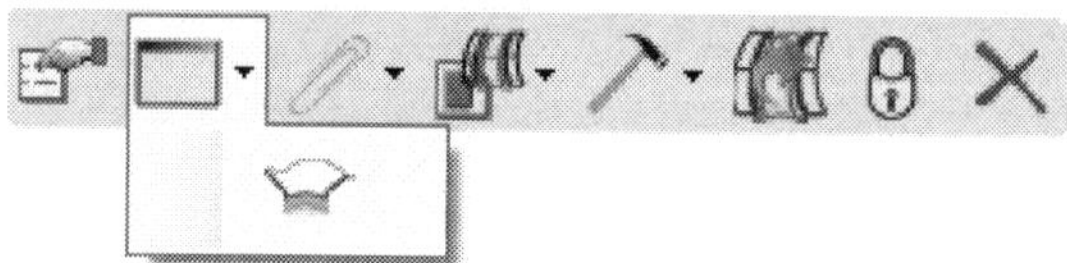

- From the drop-down, choose **Open Cross Section Model**

- Select View 7 with a <D>

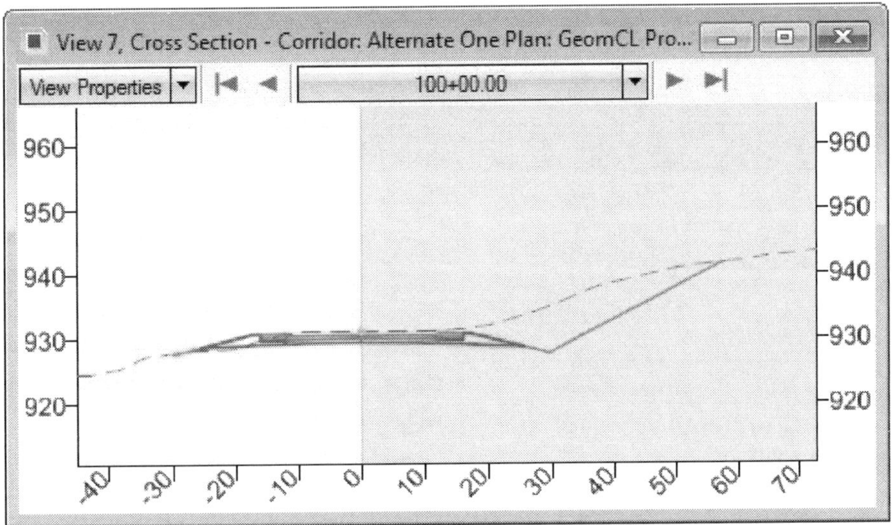

The section view is created. You can step through the sections, change the View Properties, etc.

18 Display the ROW on the sections

- Step through a few of the temporary cross sections and zoom out until you can see the right-of-way

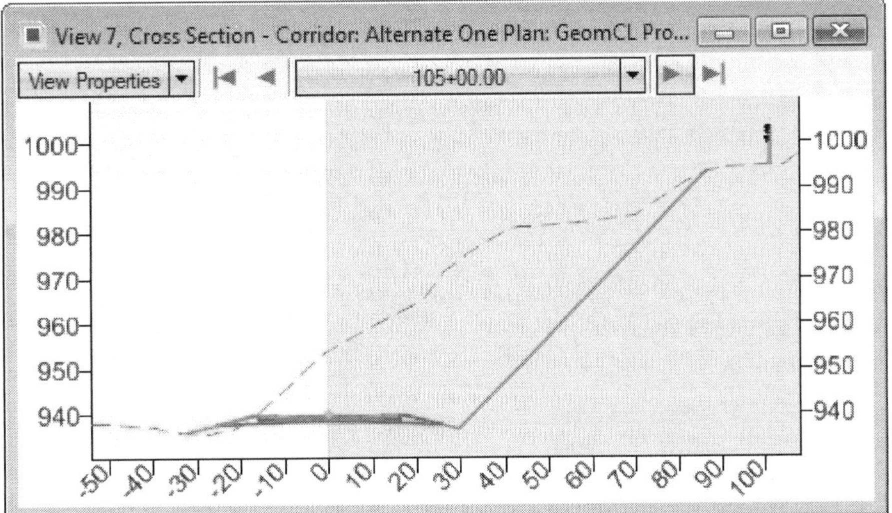

19 Dimension some segments with temporary dimensions

- Right-click in the cross section view and select **Place Temporary Dimension Line**

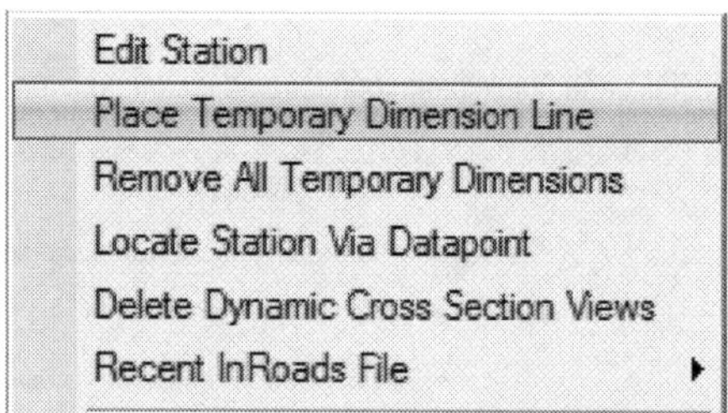

- Follow the prompts to place the dimensions

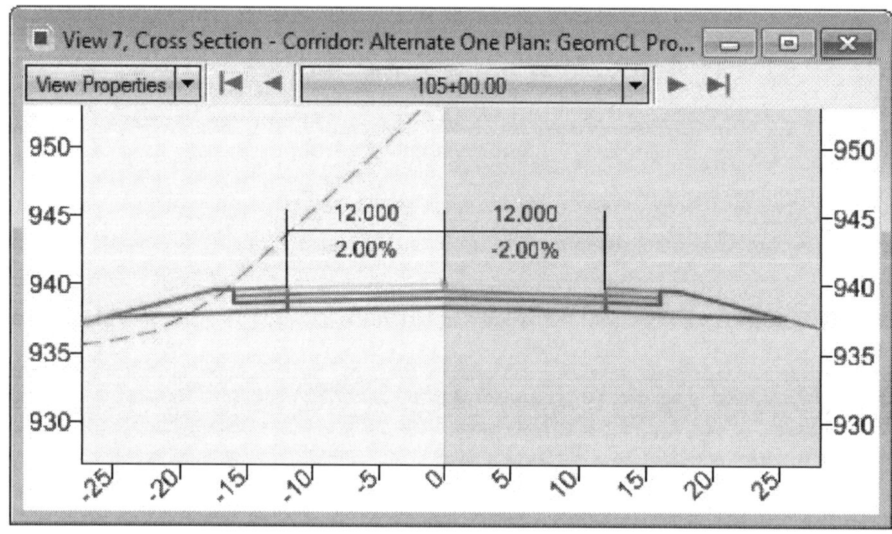

- Notice on the right-click menu, you can also jump to a location by selecting it in plan the plan view

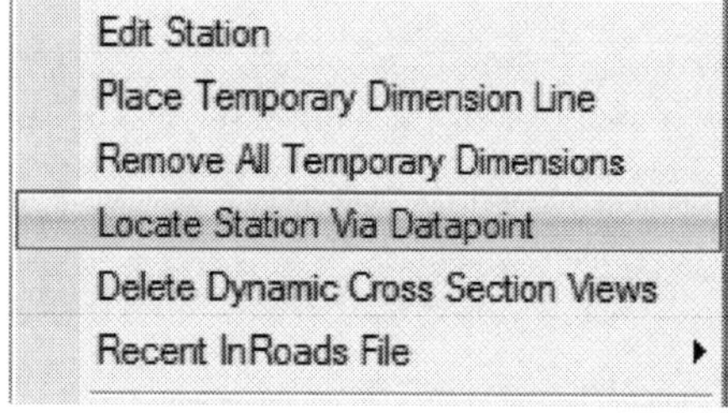

Ending

20 **Save Settings**

21 **Exit**

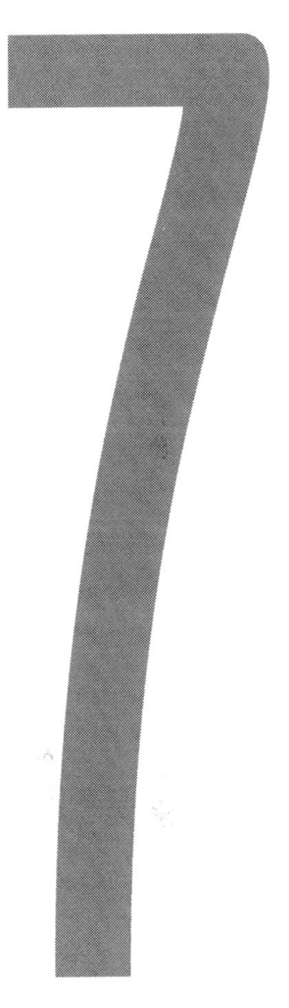

Transitions

BETWEEN TWO TEMPLATES

PARAMETRIC CONSTRAINTS

POINT CONTROLS

7 Transitions

There are multiple methods of creating transition in a corridor. Here we will look at how the three main methods are accomplished in this version of software.

Multiple templates with a specified distance between can accomplish a transition. While this method can be used for various types of transitions, what makes it unique is the ability to introduce new points, segments, and/or components into the design.

Parametric constraints are used to override the constraint values for a certain point or points in a template. The constraints in the template are given labels which act as variables. These variables allow the value of the constraint to be changed over a station range. Parametrics are unique in that if the same label is used on multiple points, then multiple values can be changed – depths of pavement, for example. Parametrics can span multiple templates as long as the same label is used.

Point controls can assign a different path to any point in the template. This path can be defined by varying the offsets from the CL, by separate geometry, by ‘following’ a feature definition, etc. Two things make point controls unique: you can alter the path of the template drop by point controlling the center, but still keep the stationing of the original alignment. You can also define a path with curves by point controlling to another alignment. Point controls can span multiple templates as long as the same point name is used.

7.1 Multiple Templates

When you are creating a corridor, you are also creating a template drop. In the last chapter, you specified the template drop to go from the beginning to the end of the alignment. You could have started and stopped the template drop elsewhere, then added additional template drops and created transitions. You can also add template drops in the middle of existing ones.

➢ Create a template drop

- **MS: Tasks > Civil Tools > Corridor Modeling > Create Template Drop**

- Select the Corridor
- Or, use **Element Selection** to highlight the corridor and on the context sensitive menu, select **Corridor Creation Tools > Create Template Drop**

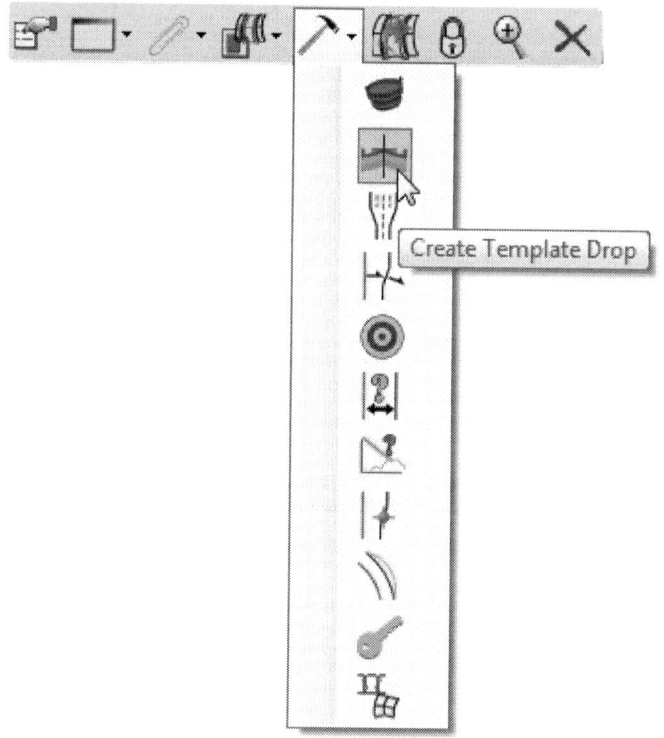

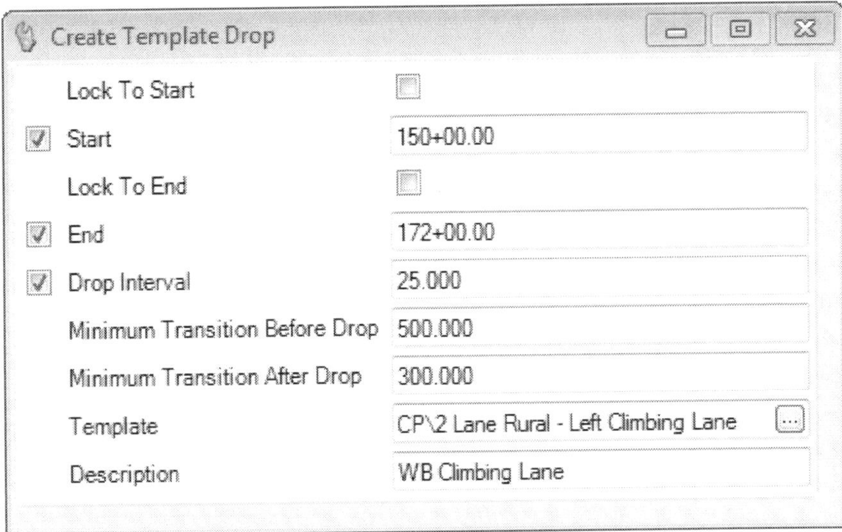

- After selecting the corridor you may either fill in the dialog or enter the information as you cycle through the heads-up prompts:

Note: You could also have selected this command from the context-sensitive menu on the corridor.

- **Template**: *The new template for this area*
- **Start Station**: *The start of the fully developed template*
- **End Station**: *The end of the fully developed template*
- **Template Drop Interval**: *how often the template is processed*
- **Minimum Transition Before Drop**: *This distance forms the transition area at the beginning. The start station minus this transition is where the transition actually starts.*
- **Minimum Transition After Drop**: *This distance forms the transition area at the ending. The end station plus this transition is where the transition actually ends and you are back to the original template.*
- **Description**: *Your choice*

The software will take a minute to process

➢ There is now a template drop at the beginning

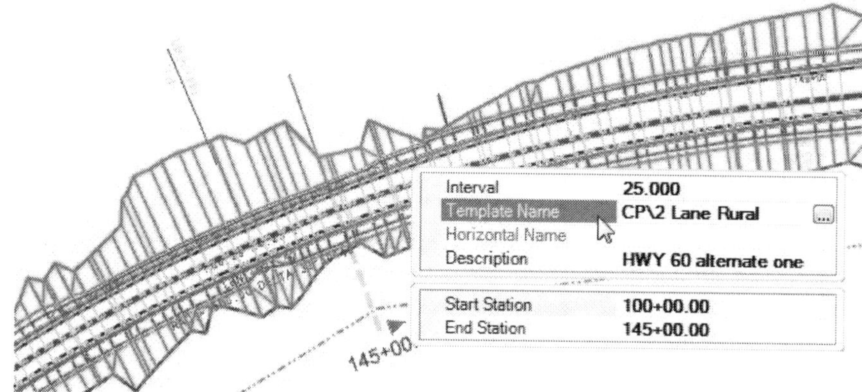

➤ A transition

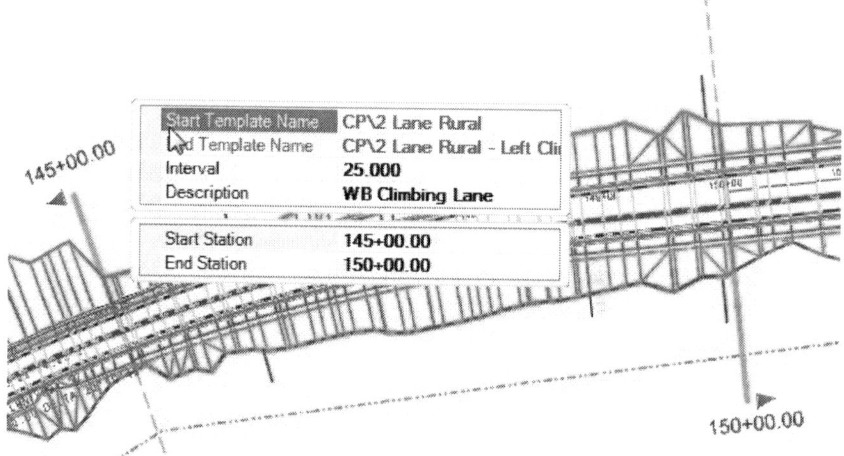

➤ A template drop in the middle

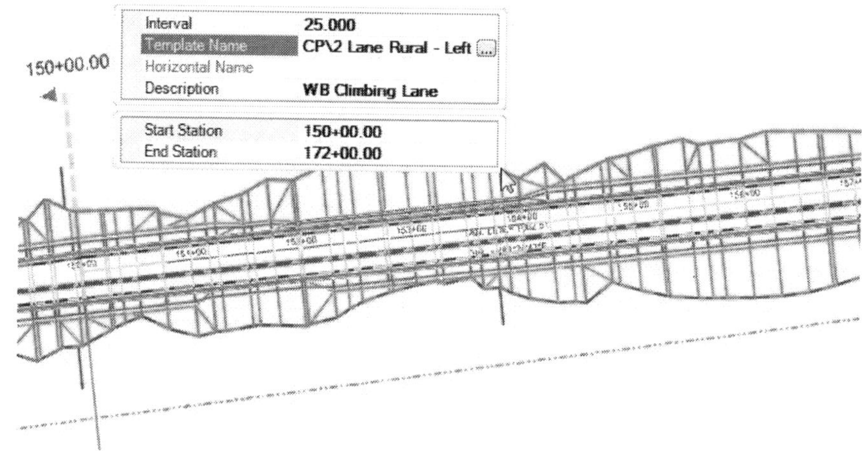

- A transition

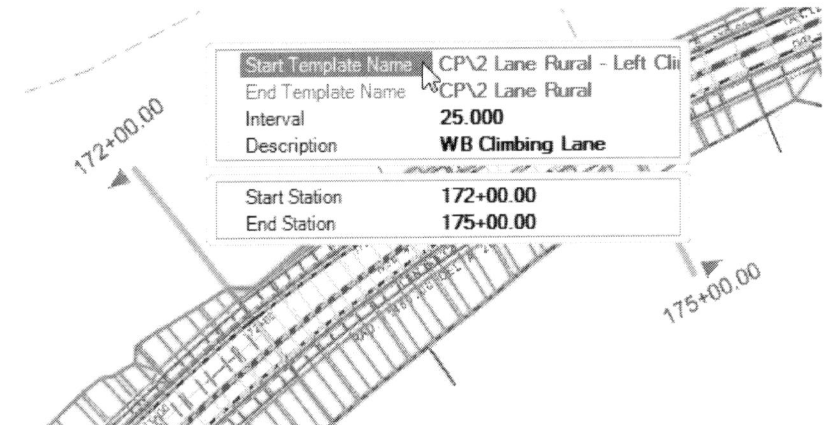

- And a template drop at the end, plus any additional template drop areas previously defined

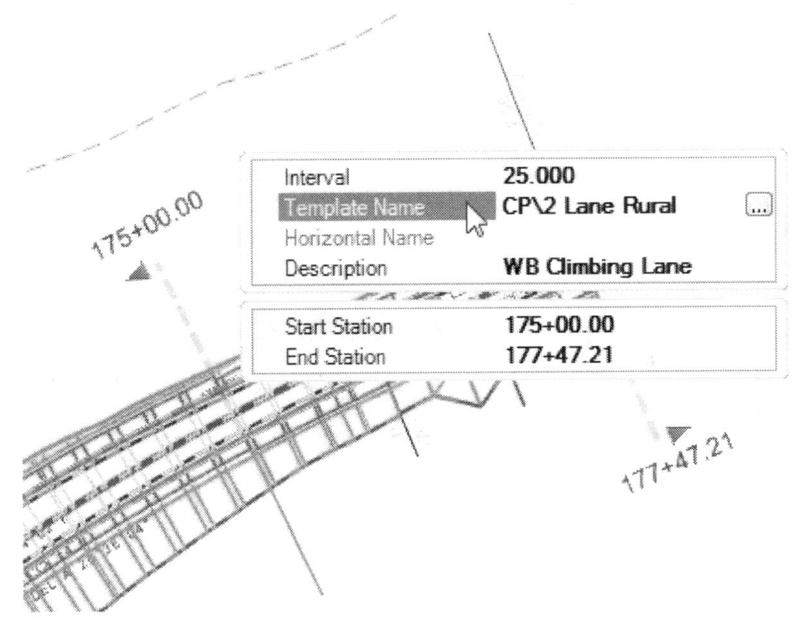

➤ Modify the transition (if necessary)

If the templates you are transitioning from/to do not have the same number of points or the points are different names, you may need to modify the transition area to define how you want things connected.

- Select the first transition and choose **Edit Transition**

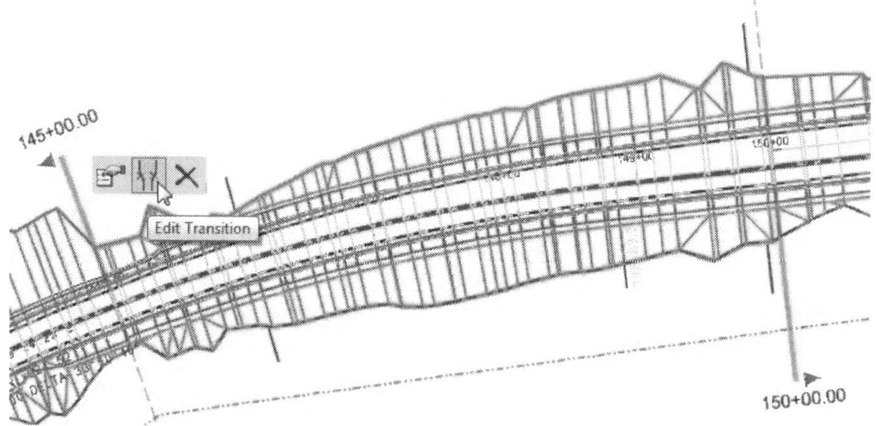

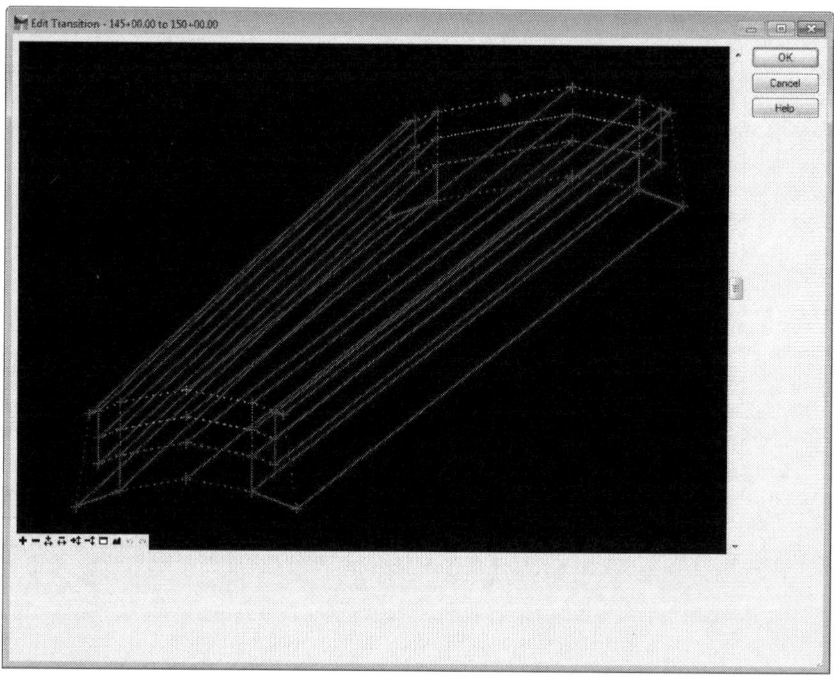

This is very similar to the transition editor in the previous version.

- Connect the points as necessary

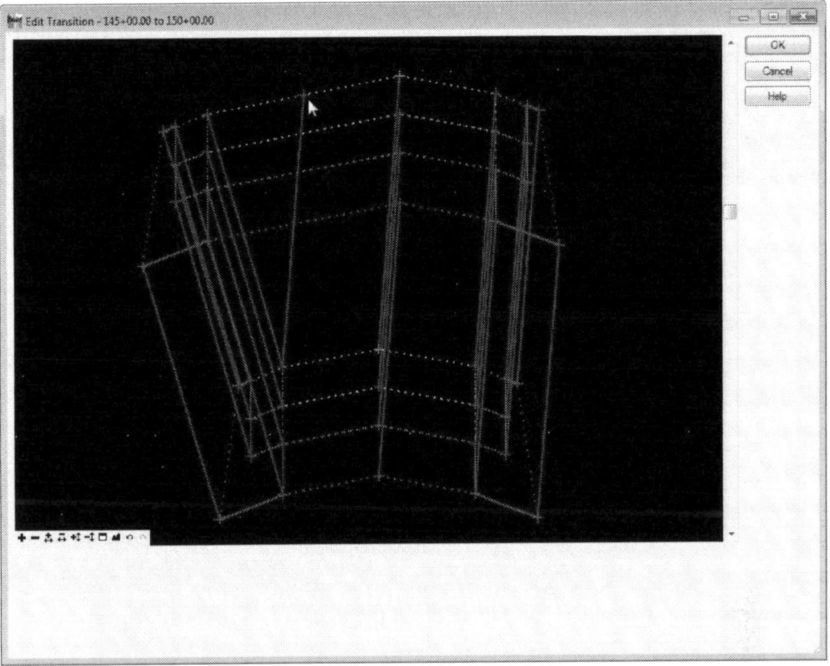

- Select **OK**
- **Delete** the ***Constraints*** as necessary
- Select **OK**

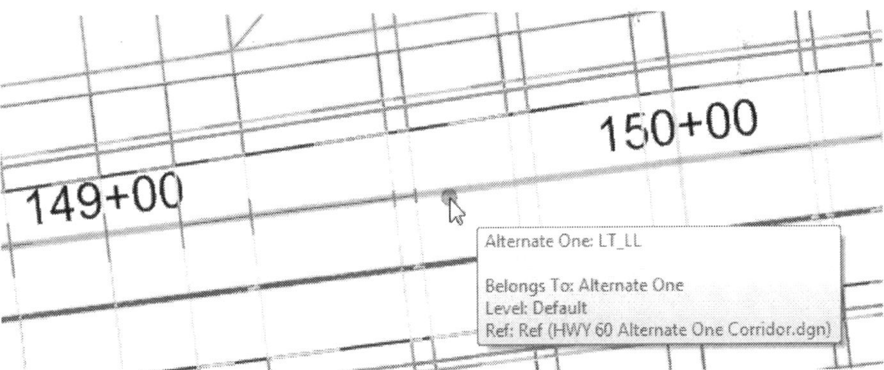

- Repeat for the transition on the other end

7.2 Parametric Constraints

The constraints in the template may be given labels which act as variables. These labels can be used to edit the value of all constraints where the label is assigned in the template editor, or in the corridor you can use Parametric Constraints to override the values from the original template. This override is based on a station range, so you can change the values along the corridor. The value at the starting station can be different than the ending station so you can create tapers using this method.

➢ Create a **Parametric Constraint** for the first taper

- **MS: Tasks > Civil Tools > Corridor Modeling > Create Parametric Constraint**

- Select the Corridor

  Or, use **Element Selection** to highlight the corridor and on the context sensitive menu, select **Corridor Creation Tools > Create Parametric Constraint**

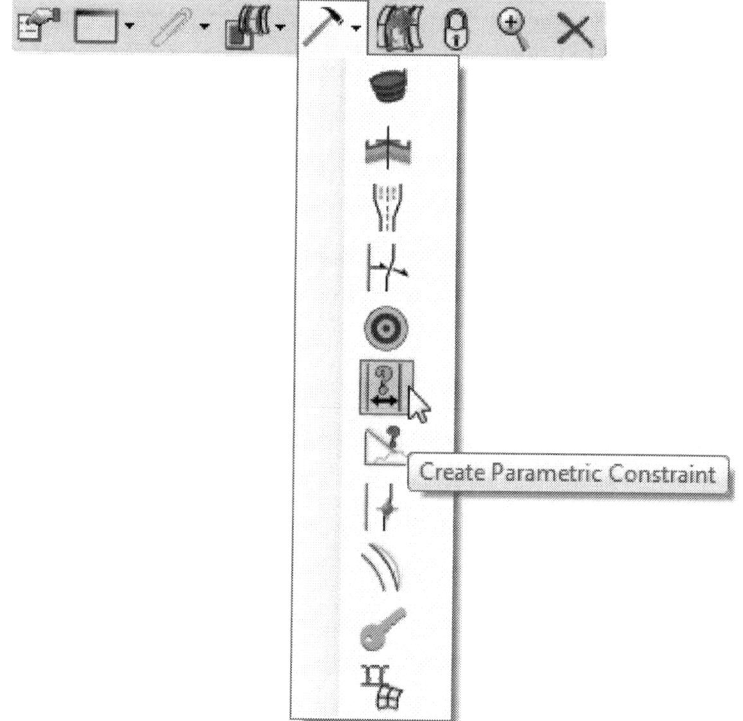

You can either enter your options through the dialog box, or the heads-up prompts

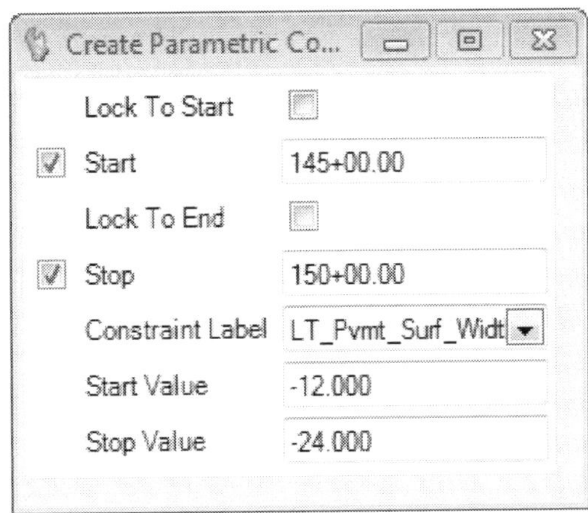

- **Start Station**: *The first station of the parametric.*
- **Stop Station**: *The final station of the parametric.*
- **Constraint Label**: *This is the label assigned to the constraint(s) you are modifying. It is assigned in the template.*
- **Start Value**: *You are replacing the constraint value which most often it is not set to 0.00, so if you are tapering, start with a value equal to the default in the template.*
- **Stop Value**: *The new constraint value at the end of the parametric.*
- Continue through the prompts, establishing them as necessary and accepting each with a **<D>**

This establishes the transition

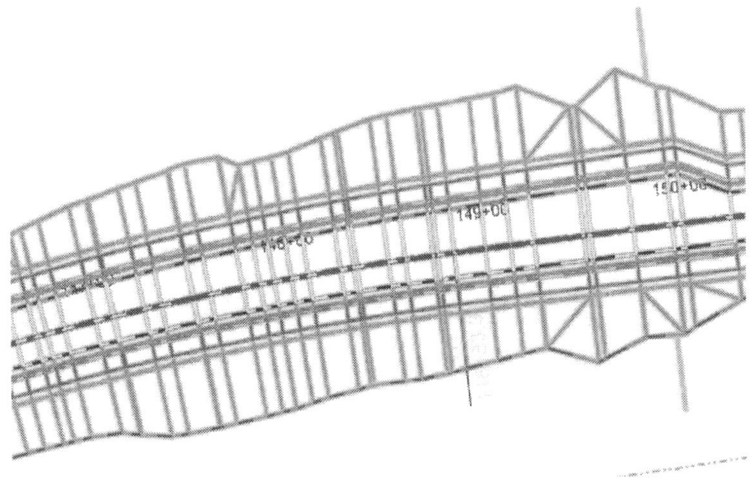

7.3 Point Controls

By default, the control point (typically the centerline) of a template follows the horizontal and vertical geometry, with all other point locations being determined by their respective constraints. These constraints can be overridden by either **Parametric Constraints** or **Point Controls**, both of which carry over from previous versions. With **Point Controls**, you can assign any point in the template to follow a different path. This path can be defined by varying the offsets from the CL, by separate geometry, by 'following' a feature definition, etc. You can rely solely on the centerline and point constraints, **Point Control** every point or anything in between.

The complexity of the job and type of transitions can help you determine the extent to which **Point Controls** are beneficial. Small jobs with little variation in widths/slopes may be easiest with few controls whereas a larger job with many variations in the template may be more easily managed with each point assigned a control.

If using separate geometry to define the path, it must be created prior to entering the command.

To define a Point Control

➢ **MS: Tasks > Civil Tools > Corridor Modeling > Create Point Control**

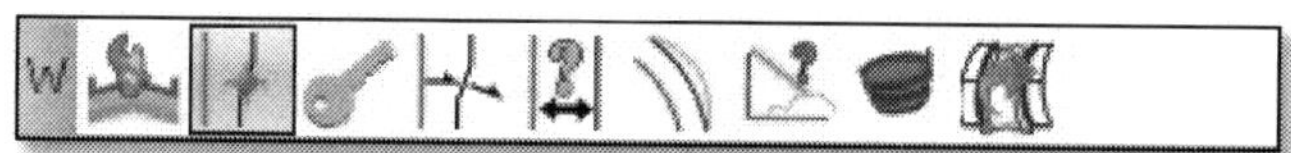

➢ Select the Corridor

Or, use **Element Selection** to highlight the corridor and on the context sensitive menu, and select **Corridor Creation Tools > Create Point Control**

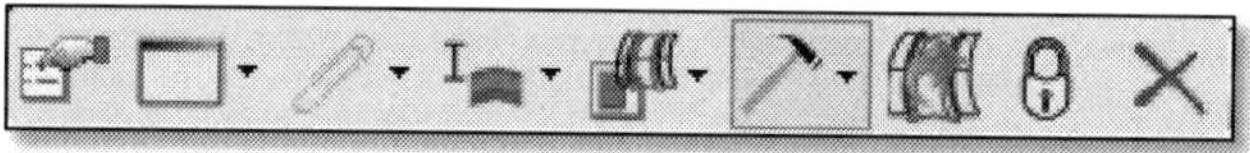

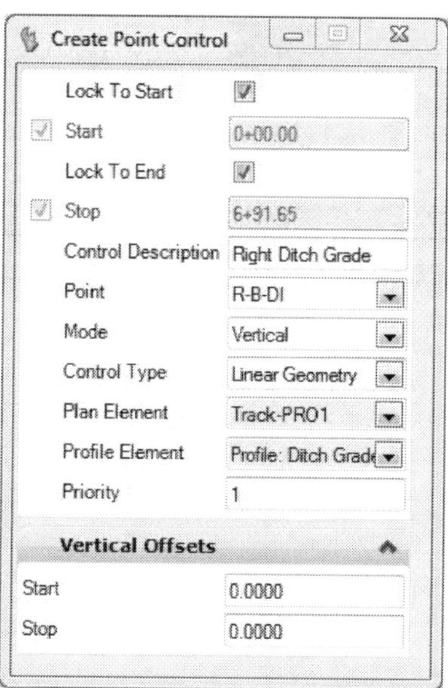

- You can either enter your options through the dialog box, or by cycling through the heads-up prompts
    - The **Start** and **Stop** Stations are along the main corridor geometry, even if you are using separate geometry for the control
    - Enter a **Description**
    - The **Point** is the template point you are controlling
    - The **Mode** can be either ***Horizontal***, ***Vertical*** or ***Both***
    - The **Control Type** will change depending upon the **Mode**

Control Type \ Mode	Horizontal	Vertical	Both	
Corridor Feature	X	X	X	Used to tie to the path of a point in another corridor.
Feature Definition	X	X	X	Used to tie to a Feature Definition. Can be multiple features with the same definition
Linear Geometry	X	X	X	Used to tie to civil geometry. May be the same as the CL with different offsets. For Vertical, can be the same horizontal as the CL with different Vertical
Elevation & Grade		X		Used to specify the elevation at the first Station and a longitudinal grade.
Elevation Difference		X		Used when you define the elevation of a point by an alignment whose elevations are the difference to the CL vertical. (Sometimes used for Super)
Superelevation		X		Used when you have defined Superelevation Control alignments for the rotation in super. Automatically used by the Superelevation commands.

- Continue through the prompts, establishing them as necessary and accepting each with a **<D>**
- When done, the **Point Control** is applied and the corridor graphics update. If dynamic cross sections are displayed, they also update.

To edit or delete an established Point Control

- **MS: Tasks > Civil Tools > Corridor Modeling > Corridor Objects**

- And then select the **Corridor**

  Or, use **Element Selection** to highlight the corridor and on the context sensitive menu, select **Corridor Creation Tools > Corridor Objects**

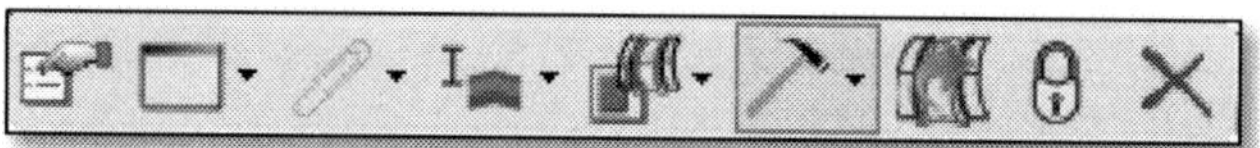

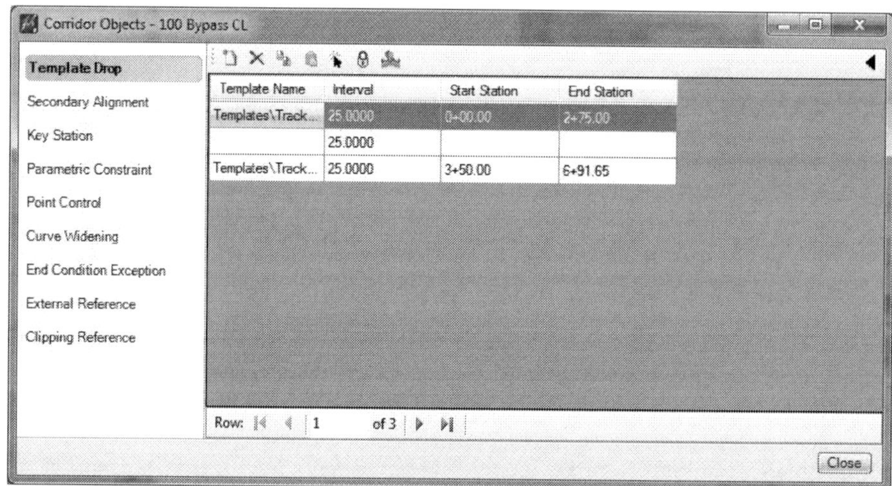

➢ Through this dialog, you can access all of the settings for the corridor. Adjust the dialog if necessary to see additional settings.

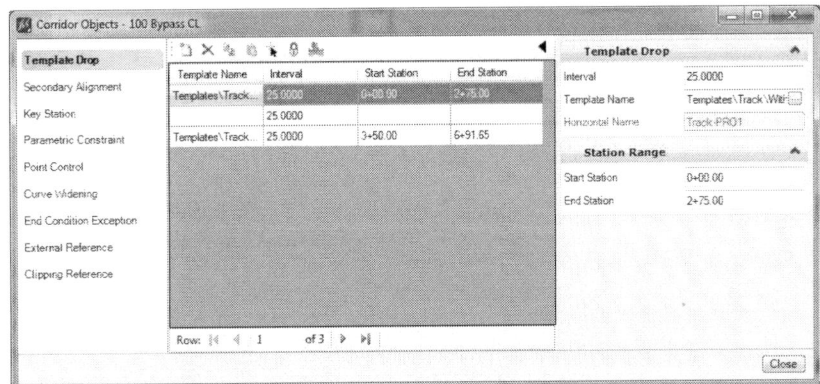

➢ Select the **Point Control** category and make any edits desired

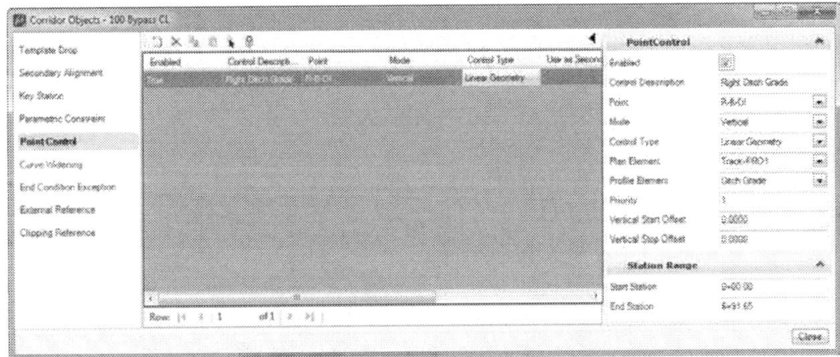

Note: Changes automatically take affect – there is no Apply button. Undo will reverse any unwanted changes.

➢ **Close** the dialog when done

Exercise 7: Transitions

Given:

- *HWY 60 Alternate One Corridor.dgn* – Previously created corridor.

Required:

For changing templates and point controls, you will add the same climbing lane to the West-bound side of the roadway. The goal is to give you a sense of how these options work by comparing the setups. The full width of the climbing lane occurs between stations 150+00 and 172+00. Tapers will occur between 145+00 and 150+00 as well as between 172+00 and 175+00.

For the Parametric Constraint example, you will vary the depth of the asphalt along the corridor.

- Accomplish transitions by:
- Using Multiple Templates
- Using Point Controls, and
- Using Parametric Constraints

Getting Started

1 Open your design file

- Start InRoads using the icon on your desktop or using the **Start** menu

2 On the MicroStation manager, set the:

- **User**: ***examples***
- **Project**: ***Bentley-Civil-Imperial***
- **Interface**: ***default***

3 Select the *HWY 60 Alternate One Corridor.dgn* and Open

4 Load the template library

- **MS: Tasks > Civil Tools > Corridor Modeling > Create Template**

- In the **Create Template** dialog, choose **File > Open** and select the *HWY 60 Templates.itl* file
- **Open**

Multiple Templates

5 Review the template

- Select the **Library** tab at the bottom of the **Active Template** area.
- In the *CP* folder, activate **2 Lane Rural – Left Climbing Lane**
- Review the template and note the extra lane on the left

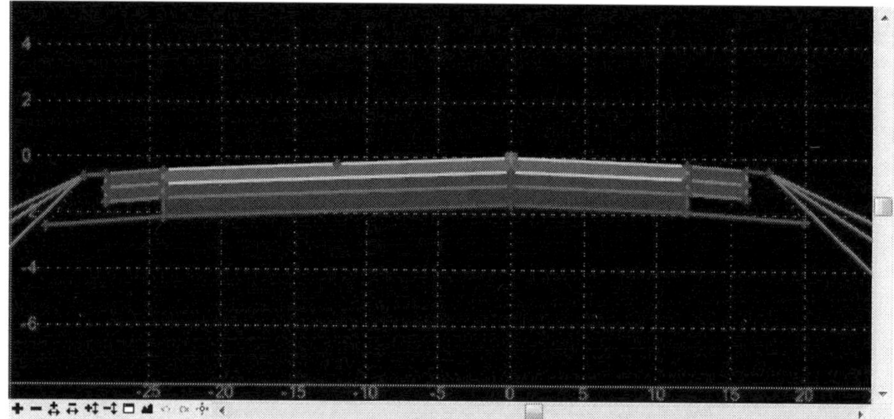

- **Close**

6 Create a template drop

- **MS: Tasks > Civil Tools > Corridor Modeling > Create Template Drop**

- Select the Corridor

- Or, use **Element Selection** to highlight the corridor and on the context sensitive menu, select **Corridor Creation Tools > Create Template Drop**

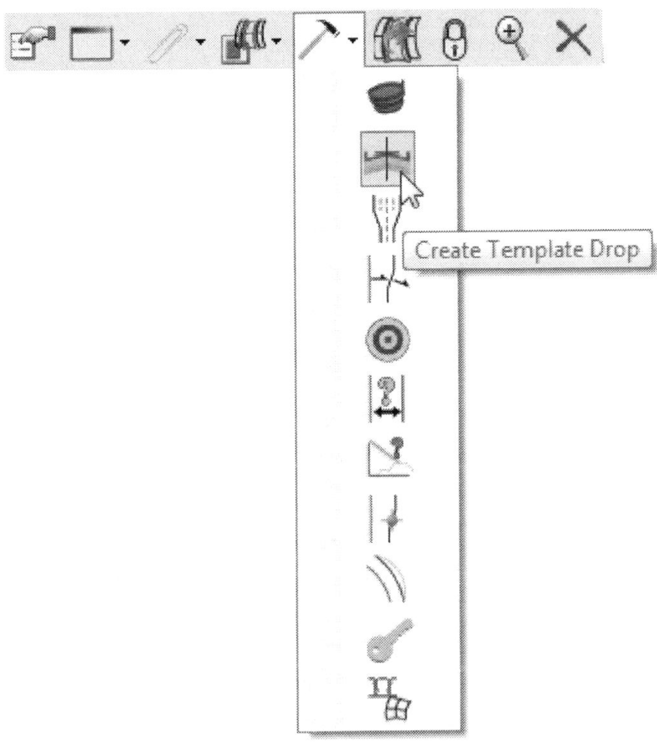

You can either enter your options through the dialog box, or the heads-up prompts

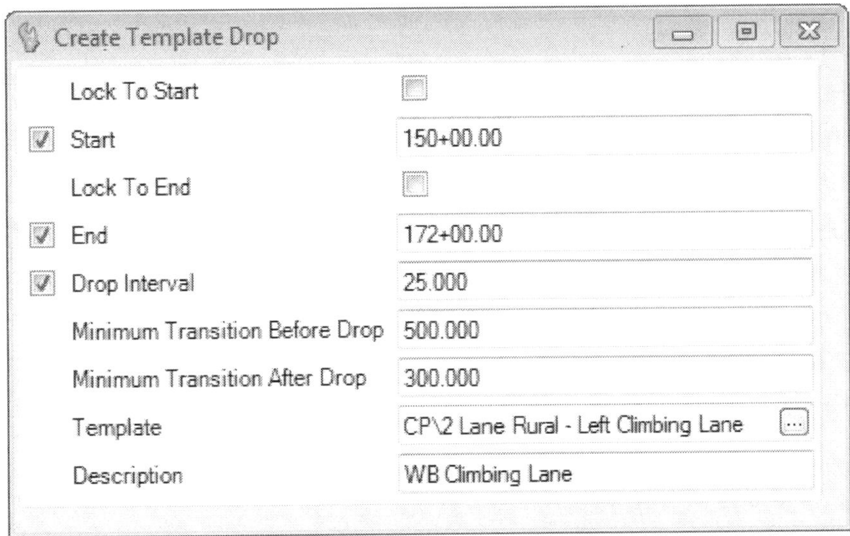

*Remember to <**Tab**> and **Accept** after each entry*

- **Template**: *CP\2 Lane Rural - Left Climbing Lane*
- **Start Station**: **150+00**
- **End Station**: **172+00**
- **Template Drop Interval**: **25**
- **Minimum Transition Before Drop**: **500**
- **Minimum Transition After Drop**: **300**

  Including transitions in and out, the lane will go from 145+00 to 175+00

- **Description**: **WB Climbing Lane**

  The software will take a minute to process

- There is now a template drop at the beginning (to see the menu shown, select the template drop handle and choose Properties)

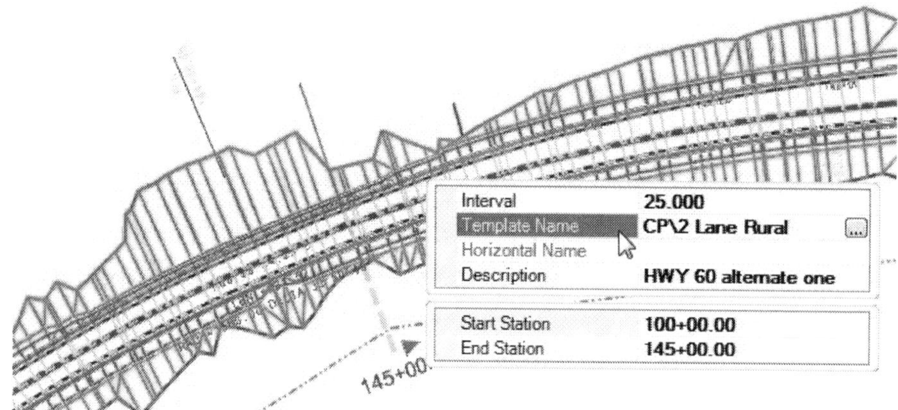

- A transition

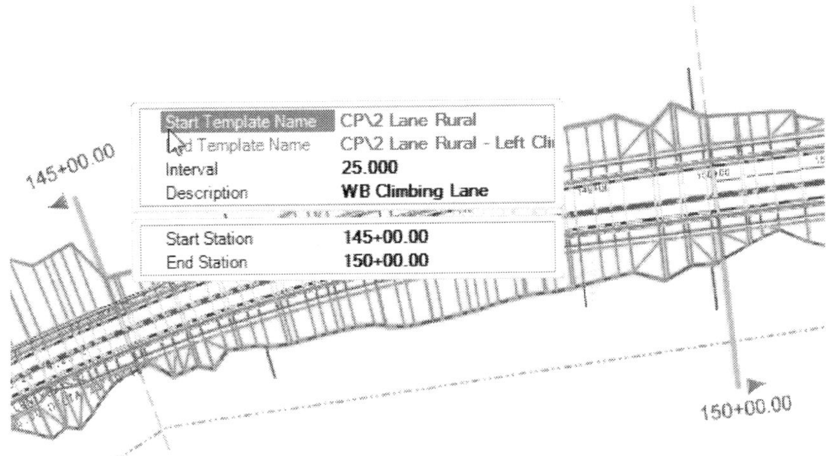

- A template drop in the middle

- A transition

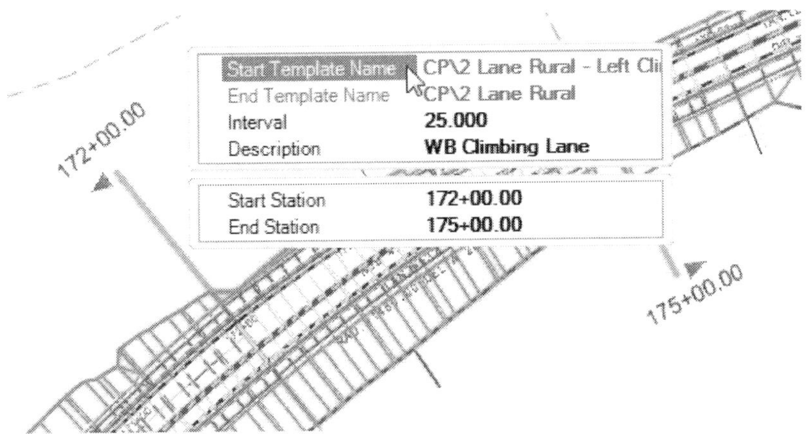

- And a template drop at the end

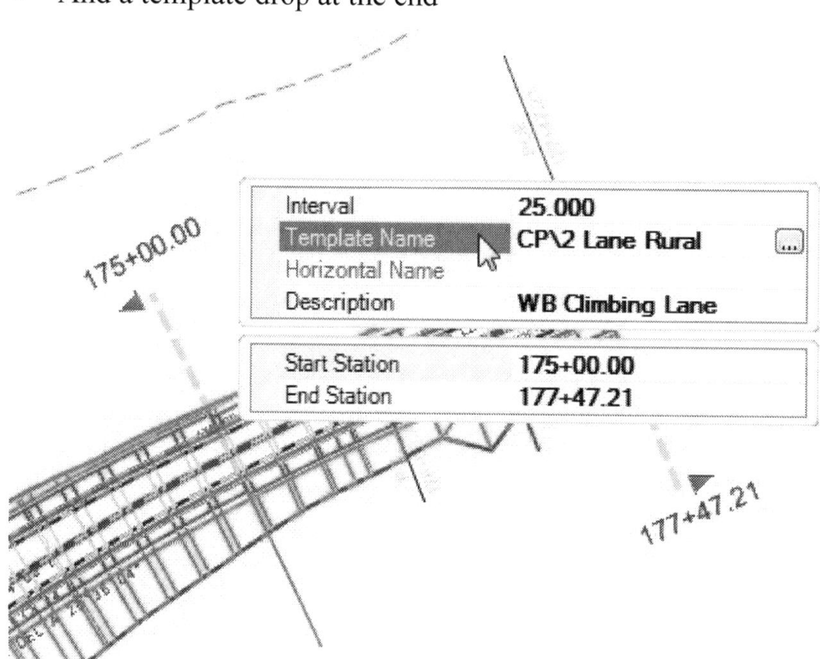

7 Modify the transition (optional)

Look at the first transition and notice the lane line does not start until the full width of the lane is achieved. If you want the lane line to join to the previous edge of pavement, use the following options. Otherwise, you may skip to the next step.

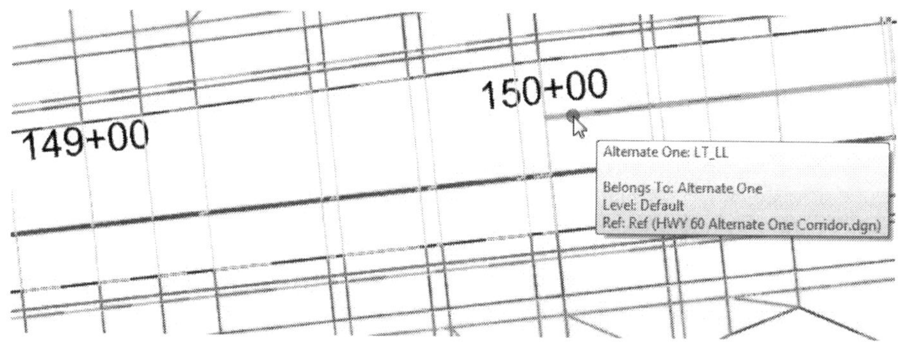

- Select the first transition and choose **Edit Transition**

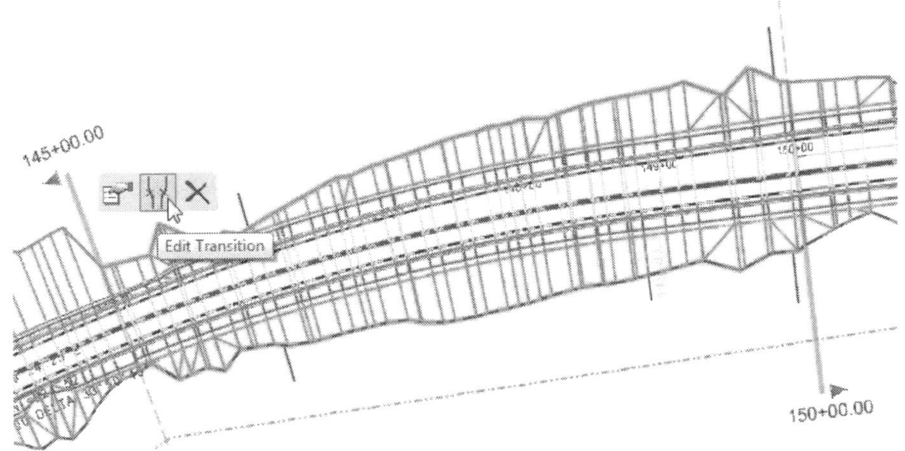

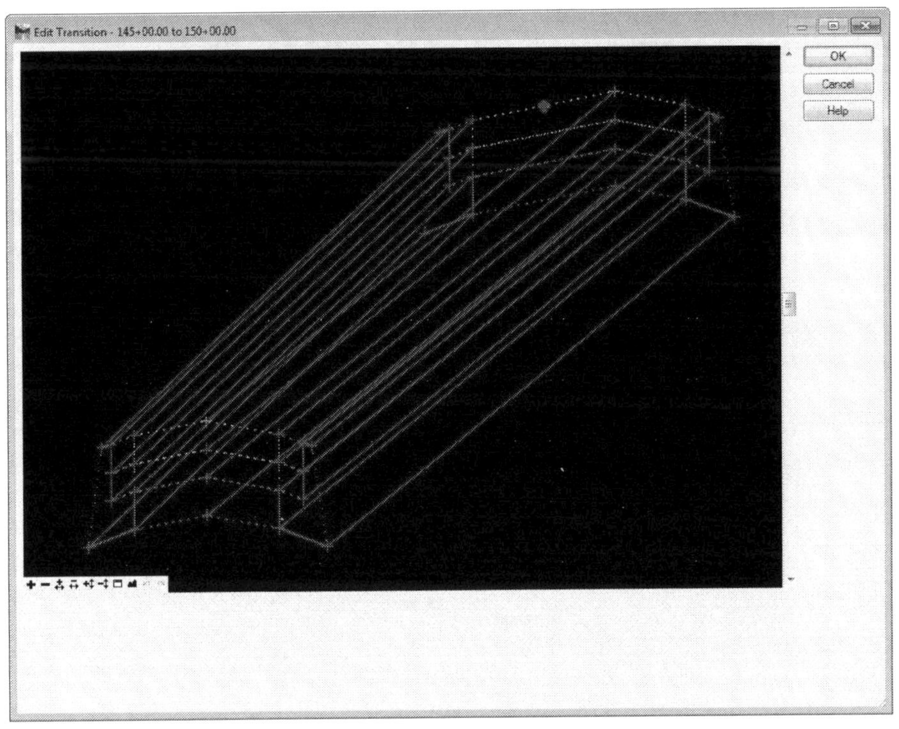

This is very similar to the transition editor in the previous version.

- Connect the lane line point to the previous EOP

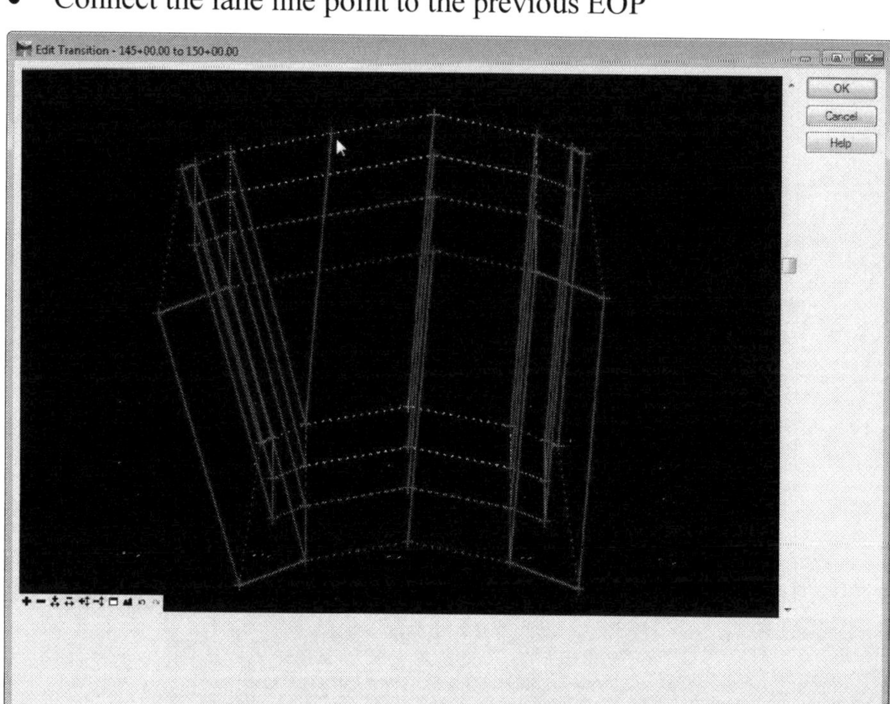

- Select **OK**
- **Delete** the ***Horizontal Constraint*** on the **LT_EOP**
- Select **OK**

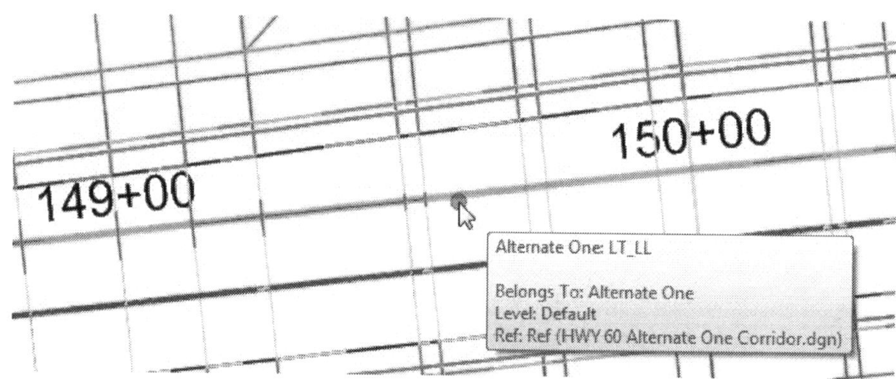

- Repeat for the other transition

8 Review the transition

- In the **Dynamic Section** view, dimension the lane and step through the stations to review the transition area

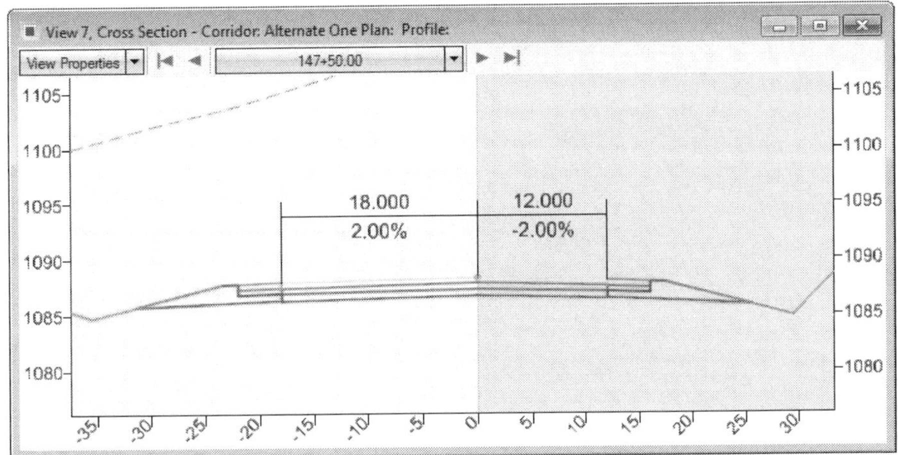

9 Next, you'll accomplish the same transition using a different method so you must first remove this method

- Select the first transition and **Delete**

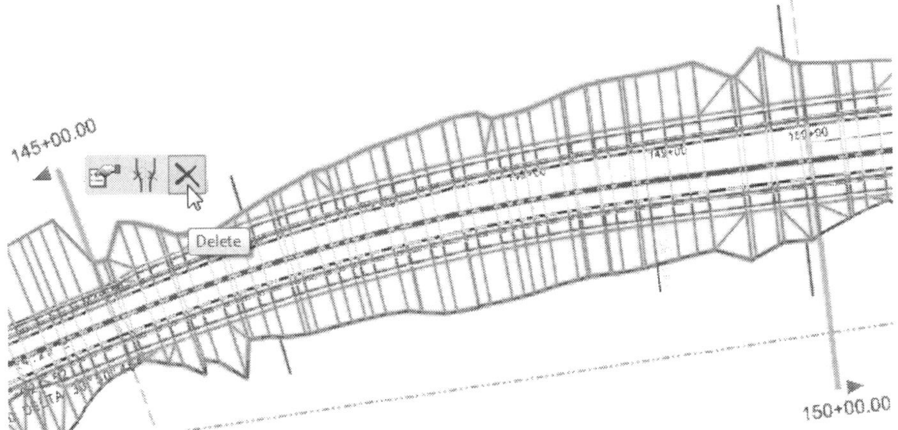

- Using the same procedure, **Delete**:
- The middle template drop
- The second transition
- The final template drop
- This will leave you with just the first template drop

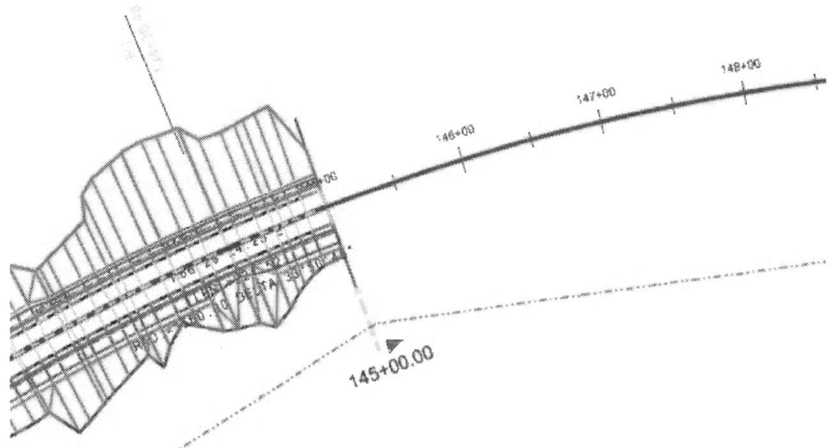

- Drag the indicator above 145+00.00 to the end of the alignment

  You could have selected 145+00.00 and typed over it with **177+47.207**

- You could also have selected **Corridor Objects …**

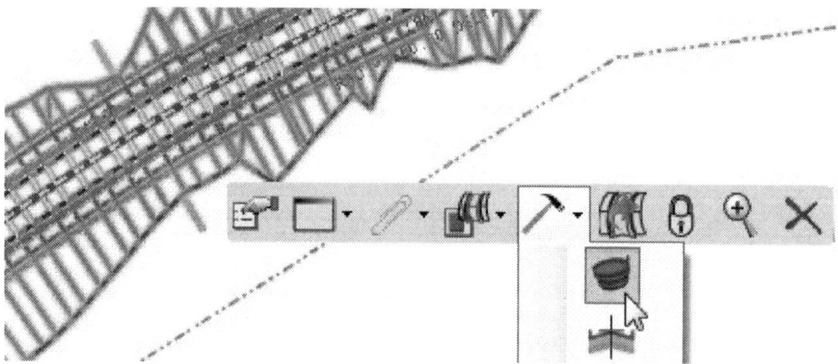

- And deleted the entries from the **Template Drop** page, then changed the **End Station** of the first drop.

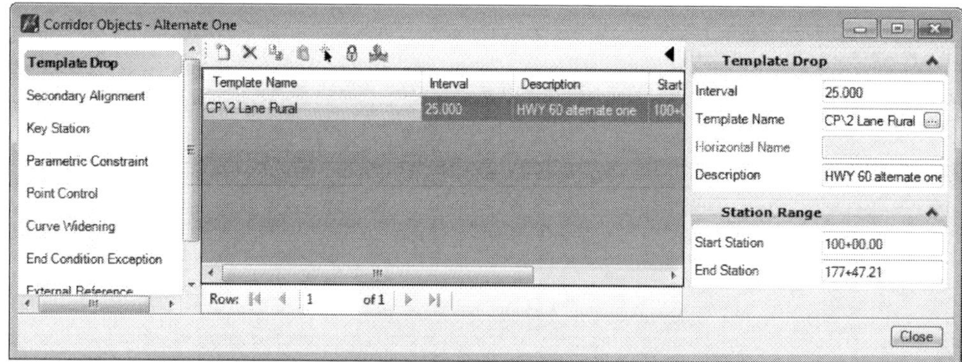

- OR, you could have used **Undo** to undo back to the start of the lab

Point Controls

By default, the control point (typically the CL) of a template follows the horizontal and vertical geometry, with all other point locations being determined by their constraints. These constraints can be overridden by either Parametric Constraints or Point Controls. With Point Controls, you can assign any point in the template to follow a different path. This path can be defined by varying the offsets from the CL, by separate geometry, by 'following' a feature definition, etc.

Here, you'll widen for a climbing lane on the West-bound side of the highway between stations 145+00 and 175+00.

Note: If using separate geometry for point controls instead of the stations and offsets from the CL, the additional geometry must be defined prior to entering the command.

10 Create a **Point Control** for the first taper

- **MS: Tasks > Civil Tools > Corridor Modeling > Create Point Control**

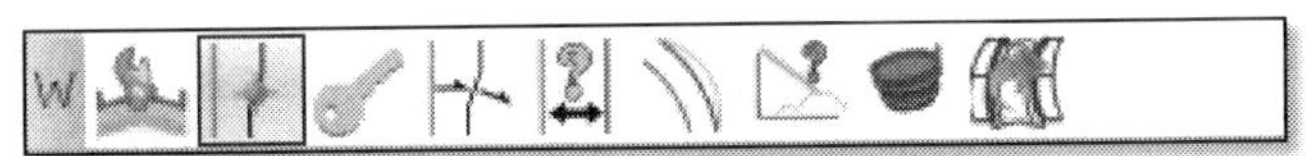

- Select the Corridor

- Or, use **Element Selection** to highlight the corridor and on the context sensitive menu, select **Corridor Creation Tools > Create Point Control**

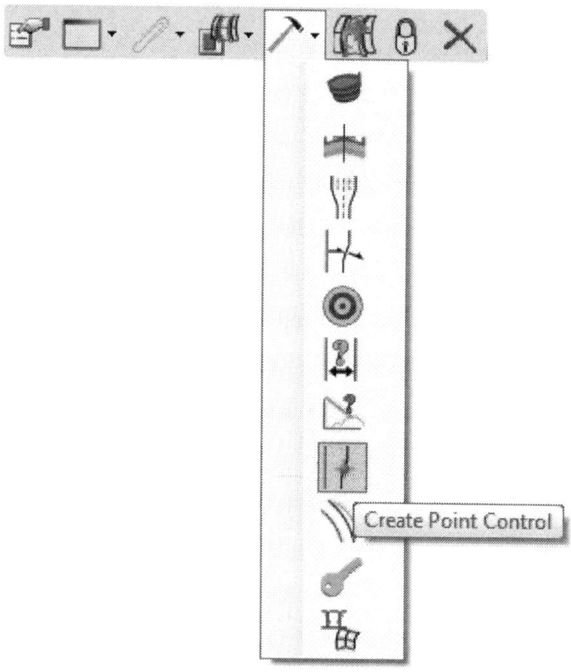

You can either enter your options through the dialog box, or the heads-up prompts

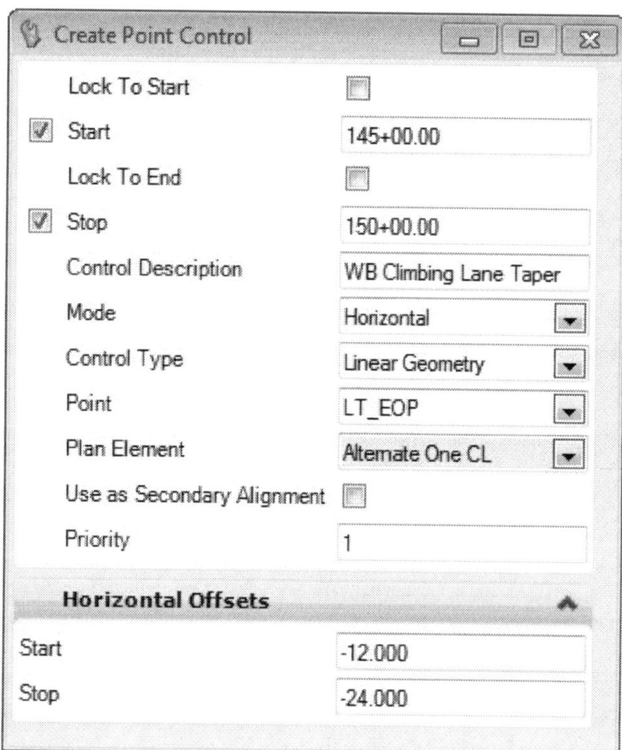

- **Start Station**: **145+00** (**<Tab>** then Accept if using Heads-up - **<End>** to unlock)
- **Stop Station**: **150+00** (**<Tab>** then Accept if using Heads-up)
- **Description**: **WB Climbing lane taper**
- **Mode**: ***Horizontal***
- **Control Type**: ***Linear Geometry***
- **Point**: ***LT_EOP***
- When prompted to ***Locate Plan or Profile Element***, select the Alternate One centerline horizontal alignment. The **Plan Element** will then show ***Alternate One CL***
- **Use as Secondary Alignment:** ***No***
- **Priority:** ***1***
- **Horizontal Offsets**: **Start**: **-12.00**, **Stop**: **-24.00**
- Continue through the prompts, establishing them as necessary and accepting each with a **<D>**

  When done, the Point Control is applied and the corridor graphics update. If the dynamic cross sections are displayed, they will also update.

  Note: Station entries sometimes don't appear to 'stick'. If you do not see the transition as shown, you can check/edit the stations on the next page.

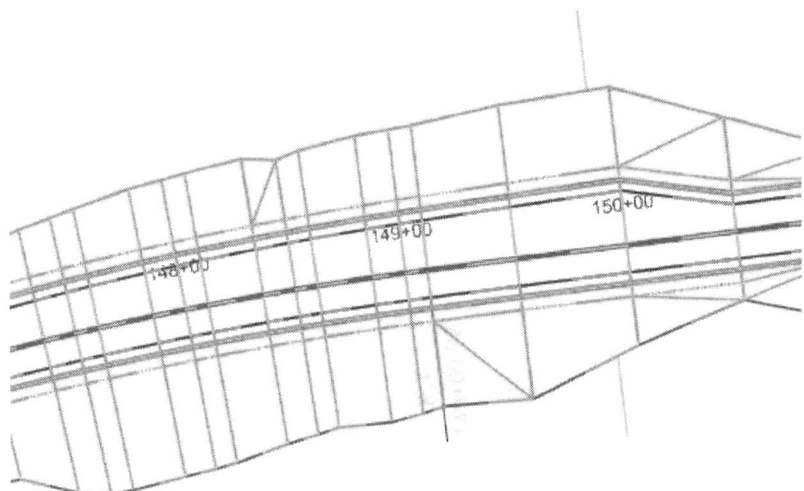

11 Add two additional point controls:

- Maintain the **24'** width from station **150+00** to station **172+00**
- Taper back from **24'** to **12'** from station **172+00** to **175+00**

12 Open the **Point Controls** for editing

- **MS: Tasks > Civil Tools > Corridor Modeling > Corridor Objects**

- And then Select the Corridor
- Or, use **Element Selection** to highlight the corridor and on the context sensitive menu, select **Corridor Creation Tools > Corridor Objects**

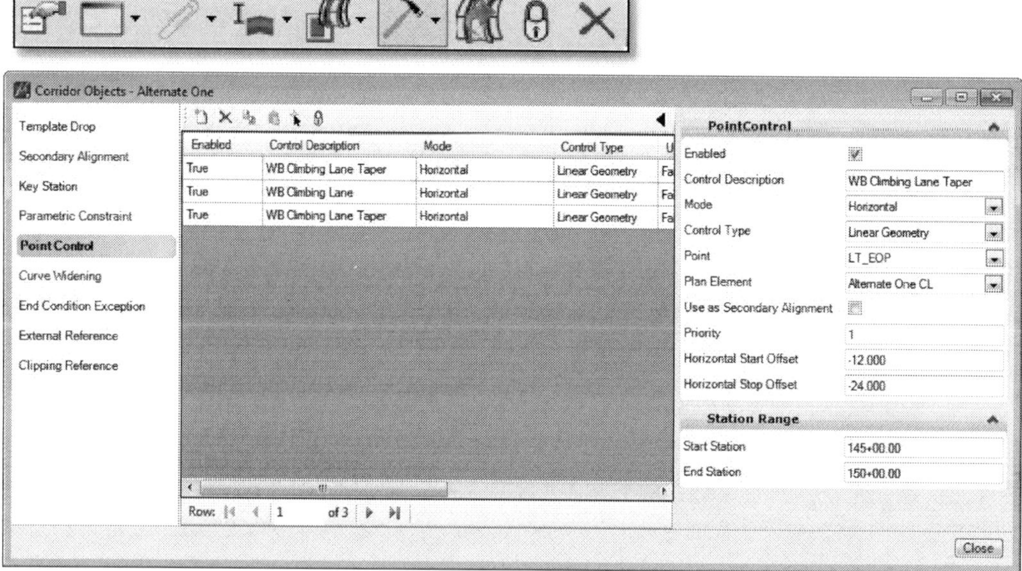

- Double-check each entry to make certain the stations and offsets are correct

  Through this dialog, you can access all of the settings for the corridor. Adjust the dialog if necessary to see additional settings.

  Note: **Undo** *will reverse any unwanted changes. Depending upon the type of change, you may need to* **Process** *the corridor.*

- Select a corridor handle and choose **Process Corridor** from the menu

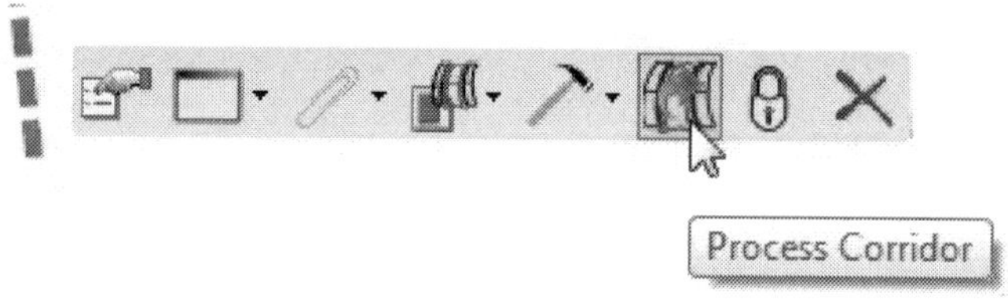

- **Close** the dialog when done

13 Review the Point Control

- Look at sections and the plan view in the area of the point control

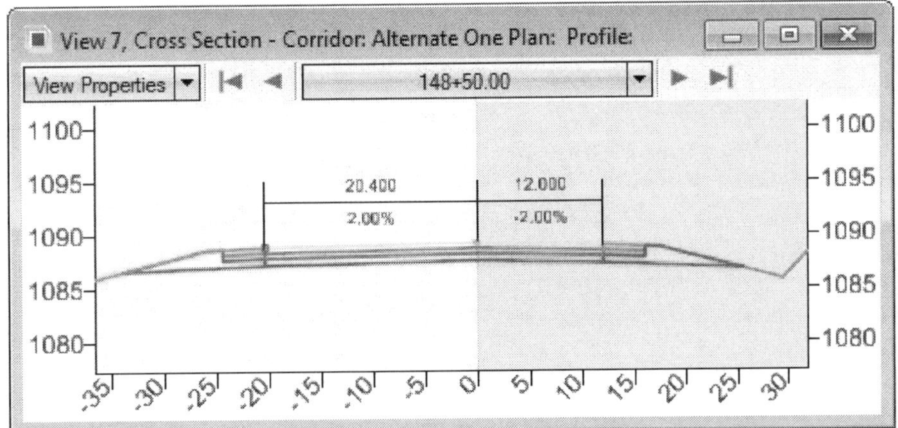

Parametric Constraints

The constraints in the template may be given labels which act as variables. These labels can be used to edit the value of all constraints where the label is assigned in the template editor, or in the corridor you can use Parametric Constraints to override the values from the original template. This override is based on a station range, so you can change the values along the corridor. The value at the starting station can be different than the ending station so you can create tapers using this method.

14 Review the template's label

- **MS: Tasks > Civil Tools > Corridor Modeling > Create Template**

- Make the *CP/2Lane Rural* template active
- **Edit** the LT_EOP_AGGR_BOT

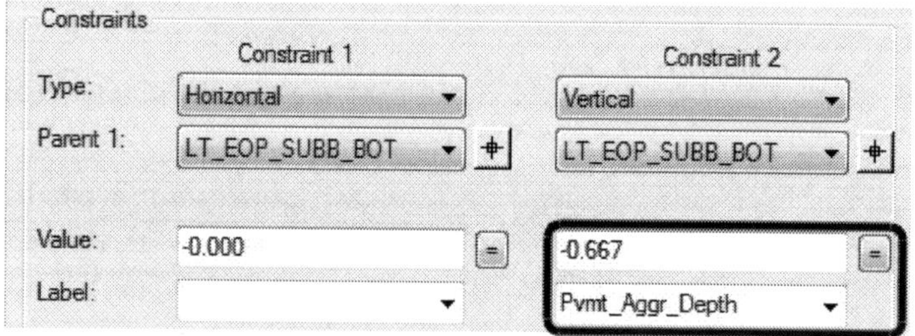

Note the Label is already established for the Vertical. Any point using this Label can be edited on the fly in the corridor.

- **Close Point Properties**
- Select the **Active Template** tab on the left
- Expand **Parametric Constraints** and highlight *Pvmt_Aggr_Depth*

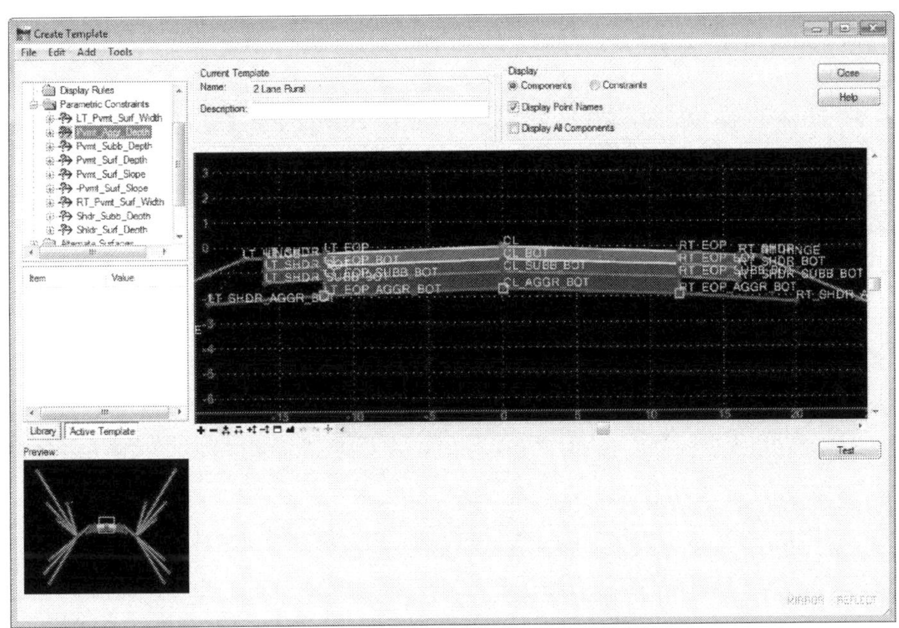

Notice that three points on the bottom of the Aggregate component highlight, indicating they all use the same label.

- **Close** the **Template Editor**

15 Create a **Parametric Constraint** for the first taper

- **MS: Tasks > Civil Tools > Corridor Modeling > Create Parametric Constraint**

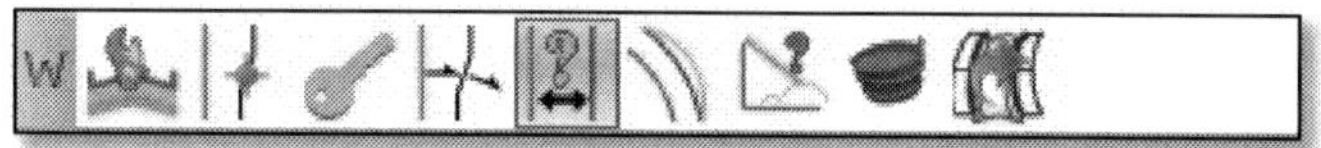

- Select the Corridor

  Or, use **Element Selection** to highlight the corridor and on the context sensitive menu, select **Corridor Creation Tools > Create Parametric Constraint**

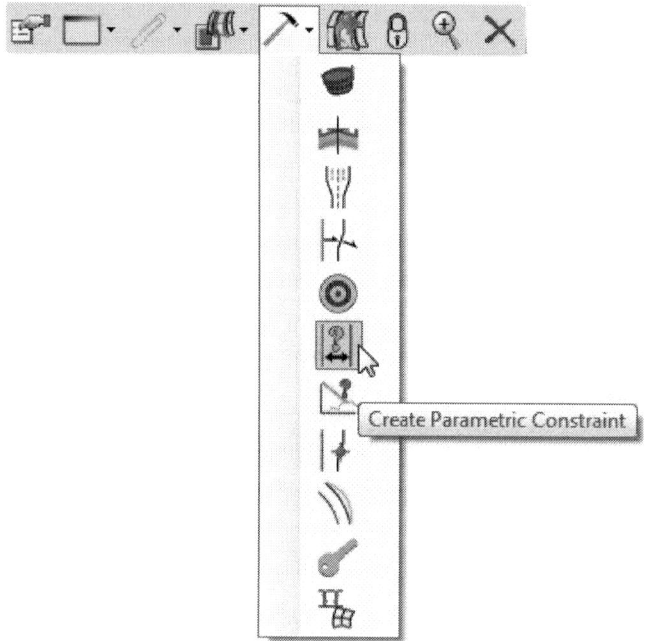

You can either enter your options through the dialog box, or the heads-up prompts

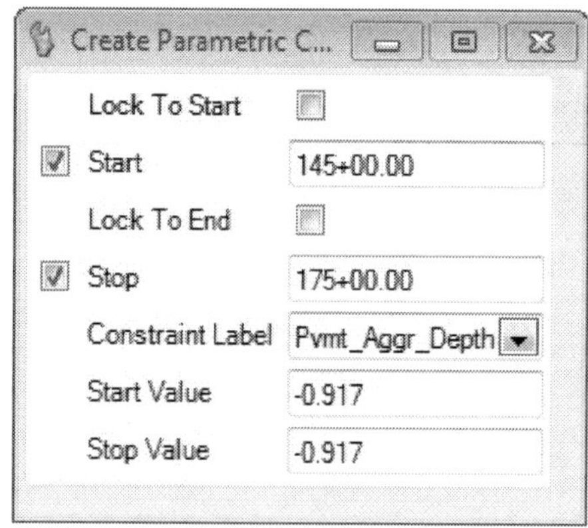

- **Start Station**: **145+00** (If using heads-up, **<End>** or **<Alt>** to unlock if necessary before entering the value **<Tab>** then **Accept** after)
- **Stop Station**: **175+00**
- **Constraint Label**: ***Pvmt_Aggr_Depth***
- **Start Value**: **-.917** (you may alternately key in -11/12)
- **Stop Value**: **-.917**
- Continue through the prompts, establishing them as necessary and accepting each with a **<D>**

16 Review the **Parametric Constraint**

- Look at sections before and after the parametric constraint starts

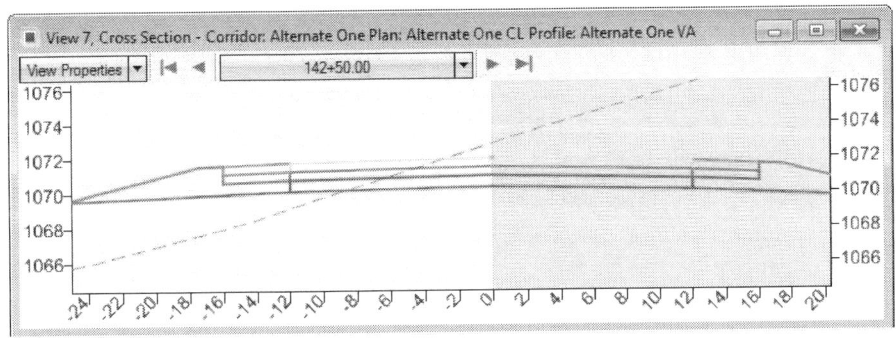

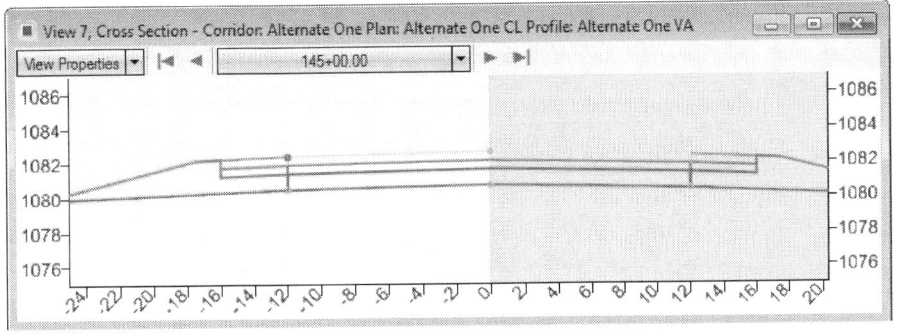

Notice the aggregate is thicker in the parametric area. Also note the green markers indicating the points that are parametrically controlled. Purple markers indicate points that are point controlled.

17 Open the **Parametric Constraints** for review and editing

- **MS: Tasks > Civil Tools > Corridor Modeling > Corridor Objects**

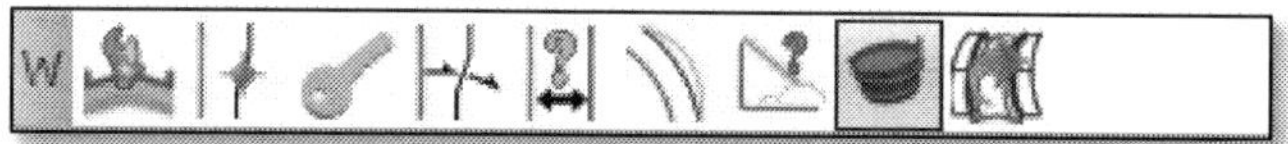

- And then Select the Corridor
- Or, use **Element Selection** to highlight the corridor and on the context sensitive menu, select **Corridor Creation Tools > Corridor Objects**

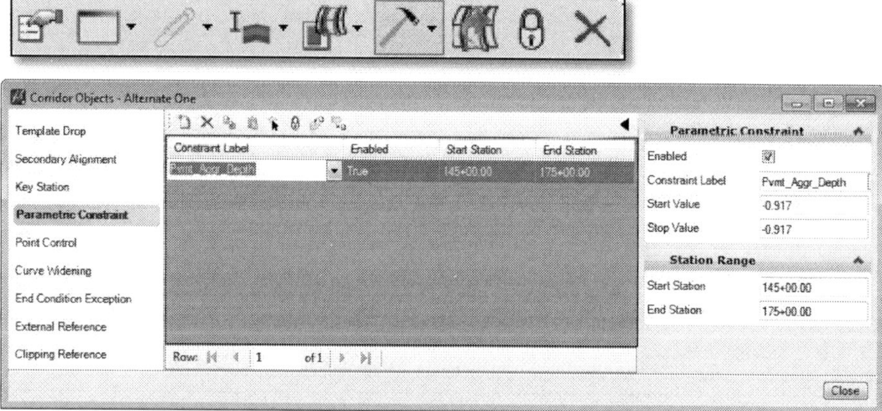

Through this dialog, you can access all of the settings for the corridor. Adjust the dialog if necessary to see additional settings.

Note: **Undo** *will reverse any unwanted changes. Depending upon the type of change, you may need to* **Process** *the corridor.*

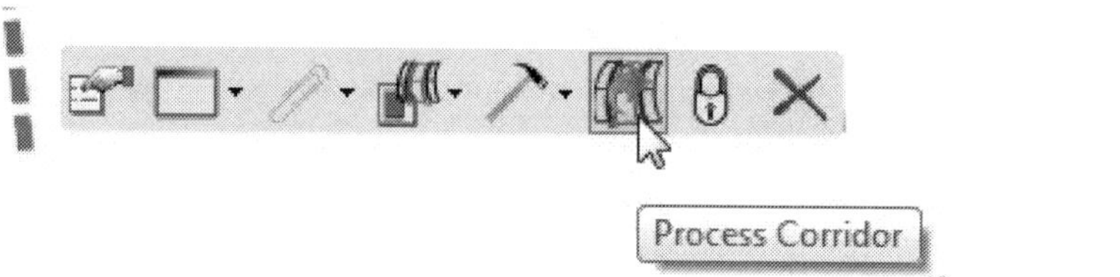

- **Close** the dialog when done

Ending

18 **Save Settings**

19 **Exit**

Superelevation

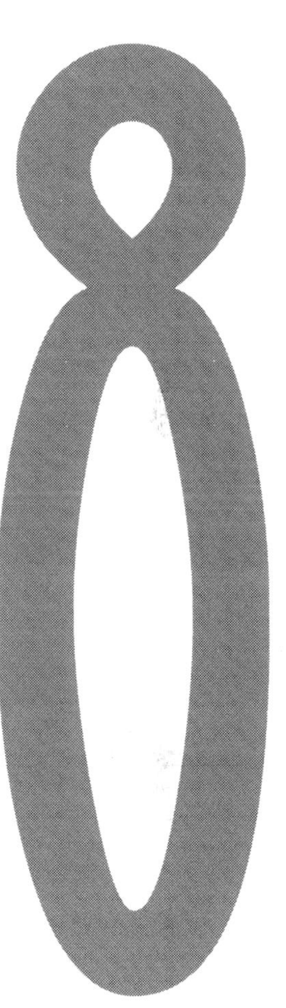

DEFINE SUPER SECTIONS

CREATE SUPER LANES

CALCULATE SUPERELEVATION

ASSIGN SUPER TO A CORRIDOR

8 Superelevation

Superelevation is handled very differently in SS4 than in previous versions. The Superelevation is represented graphically in the plan view and can be created in a separate MicroStation model or even in a separate DGN that has your horizontal alignment referenced. After the super is created, the model can be referenced and applied to your corridor.

- The horizontal alignment must created
- The horizontal alignment must be in the active model or referenced into the active model

Note: If you want to see color-shaded lanes, select ***Workspace > Preferences > View Options – Civil*** *and toggle the* ***Superelevation Settings*** *for* ***Fill*** *to* ***Color Shaded Fill***.

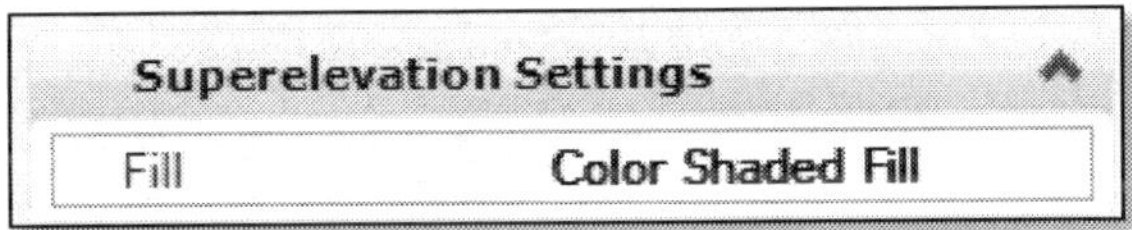

The basic workflow for Superelevation is to:

- Define Sections
- Define Lanes
- Calculate Transitions and
- Review/Edit.

Once you start the process, the software automatically steps you through the different commands to complete the Superelevation, although you may select each step individually.

8.1 Superelevation

Define Superelevation Sections

A section is the station range for one design criteria. It can be the entire alignment, an individual curve or anything in between. Use different sections when the design criteria changes along the alignment (different rates or different lane widths, for example) or if you want more flexibility in editing the Superelevation later.

➢ Select the level for your Superelevation graphics by setting the active MicroStation level

➢ **MS:Tasks > Corridor Modeling > Create Superelevation Sections**

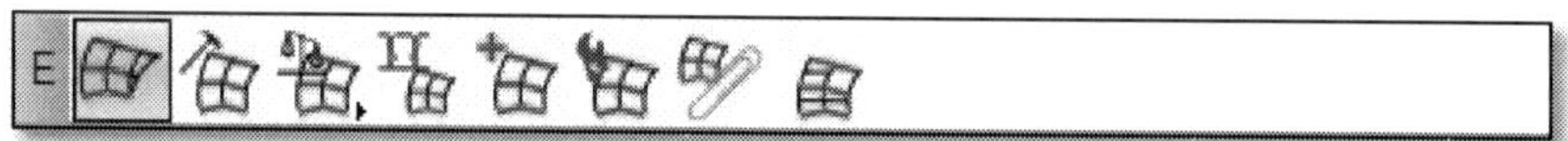

➢ Follow the heads-up prompts or use the dialog box to define:

- **Name** of the section – this will include both left and right Superelevation lanes
- **Locate Reference Element** – this is the horizontal alignment
- **Start Station** – for this section; you can **<ALT>** to lock to the beginning of the alignment
- **Stop Station** – for this section; you can **<ALT>** to lock to the end of the alignment
- **Minimum Tangent Length** – if the tangent is shorter than this, adjacent curves will be placed in the same section. A zero value means each curve is in a different section.

After stepping through the prompts, a MicroStation element is created that encompasses the section. This element is used to graphically identify the section when needed in the future.

The software will automatically continue with the next command …

Create Superelevation Lanes

Lanes are defined as one width following the same Superelevation criteria. A two-lane roadway would have two Superelevation lanes, one for each side. A four-lane roadway where each side acts as a single cross slope for rotation could also be defined with two Superelevation lanes.

If you stopped after the previous step, choose

➢ **MS:Tasks > Corridor Modeling > Create Superelevation Lanes**

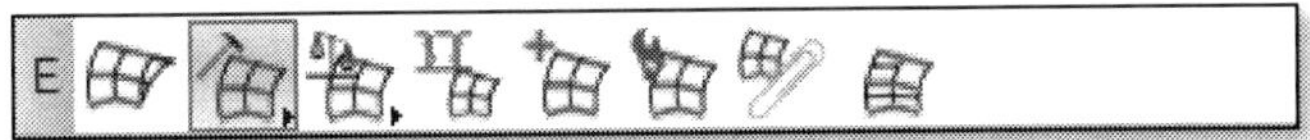

➢ Continue following the heads-up prompts or use the dialog box to define:

- **Name** – This is the lane name, so you can use R or L as a prefix to help distinguish them later
- **Side of Centerline** – Obviously, **Left** or **Right**
- **Inside Edge of Offset** – This is the distance from the centerline to the inside edge of the lane
- **Width** – The lane width
- **Normal Cross Slope** – Whatever the normal crown is for the template

➢ Repeat for each lane (the prompts will cycle through repeatedly for you to add other lanes – Reset when you cycle back to the original prompt but are done adding lanes)

The software will automatically continue with the next command …

Calculate Superelevation

This command is where you tell the software what standards file to use for Superelevation.

*Note: Reset here and then choose **Import Superelevation** if you want to import a text file or spreadsheet.*

If you stopped after the previous step, choose

- ➢ **MS:Tasks > Corridor Modeling > Calculate Superelevation**

- ➢ Continue following the heads-up prompts or use the dialog box to define:

  - **Standards File Name** – the SEP or SRL file for your super rates from your CAD configuration (SEP is shown here)

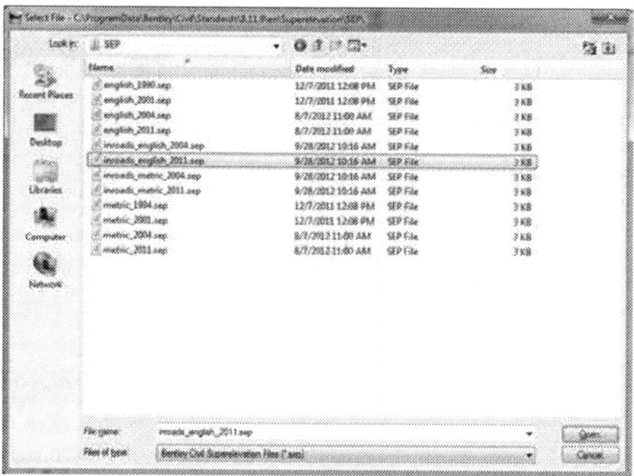

  - **e Selection** – Choose the max super rate and design speed file for this section
  - **L selection** – Choose the number of lanes
  - **Design Speed** – This will default based on the e Selection you made above
  - **Transition ID** – Select the transition type for this section
  - **Number of Lanes** – Choose the number of lanes
  - **Facility** – Select ***Divided*** or ***Undivided***

- **Open Editor** – Toggle on if you want the Superelevation Editor to open when the calculations are finished; you can always open the editor later if desired (If you open the editor, it will not progress to the next step automatically, but you can select the command later from the menu.)

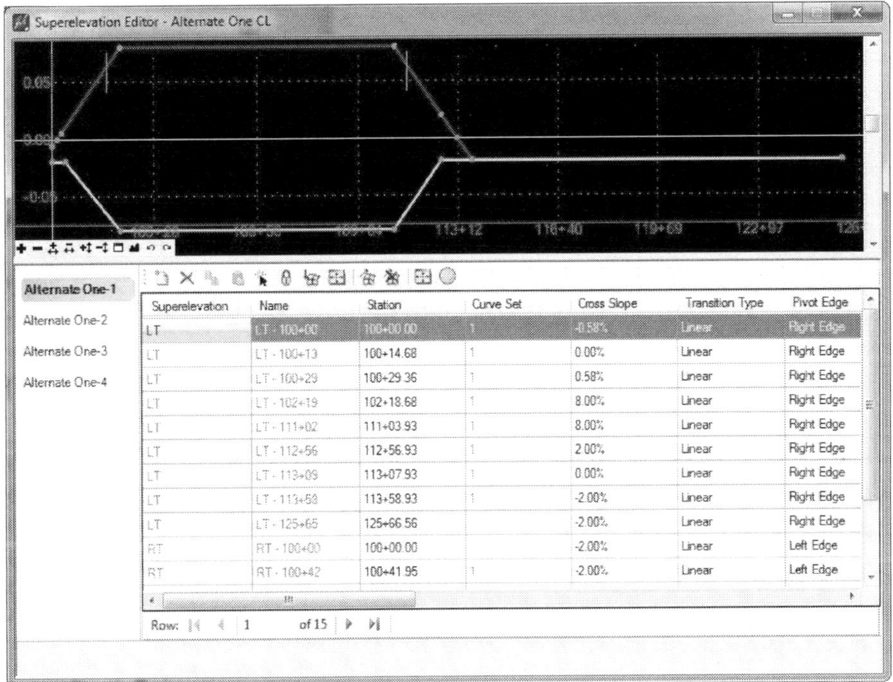

If you did not open the editor, the software will automatically continue with the next command …

➢ To open the **Editor** later, choose:

➢ **MS:Tasks > Corridor Modeling > Superelevation Editor**

Assign Superelevation to Corridor

If you stopped after the previous step, choose

➢ **MS:Tasks > Corridor Modeling > Assign Superelevation to Corridor**

➢ If you are continuing from the previous command, select the corridor to assign the Superelevation.

➢ If the corridor is in a separate DGN, you'll need to select the command from the menu.

➢ The **Associate Superelevation** box will appear and you can check to ensure the proper Superelevation objects are assigned to the proper points. If you assign **Super flags** in your template, it will use those points. If you did not, it will use the points closest to the width defined in the lanes.

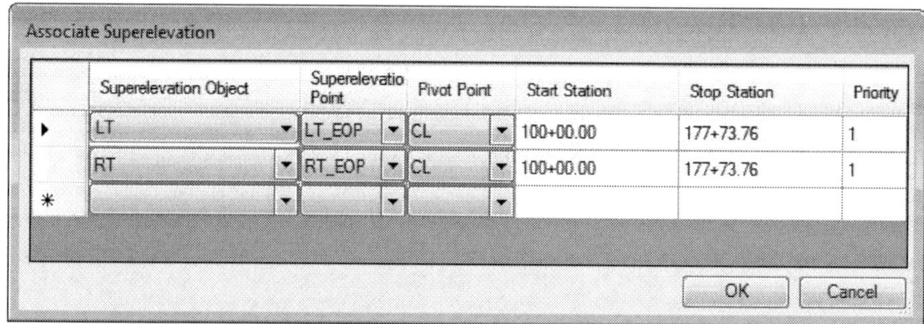

Note: You must be in the model where the corridor resides. If you have to switch models, you must select the command from the task bar. If you opened the editor in the last step, you will also need to select the command from the task bar.

➢ If you are assigning to more than one Section, you can highlight them before choosing the command. It does not matter if other graphics are in the selection set, as it only looks at super.

Exercise 8: Superelevation

Given:

- *HWY 60 Alternate One Geometry.dgn* – Horizontal and Vertical Alignments for Alternate One
- *HWY 60 Alternate One Corridor.dgn* – Corridor with Terrain and Alignments referenced

Required:

- Create a new design file
- Attach the Geometry as a reference
- Establish Superelevation based on your Design Criteria
- Create Superelevation Sections
- Create Superelevation Lanes
- Calculate Superelevation
- Assign Superelevation to the Corridor

Getting Started

1 Start InRoads using the icon on your desktop or using the **Start** menu

2 On the MicroStation manager, set the:

- **User**: ***examples***
- **Project**: ***Bentley-Civil-Imperial***
- **Interface**: ***default***

3 Create a new file

- Select the **New** File icon

- Browse to select the seed file *Seed2D-InRoads-Imperial.dgn* and select **Open**

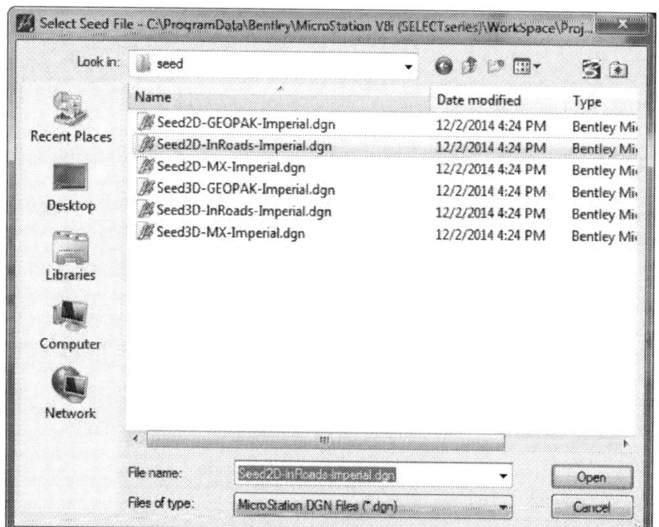

- Key in the File Name: **HWY 60 Alternate One Super.dgn**
- Select **Save**

4 Open the new file

5 Reference *HWY 60 Alternate One Geometry.dgn* with **no nesting**

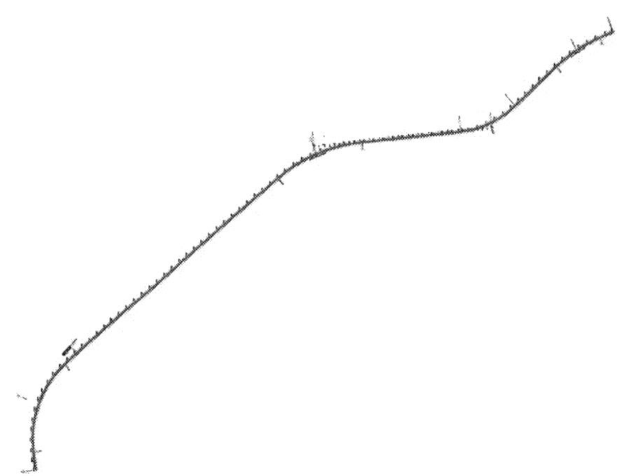

To create the Superelevation, you need nothing but the horizontal geometry referenced to the DGN file. Because of this, someone can reference the geometry and work on Superelevation at the same time someone else references the geometry and creates the corridor.

Note: The primary Superelevation commands may be chosen from the Task Menu

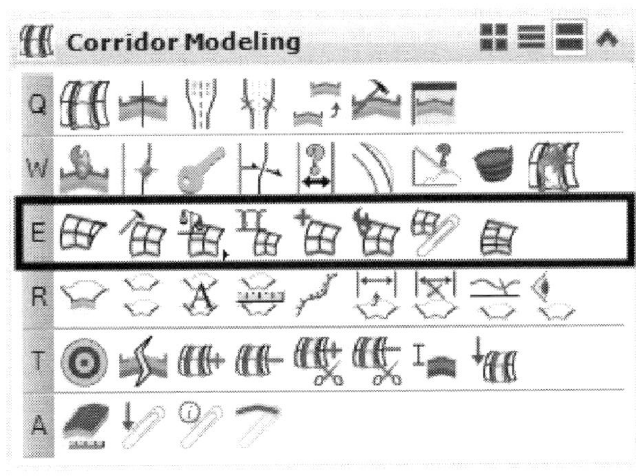

OR

From the context sensitive menu on the Corridor pop-up if you're in the corridor file.

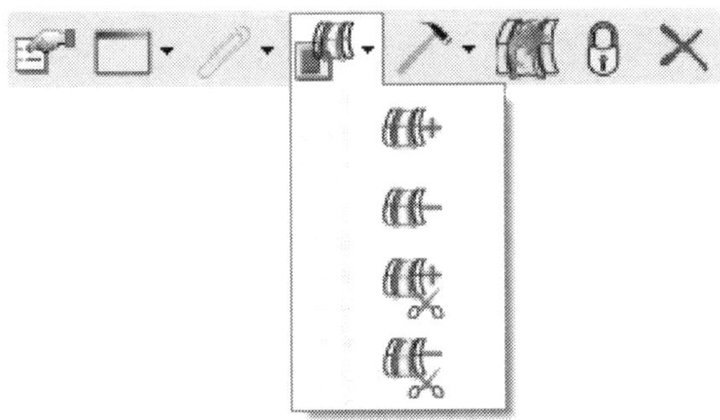

Superelevation Sections

6 Define Superelevation Sections

A section is the station range for one design criteria. It can be the entire alignment or an individual curve. Use different sections when the design criteria changes along the alignment (different rates or different lane widths, for example) or if you want the flexibility of editing one section later.

- Make **Draft_Corr_Superelevation** the active MicroStation level

- **MS: Tasks > Civil Tools > Corridor Modeling > Create Superelevation Sections**

7 Follow the heads-up prompts or use the dialog box to define:

- **Name** of the section – **Alternate One**
- **Locate Reference Element** – **<D>** on the Horizontal Alignment
- **Start Station** – **<ALT>** to lock to the beginning of the alignment
- **Stop Station** – **<ALT>** to lock to the end of the alignment
- **Minimum Tangent Length** – **100**

After stepping through the prompts, a MicroStation element is created that encompasses the sections. This element is used to graphically identify each section when needed in the future.

The software automatically continues with the next command ...

Superelevation Lanes

8 Create Superelevation Lanes. Continue following the heads-up prompts or use the dialog box to define:

- **Name** – **RT**
- **Side of Centerline** – **Right**
- **Inside Edge of Offset** – **0**
- **Width** – **12**

Note: This is the width of the shape, not the lane. You can make this as wide as you would like – the wider, the easier to see.

- **Normal Cross Slope** – **-2%**

Note: Unlike previous version, this command requires you enter the percentage. -.02 will be interpreted as -.02%.

- Repeat for the Left side changing the input as necessary (the prompts automatically cycle through again)
- **<R>** when done with the left

The software automatically continues with the next command ...

Superelevation Calculation

9 Calculate Superelevation.

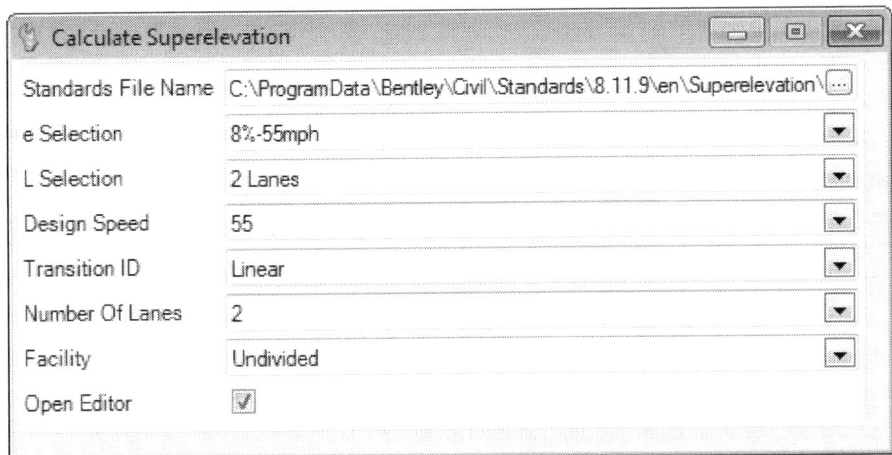

- Continue following the heads-up prompts or use the dialog box to define:
- Standards File Name – Use **<Alt>** and the down arrow to browse for the *SEP* file as shown.

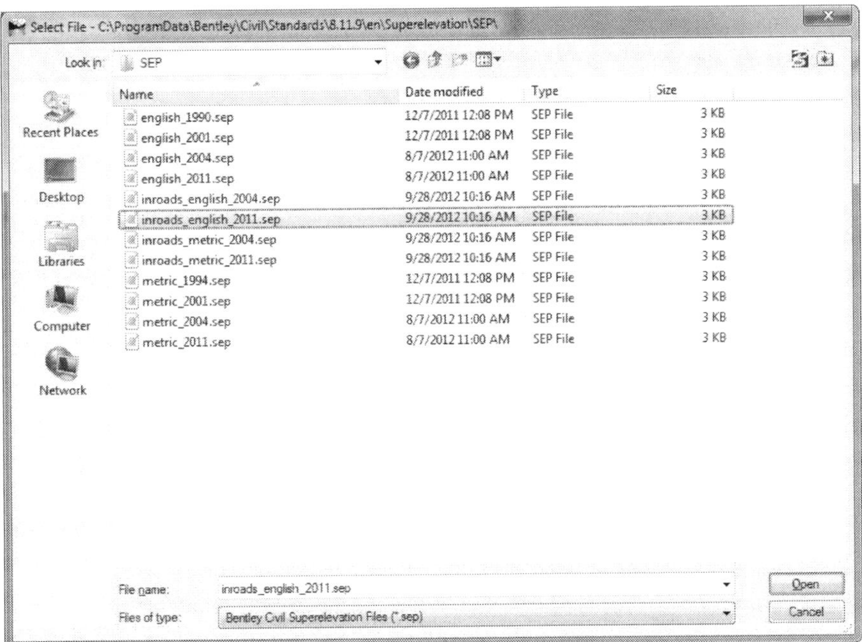

- **Open**
- **e Selection** – ***8% - 55mph***
- **L selection** – ***2 Lanes***
- **Design Speed** – **55**

- **Transition ID** – ***Linear***
- **Number of Lanes** – **2**
- **Facility** –***Undivided***
- **Open Editor** – ***Yes***

  If you say no, the software automatically continues with the next command and asks you to select the corridor. Since yours is now in a different DGN, we'll pause here and review the Superelevation. Any edits to the super must be completed in this design file.

10 Review the Superelevation

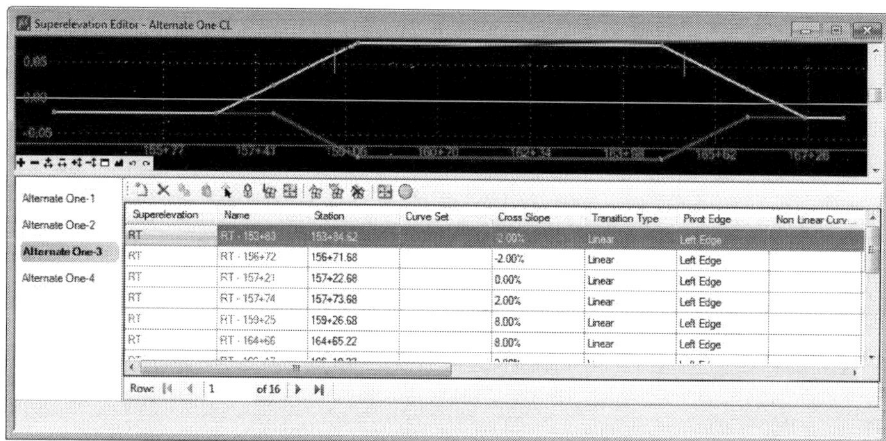

- Highlight and review the different Superelevation sections. From this dialog, you can make changes to the stations, cross slopes, etc. You can also add sections.
- Close the dialog when you are finished reviewing the **Superelevation Editor**.

11 Graphically review the Superelevation

- Select **Workspace > Preferences > View Options – Civil** and toggle the **Superelevation Settings** for **Fill** to ***Color Shaded Fill*** if it's not already set
- Open **View Attributes** and toggle on ***Fill***
- Zoom into one or more of the curves

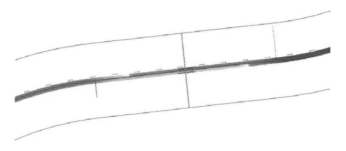

The color coding indicates the Superelevation cross slope. Slopes to the right are red/orange/yellow while slopes to the left are blue/teal/green.

- **Save Settings**

Superelevation Assignment

12 Assign Superelevation to the Corridor

- Open the *HWY 60 Alternate One Corridor.dgn* file.
- Reference *HWY 60 Alternate One Super.dgn*, with **No Nesting**
- Toggle on **Fill** in **View Attributes**

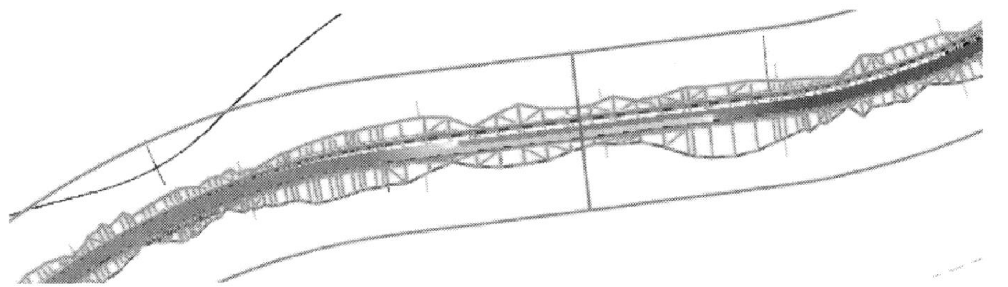

- Put the four superelevation sections into a selection set

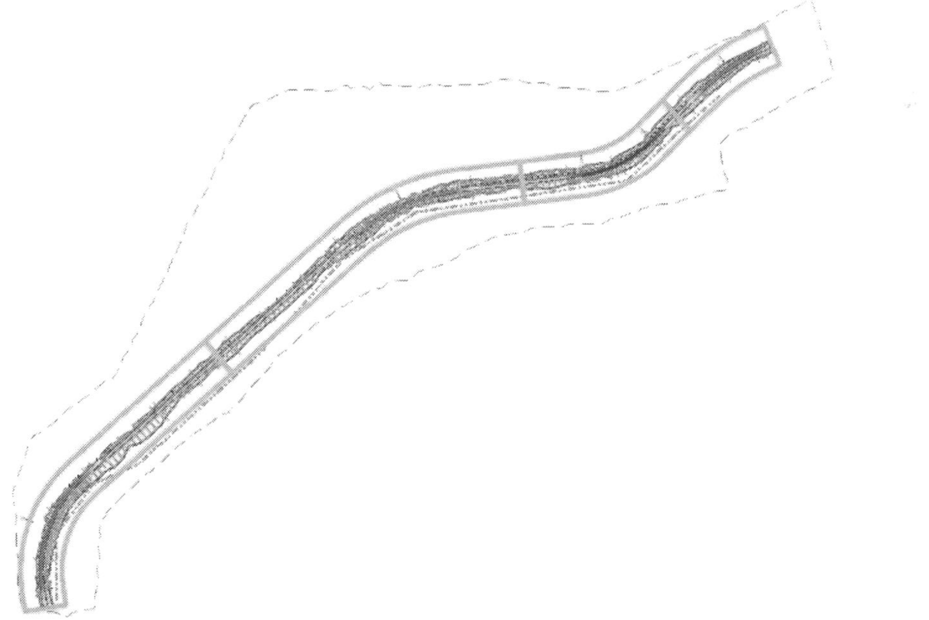

Since you are assigning to more than one Section, you can highlight them before choosing the command. It does not matter if other graphics are in the selection set, as it only looks at super.

- **MS: Tasks > Civil Tools > Corridor Modeling > Assign Superelevation to Corridor**

- **<D>** to use the selected elements
- Select the corridor

The Associate Superelevation dialog appears. This shows the Super Lane and corresponding point on the template as well as the Pivot Point. If something does not appear to be assigned to the correct point, you can change it before proceeding.

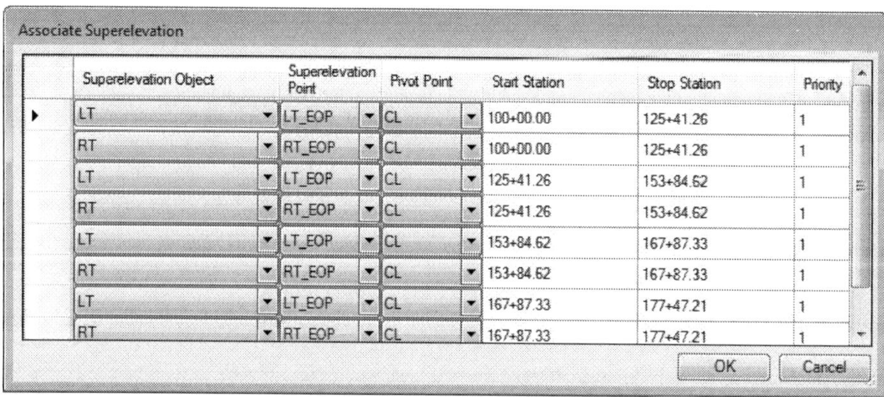

Associate Superelevation

Superelevation Object	Superelevation Point	Pivot Point	Start Station	Stop Station	Priority
LT	LT_EOP	CL	100+00.00	125+41.26	1
RT	RT_EOP	CL	100+00.00	125+41.26	1
LT	LT_EOP	CL	125+41.26	153+84.62	1
RT	RT_EOP	CL	125+41.26	153+84.62	1
LT	LT_EOP	CL	153+84.62	167+87.33	1
RT	RT_EOP	CL	153+84.62	167+87.33	1
LT	LT_EOP	CL	167+87.33	177+47.21	1
RT	RT_EOP	CL	167+87.33	177+47.21	1

OK Cancel

- Choose **OK**

The Superelevation is applied to the corridor and the corridor is reprocessed.

- Clear the selection set and then **Zoom in** on one of your curves in plan view

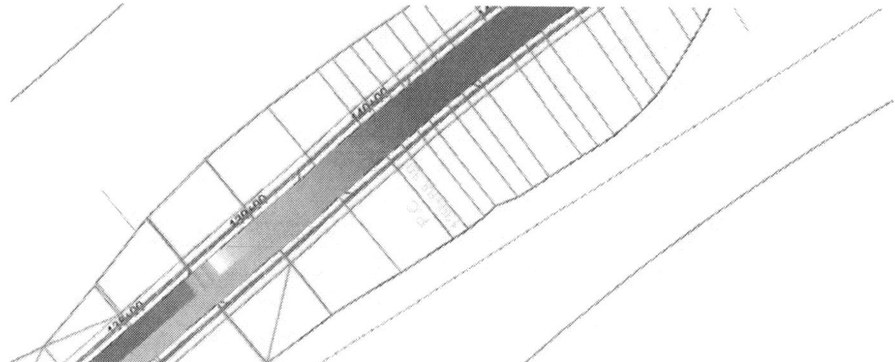

Superelevation Modification

13 Review cross sections

- Open the cross section view and step through some sections to see the results of the Superelevation.
- **<R>** in the cross section view and choose **Place Temporary Dimension Line**
- Dimension the travel lanes, then step through some of the curves to see the results

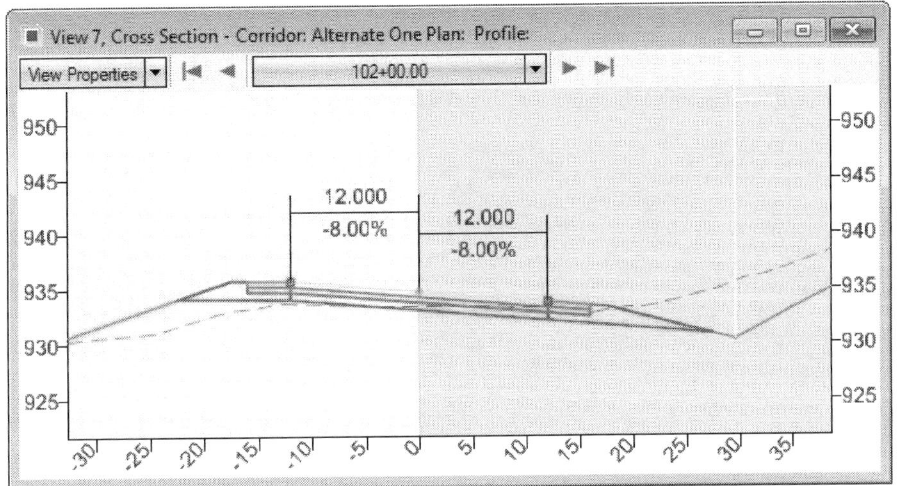

14 Modify the Superelevation

The existing roadway is already in partial rotation both at the beginning of the project and at the end, so you must modify the Superelevation accordingly.

- **Save Settings**
- Return to the *HWY 60 Alternate One Super.dgn* file
- **MS: Tasks > Civil Tools > Corridor Modeling > Superelevation Editor**

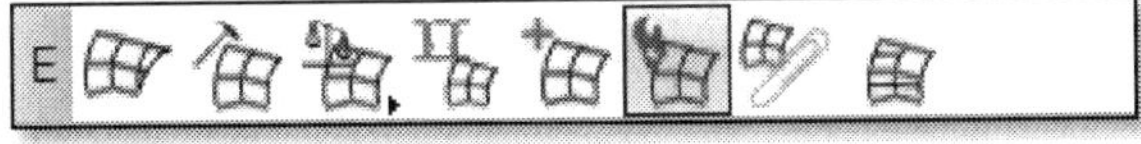

- Select the first Superelevation section

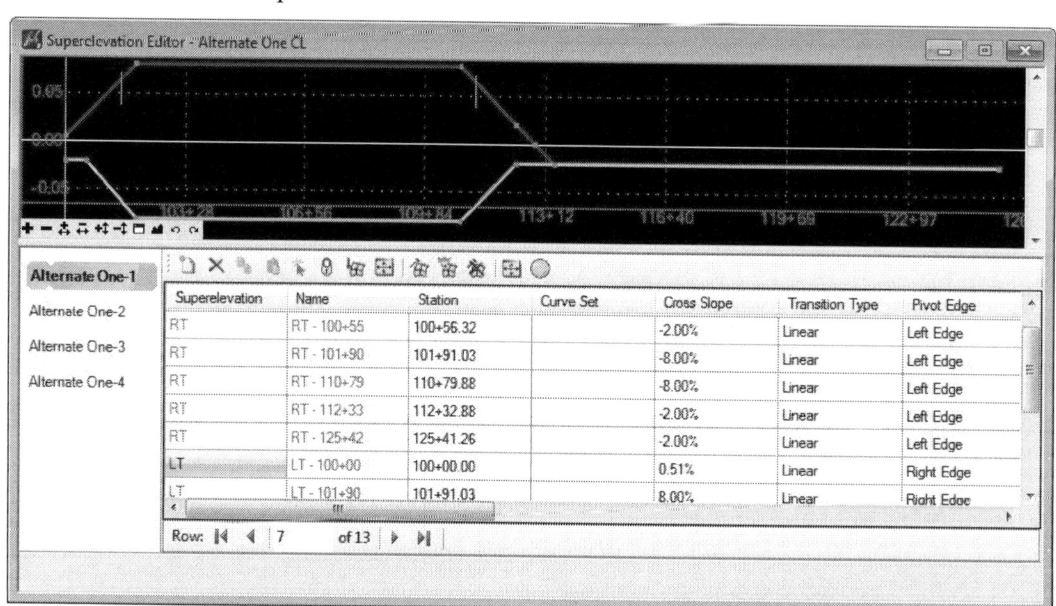

Notice the alignment was not long enough to complete the super transition on the outside, so the Left lane does not start at a -2% slope. In this case, we actually want to match the existing conditions at the start of the model.

- Look at the first **RT** station
- Change the slope to **-0.5%** to match the existing conditions.
- Repeat for the first **LT** station
- Right click on the second RT station and Delete it
- **Close** the dialog when done

Note: This is just an example of how you can edit the Superelevation. You would most likely be making other edits here as well to develop the needed super.

15 Review the changes to Super

- Open the *HWY 60 Alternate One Corridor.dgn* file
- Open the Cross Section view
- Go to cross section ***100+00***
- Place Temporary Dimensions on the travel lanes to review the results of your edits

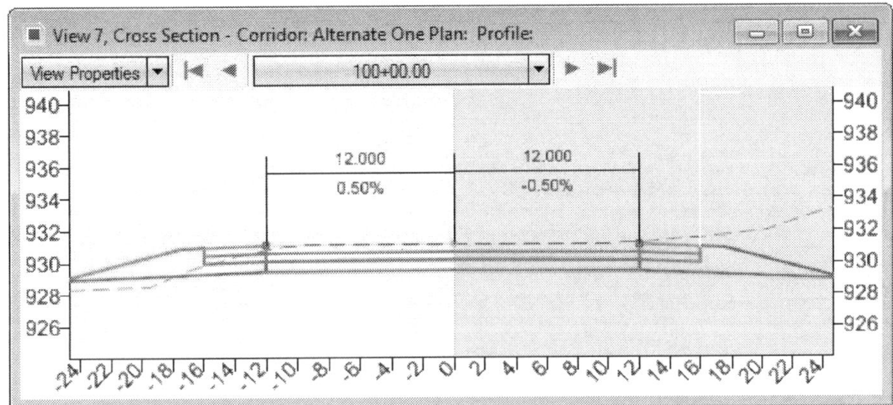

Note: Since the Superelevation was already referenced to the file, it is automatically updated when you return to the corridor.

- Place Temporary Dimensions on the shoulders and step through some of the sections.

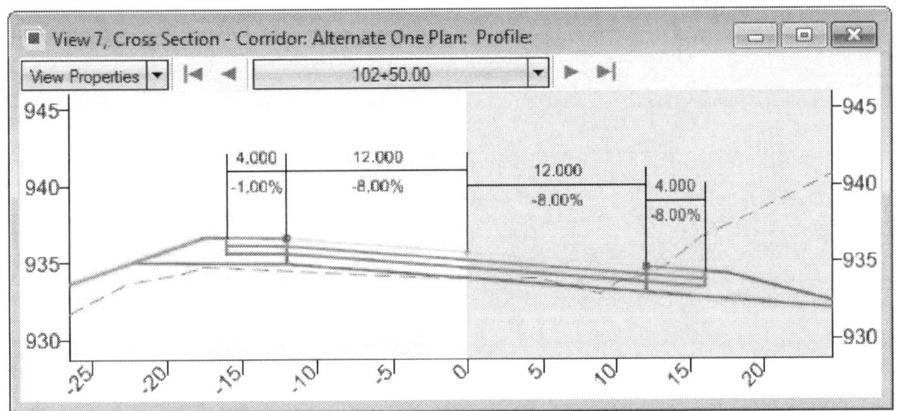

Note the Rollover lock previously established in the template is automatically applied here. If you want more control over the rollover, you can set up the shoulder as a separate superelevated lane.

Ending

16 **Save Settings**

17 **Exit**

Civil Cells

WHAT ARE CIVIL CELLS?

PLACING CIVIL CELLS

EDITING / UPDATING CIVIL CELLS

9 Civil Cells

Civil Cells are similar to regular MicroStation cells in that they prevent you from having to complete repetitive tasks over and over, but they go beyond just graphics. Civil cells perform actions that create geometry and/or corridors, terrains, etc. Creating a cell you basically start with civil geometry (reference elements) and anything ruled from that geometry can be part of the cell. To place the cell, you create a new set of reference geometry and identify it as the location of the cell. All the actions that were used on the reference geometry to create the cell are then applied to the new geometry. Since the actions are all performed again and not just copied into the DGN, the original reference and new reference geometry do not have to be the same size or shape.

For example, create a simple line with Civil Geometry.

Offset the line

Create a civil cell with the first line as the Reference Element

Create a new Civil Geometry

Place the civil cell and the same action is taken on the new reference as on the original, much like running a macro.

9.1 Placing a Civil Cell

➢ **MS: Tasks > Civil Tools > Civil Cells > Place Civil Cell**

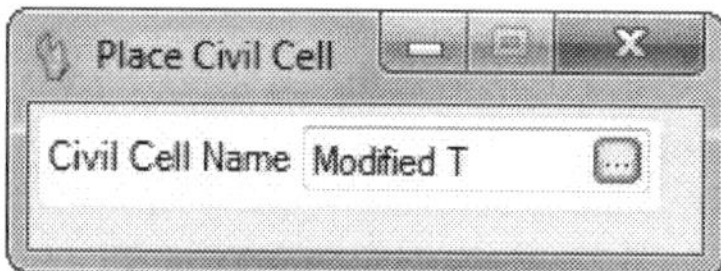

➢ Use the **Browse …** button to open the **Civil Cell** dialog

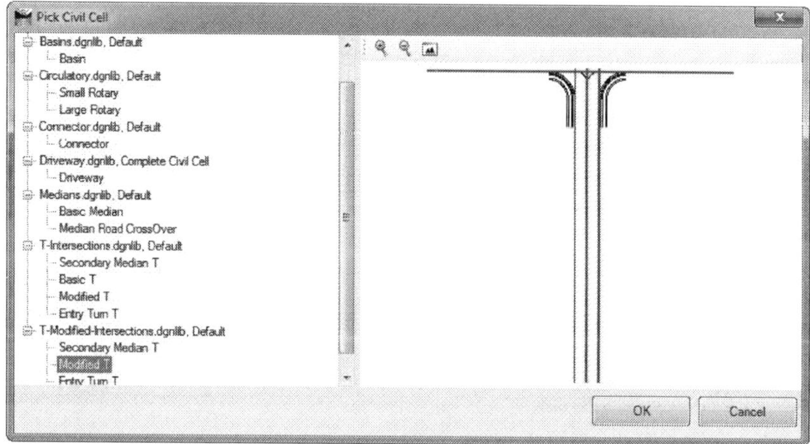

➢ All of the civil cell *DGNLIBs* in the configuration are listed. Expand the one that you want and highlight it. The graphic shows the civil cell in black, and in red the reference elements which you will be prompted to identify during placement. These must be created prior to placing the civil cell.

➢ Highlight and **OK** the civil cell that you would like to place

➢ Select the first reference element as prompted

➢ Continue through the reference elements, selecting them graphically and following the other prompts to change the orientation, etc.

➢ Once the civil cell is placed, you can edit any of the civil elements as normal and the cell updates. The civil cell can also be dropped back to its basic elements.

➢ If you already have civil cells in your file, after you choose **Place Civil Cell**, you can identify an existing one to place it elsewhere, rather than having to go to the *DGNLIB* and choose the same cell again.

Exercise 9: Place a Civil Cell

Given:

- *HWY 60 Alternate One Geometry.dgn* – Previously created proposed alignment.
- *HWY 60 Alternate One Corridor.dgn* – Previously created corridor.
- *Entrance_Rural.dgnlib* – Bentley's entrance Civil Cell

Required:

- Place a previously created Civil Cell
- Modify the Civil Cell parameters
- Modify the Civil Cell location

Getting Started

1 Open your design file

- Start InRoads using the icon on your desktop or using the **Start** menu

2 On the MicroStation manager, set the:

- **User**: ***examples***
- **Project**: ***Bentley-Civil-Imperial***
- **Interface**: ***default***

3 Select the *HWY 60 Alternate One Geometry.dgn* and Open

4 Attach the raster images for reference

- **MS: Primary toolbox > Raster Manager**
- Make sure the **Default** model in view 1 is active
- **File > Attach > Raster**
- Set the **Look in** folder to *c:\Projects\HWY_60\Images*
- Use **<Ctrl>** to select all four *TIF* files or if you have a slower machine, just use *4.tif*

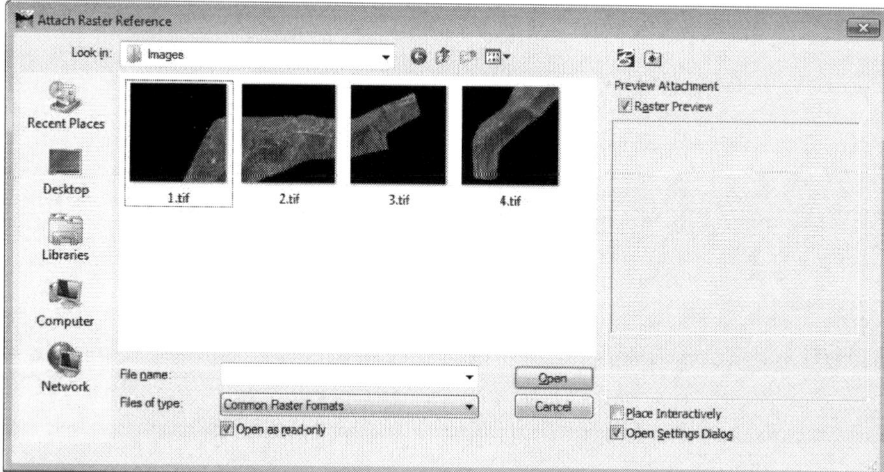

- Select **Open**
- In the **Raster Attachment Options** box, select **Attach**
- **Close** the **Raster Manager**

5 Zoom into the area between stations 112+00 and 114+00.

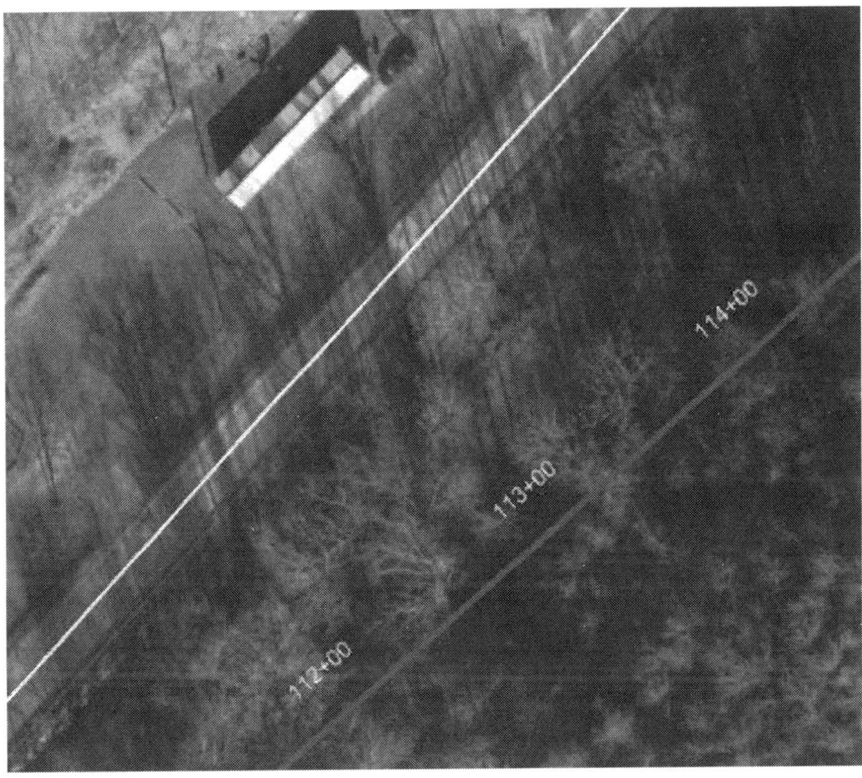

Civil Cell Reference Geometry

6 Using Civil Geometry, draw a horizontal alignment along the existing edge of the road to form the back of the entrance.

- Set the **Feature Definition** to ***Linear > Geometry > Geom_Secondary*** and make sure **Use Active Feature Definition** is turned ***on***

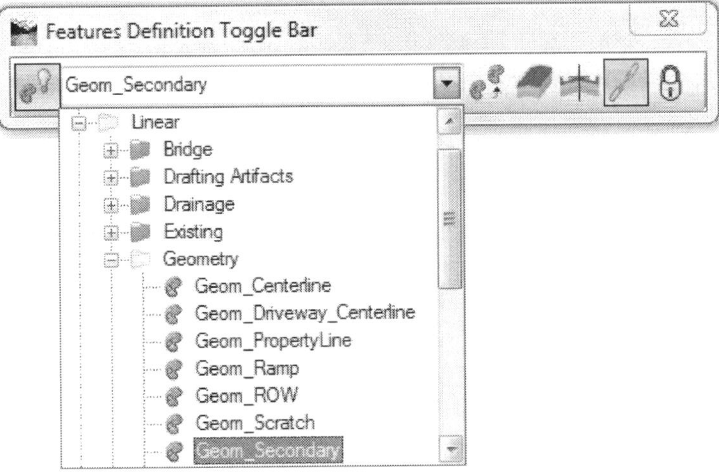

- **MS: Tasks > Civil Tools > Horizontal Geometry > Line Between Points**

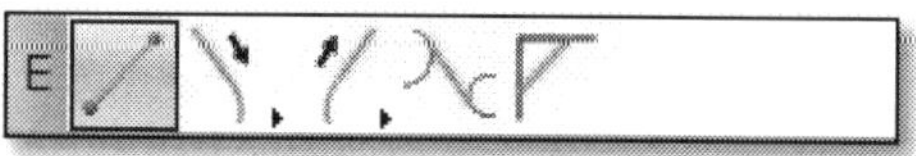

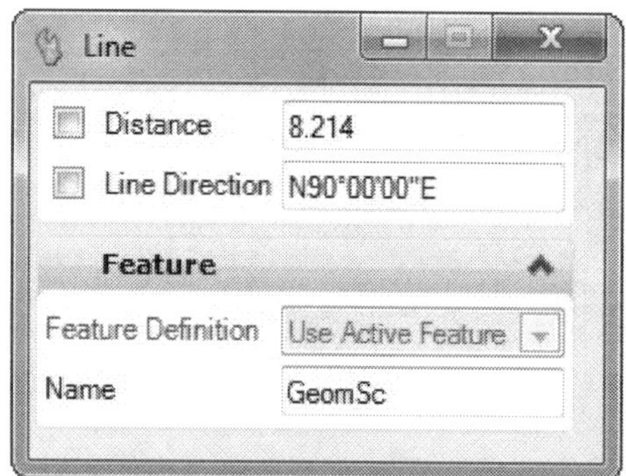

- Sketch a 200' line along the existing edge of pavement approximately between stations 112+00 and 114+00 (the length and direction do not have to be exact)

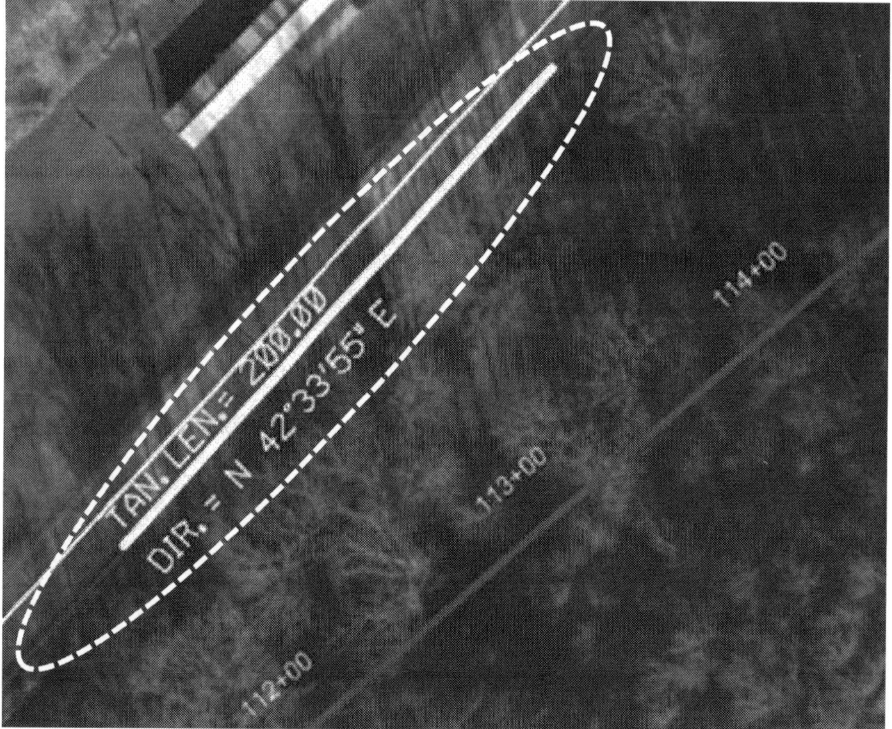

7 Create the centerline of an entrance

- Set the **Feature Definition** to ***Geom_Driveway_Centerline***

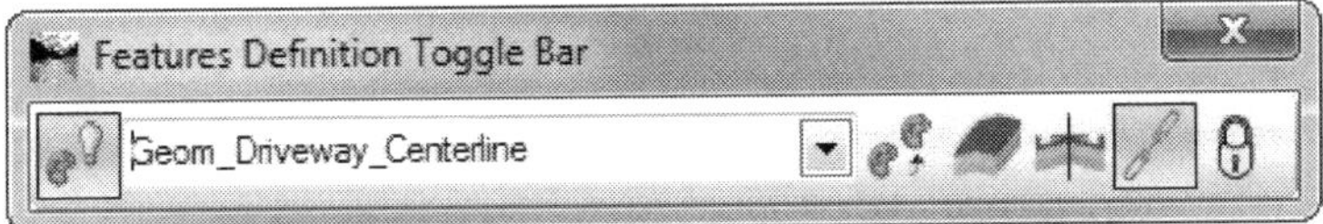

- **MS: Tasks > Civil Tools > Horizontal Geometry > Line to Element**

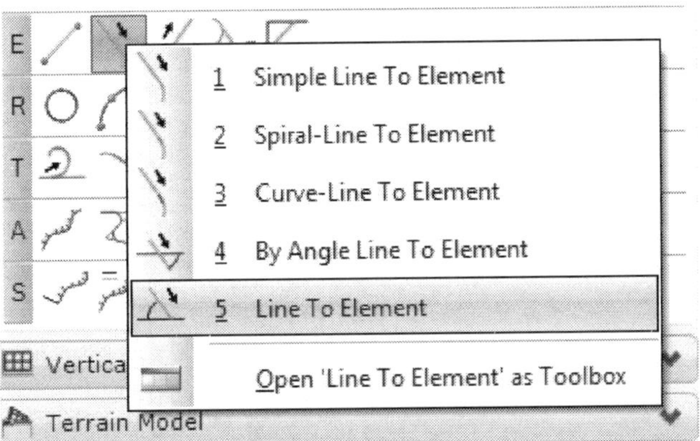

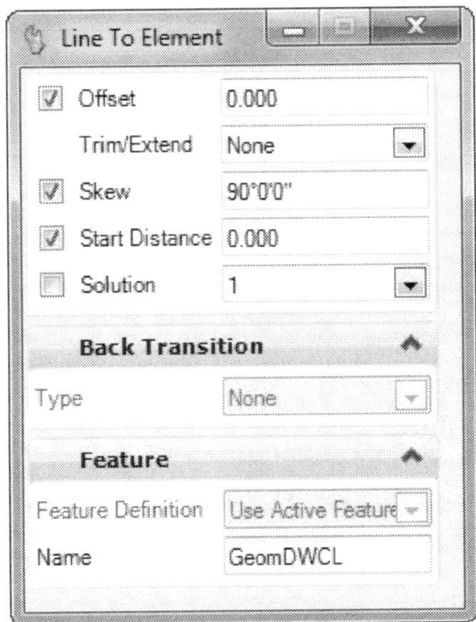

You may either set the dialog up as shown, or change the values as you step through the heads-up prompts.

- *Locate Element*: Choose the proposed centerline HWY 60 Alternate One CL
- *Enter Offset*: **0.00**
- **<D>** to Accept

- *Enter EndPoint*: At approximately 113+00, choose a point close to the centerline of the existing roadway

- **Skew**: **90^0'0" <D>**
- **Start Distance**: **0.000 <D>**
- **Trim/Extend**: **None <D>**

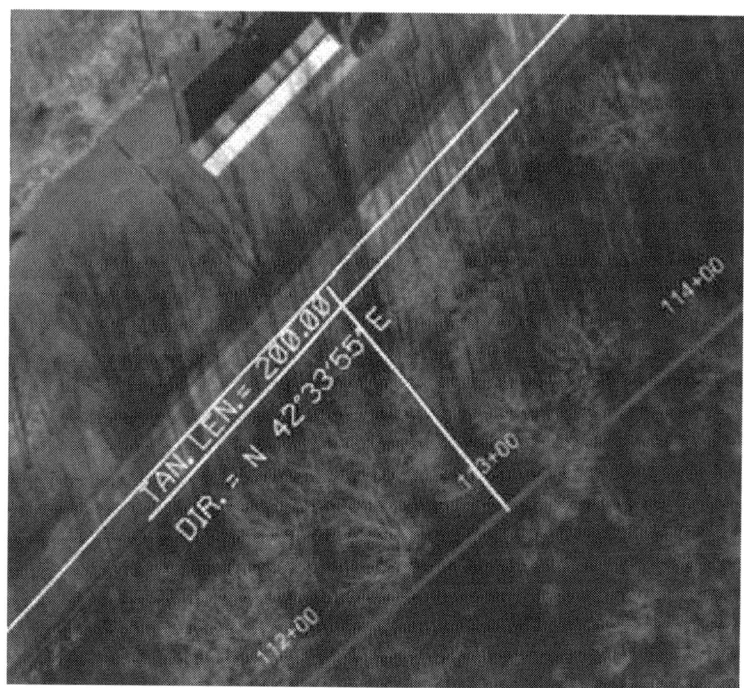

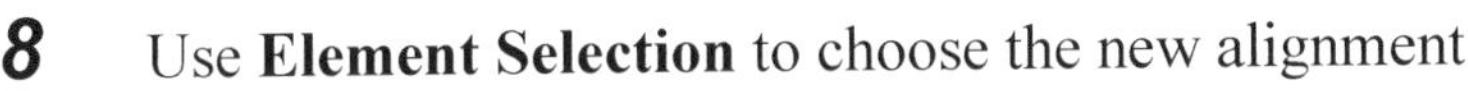

8 Use **Element Selection** to choose the new alignment

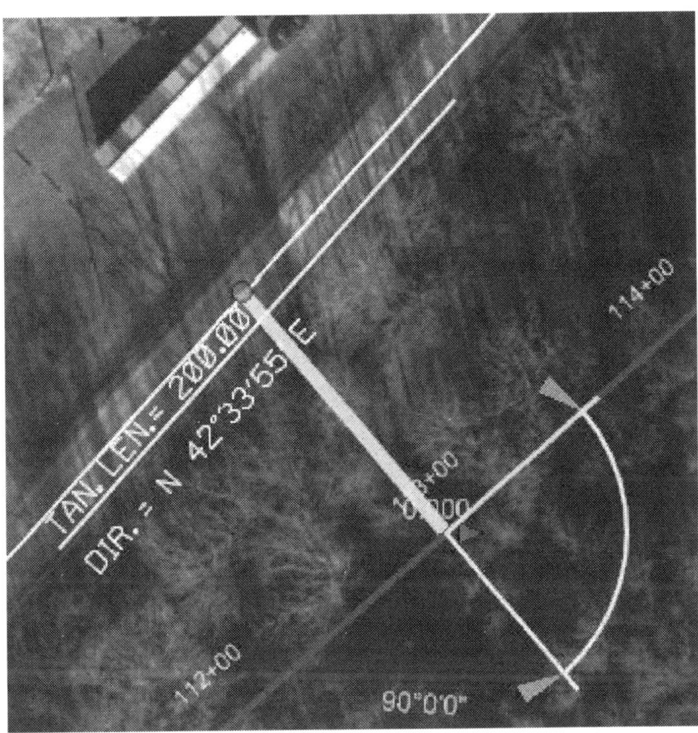

Note that you can change the Skew, Offset or End Point.

9 **Detach** the Rasters and **Save Settings**

10 Open *HWY 60 Alternate One Corridor.dgn*

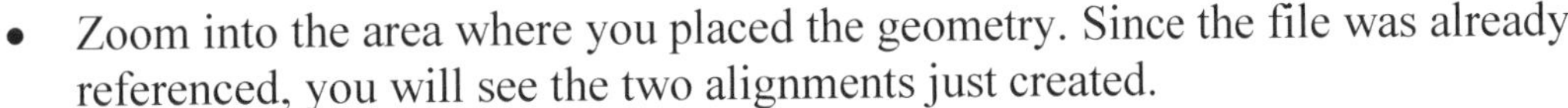

- Zoom into the area where you placed the geometry. Since the file was already referenced, you will see the two alignments just created.

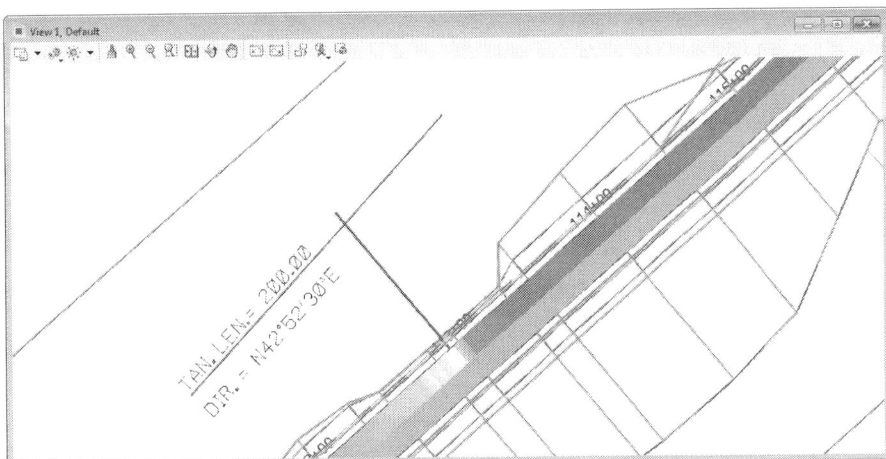

Civil Cell Placement

11 Place a civil cell

- **MS: Tasks > Civil Tools > Civil Cells > Place Civil Cell**

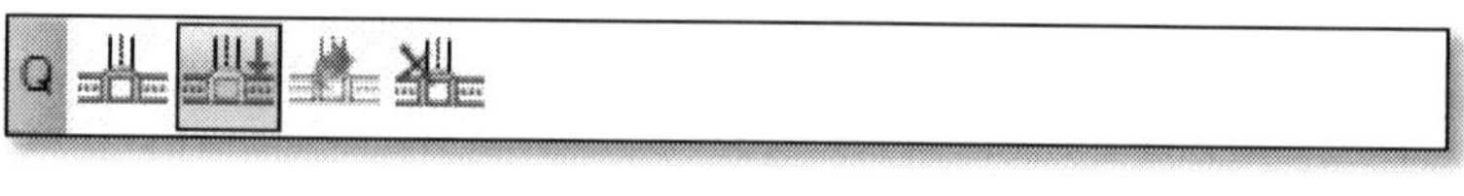

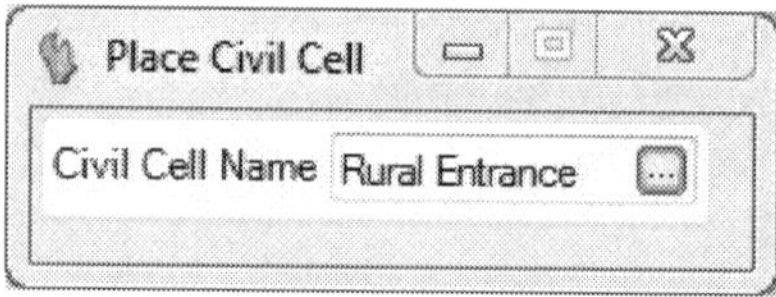

- Select the **...** button and then select the *Rural Entrance* from the *Entrance_Rural.dgnlib* file

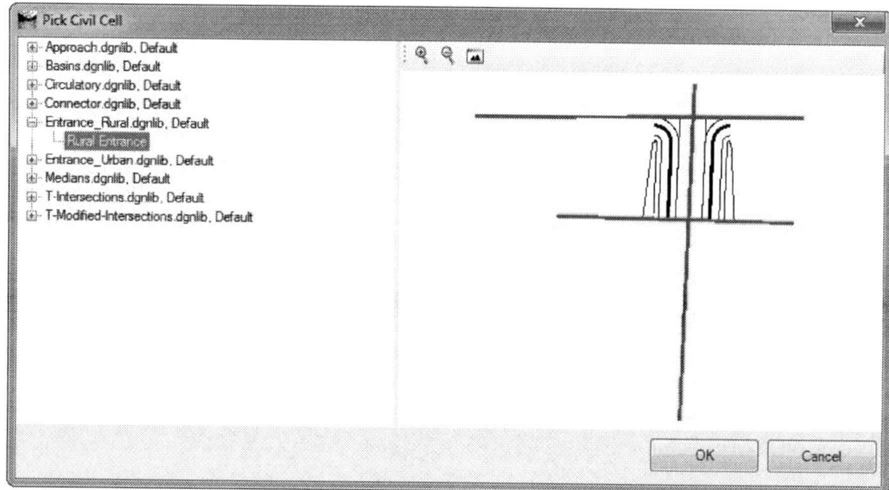

- **OK**

  Follow the heads-up prompts

- *Locate Reference Element: Entrance Centerline*: Choose the alignment that extends from the Existing roadway to the Proposed
- *Locate Reference Element: Mainline Edge Pavt.*: Choose the edge of pavement from the corridor

You may need to hover over it to make certain you are choosing the correct element.

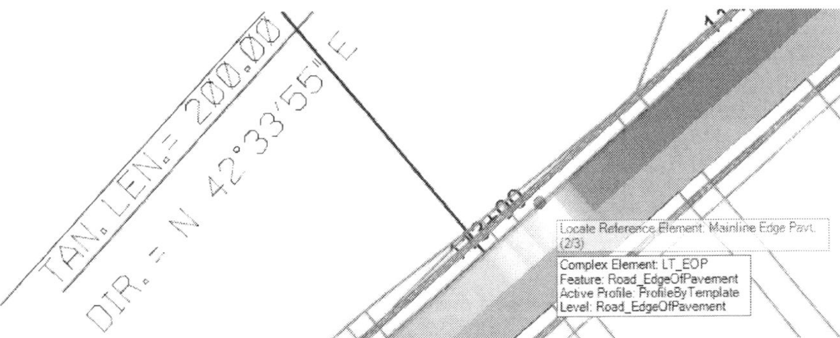

- *Locate Reference Element: Entrance Back*: Choose the alignment you created along the Existing Edge of Pavement
- **Reset** *to Skip Alternatives* (there are none for this case)
- *Select Corridors to be Clipped*: Choose one of the handles for the proposed corridor, then **Reset** to Complete

  Note: The corridor does not have to be clipped at this time. It can be clipped later, or the template through this area may be modified to remove the unnecessary components using display rules, end condition exceptions, etc.

- **<D>** to Accept the Civil Cell Placement

  Be patient! The software will go into a processing mode for a minute to create the entrance and model it, along with clipping the mainline.

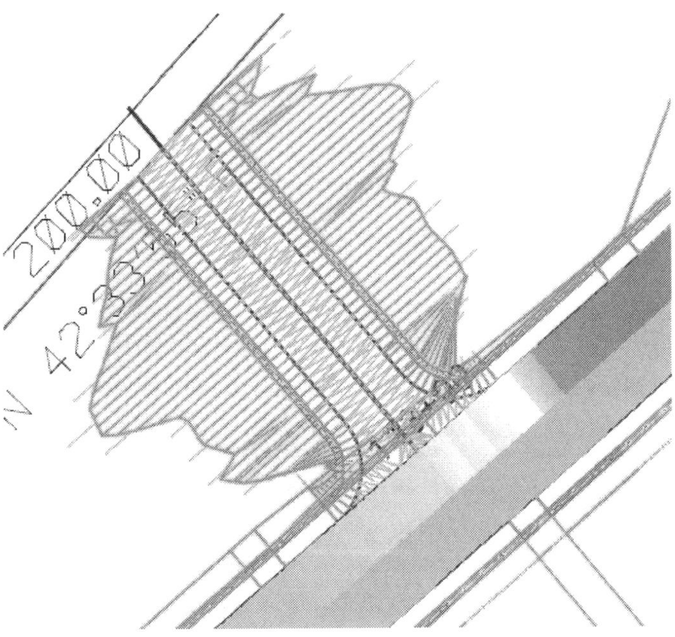

12 If the Cell did not place correctly, you can Undo or you can select the Cell and choose **Delete**

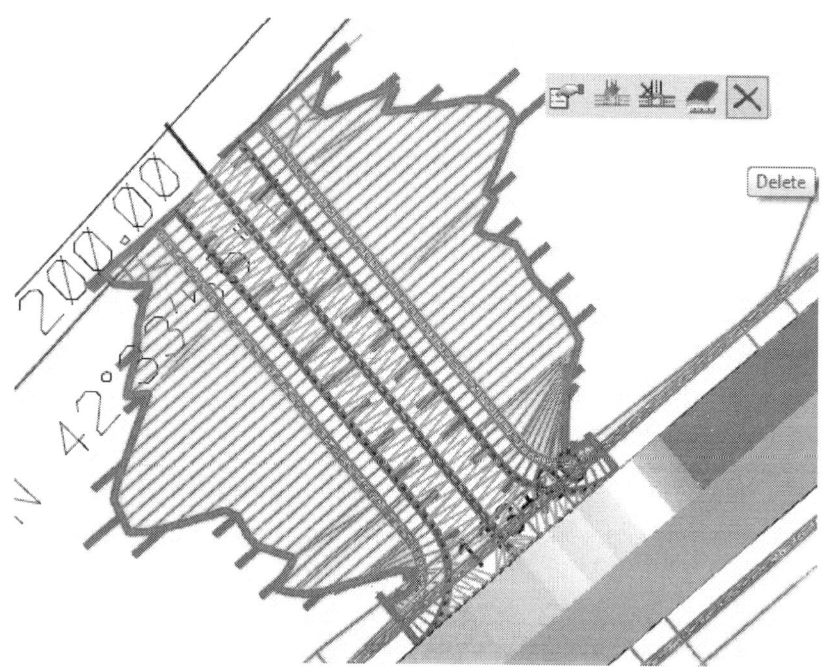

13 Open the 3D model and look at the cell

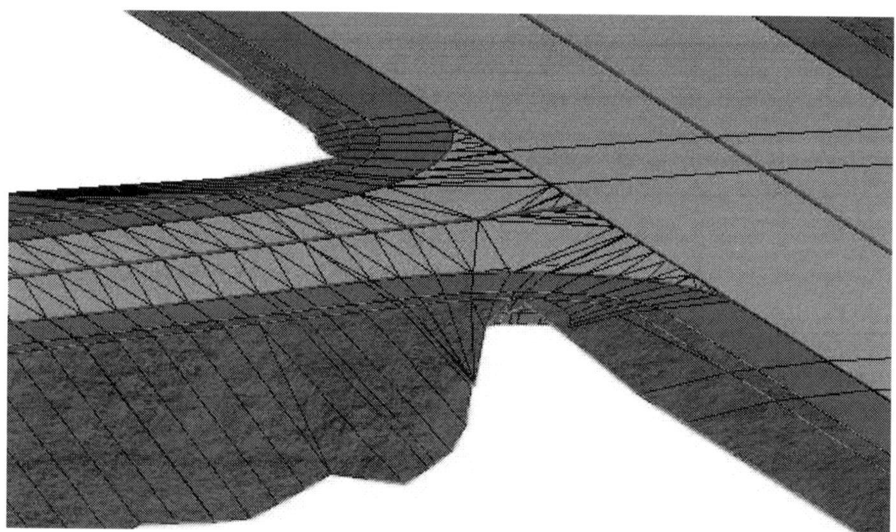

Note how the entrance ties into the proposed edge of pavement even through the Superelevation transition. Depending upon how the slopes tie in, there may be additional clean-up required.

Civil Cell Edits

14 Back in the Default (2D) model, select the *RT_DW_Edge* line (first geometry line beside the entrance centerline) in the plan view

Since the Civil Cell was built with Civil Geometry, it remembers the rules used to create it and you can now adjust those rules.

- Using the **Offset** in the ***center*** of the cell, change the value to **5**.
- Repeat for the other side, making it **– 5** (make sure to include the negative sign)

- Change the radius of the upper return to 25 and note how everything adjusts accordingly.

15 Right-Click on the Entrance Alignment and choose **Activate**

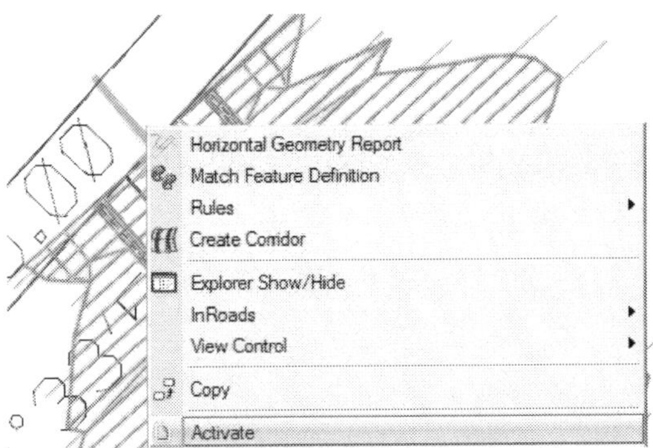

This activates the reference file where the alignment was created. Everything in the current file turns gray, since it is no longer active. You can now edit the alignment.

- Select the entrance alignment and change the **Skew** to **80^** and the civil cell updates to the new location and heals the corridor

Note: If the civil cell does not automatically update, Deactivate the reference and process the corridor.

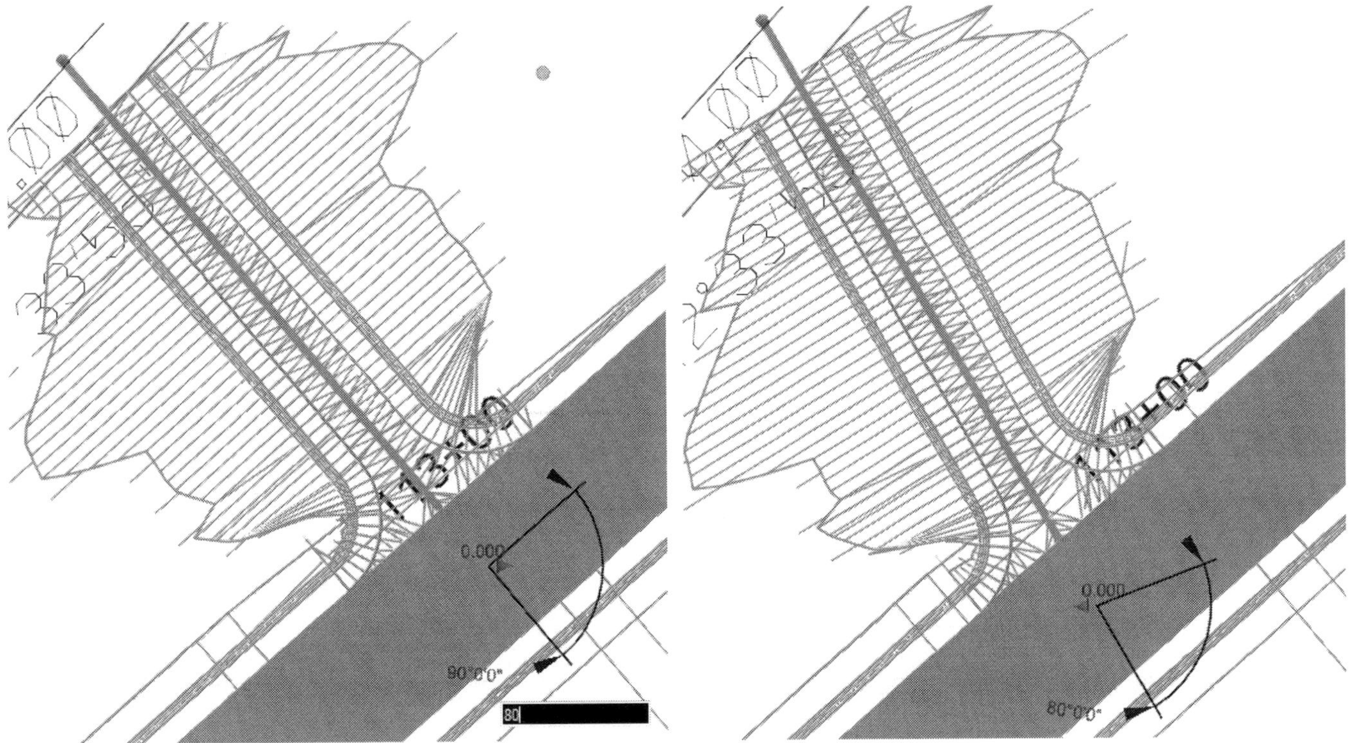

- Change the skew back to **90^00'00"**

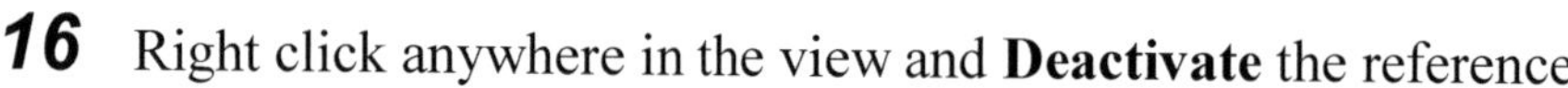

16 Right click anywhere in the view and **Deactivate** the reference

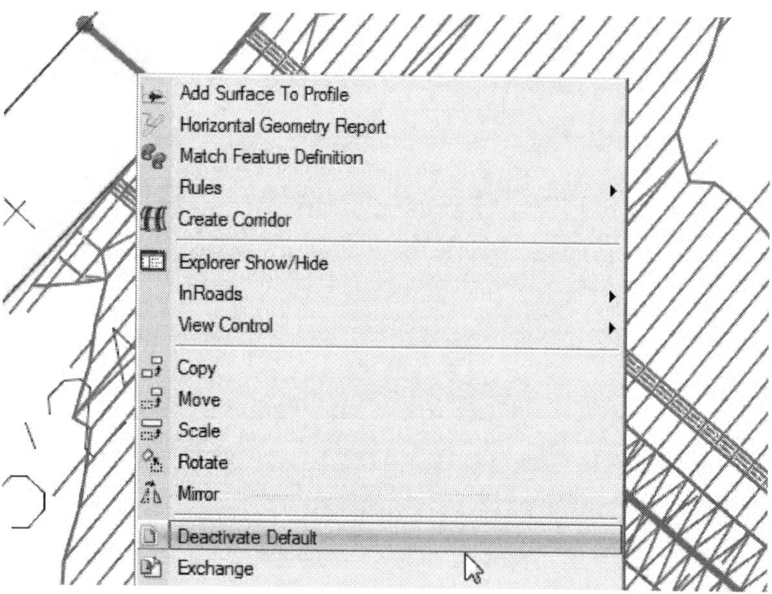

Ending

17 **Save Settings**

18 **Exit** MicroStation.

If asked to save the geometry project, select ***No***

Cross Sections

CREATING CROSS SECTIONS

ANNOTATING CROSS SECTIONS

CALCULATING VOLUMES

10 Cross Sections

The dynamic sections created for review purposes during your design are not printable. Therefore, you must create a set of sections whenever you want to plot to paper or PDF.

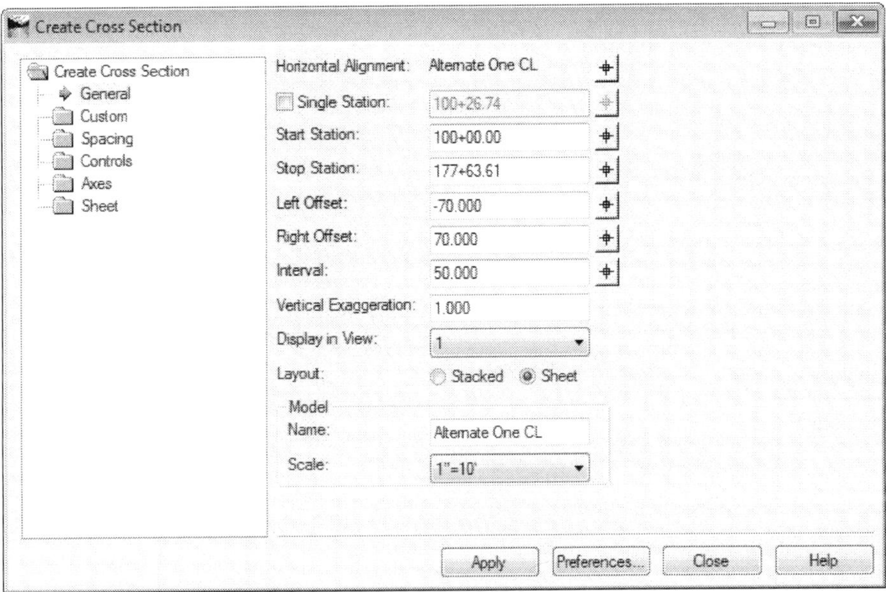

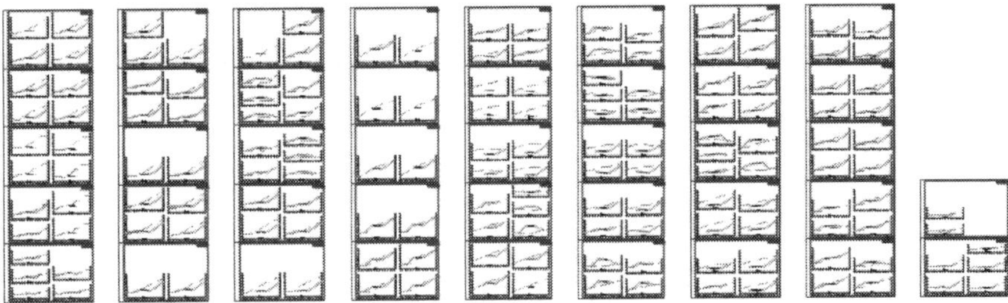

10.1 Creating cross sections

When creating cross sections, the current **Design Stage** of the corridor affects what you will see in the resulting sections. To see the proposed surface, you must have one of the Design Stages that includes more than just the linear features. For example, you can use **Final** or **Design**. Here, we'll use Stage **4 Final w/Linear + Meshes**.

➢ **MS: Tasks > Civil Tools > Corridor Modeling > Create Cross Sections**

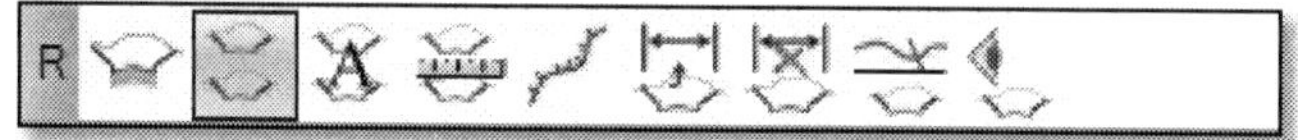

➢ Select the horizontal geometry you want to cut sections along

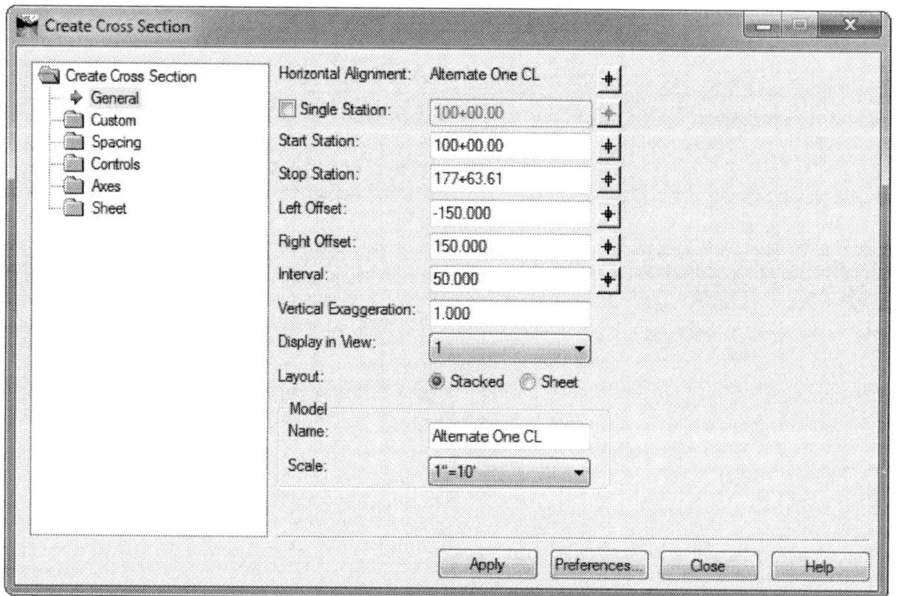

- Select **Preferences** and choose the preference that you would like to use, then **Load**
- Make any changes to the settings you wish
- Select the View for the initial display (you can see them in any view later)
- Key in a **Name** for the **Model** (or you can accept the default name)

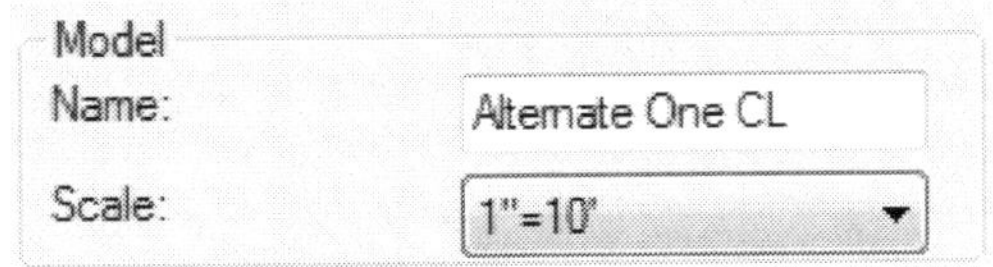

- Choose **Apply**

A MicroStation model is created for each set of cross sections. The preferences are set up to use an Annotation Scale. The text does have Annotation Scale turned on, so changes to the Drawing Scale will change the text.

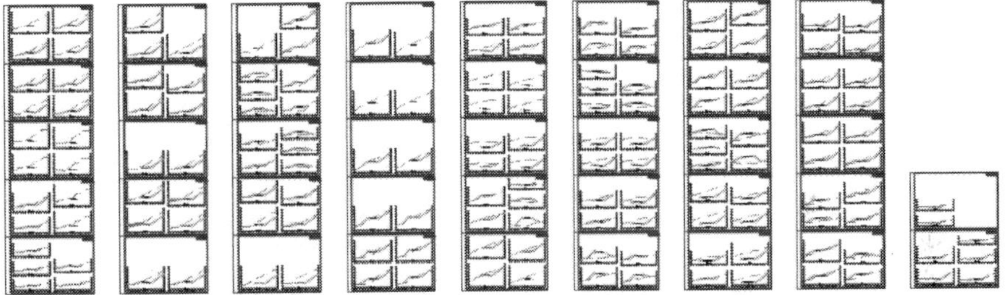

- You can return to this model any time you want to review, annotate or plot the sections.

10.2 Annotating Cross Sections

Once the sections are cut, you may annotate them very similar to the way you annotated in previous versions.

➢ **MS: Tasks > Civil Tools > Corridor Modeling > Annotate Cross Sections**

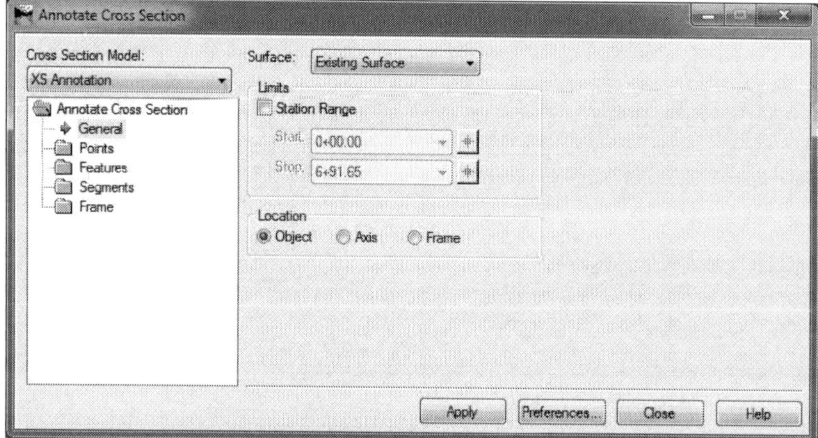

➢ Specify the **Cross Section Model** that you would like to Annotate

➢ Select **Preferences** and **Load** the appropriate preference

To annotate specific features

➢ Select the **Features** category

➢ Select **Annotate**

➢ Choose the **Crossing Feature** or **Features** you would like to annotate

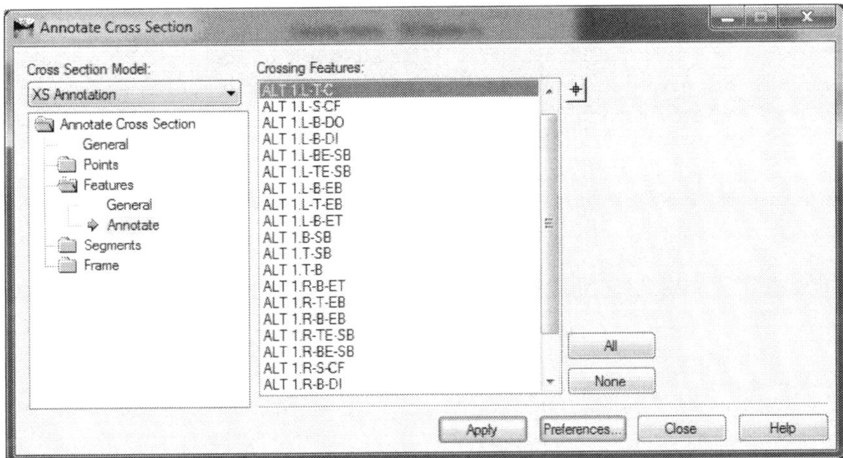

➢ Choose **Apply**

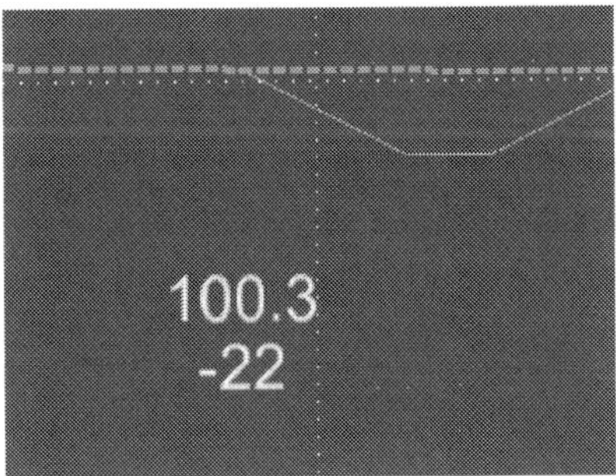

➢ **Close** the dialog when done

10.3 Calculate Volumes

There are multiple methods you can use to calculate volumes. Here, we'll look at a couple of them.

End-Area from Sections

To use this method, first create a set of cross sections showing the existing and proposed design.

➢ **MS: Tasks > Civil Tools > Corridor Modeling > End Area Volume**

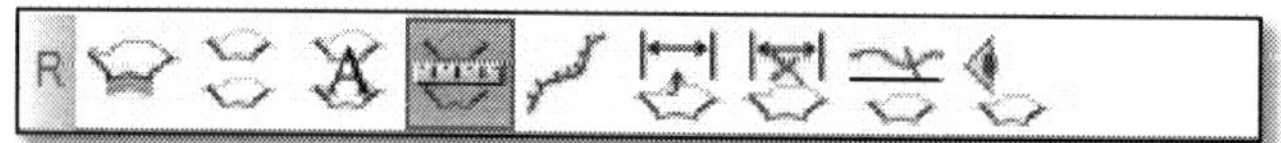

➢ Follow the heads-up prompt to choose the horizontal alignment

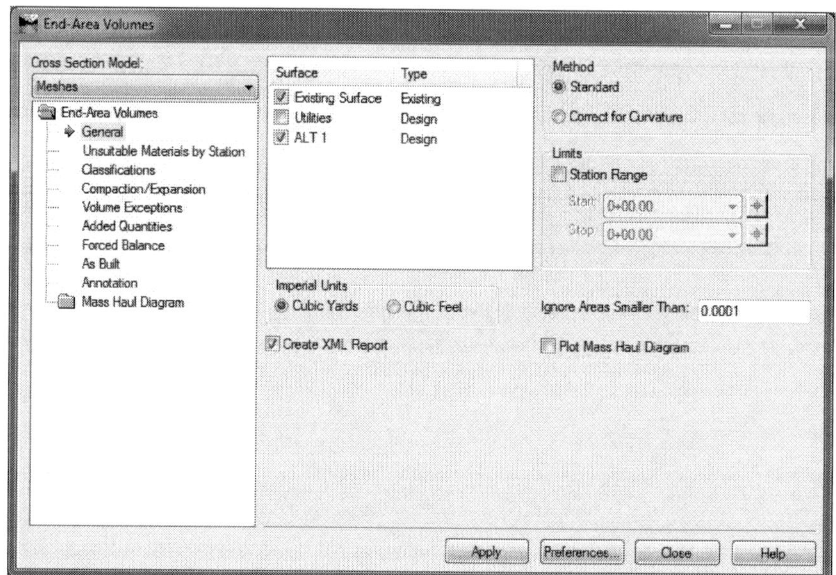

➢ Select **Preferences** and **Load** the appropriate preference

➢ Make any changes you wish to the settings

➢ Choose **Apply**

➤ If **Create XML Report** is toggled on, the **Report Browser** opens automatically and a report is shown.

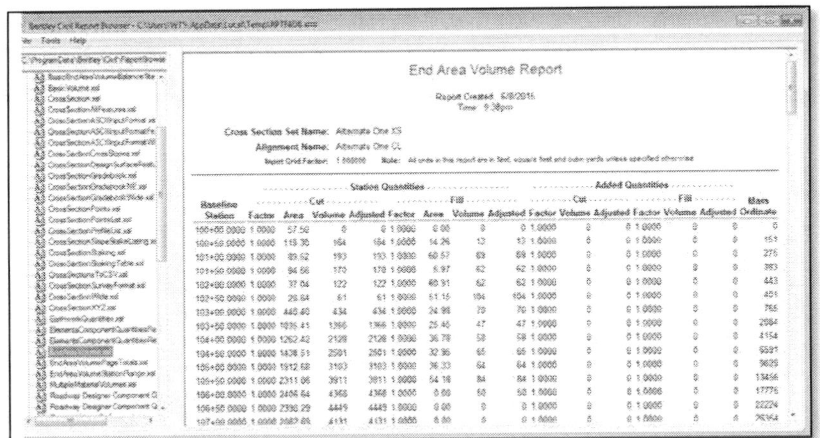

End Area Volume Report

Report Created: 6/8/2016
Time: 9:38pm

Cross Section Set Name: Alternate One XS
Alignment Name: Alternate One CL

Baseline Station	Station Quantities: Cut Factor	Cut Area	Cut Volume	Cut Adjusted	Fill Factor	Fill Area	Fill Volume	Fill Adjusted	Added Quantities: Cut Factor	Cut Volume	Cut Adjusted	Fill Factor	Fill Volume	Fill Adjusted	Mass Ordinate
100+00.0000	1.0000	57.50	0	0	1.0000	0.00	0	0	1.0000	0	0	1.0000	0	0	0
100+50.0000	1.0000	113.30	164	164	1.0000	14.26	13	13	1.0000	0	0	1.0000	0	0	151
101+00.0000	1.0000	89.52	193	193	1.0000	60.57	69	69	1.0000	0	0	1.0000	0	0	275
101+50.0000	1.0000	94.56	170	170	1.0000	5.97	62	62	1.0000	0	0	1.0000	0	0	383
102+00.0000	1.0000	37.04	122	122	1.0000	60.91	62	62	1.0000	0	0	1.0000	0	0	443
102+50.0000	1.0000	28.84	61	61	1.0000	51.15	104	104	1.0000	0	0	1.0000	0	0	401
103+00.0000	1.0000	440.40	434	434	1.0000	24.98	70	70	1.0000	0	0	1.0000	0	0	765
103+50.0000	1.0000	1036.41	1366	1366	1.0000	25.40	47	47	1.0000	0	0	1.0000	0	0	2084
104+00.0000	1.0000	1262.42	2128	2128	1.0000	36.78	58	58	1.0000	0	0	1.0000	0	0	4154
104+50.0000	1.0000	1438.51	2501	2501	1.0000	32.36	65	65	1.0000	0	0	1.0000	0	0	6591
105+00.0000	1.0000	1912.68	3103	3103	1.0000	36.33	64	64	1.0000	0	0	1.0000	0	0	9625
105+50.0000	1.0000	2311.06	3911	3911	1.0000	54.18	84	84	1.0000	0	0	1.0000	0	0	13456
106+00.0000	1.0000	2404.64	4368	4368	1.0000	0.00	50	50	1.0000	0	0	1.0000	0	0	17775
106+50.0000	1.0000	2398.29	4449	4449	1.0000	0.00	0	0	1.0000	0	0	1.0000	0	0	22224
107+00.0000	1.0000	2087.65	4131	4131	1.0000	0.00	0	0	1.0000	0	0	1.0000	0	0	26354

➤ You may change the format by selecting another option from the list at the left

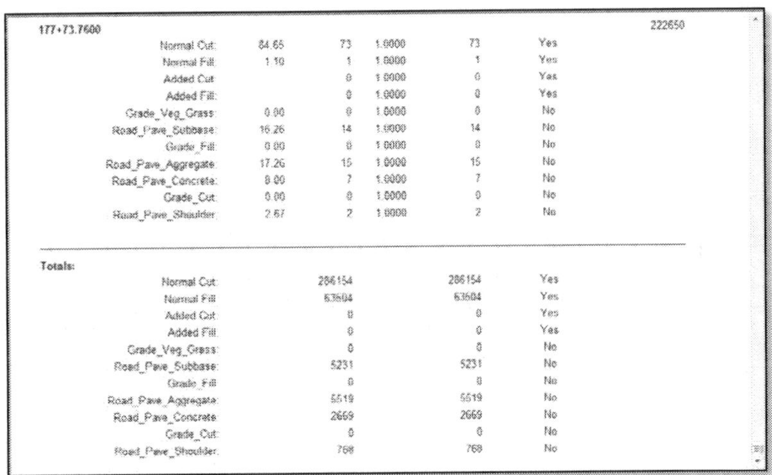

177+73.7600						222650
Normal Cut:	84.65	73	1.0000	73	Yes	
Normal Fill:	1.10	1	1.0000	1	Yes	
Added Cut:		0	1.0000	0	Yes	
Added Fill:		0	1.0000	0	Yes	
Grade_Veg_Grass:	0.00	0	1.0000	0	No	
Road_Pave_Subbase:	16.26	14	1.0000	14	No	
Grade_Fill:	0.00	0	1.0000	0	No	
Road_Pave_Aggregate:	17.26	15	1.0000	15	No	
Road_Pave_Concrete:	8.00	7	1.0000	7	No	
Grade_Cut:	0.00	0	1.0000	0	No	
Road_Pave_Shoulder:	2.67	2	1.0000	2	No	
Totals:						
Normal Cut:		286154		286154	Yes	
Normal Fill:		63604		63604	Yes	
Added Cut:		0		0	Yes	
Added Fill:		0		0	Yes	
Grade_Veg_Grass:		0		0	No	
Road_Pave_Subbase:		5231		5231	No	
Grade_Fill:		0		0	No	
Road_Pave_Aggregate:		5519		5519	No	
Road_Pave_Concrete:		2669		2669	No	
Grade_Cut:		0		0	No	
Road_Pave_Shoulder:		768		768	No	

Notice in the report above, there is a category for Grade_Veg_Grass, Grade_Cut and Grade_Fill, none of which contain volumes.

These could have been eliminated from the report by selecting the ***Classifications*** *category in* ***End Are Volumes*** *and toggling the* ***Classification*** *to* **Ignore**.

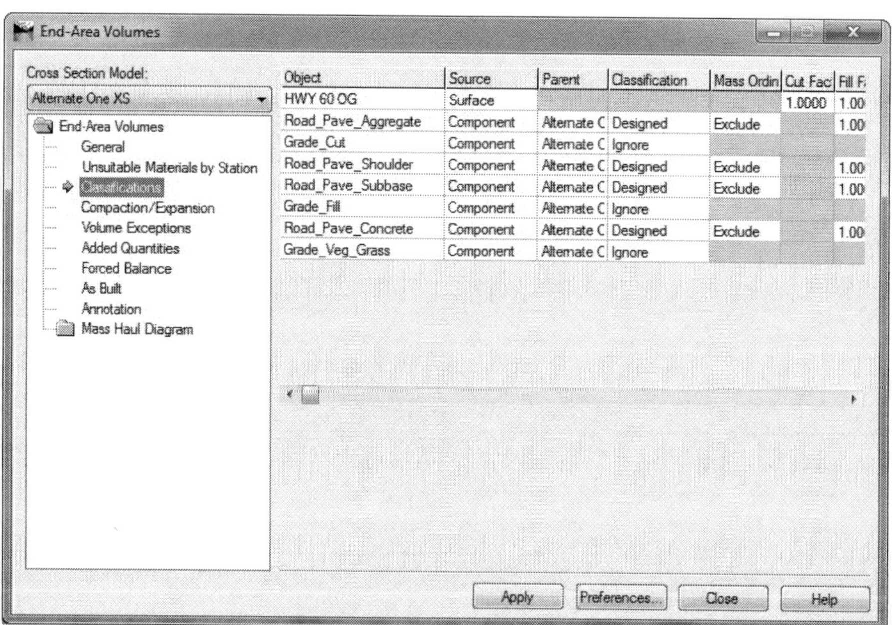

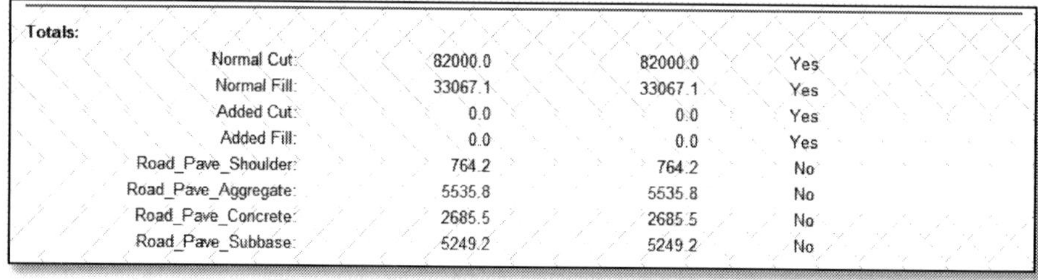

Totals:

Normal Cut:	82000.0	82000.0	Yes
Normal Fill:	33067.1	33067.1	Yes
Added Cut:	0.0	0.0	Yes
Added Fill:	0.0	0.0	Yes
Road_Pave_Shoulder:	764.2	764.2	No
Road_Pave_Aggregate:	5535.8	5535.8	No
Road_Pave_Concrete:	2685.5	2685.5	No
Road_Pave_Subbase:	5249.2	5249.2	No

Component Volumes

Another method of computing volumes it to use **Component Quantities**

➢ **MS: Tasks > Civil Tools > Corridor Modeling > Component Quantities**

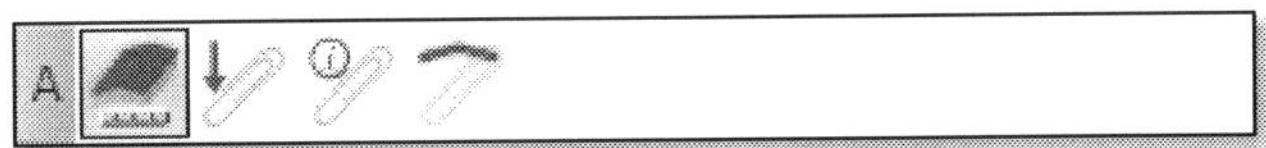

➢ Follow the head-up prompt to select the corridor

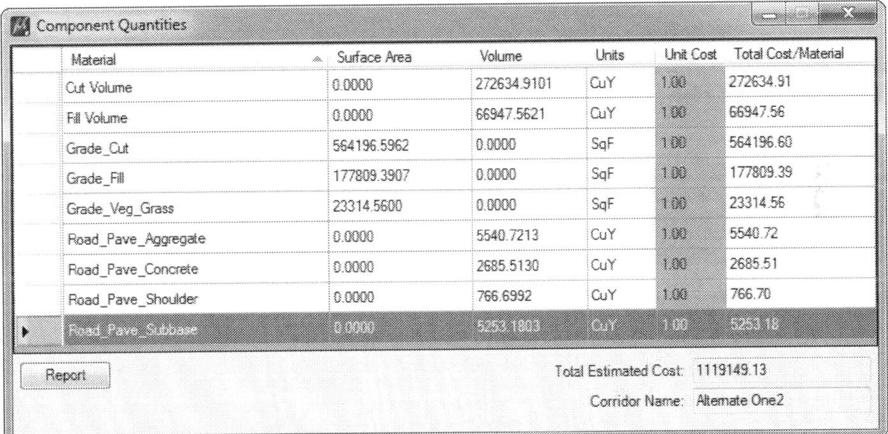

Material	Surface Area	Volume	Units	Unit Cost	Total Cost/Material
Cut Volume	0.0000	272634.9101	CuY	1.00	272634.91
Fill Volume	0.0000	66947.5621	CuY	1.00	66947.56
Grade_Cut	564196.5962	0.0000	SqF	1.00	564196.60
Grade_Fill	177809.3907	0.0000	SqF	1.00	177809.39
Grade_Veg_Grass	23314.5600	0.0000	SqF	1.00	23314.56
Road_Pave_Aggregate	0.0000	5540.7213	CuY	1.00	5540.72
Road_Pave_Concrete	0.0000	2685.5130	CuY	1.00	2685.51
Road_Pave_Shoulder	0.0000	766.6992	CuY	1.00	766.70
Road_Pave_Subbase	0.0000	5253.1803	CuY	1.00	5253.18

➢ The volume is computed based on the corridor itself instead of sections. Any components that are closed result in a quantity. Any components that are not result in an area. You can type Costs into the **Unit Cost** field and the **Total Estimated Cost** at the bottom updates.

➢ Select **Report** to see a station by station report, similar to the **End Area** report

Exercise 10: Cross Sections

Given:

- *HWY 60 Alternate One Corridor.dgn* – Corridor with Terrain, Alignments and Superelevation referenced

Required:

- Attach the ROW as a reference if not already attached
- Set the appropriate Design Stage
- Create Cross Sections
- Annotate the Cross Sections (nearly identical to SS2)
- Compute End Area Volumes (nearly identical to SS2)

Getting Started

1 Start InRoads using the icon on your desktop or using the **Start** menu

2 On the MicroStation manager, set the:

- **User**: **examples**
- **Project**: **Bentley-Civil-Imperial**
- **Interface**: **default**

3 Open the File: *HWY 60 Alternate One Corridor.dgn*

- Reference the *HWY 60 Alternate One ROW.dgn* file with no nesting if it's not already referenced.

4 Set the Design Stage

- Select the Corridor
- On the menu, select **Properties**

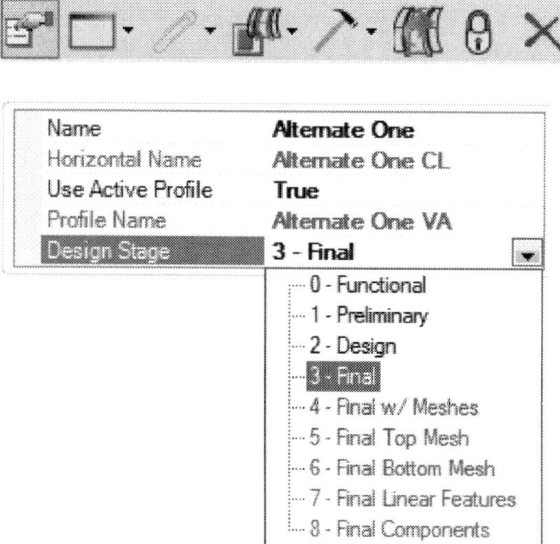

- Change the **Design Stage** to ***3 - Final***

Cross Section Creation

5 Create Cross Sections

- **MS: Tasks > Civil Tools > Corridor Modeling > Create Cross Sections**

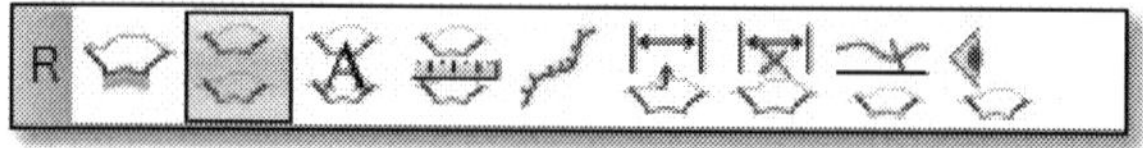

- When prompted, select the Horizontal Alignment

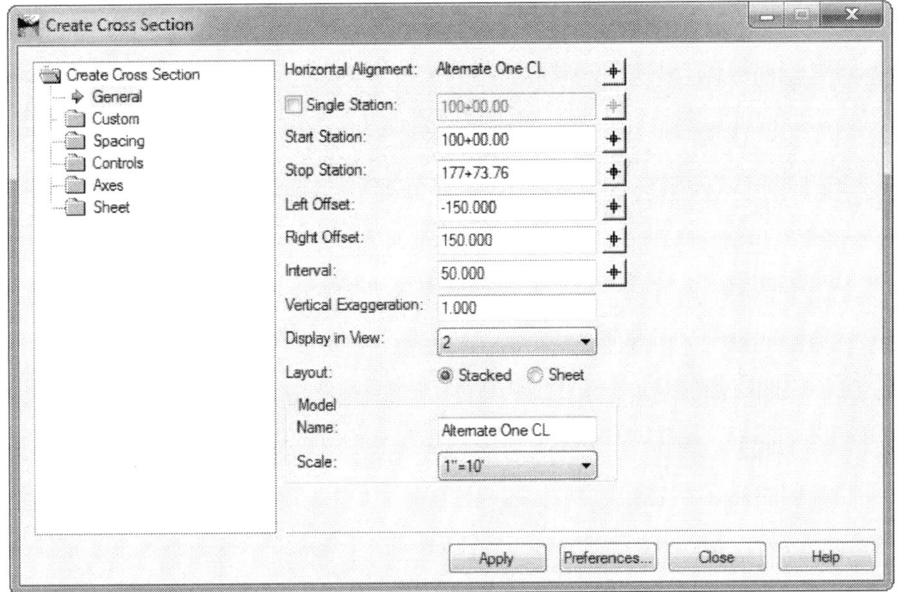

- Select **Preferences**

- Load **Stacked – w/Grid and Axis**

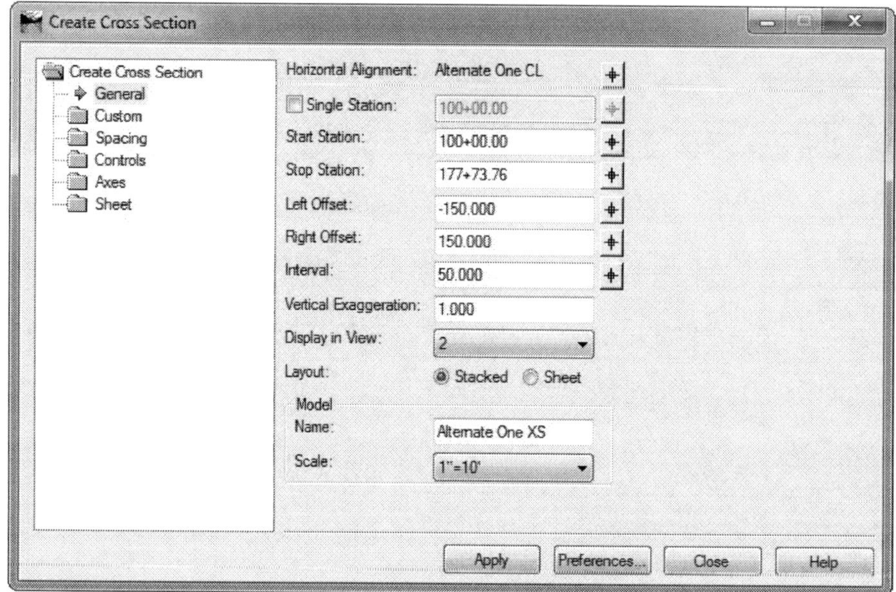

- Change the **Model Name** to **Alternate One XS**

  Note a new MicroStation model is created for the cross sections, within the active design file.

- Choose **Apply**

  The new model is created and displayed containing the cross sections.

- Close the **Create Cross Section** box

Using SS3 and cells appear too large?

Look at the Right of Way cell. If it appears too large, it may be because the text scale factor was erroneously applied to the cell (commonly happens in earlier versions of InRoads). If that has happened with yours (or additional cells like utilities) follow the next step. Otherwise, **skip this step**.

6 Correct the cell size ***if necessary***

- **MS Tasks > Drawing > Replace Cells**

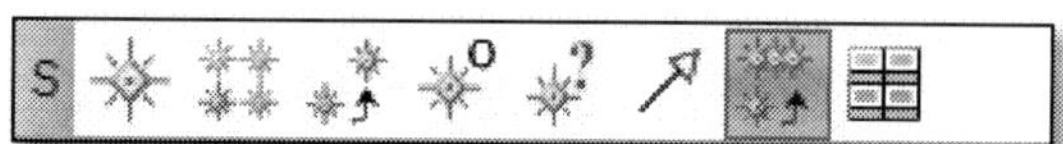

- Set the **Method** to ***Update***
- **Mode** to ***Global***
- Then select one of the Right of Way cells

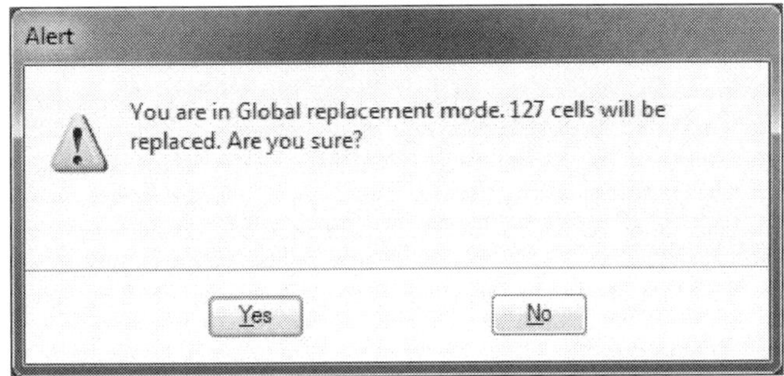

- When the Alert appears select **Yes** (your number will vary)

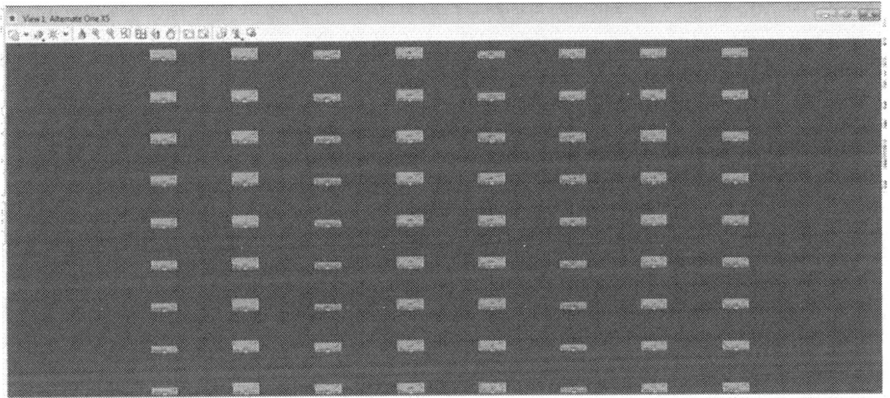

- Zoom in and review some of the section

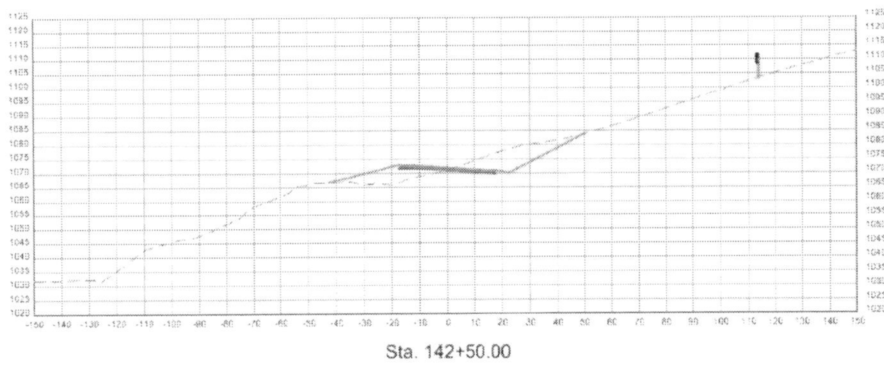

- You can change the **Drawing Scale** to change the size of the text if desired.

Cross Section Annotation

7 Annotate Cross Sections

- **MS: Tasks > Civil Tools > Corridor Modeling > Annotate Cross Sections**

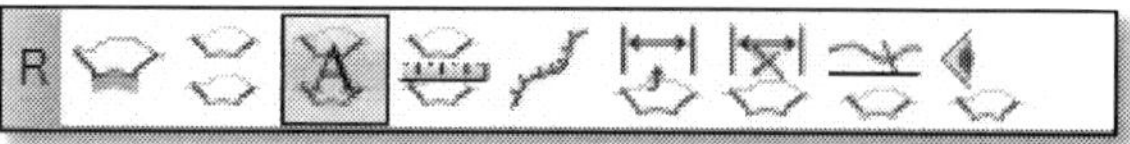

- If you have created more than one set of sections, make certain the Cross Section Model listed is the one you want to annotate

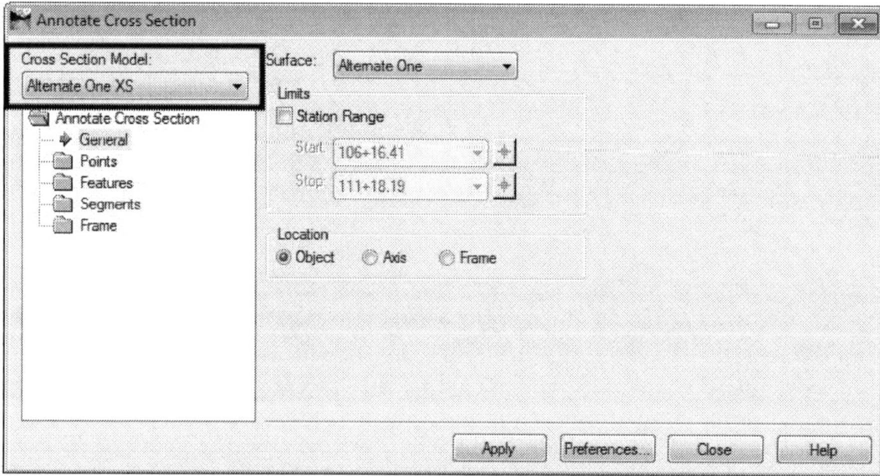

- Set the **Surface** to ***Alternate One***
- Select **Points** and toggle off **Include Points**
- Select **Features** and toggle off **Include Features**
- Select **Segments** and toggle on **Include Segments**
- **Apply** and zoom in on one section to see the results.

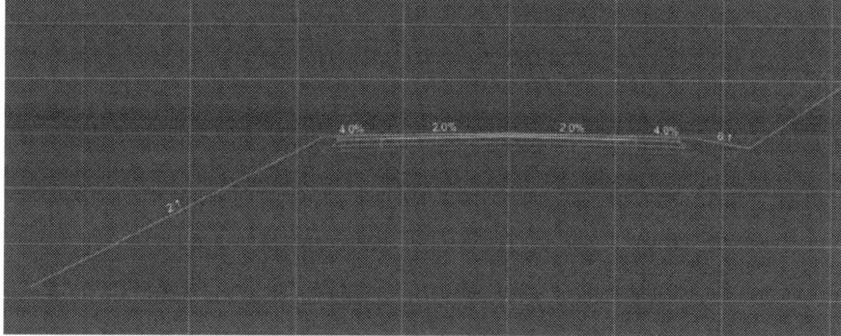

- **Undo** and then change any settings you'd like before Applying Again.
- **Undo** once again and choose **Features**

- Toggle on **Include Features**
- Select **Annotate** and highlight the **EOPs** and the **Construction Limits**

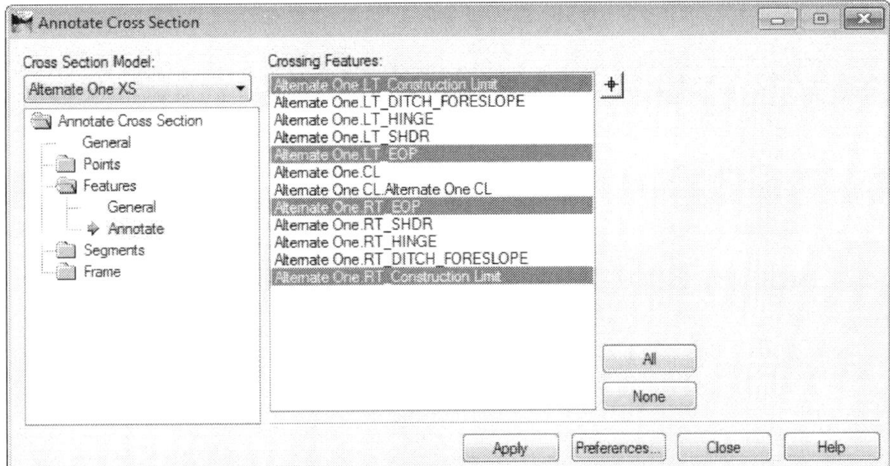

- **Apply** and zoom into one of the sections to see the results

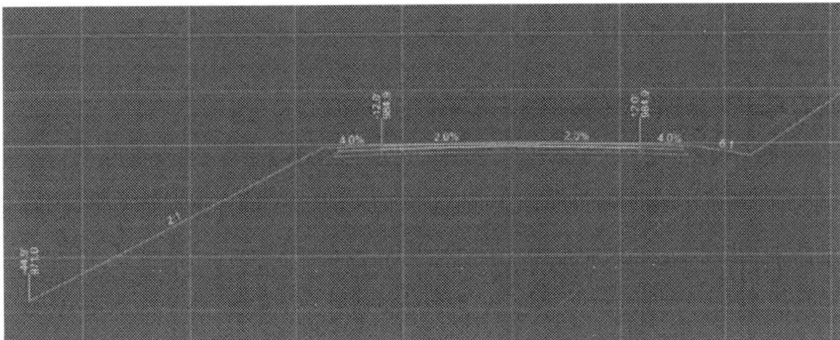

- Continue experimenting with any other annotations you would like
- **Close** the dialog when done

End Area Volumes

8 Compute End Area Volumes

- **MS: Tasks > Civil Tools > Corridor Modeling > End Area Volume**

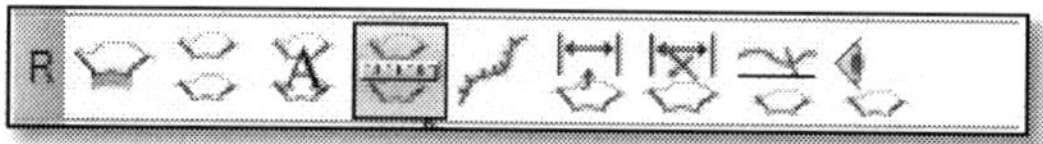

- Make certain the correct Cross Section **Model** is selected

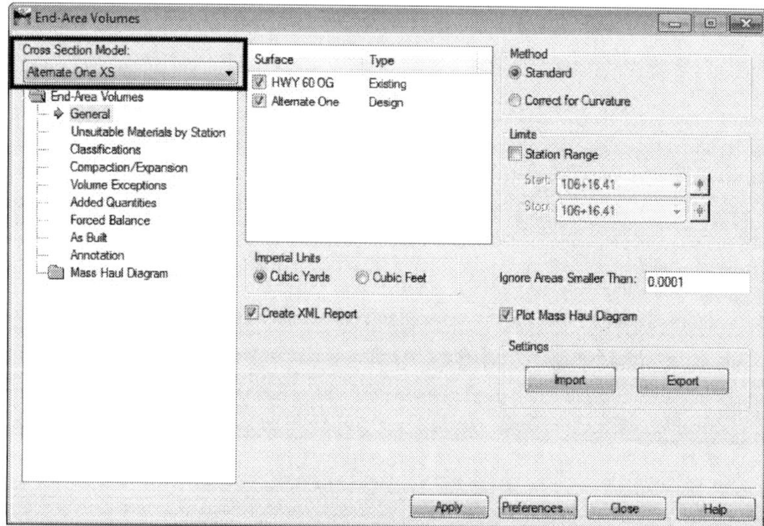

- Choose **Apply**

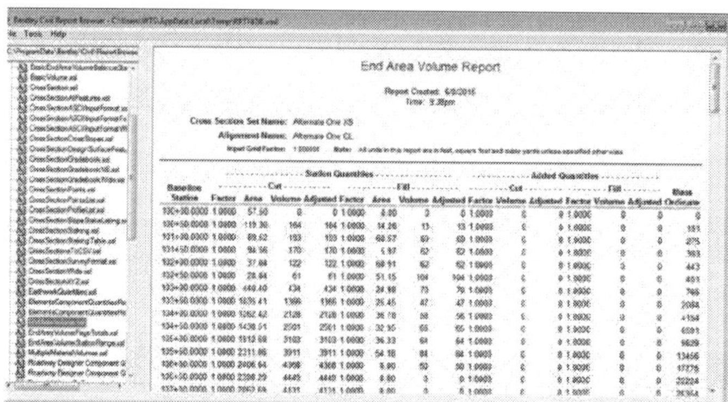

A report is generated and shown in the Report Browser

- On the left of the **Report Browser**, scroll down and choose *Volumes.xsl*
- Now, scroll to the bottom of the report and note the quantities for your different components.
- **Close** the open dialogs

Ending

9 **Save Settings**

10 **Exit** MicroStation

Proposed Terrain Models

CREATING A TERRAIN FROM A CORRIDOR

CREATING A TERRAIN MODEL FROM ALTERNATE SURFACE

11 Proposed Terrain Models

The corridors created in the modeling process may be made up of linear features, components and even meshes but do not automatically create terrain models. You do not need the terrain models for cross sections and volumes, but you do need them for contours. You will also need them if you are taking the models back to the legacy format of DTMs as discussed in the next chapter.

11.1 Creating a Terrain Model from a Corridor

You must already have a set of features and/or a Mesh for either the Subgrade, Finished Grade or Both for the proposed corridor, although they may be in a reference. If you are in a 2D MicroStation model, when you create the terrain model, it will automatically create and reference a 3D model for the terrain, however it is strongly encouraged to create terrains in a 3D model to start with.

To create the Terrain Model

- **MS: Tasks > Civil Tools > Terrain Model > Create Terrain Model by Graphical Filter**

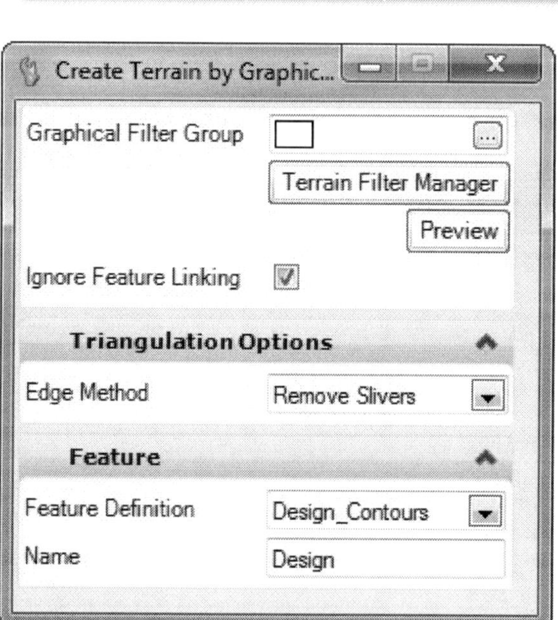

- Select the **Browse (...)** button next to the Graphical Filter Group
- In the **Graphical Filters** category, typically select either ***Design – Road Finished Grade*** or ***Design – Roads Subgrade***
- Make certain the MicroStation model containing the 3D mesh is active
- Select **Preview** to make certain the mesh highlights

- Set the desired **Edge Method** for the terrain
- Select a **Feature Definition**
- Key in a **Name**

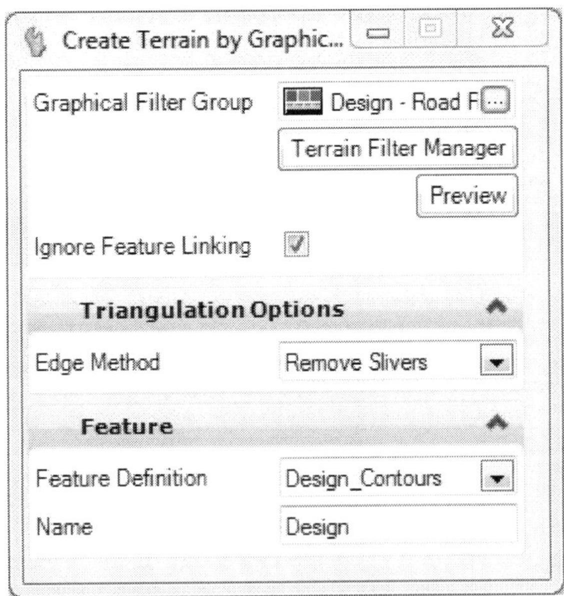

- Follow the heads-up prompts to accept your settings

The terrain is created. This is just one method and it is basically using the selection filter to create a set of graphics for loading into a terrain. You can also load the graphics individually.

11.2 Creating an Alternate Surface

When templates are created, you can specify points that you want to go into an alternate surface. You do not need alternate surfaces for volume computations, as they can be performed from the components in the template. However, there are instances where you may need to create a surface for contouring or grading that is made up of specific points.

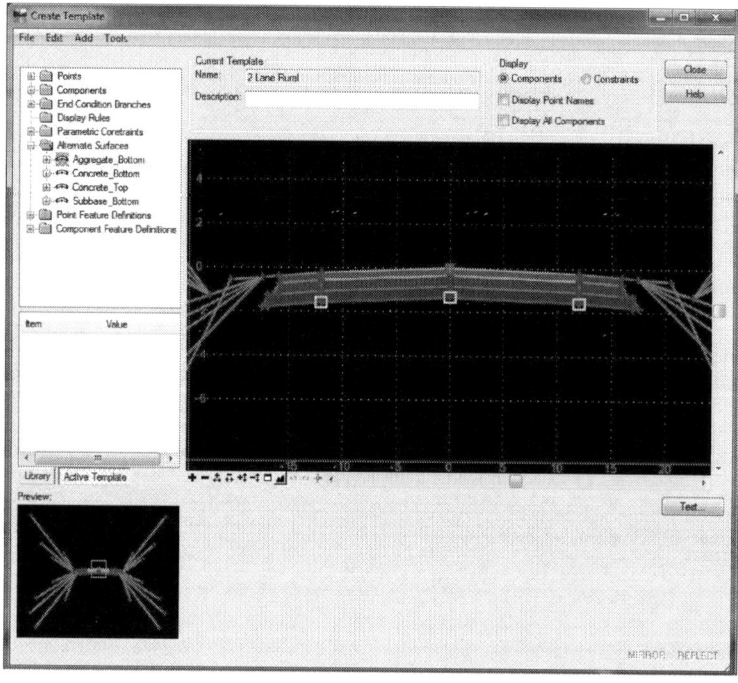

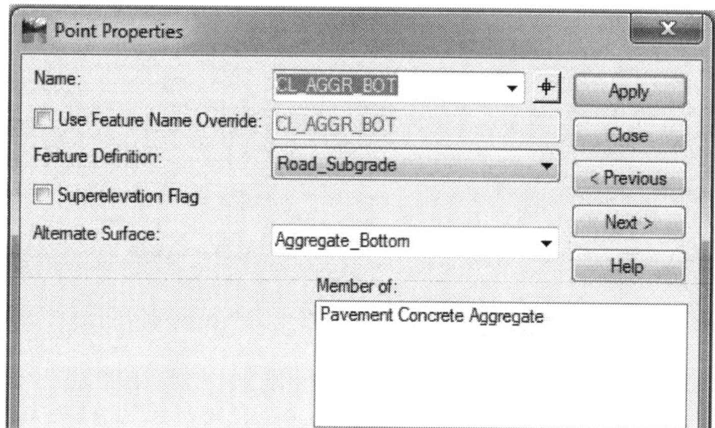

To create the alternate surface(s)

- **MS: Tasks > Civil Tools > Terrain Model > Create Corridor Alternate Surfaces**

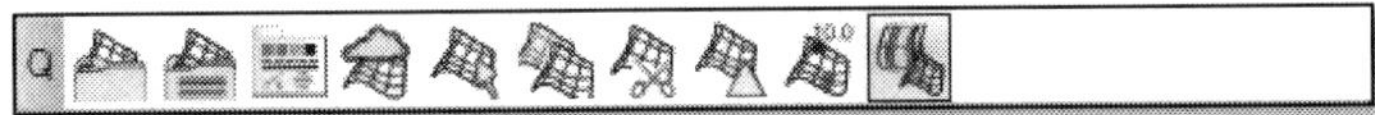

- Follow the heads-up prompt to choose the corridor
- The templates are processed and any noted alternate surfaces are created as terrain models

Exercise 11: Creating Proposed Terrain Models

Given:

- *HWY 60 Alternate One Corridor.dgn* – Corridor with Terrain, Alignments and Superelevation referenced

Required:

- Create a Terrain Model from your Proposed Surface
- Create Terrain Models from your Proposed Alternate Surfaces

Getting Started

1. Start InRoads using the icon on your desktop or using the **Start** menu
2. On the MicroStation manager, set the:
    - **User**: ***examples***
    - **Project**: ***Bentley-Civil-Imperial***
    - **Interface**: ***default***
3. Open the *HWY 60 Alternate One Corridor.dgn* file

Terrain Model from a Corridors

4 Set the **Design Stage**

- Select the Corridor
- On the menu, select **Properties**

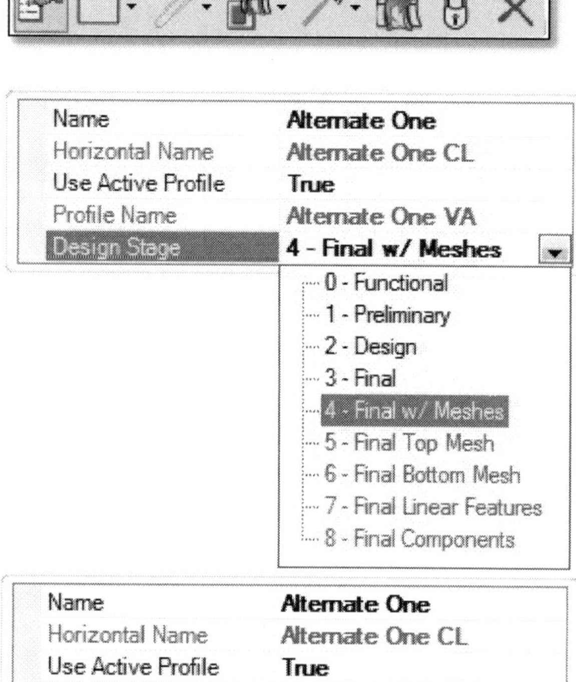

- Change the **Design Stage** to ***4 – Final with Meshes***

  This creates the component along with meshes for the top and bottom layers of the templates. In the next series of steps, you will create a terrain model from linear features, so make sure the design stage is one that contains the linear features.

5 Create a new file for the proposed terrain

- Select the **New** File icon
- Browse to select the seed file *Seed3D-InRoads-Imperial.dgn* and select **Open**

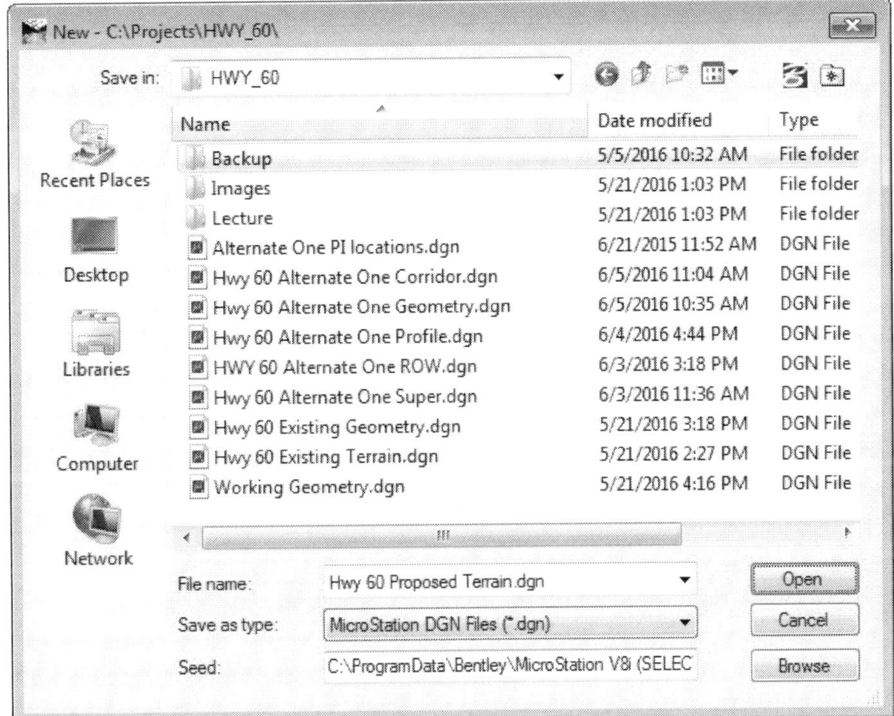

- Key in the File Name: **HWY 60 Proposed Terrain.dgn**
- Select **Save**

6 Open the new file

7 Reference *HWY 60 Alternate One Corridor.dgn* ***Coincident World*** with a **Nested Depth** of **1**

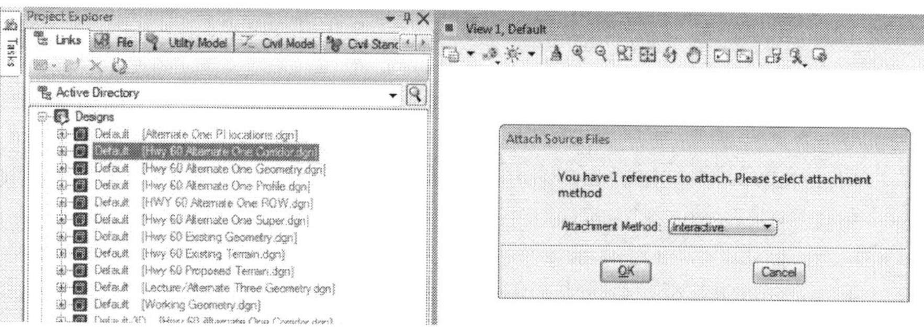

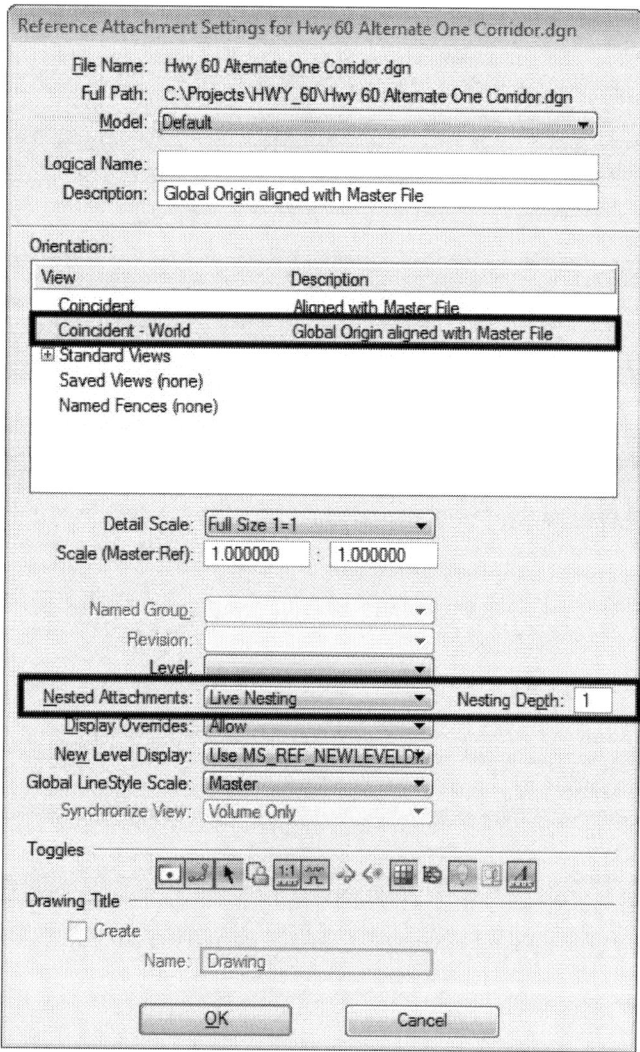

8 **Fit** the View

9 **MS: Tasks > Civil Tools > Terrain Model > Create Terrain Model by Graphical Filter**

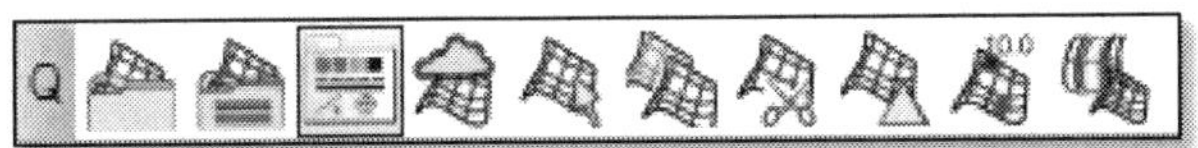

- Choose the browse (**...**) next the **Graphical Filter Group**

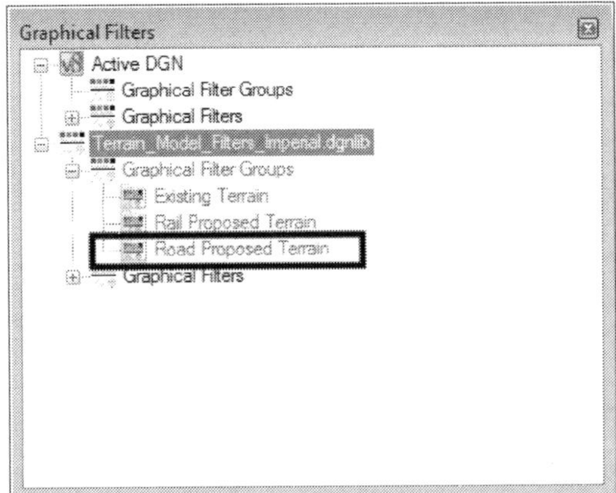

- Expand the *Terrain_Model_Filters_imperial.dgnlib* ***Graphical Filter Groups*** and choose ***Road Proposed Terrain***

  This filter group is composed of two filters – one that includes the linear features (loaded as break lines) and one that includes the limits of construction (loaded as boundaries).

- Set the other options as shown
- Follow the heads-up prompts to Accept the settings with a **<D>**

  The Terrain Model is created

10 View the proposed 3D terrain model

- Open View 8 and **Fit** the view
- Turn ***off*** the *HWY 60 Alternate One Corridor* reference
- Dynamically rotate the view to examine the new proposed 3D terrain model

- From the terrain properties, experiment turning some of the terrain displays **On** and **Off**

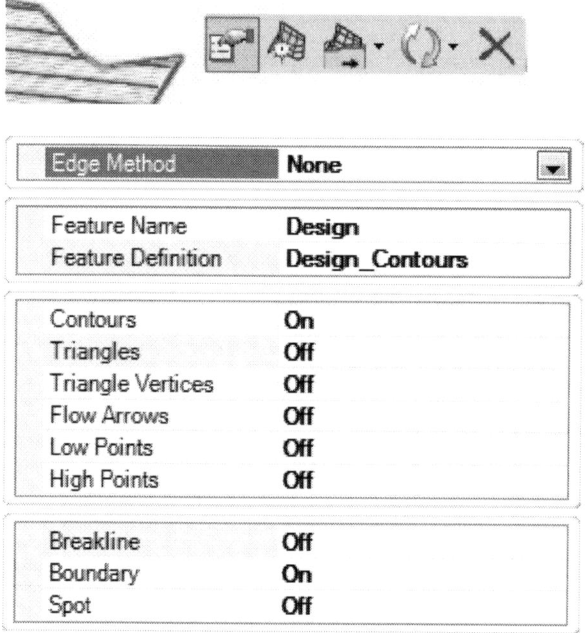

- Choose **File > Save Settings**

Terrain Model from Alternate Surfaces

11 Select **File > New**

- Ensure the seed file is *Seed3D-InRoads-Imperial.dgn*
- Key in the File Name: **HWY 60 Proposed Subgrade Terrain.dgn**
- Select **Save**

  The new file is created and opened.

12 Reference your corridor

- Be sure to use **Nesting** with a depth of **1** so you get the 3D model as well as the Terrain model
- Make the Existing Terrain active

  The terrain must be active because in the next step because the corridor will be processed.

  This would also create a 3D Model in the current file if you were in a 2D Model.

13 **MS: Tasks > Civil Tools > Terrain Model > Create Corridor Alternate Surface**

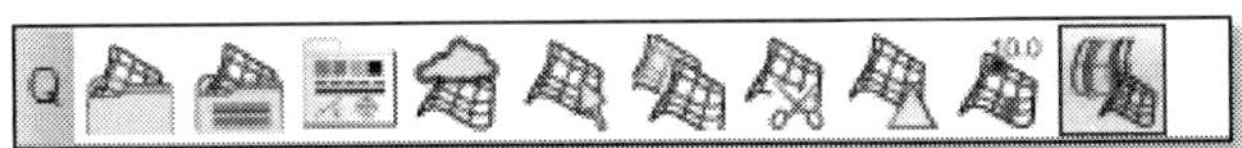

- Select the Corridor

  The corridor is processed and any Alternate Surfaces designated in the templates are created.

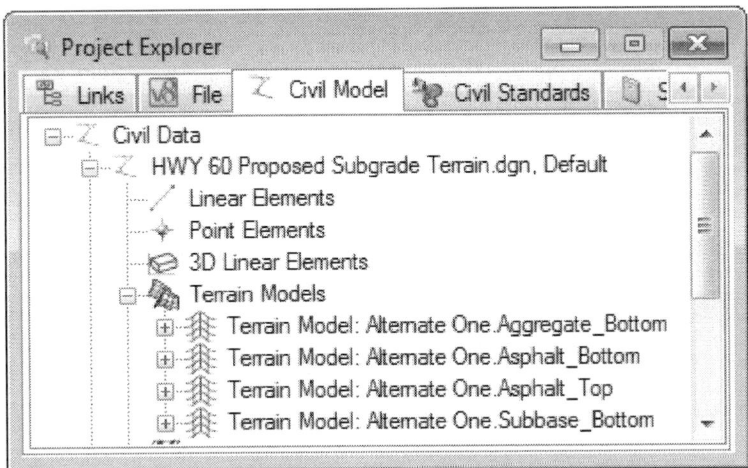

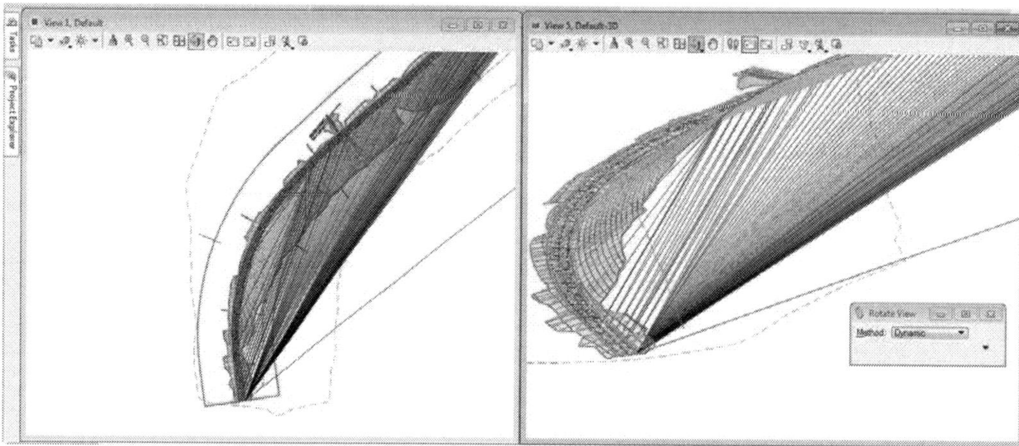

- Open View 5

  Note there is not a boundary, so the triangles extend outside the proposed model.

- Toggle off the Corridor reference display

  The terrain model is linked to the corridor so any changes to it are reflected in the terrain. Detaching the reference would break this link.

- Expand the list of terrain models from the **Project Explorer Civil Model** tab
- Right click on the first subgrade terrain and select **Properties**

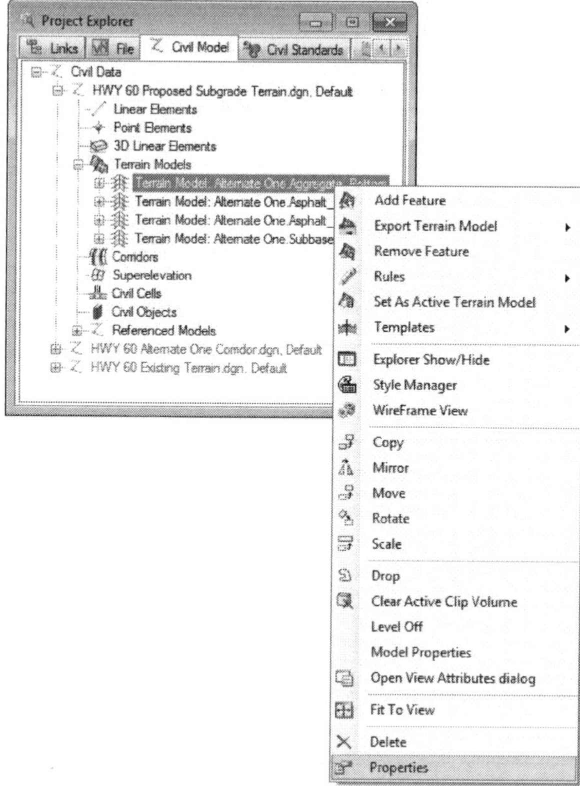

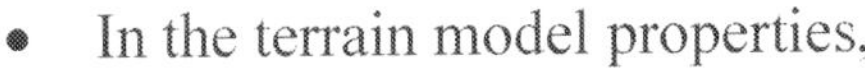

- In the terrain model properties,

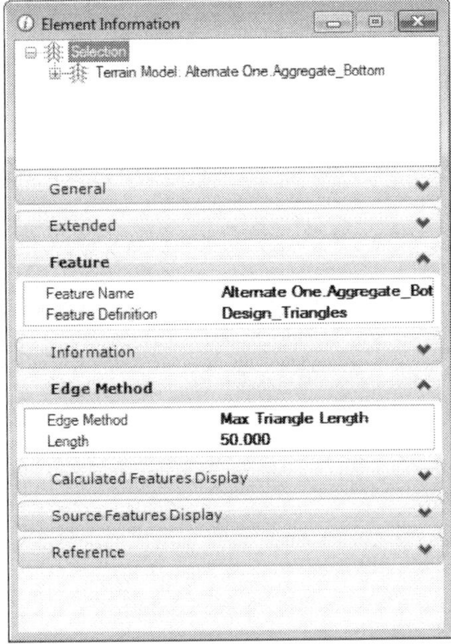

- Under the **Feature** category, set the Feature Definition to ***Design_Triangles***
- Under the **Edge Method** category, set the Edge Method to ***Max Triangle Length*** and the Length to 50
- Repeat for each additional subgrade surface

  Note: You may select multiple surfaces and then choose Element Information instead of properties to change more than one at a time.

- Review the results

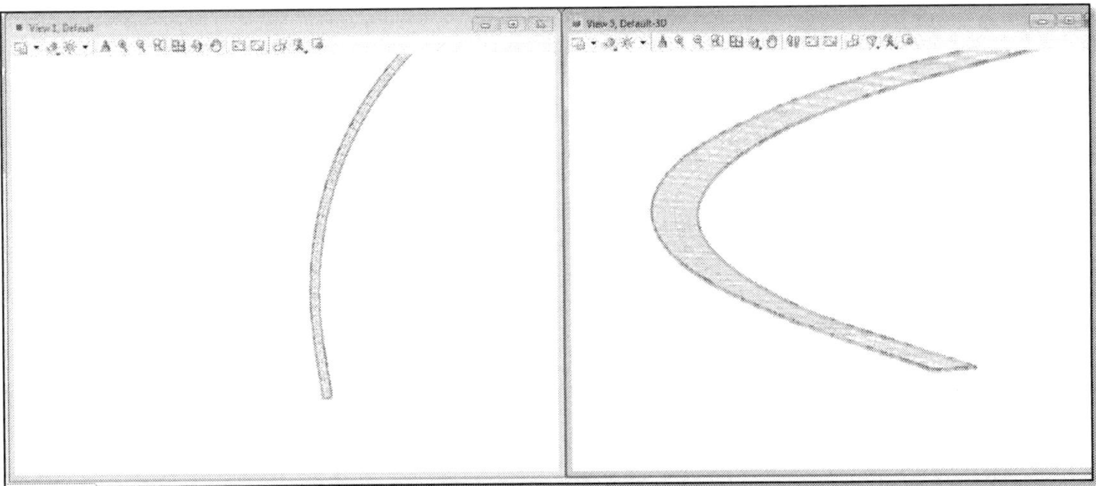

Ending

14 Save Settings

15 Exit

Native Data

Creating an ALG from Civil Geometry

Creating a DTM from a Terrain Model

Creating Profiles for Printing

12 Creating Native Data

This version of InRoads is transitioning from storing data in external files to storing data in the MicroStation DGN file. However, there are some commands in InRoads that require you to have the old format or external files – ALG for geometry and DTM for surfaces. These are commonly referred to as Legacy or Native Data formats.

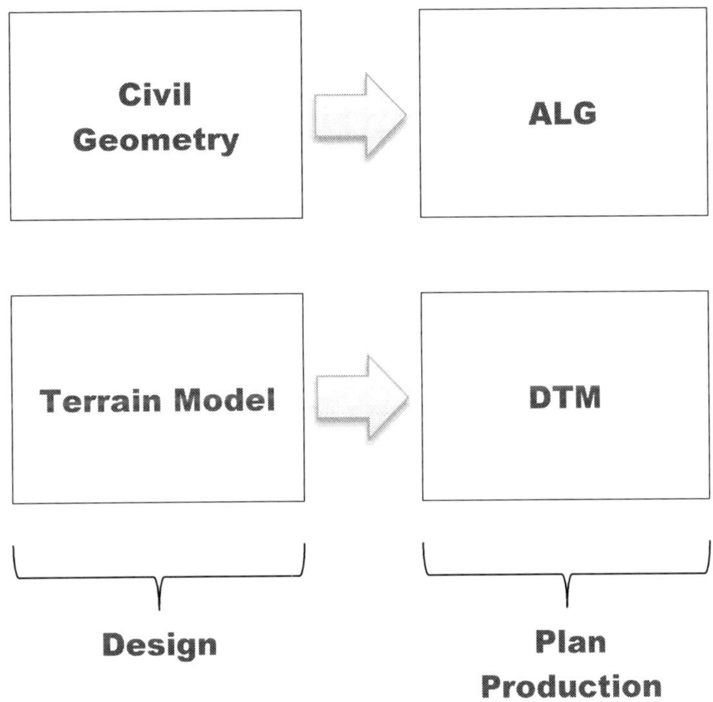

12.1 Creating an ALG from Civil Geometry

There are some functions in InRoads SS4 that require the use of legacy commands, such as stationing (unless using Automatic Stationing), generating profiles for plan production and using the **Plan/Profile Generator**. This involves taking your civil geometry and storing it in the ALG and can be accomplished in a couple of different ways.

If the feature definition assigned to the geometry has **Auto Export** set to **True**, the geometry is automatically stored and updated in the ALG. Changes to the ALG using legacy commands will NOT be reflected in the Civil Geometry.

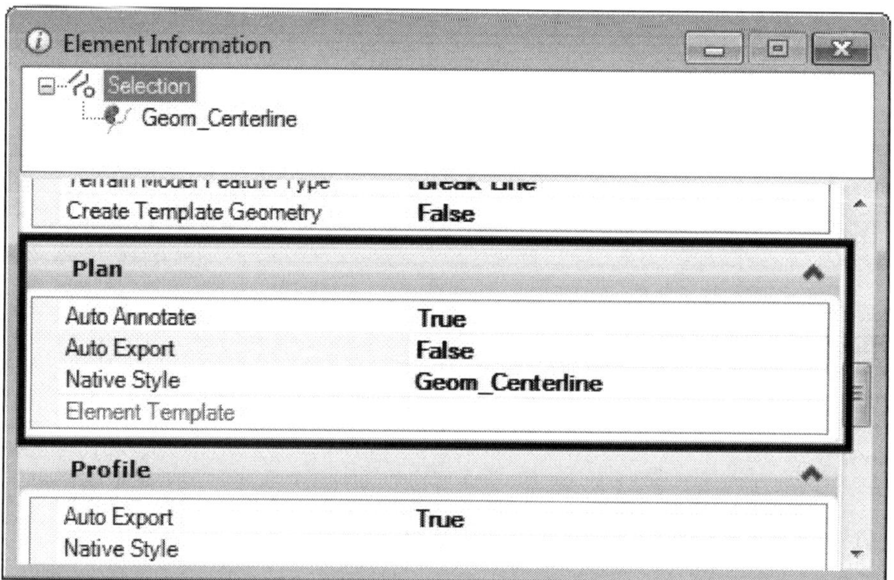

If the Civil Geometry is using a feature definition with **Auto Export** set to **False**,

➢ You must have the desired ALG loaded and active

➢ **MS: Tasks > Civil Tools > General Geometry > Export to Native**

➢ When prompted, select the **Civil Geometry** you want to include in the ALG

➢ Continue to select geometry, and **<R>** when done

The alignment(s) are now part of the ALG. If the horizontal has a corresponding vertical, it will also be added to the ALG.

Warning: Edits to the civil geometry will NOT be reflected in the ALG and vice versa since the Auto Export is set to False.

12.2 Creating DTM from Terrain Model

The terrain model may be in either the active MicroStation model or a referenced to the active model.

➤ Select the terrain model

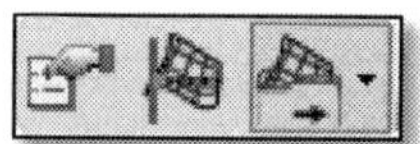

➤ On the context-sensitive menu, select **Export Terrain Model**

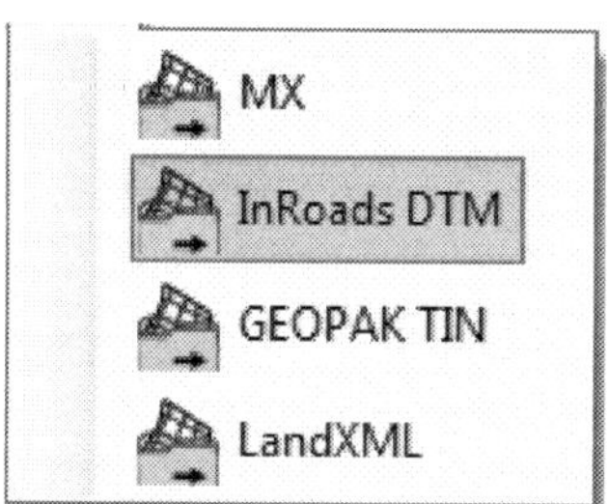

➤ Choose **InRoads DTM**

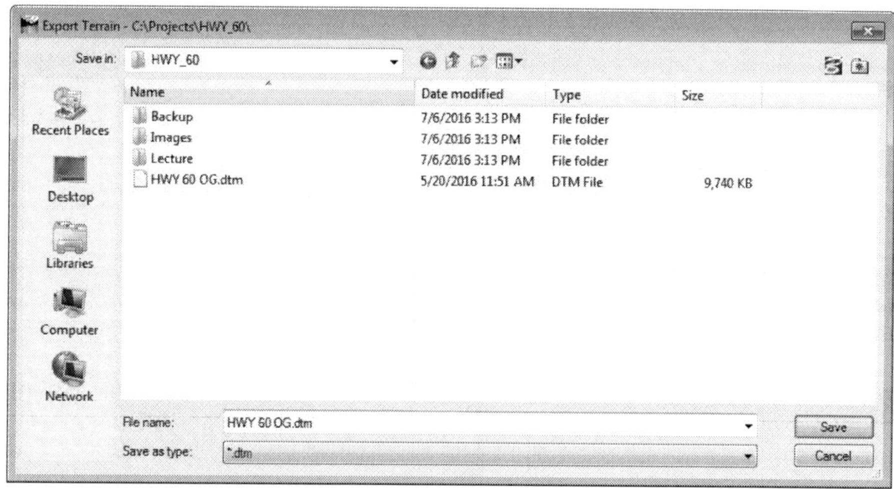

➤ Specify a **File Name** and select **Save**

*Alternately, you can choose **MS: Tasks > Civil Tools > Terrain Model > Export to File** and then select the terrain model.*

12.3 Stationing an Alignment

The stationing for a Civil Geometry alignment is controlled by the Feature Definition. If it is set to **Auto Annotate**, the alignment will always have up to date stationing as long as the Stationing dialog contains a preference name that matches the Feature Definition Name.

If you have exported your alignment to an ALG, it is just like previous versions.

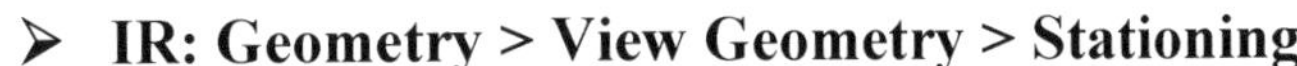

➤ **IR: Geometry** > **View Geometry** > **Stationing**

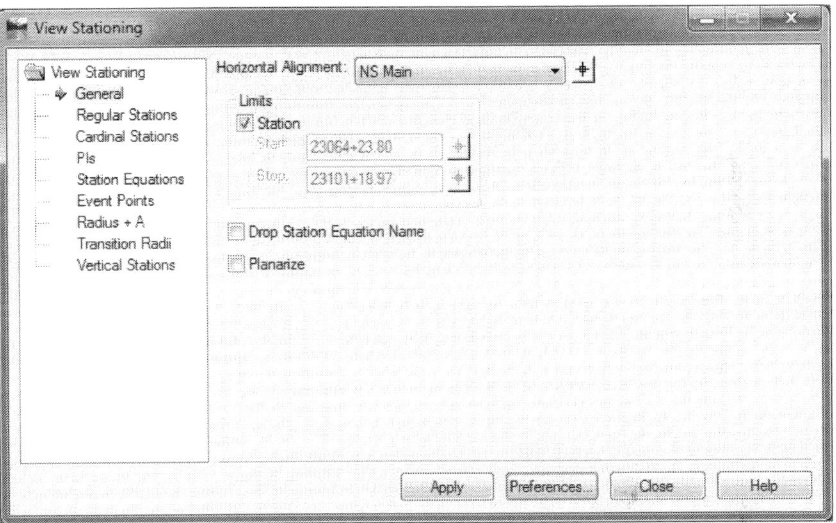

➤ Using the drop-down, select the **Horizontal Alignment**

➤ Select **Preferences** choose the appropriate one and **Load**

➤ Close the **Preference** box

➤ On the **View Stationing** box, choose **Apply**, then **Close**

The stationing is annotated on the horizontal alignment

12.4 Creating a Profile for Plan Production

The alignment must already be part of the ALG

The terrain must be exported to a DTM

➢ **IR: Evaluation > Profile > Create Profile**

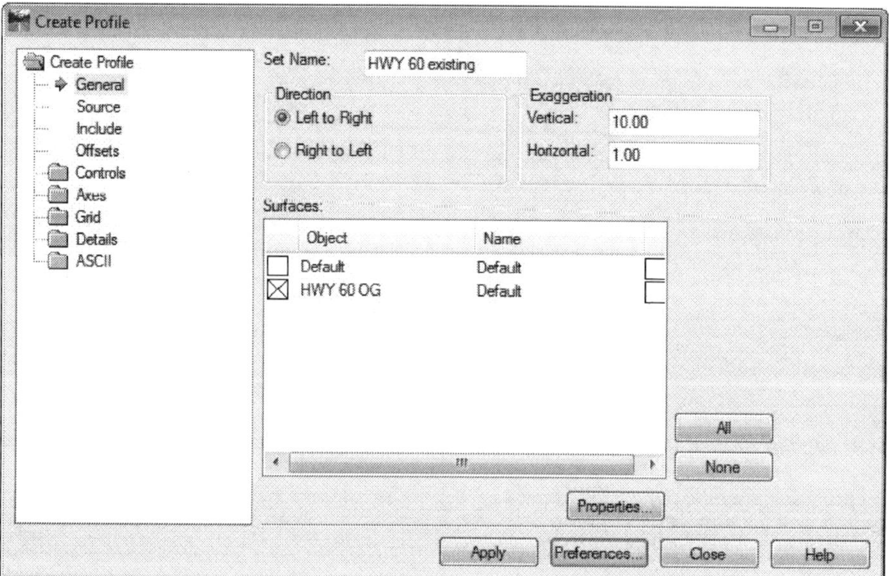

➢ Select **Preferences** and load the appropriate preference

➢ Toggle on the Surface(s) you wish to show on your profile

➢ On the **Source** tab, make certain the appropriate horizontal alignment is listed

➢ Choose **Apply**

➢ **<D>** where you would like the lower left corner of your Profile

➢ The profile is displayed in the design file and can be annotated and plotted as needed

12.5 Annotating a Vertical Alignment

The alignment must already be part of the ALG

The profile must already be created in the DGN

At this point, the Vertical Annotation is almost identical to previous versions.

➢ **IR: Geometry > View Geometry > Vertical Annotation**

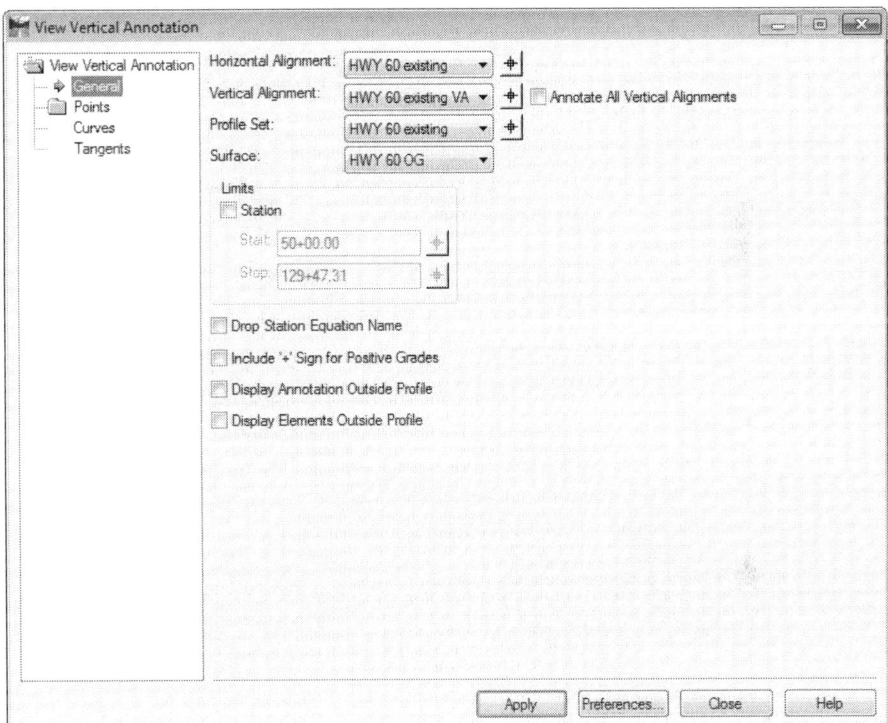

➢ Select **Preferences** and **Load** the appropriate preference

➢ Make certain the Horizontal Alignment, Vertical Alignment, Profile Set and Surface are appropriately selected

➢ Choose **Apply** and **Close**

The vertical alignment is now annotated in the selected profile.

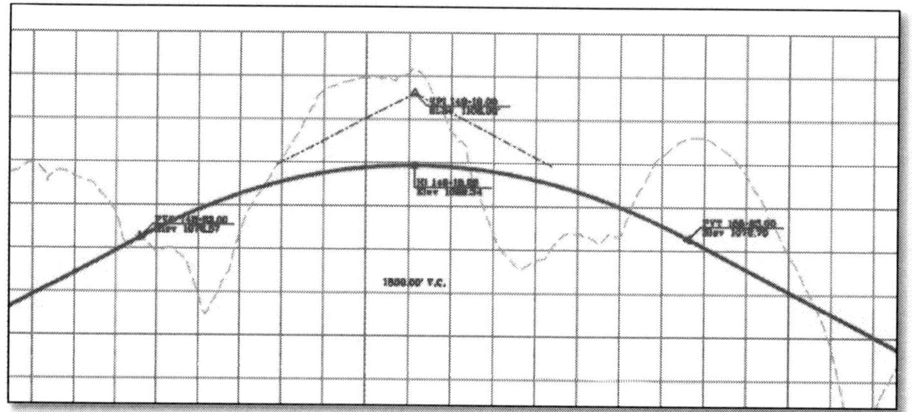

12.6 Plan Graphics for Plan Sheets

The corridor graphics are intelligent and cannot be manipulated as regular MicroStation graphics, such as modifying a construction limit. If you need to perform these types of tasks, one solution is to file fence the graphics into another DGN.

➢ Place a fence around the plan view graphics

➢ **MS: Copy/Move Fence Contents to file**

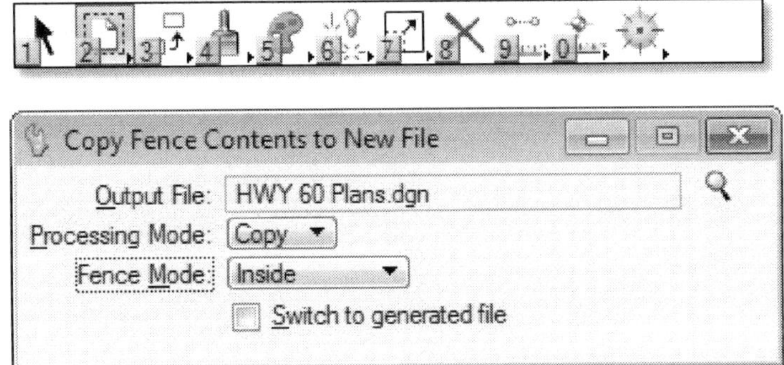

➢ Use the **Browse** icon to specify a location and name for the file.

➢ <D> to **Accept**

The new file will be made up of 'dumb' versions of the corridor graphics and all association with the corridor will be lost.

Exercise 12: Creating Native Data

Given:

- *HWY 60 Alternate One Corridor.dgn* – Corridor with Terrain, Alignments and Superelevation referenced

Required:

- Create an ALG from your Civil Geometry
- Create a DTM from your Existing Terrain
- Create a DTM from your Proposed Terrain
- Create DTMs from your Proposed Alternate Terrains

Getting Started

1 Start InRoads using the icon on your desktop or using the **Start** menu

2 On the MicroStation manager, set the:

- **User**: ***examples***
- **Project**: ***Bentley-Civil-Imperial***
- **Interface**: ***default***

3 Open the File: *HWY 60 Alternate One Geometry.dgn*

ALG from Civil Geometry

Depending upon which Feature Definition you are using, alignments may be automatically placed in the active ALG. If not, follow these steps to create alignments in an ALG.

4 Right-click and show the **InRoads Explorer** if it is hidden.

5 On the Explorer menu, select **File > New > Geometry**

- **Type**: ***Geometry Project***
- **Name**: **HWY 60 Proposed**
- **Description**: **Alternates for HWY 60**
- Choose **Apply**, then **Close**

6 Export to Native Geometry

Note: If you're using a feature definition which is set to ***Auto Export:*** **True**, *you can skip this step.*

- **MS: Tasks > Civil Tools > General Geometry > Export to Native**

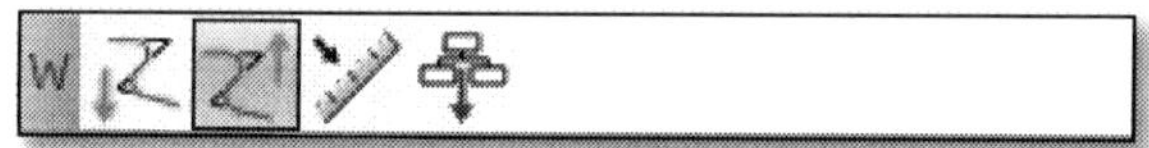

- Select the Horizontal Alignment
- **<R>** to complete the export

7 Verify and save the ALG

- Expand the geometry project and note the alignment is now part of the ALG

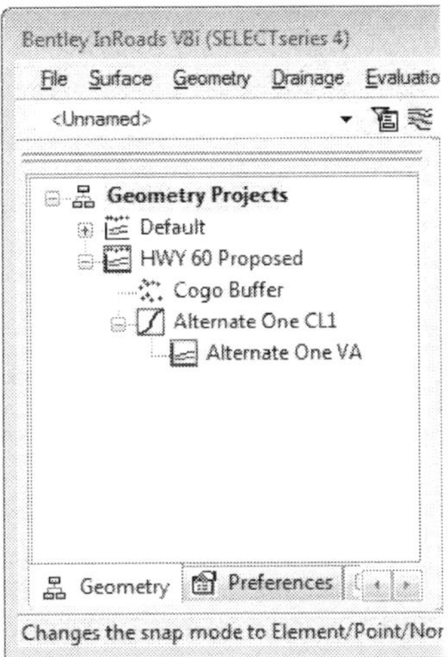

- Right-click on the *HWY 60 Proposed* name and save the ALG to your project folder.

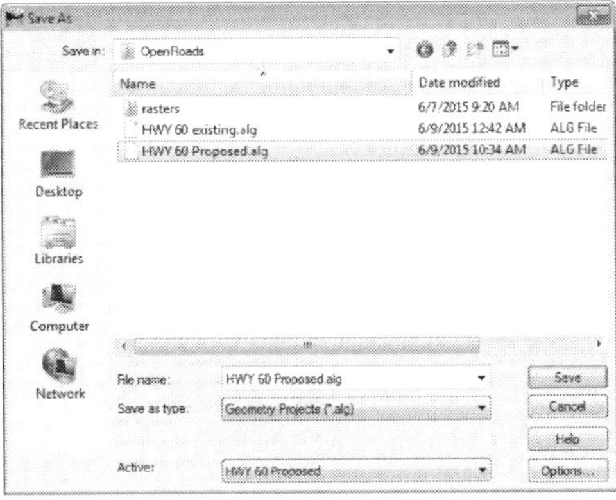

DTM from Terrain Model - Existing

8 **MS: Tasks > Civil Tools > Terrain Model > Export to File**

- Select the ***Terrain HWY 60 OG***
- Select the **Export Format *InRoads DTM (.dtm)***
- Accept with a **<D>** in any view

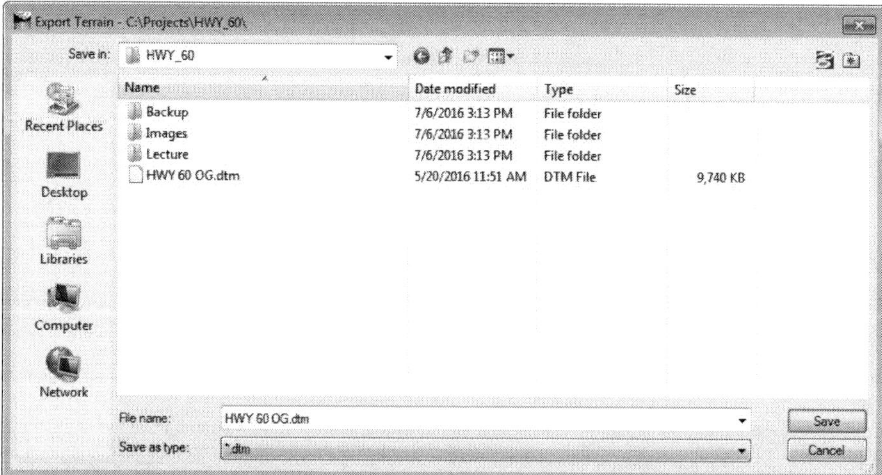

- The **Export Terrain** dialog appears. Here you can key in a name for the file. Since we originally created this Terrain Model from a DTM, there is no need to continue.
- **Cancel** to exit the command.

DTM from Terrain Models - Proposed

You could create the DTM the same way shown earlier, or you can try another method as shown here.

9 Open the file *HWY 60 Proposed Terrain.dgn*

10 Go to **Project Explorer**

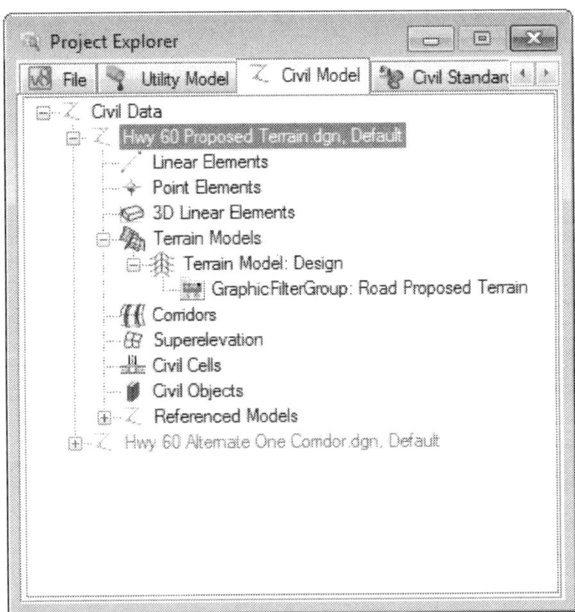

- Select the **Civil Model** tab and expand the design file and then ***Terrain Models***

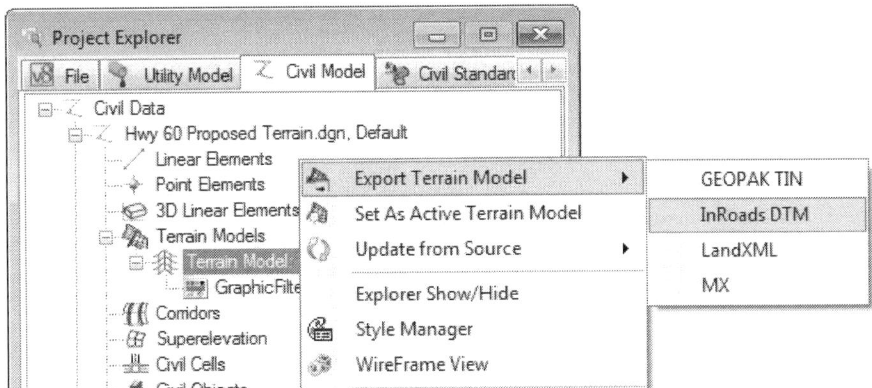

- Right-click on the ***Terrain Model: Design*** and choose **Export Terrain Model > InRoads DTM**

- Navigate to the project folder and key in the name *HWY 60 FG.dtm*

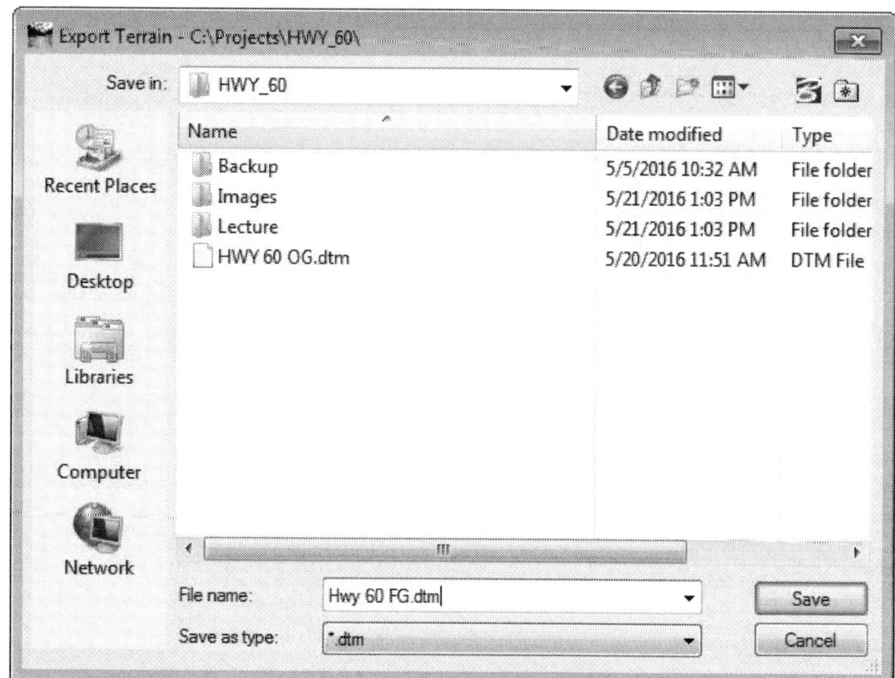

- Choose **Save**

11 Create DTMs from the proposed subgrades

- Open the file *HWY 60 Proposed Subgrade Terrain.dgn*
- Repeat the process above to create DTMs for each of the proposed subgrades (alternate surfaces)

Creating Profiles for Printing/Plotting

12 Select **File > New**

- Verify the seed file is *Seed2D-InRoads-Imperial.dgn*
- Key in the ***File Name***: **HWY 60 Alternate One Profile.dgn**
- Select **Save**

13 **Open** the new file

14 Right-click and Show the **InRoads Explorer** if it is not shown.

15 Select **File > Open**

- From the **Open** dialog, select *HWY 60 existing.alg* and *HWY 60 OG.dtm*
- Set the geometry project **HWY 60 Proposed** active

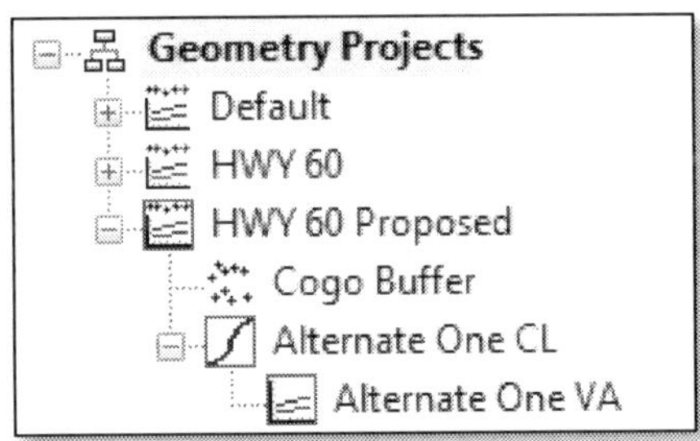

16 Choose **Evaluation > Profile > Create Profile**

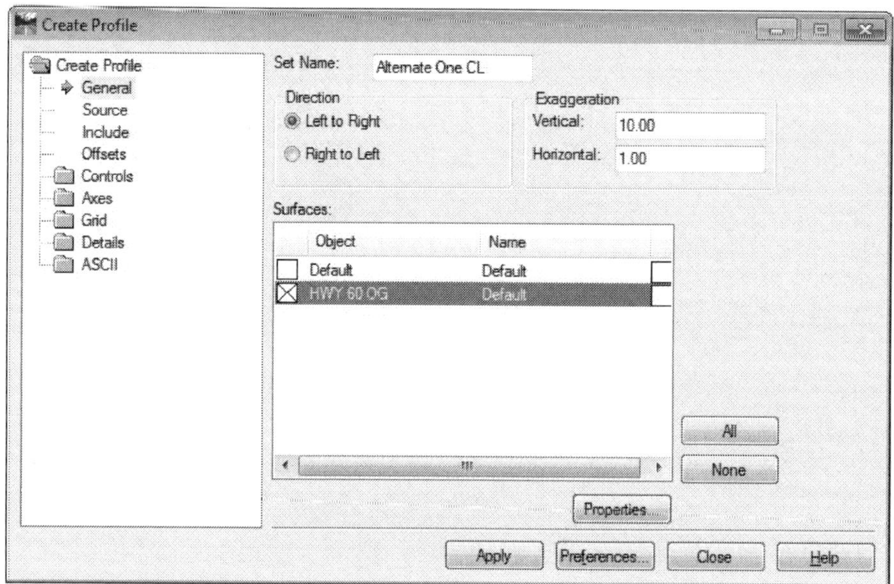

- Highlight the **HWY 60 OG** and choose **Properties**

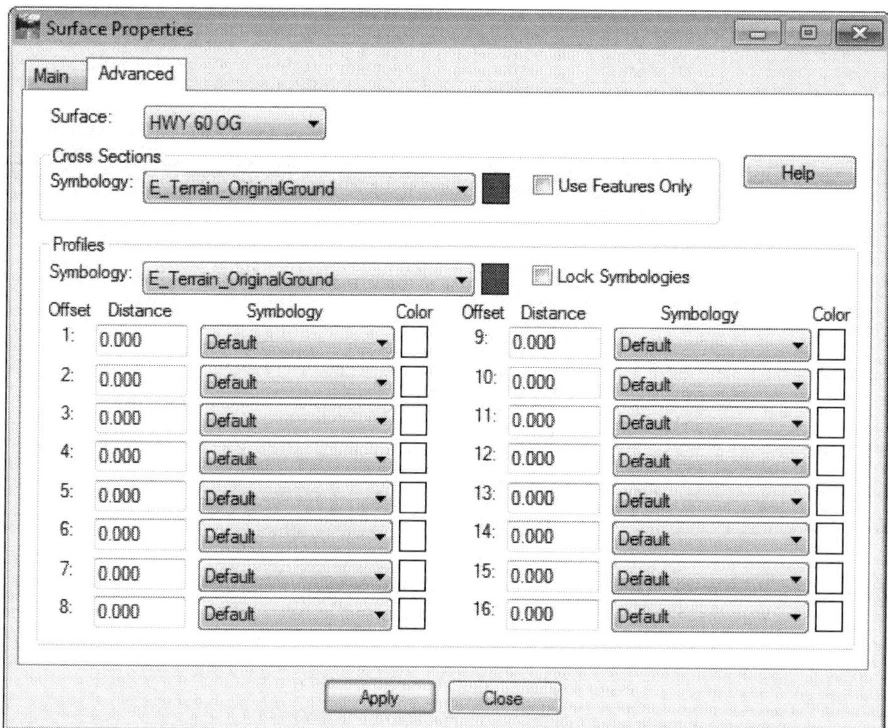

- Under **Profile Symbology**, choose ***E_Terrain_OriginalGround*** (You can set the cross section symbology also while you're here if you'd like.)
- Choose **Apply**, then **Close**
- Set the **Vertical Exaggeration** to **5**

- Apply and **<D>** for the lower left corner of the profile

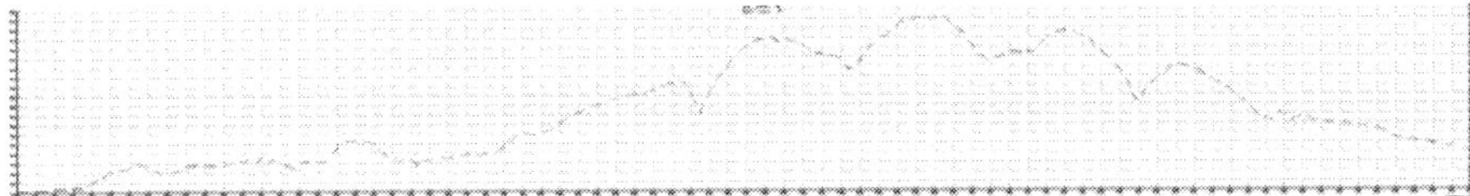

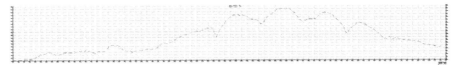

Note the profile command is a legacy command so there is little difference from the previous version.

17 Annotate the Vertical Alignment

- Choose **Geometry > View Geometry > Vertical Annotation**

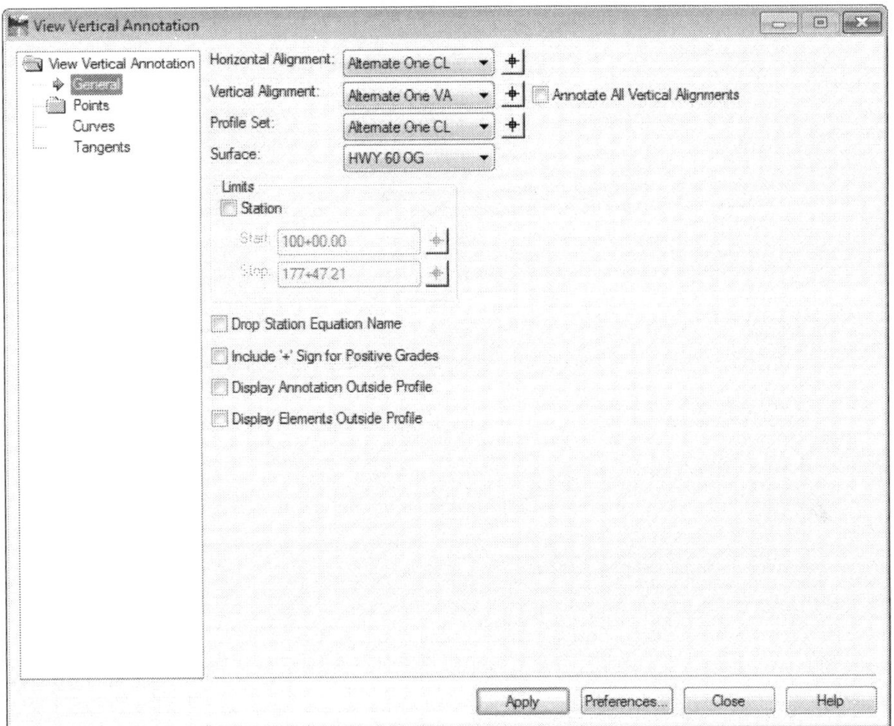

- Make certain the correct ***Alignments*** and ***Profile Set*** are selected.
- **Apply** and the Vertical Alignment is displayed and annotated on the Profile.

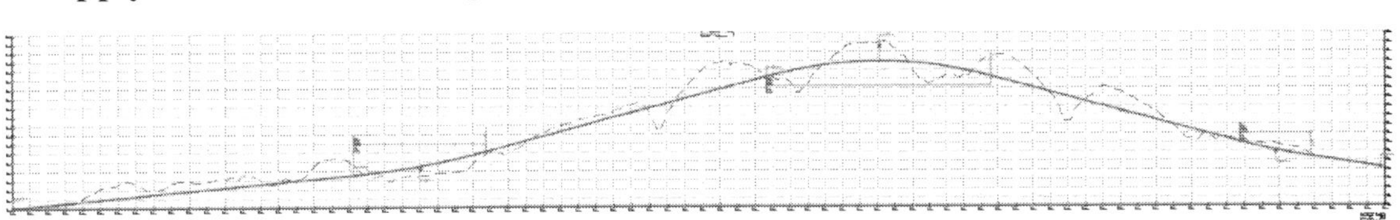

Ending

18 **Save Settings**

19 **Exit** MicroStation

Congratulations! You have now completed the basic workflow for upgrading to InRoads SS4.

Be sure to check out

www.civilCADconsultant.com

for tips and tricks and

www.CADProdinc.com

for information on additional training options.

Index

D

E

F

G

H

I

U

V

W

Made in the USA
Charleston, SC
30 January 2017